ADVANCES IN
MOTIVATION SCIENCE

Advances in
MOTIVATION SCIENCE

Series Editor

ANDREW J. ELLIOT
Department of Clinical & Social Sciences in Psychology
University of Rochester, USA

Sponsored by The Society for the Study of Motivation

Amsterdam • Boston • Heidelberg • London
New York • Oxford • Paris • San Diego
San Francisco • Singapore • Sydney • Tokyo
Academic Press is an imprint of Elsevier

Academic Press is an imprint of Elsevier
225 Wyman Street, Waltham, MA 02451, USA
525 B Street, Suite 1800, San Diego, CA 92101-4495, USA
125 London Wall, London EC2Y 5AS, UK
The Boulevard, Langford Lane, Kidlington, Oxford OX5 1GB, UK

First edition 2015

Notices
Knowledge and best practice in this field are constantly changing. As new research and
experience broaden our understanding, changes in research methods, professional practices,
or medical treatment may become necessary.

Practitioners and researchers must always rely on their own experience and knowledge in
evaluating and using any information, methods, compounds, or experiments described
herein. In using such information or methods they should be mindful of their own safety and
the safety of others, including parties for whom they have a professional responsibility.

To the fullest extent of the law, neither the Publisher nor the authors, contributors, or editors,
assume any liability for any injury and/or damage to persons or property as a matter of
products liability, negligence or otherwise, or from any use or operation of any methods,
products, instructions, or ideas contained in the material herein.

ISBN: 978-0-12-802270-2
ISSN: 2215-0919

For information on all Academic Press publications
visit our website at http://store.elsevier.com/

Working together
to grow libraries in
developing countries

www.elsevier.com • www.bookaid.org

CONTENTS

List of Contributors   *ix*

1. **Balancing Rewards and Cost in Relationships: An Approach–Avoidance Motivational Perspective**   **1**

   Shelly L. Gable

   1. Social Ties, Health, and Well-being   2
   2. Relationships Giveth, Relationships Taketh Away   5
   3. Appetitive and Aversive Motivation in Animals and Humans   8
   4. Approach–Avoidance Social Motivation   10
   5. Approach and Avoidance Motivation and Outcomes   14
   6. Mediating Links Between Social Motivation and Outcomes   17
   7. Moderators of Approach and Avoidance Social Motivation Processes   21
   8. Future Directions   22
   9. Concluding Comments   24
   Acknowledgments   24
   References   24

2. **Between Persistence and Flexibility: The Yin and Yang of Action Control**   **33**

   Bernhard Hommel

   1. Introduction   34
   2. The Will   35
   3. The Ego   39
   4. Control as Balance   43
   5. The Metacontrol State Model   46
   6. The Plasticity of Control States   49
   7. Short-term Biases of Cognitive Control   50
   8. The Impact of Learning, Experience, and Culture on Cognitive Control   54
   9. Conclusions   60
   Acknowledgments   61
   References   61

3. The Architecture of Goal Systems: Multifinality, Equifinality, and Counterfinality in Means—End Relations   69

Arie W. Kruglanski, Marina Chernikova, Maxim Babush, Michelle Dugas and Birga M. Schumpe

1. Introduction   70
2. Multifinality   71
3. Equifinality   78
4. Counterfinality   88
5. Recapitulation and Conclusion   94
References   96

4. Breaking the Rules: A Historical Overview of Goal-Setting Theory   99

Edwin A. Locke and Gary P. Latham

1. Early Development: Laying the Groundwork for Goal-Setting Theory   100
2. An Inductive Approach to Theory Building   103
3. Empirical Findings   105
4. Learning from Field Experiments: Latham   107
5. Goal-Setting Studies by Others   111
6. The Theory: 1990   112
7. The Theory Expanded: 2013   115
8. Observations on Theory Building   118
9. Future Directions   119
10. Conclusions   120
References   121

5. The Big-Fish–Little-Pond Effect, Competence Self-perceptions, and Relativity: Substantive Advances and Methodological Innovation   127

Herbert W. Marsh and Marjorie Seaton

1. Introduction   128
2. The Importance of Self-concept   130
3. A Historical Perspective on Self-concept   132
4. The BFLPE Model   134
5. Extended Empirical Support for BFLPE Generalizability   141
6. New Theoretical Directions: Integrating the BFLPE with Alternative Theoretical Perspectives   155
7. Methodological Innovation and the BFLPE   163
8. Substantive Implications for Policy Practice   170

9. Limitations and Directions for Future Research   173
Acknowledgments   175
References   176

6. On the Panculturality of Self-enhancement and Self-protection Motivation: The Case for the Universality of Self-esteem   185

Constantine Sedikides, Lowell Gaertner and Huajian Cai

1. Introduction   187
2. The Controversy   188
3. The Cultural Relativism Perspective   189
4. The Extended Self-enhancement Tactician Model (SCENT-R): Foundational
   Tenets   191
5. The Extended Self-enhancement Tactician (SCENT-R) Model: Key Postulates 200
6. Discussion   219
7. Research Agenda   223
8. Coda   225
References   226

Index   243

LIST OF CONTRIBUTORS

Maxim Babush
University of Maryland, College Park, MD, USA

Huajian Cai
Chinese Academy of Sciences, Beijing, China

Marina Chernikova
University of Maryland, College Park, MD, USA

Michelle Dugas
University of Maryland, College Park, MD, USA

Shelly L. Gable
Department of Psychological & Brain Sciences, University of California Santa Barbara, Santa Barbara, CA, USA

Lowell Gaertner
Department of Psychology, University of Tennessee, Knoxville, TN, USA

Bernhard Hommel
Cognitive Psychology Unit & Leiden Institute for Brain and Cognition, Leiden University, Leiden, The Netherlands

Arie W. Kruglanski
University of Maryland, College Park, MD, USA

Gary P. Latham
Rotman School of Management, University of Toronto, Toronto, ON, Canada

Edwin A. Locke
R.H. Smith School of Business, University of Maryland (Emeritus), College Park, MD, USA

Herbert W. Marsh
Australian Catholic University, Stratfield, NSW, Australia; King Saud University, Riyadh, Saudi Arabia; University of Oxford, Oxford, UK

Birga M. Schumpe
Helmut-Schmidt University, Hamburg, Germany

Marjorie Seaton
Australian Catholic University, Stratfield, NSW, Australia

Constantine Sedikides
School of Psychology, University of Southampton, Southampton, UK

CHAPTER ONE

Balancing Rewards and Cost in Relationships: An Approach—Avoidance Motivational Perspective

Shelly L. Gable
Department of Psychological & Brain Sciences, University of California Santa Barbara,
Santa Barbara, CA, USA
E-mail: shelly.gable@psych.ucsb.edu

Contents

1. Social Ties, Health, and Well-being   2
   1.1 The Effects of Social Isolation   2
   1.2 A Basic Social Motive   4
2. Relationships Giveth, Relationships Taketh Away   5
3. Appetitive and Aversive Motivation in Animals and Humans   8
4. Approach—Avoidance Social Motivation   10
   4.1 Model of Approach and Avoidance Social Motives and Goals   11
5. Approach and Avoidance Motivation and Outcomes   14
6. Mediating Links Between Social Motivation and Outcomes   17
   6.1 Attention   18
   6.2 Cognitive Biases   19
   6.3 Weight of Social Information   20
7. Moderators of Approach and Avoidance Social Motivation Processes   21
8. Future Directions   22
9. Concluding Comments   24
Acknowledgments   24
References   24

Abstract

Social bonds have a profound effect on health and well-being. It is clear that people have a fundamental need to form and maintain social bonds, but interpersonal relationships present potential threats as well as potential incentives. In this article, I review a model of approach and avoidance social motivation (Gable, 2006) that accounts for people's tendencies to both approach the incentives and avoid the threats in their social worlds. I also review research that has tested different aspects of the model including the consequences of approach and avoidance social motivation, mediators

Advances in Motivation Science, Volume 2
ISSN 2215-0919
http://dx.doi.org/10.1016/bs.adms.2015.06.001

that link motivation to these outcomes, and moderators of these processes. The article concludes by examining gaps that persist in the literature.

The truth is, everyone is going to hurt you. You just got to find the ones worth suffering for.

Quote widely attributed to Bob Marley[1]

As the opening quote states, relationships with other people involve both pleasure and pain. The key, according to Marley, is to figure out in which relationships the benefits exceed the costs, preferably by a wide margin. Of course a rational response to this challenge is to simply take a pass on social bonds, find benefits outside the context of familial ties, friendships, and romantic relationships, thereby avoiding these potential costs completely. However, empirical data have been accumulating that lead to the inescapable conclusion that social isolation is not a good recipe for health and happiness for humans; in short, people need people.[2]

1. SOCIAL TIES, HEALTH, AND WELL-BEING

1.1 The Effects of Social Isolation

The most compelling evidence that humans need social connections comes from studies that examine what happens to people when they are not able to form or maintain adequate interpersonal bonds. For example, there is a good deal of evidence that social relationships are a strong predictor of health. Perhaps, most illustrative of this evidence is the meta-analysis in which Holt-Lunstad and her colleagues quantified the profound effect that social bonds have on mortality (Holt-Lunstad, Smith, & Layton, 2010). Their meta-analysis included 148 longitudinal epidemiological studies that examined the associations among the existence or quality of social bonds and the outcome of mortality (excluding studies that examined death by suicide or injury). The time between assessment of predictors and mortality in the studies included in Holt-Lunstad et al. (2010) review ranged from 3 months to 58 years, with an average of 7.5 years. Overall their

---

[1] The author is aware that many people (especially fans of Bob Marley) doubt the origin of this quote was, in fact, Bob Marley. Whoever said it, however, captured perfectly the content described in this chapter.

[2] Clearly, there are individual differences in people's preferences for social contact and examples of people thriving with very limited social contact. However, the data show that by a large margin social isolation is not preferred by people and solitary confinement remains one of the most severe punishments a society can inflict on its individuals.

meta-analysis revealed a strong link between having social connections with others, especially high-quality connections, and mortality. The effect sizes ranged depending upon the indicator of social ties, but there is no doubt that social ties are as powerful (or in most cases, more powerful) a predictor of death as other well-established mortality risks, such as excessive alcohol use, obesity, and failure to treat hypertension (Holt-Lunstad et al., 2010). Of particular note here is that studies that included measures of social isolation and loneliness showed that those who perceived a lack of social ties were 40% more likely to be dead at follow-up than those who reported feeling connected to others. Although the mechanisms linking social isolation with poor health outcomes are not yet fully understood, recent studies have begun to tackle these critical questions (e.g., Shankar, McMunn, Banks, & Steptoe, 2011).

Just as there is no question that there is a robust link between physical health and social isolation, there is also no dispute in the empirical record that there is a strong link between social isolation and *psychological health*. For example, there is a long history of the documented association between feelings of social isolation and depression (e.g., Shaver & Brennan, 1991). Perhaps, the first systematic empirical publication in the field on the topic of relationships and psychological health was Durkheim's (1897) archival study of church records in Europe in which he found an association between a lack of social ties and risk for suicide. In addition to the observed associations between social isolation and mood disturbances, there are also well-documented links between loneliness and other psychological disorders, such as schizophrenia, personality disorders, and substance abuse (e.g., Akerlind, Hörnquist, & Hansson, 1987; Neeleman & Power, 1994; Overholser, 1992). Moreover, studies also suggest that the social isolation and psychological distress relation is reciprocal, such that social isolation increases risks for disorders and disorders exacerbate isolation (e.g., Ernst & Cacioppo, 1999).

Turning from clinical findings on disorders and focusing on psychological well-being more broadly, the empirical literature also finds that there is a strong negative association between loneliness and well-being (e.g., Helliwell & Putnam, 2005; VanderWeele, Hawkley, Thisted, & Cacioppo, 2011). The link between social isolation and well-being crosses the life span; evidence for this negative association has been documented in older adults (e.g., Chen & Feeley, 2014), young adults (e.g., Sherman, Lansford, & Volling, 2006), adolescents (e.g., Rönkä, Rautio, Koiranen, Sunnari, & Taanila, 2014), and children (e.g., Bradshaw, Hoelscher, & Richardson,

2007). Due to the strength and consistency of the ties between social isolation and happiness, empirical studies often use measures of loneliness as indicators, or as the operationalization, of well-being, while many theoretical approaches include social bonds in the very definition of psychological well-being (e.g., Keyes, 1998; Ryff, 1995).[3]

1.2 A Basic Social Motive

The links that social isolation shares with health and well-being are very likely rooted in human evolutionary history. It is clear that modern humans evolved in a rich social context; the presence of benevolent social bonds increased fitness (e.g., Beckes & Coan, 2011). We were designed by selection to live in social habitats, and social isolation puts stress on the system (Beckes & Coan, 2011). It should not be a surprise then that just as we are motivated to obtain food and water, and to reproduce, humans also seem to possess a powerful *motivation* to identify, cultivate, and keep interpersonal relationships (e.g., Baumeister & Leary, 1995; Cantor & Malley, 1991; Gere & MacDonald, 2010; McAdams, 1982).

These interpersonal relationships can take many forms, such as attachment, mating, coalition, or communal bonds because different relationships vary in structure and function (Bugental, 2000; Fiske, 1992). Regardless of the ultimate form, the motivation to bond with other people is powerful and pervasive, and likely operates both within our conscious control as well as outside of our awareness (e.g., Epley, Akalis, Waytz, & Cacioppo, 2008; McAdams, 1982). For example, people routinely list having and maintaining close relationships as one of their important life goals (e.g., Emmons, 1999), and people who chronically place other goals (e.g., wealth) above social goals have poorer mental and physical health than those who prioritize their social goals (Kasser & Ryan, 1996). Another example of the basicness of this motive is the automatic tendency to ascribe human characteristics to inanimate objects; a tendency that becomes more pervasive in people whose social needs are thwarted (Epley, Akalis, et al., 2008; Epley, Waytz, Akalis, & Cacioppo, 2008). The *fundamental need to belong*, as Baumeister and Leary (1995) described it, is so pervasive that prominent theories of human functioning explicitly state that the social motive is one of only a handful of basic human needs (e.g., Deci & Ryan, 2000).

---

[3] Eudoimonic models of well-being include social relationship quality as is an integral component of well-being (e.g., Ryff, 1995) while hedonic models of well-being posit that social ties are one of the most, if not the most, important predictors of well-being (e.g., Diener, 2000).

In addition, social motives direct cognition, affect, and behavior not only when we are bonding with other people. Rather, our fundamental need to belong influences our thoughts, feelings, and actions beyond the boundaries of our interactions with others and in domains once thought to be independent of any social context. For example, social motives and the status of our social needs influence psychological processes in domains such as performance on achievement tasks or judgments in risk in different recreational activities (e.g., Cavallo, Fitzsimons, & Holmes, 2009). Moreover, the influence that social motives and goals have on how we think, feel, and act in nonsocial contexts often occurs without our explicit knowledge (Shah, 2003).

2. RELATIONSHIPS GIVETH, RELATIONSHIPS TAKETH AWAY

As the previous section makes clear, there is a solid theoretical and empirical foundation suggesting that people are motivated to form and maintain stable interpersonal bonds and that this motivation influences broad psychological processes in social and nonsocial contexts. The data also show that the failure to meet social needs is detrimental to health and well-being in that social isolation and loneliness predict mortality, become risk factors for psychological disorders, and are practically synonymous with poor well-being. However, the literature also is clear that the presence or absence of relationships per se is not a good predictor of either feelings of social isolation or the health and well-being outcomes reviewed above. Rather, it is the quality of relationships that are important (e.g., Holt-Lunstad et al., 2010; Uchino, 2013).

Critical for the current point is that not all relationships, and not all aspects of a given relationship, are good for health and well-being. Social relationships can provide people with many benefits such as companionship, social support, and opportunities for growth; these qualities are, on average, positively associated with health and well-being and negatively associated with feelings of social isolation and loneliness (Cohen & Willis, 1985; Lakey & Cassady, 1990). However, relationships are also rife with potential costs such as abandonment, exploitation, and conflict; and these qualities are, on average, negatively associated with health and well-being and positively associated with feelings of loneliness and isolation (e.g., Segrin & Flora, 2000; Kiecolt-Glaser & Newton, 2001; Miller, Rohleder, & Cole, 2009). Although there are exceptions (e.g., Rafaeli, Cranford, Green, Shrout, &

Bolger, 2008), the majority of empirical work either focuses on the potential rewards of close relationships or the potential costs of close relationships.

By far, the vast majority of studies have focused on examining the potential costs of relationships (see Fincham & Beach, 2010; Reis & Gable, 2003). These costs are real, in that they can have a profound effect on psychological and physical functioning. For example, conflict in relationships contributes to psychopathological symptoms such as depression, anxiety, and substance abuse (e.g., Davila, Bradbury, Cohan, & Tochluk, 1997; Whisman, 2001; Whisman, Uebelacker, & Settles, 2010). Marital conflict, in particular, has been shown to increase the likelihood of cardiac death (Eaker, Sullivan, Kelly-Hayes, D'Agostino, & Benjamin, 2007; Wilcox, Kasl, & Berkman, 1994), and interpersonal stressors increase the susceptibility to the common cold virus (Cohen, Doyle, Skoner, Rabin, & Gwaltney, 1997). Hostility and conflict in dyadic relationships are associated with significant health consequences such as poorly regulated immune responses and unhealthy cardiovascular reactivity (Kiecolt-Glaser, 1999; Uchino, Holt-Lunstad, Uno, & Flinders, 2001). Other potential costs such as fears of and experiences with rejection and abandonment also have well-documented detrimental links to psychological health (e.g., Baron et al., 2007; Downey, Feldman, & Ayduk, 2000; Mikulincer, 1998). Of course, some of the most direct threats that relationships with others pose are threats to physical safety. Abusive relationships and intimate partner violence have profound detrimental effects on psychological and physical health, and pose a social and economic challenge to the community at large (e.g., Ellsberg, Jansen, Heise, Watts, & García-Moreno, 2008).

Balancing out these heavy risks are the equally real potential rewards of social bonds. The benefits of a responsive caregiver for the health and well-being of infants and children is widely documented by attachment theorists (e.g., Bowlby, 1982; Feeney, 2000). Another such reward that is well documented is social support, which is the receipt of aid or comfort in times of need or the perception that others would be available for aid and comfort in future times of need (Cutrona, Russell, & Rose, 1986). Social support has been consistently and broadly linked to both mental and physical health processes (e.g., Cohen & Willis, 1985; Dunkel-Schetter & Bennett, 1990; Lakey & Cassady, 1990). For example, supportive bonds with others predict recovery from illness and a return to independent functioning after an illness (e.g., Wilcox et al., 1994). In the meta-analysis by Holt-Lunstad et al. (2010), the strongest predictor of mortality was the quality of responsive and supportive relationships—people who had responsive relationships were likely to live longer than those who did not. More broadly, people tend to turn to others to aid in the management of everyday emotions and having a broad range of social bonds who are able to effectively aid in emotion regulation is positively associated with well-being (Cheung, Gardner, & Anderson, 2015).

However, the rewards of social bonds are also apparent even outside the context of stressors or the management of negative emotions. Work on capitalization has clearly shown that people turn to others when good events happen and the availability of others who respond supportively in this context is associated with increases in personal resources, such as positive emotion, well-being, and self-esteem beyond the effect of the event itself (e.g., Gable, Gosnell, Maisel, & Strachman, 2012; Gable, Reis, Impett, & Asher, 2004). Similarly, close others can facilitate one's ideal personal development (Rusbult, Kumashiro, Kubacka, & Finkel, 2009) and personal goal pursuit (Feeney & Collins, 2015).

Across these diverse literatures, it is clear that some aspects of close relationships provide powerful boons to psychological and physical health, whereas other aspects of social bonds and close relationships pose significant risks to health and well-being. Ironically, there is evidence that the impact of toxic costs in relationships is actually heavier when the same relationship also provides many benefits (e.g., Uchino et al., 2001). This double-edged sword that comes with social bonds, especially close bonds, are not only well documented by science but also widely known by writers, artists (such as the author of the quote that opened this paper), and laypersons alike. For example, in large-scale surveys of people asked about what gives meaning and happiness to their lives, the majority cited relationships (e.g., Klinger, 1977). On the other hand, people are equally quick to name relationships in surveys that ask them to describe what is going wrong in their lives (Veroff, Kulka, & Douvan, 1981).

In short, it is clear to researchers and laypersons alike that social bonds simultaneously provide the potential for rewards and threats. Moreover, because humans have a fundamental need to form and maintain social connections, and social isolation is in itself detrimental to health and well-being, choosing to avoid risk by foregoing the potential benefits and going it alone is also a poor choice. Recognizing this structure, my colleagues and I have been investigating a model of social motivation that can simultaneously account for the regulation of incentives and threats (Gable, 2006; Gable & Impett, 2012). This model draws heavily from prior work on approach and avoidance motivation more broadly and from approach and avoidance models applied to other domains, such as the achievement domain (e.g., Elliot, 2006; Gray, 1990; Higgins, 1998). It is worth reviewing the fundamental premises of approach—avoidance motivational frameworks that form the foundation of our social motivation model.

3. APPETITIVE AND AVERSIVE MOTIVATION IN ANIMALS AND HUMANS

There is a long and prolific history of theory and research that posits separate systems of motivation, one that approaches potential incentives and rewards and another which avoids potential threats and punishments. Early theorizing and operationalization of these systems can be seen in Pavlov's (1927) work. He described one physiologically based system that functioned to orient the organism toward a positive stimulus and another that functioned to orient the organism away from the stimulus. Thirty years later, Schneirla (1959) outlined evidence that the distinct approach and withdrawal systems were present across diverse species and were rooted deep in our evolutionary ancestry. Approach and avoidance behavioral models appeared consistently in the early social and personality psychological literature such as Lewin's (1935) description of the approach—avoidance conflict and Miller's (1961) empirical lab work on the topic. Later work that focused more specifically on *motivation* also posited separate approach and avoidance systems.

One of the most detailed motivational models was Gray's (1987, 1990), which outlined separate appetitive and aversive motivational systems that he coined the behavioral activation system (BAS) and the behavioral inhibition system (BIS).[4] His research suggested that the BIS inhibits behavior in response to signals of punishment, and the BAS activates behavior in response to signals of reward. Similarly, Carver and Scheier's (1990) model of self-regulation makes the distinction between behavior aimed at reducing the discrepancies between internal goals and external stimuli (i.e., approaching positive outcomes) and behavior aimed at enlarging the discrepancies between internal goals and external stimuli (i.e., avoiding negative outcomes). Their model also elegantly predicts which emotions are likely to be experienced in response to movement toward and away from goals. Higgins'

---

[4] Later refinements of Gray's model posit that the BIS system functions to monitor conflicts within BAS and between BAS and a separate aversive system referred to as a flight/fight system (see Corr, 2008).

(1998) constructs of promotion-focused orientations and prevention-focused orientations also are consistent with approach—avoidance frameworks. In Higgins' model, promotion-focused goals are those aimed at approaching gains while prevention-focused goals are those aimed at avoiding losses. Connecting work on dispositional differences in motivational strength with work on short-term goals, Elliot (2006) also proposed a hierarchical model in which underlying distal approach and avoidance motivations give rise to more proximal and cognitively accessible approach and avoidance goals, respectively.

Early approach and avoidance motivation models also recognized that these two systems were independent and likely functioned via separate biological pathways. For example, Gray specified separate neurocircuitry for each system, largely based on his work with animals (although other researchers examined these neural underpinnings in humans). In early human work, Sutton and Davidson (1997) found that individual differences in the strength of BIS and BAS predicted differences in resting prefrontal asymmetry as assessed with psychophysiological measures (i.e., EEG technology), with higher BAS showing relative left prefrontal activation, and higher BIS showing relative right prefrontal activation (see also Sobotka, Davidson, & Senulis, 1992). Similarly, Amodio and colleagues investigated the neurocognitive components of BIS and BAS and found that BAS was related to asymmetries in frontal activity (greater left hemisphere activity) and they also found that BIS strength predicted neural activity in response to conflict monitoring tasks (Amodio, Master, Yee, & Taylor, 2008). More broadly speaking, however, many researchers have documented evidence for distinct neural circuitry associated with the evaluation of rewards and threats, approach and avoidance motivation, and the emotional systems that are consonant with these motivations (e.g., Berntson & Cacioppo, 2008, pp. 307—321; Hoebel, Avena, & Rada, 2008; Lang & Bradley, 2008).

The neurocognitive evidence for the relative independence of approach and avoidance systems is consistent with the evidence that they operate via different processes. For example, Gable, Reis, and Elliot (2000) found that individual differences in the strength of approach motivations (operationalized by Gray's BAS) and avoidance motivation (operationalized by Gray's BIS) had distinct associations with positive and negative emotions. In addition, these associations emerged via different processes such that high BIS sensitivity was associated with negative emotions primarily through differential sensitivity (the degree of reaction to the occurrence of negative stimuli), and BAS sensitivity was associated with positive emotions primarily through differential exposure (the frequency of experiencing positively valenced events). Also consistent with the separate systems interpretation, using a basic visual attention task, Derryberry and Reed (1994) found that individuals with strong approach motivation were more biased toward positive cues, but not necessarily less biased toward negative cues, whereas those with strong avoidance motivation were more biased toward negative cues, but not necessarily less biased toward positive cues. Also, Higgins, Shah, and Friedman (1997) have shown that promotion-focused goals are related to emotions that vary on a cheerfulness to dejection continuum, whereas prevention-focused goals are related to emotions that vary on a quiescence to agitation continuum. So, for example, failing to reach a promotion-focused goals predicts disappointment but not anxiety, and failing to reach a prevention-focused goal predicts anxiety but not disappointment. In total, the physiological and behavioral evidence indicates the two forms of motivation are independent systems.

4. APPROACH—AVOIDANCE SOCIAL MOTIVATION

Thus far I have reviewed models of behavior and motivation that are domain-general, presumably applying equally across domains. In other words, these models do not make explicit distinctions among, for example, threats to physical safety, loss of a relationship, or failure at a task. Although there is good evidence that threats and rewards across domains may involve similar neural pathways (e.g., Eisenberger, Lieberman, & Williams, 2003) it is also fruitful to examine motives and goals within a given domain. For example, careful consideration of approach and avoidance achievement motives and goals has yielded considerable insight into behavior and outcomes within the domain (e.g., Elliot, 1997, p. 243). However, the majority of theoretical and empirical work on the topic has not simultaneously examined reward-based and threat-based social motives and goals. This oversight exists despite the fact that social relationships routinely present rewards and threats and that social motivation is considered a primary human motive, (e.g., Deci & Ryan, 2000) long holding the interests of researchers.

In fact, early work on social motivation took the position that the need for affiliation was rooted squarely in the desire to avoid being rejected, alone, or hurt by others (Atkinson, Heyns, & Veroff, 1954; DeCharms, 1957; Shipley & Veroff, 1952). Not surprisingly, findings were difficult to interpret within this framework; for example, early measures of this rejection-based need for affiliation were negatively correlated with popularity but positively correlated with self-confidence (Atkinson et al., 1954). Over the years, some models of social motivation and behavior in interpersonal relationships have focused either on threat-based motivation or on incentive-based motivation. Illustrating the former, work by Downey and her colleagues (Downey, Freitas, Michaelis, & Khouri, 1998) on what she has termed rejection sensitivity is one such example. Rejection sensitivity is the tendency to anxiously expect and intensely react to rejection by significant others. Several studies have found that those who are high on a measure of rejection sensitivity show more negative behavior and hostility after perceived or actual rejection, and their negative feelings after conflict or rejection linger longer (Ayduk, Downey, Testa, Yen, & Shoda, 1999; Downey et al., 2000). Work examining incentive-based social motivation is rare; however, one exception is work by Aron and Aron (1997). Their model of self-expansion outlines a motivation toward growth by including the resources and characteristics of other in the self-concept (Aron & Aron, 1997).

One line of research did, however, make the distinction between approach and avoidance social regulation (e.g., Boyatzis, 1973; Mehrabian, 1976). Specifically, measures of the strength of two social motives were developed, one based on expectations of positive outcomes, the need for affiliation, and one based on expectations of punishments or negative outcomes, the fear of rejection (Mehrabian & Ksionzky, 1974; Russell & Mehrabian, 1978). Assessing separate approach and avoidance social motives in this way did clarify some of the earlier findings. For example, approach social motive strength was positively associated with self-confidence, and avoidance social motive strength was positively associated with negative evaluation by others. Despite the initial promise of this work that *simultaneously* examined both reward- and threat-based reasons as motivation for behavior, similar approaches to the topic have not been common in the literature. Moreover, there has been very little work that has gone beyond models of underlying motivation and examined short-term, cognitively accessible social goals.

4.1 Model of Approach and Avoidance Social Motives and Goals

Based on models of approach—avoidance motivation more broadly and building on work on social motivation more specifically, Gable (2006) proposed a model of social motivation that simultaneously examined incentive and threat regulation in social bonds. A representation of this model is depicted in Figure 1. In this model, individual differences in the strength of approach motivation, such as BAS and need for affiliation, combine with signals of incentives[5] in the current social environment to predict the adoption of approach social goals. In turn, these goals direct behavior in the service of realizing the potential rewards of social bonds, such as companionship, support, and intimacy. Likewise, individual differences in the strength of avoidance motivation, such as BIS and fear of rejection, combine with signals of threats in the current environment to predict the adoption of avoidance social goals.[6] In turn, these avoidance goals direct behavior in the service of minimizing the potential threats of social bonds, such as rejection, conflict, and betrayal. For example, consider the first week of living in a dorm for a new student at college. If the student has strong approach motives and/or has fairly warm initial interactions with her classmates, then she is more likely to adopt goals that are focused on obtaining rewards—approach goals—such as making friends and having fun interactions. Progress is defined as obtaining these incentives. On the other hand, if the student has strong avoidance motivation and/or has had abrupt and cold initial interactions with her new classmates, she is likely to adopt goals aimed at minimizing future threats—avoidance goals—such as not being alone and not having conflicts with others. Finally, her overall assessment of the quality of her social life (e.g., loneliness, well-being) is some combination of the presence of incentives/rewards and the absence of threats/punishments.[7] Although in both of these hypothetical scenarios the content of the goals is similar, the manner in which the goals are framed makes a considerable difference. Specifically, as discussed in subsequent sections, the framing of the goals directs attention, influences the interpretation of social information, affects memory, directs behavior, and dictates how the presence and absence of incentives and threats are factored into global judgments of the quality of social life.

---

[5] Signals of incentives and threats in the current environment include the threats and incentives that recent social interactions have provided.

[6] In addition to individual differences in underlying motives and the current social environments other factors influence the adoption of approach and avoidance goals. These factors are viewed as moderators and discussed in a subsequent section devoted to moderators.

[7] There is also evidence that approach and avoidance motivation influences the manner in which incentives and threats are factored into overall judgments. This evidence is reviewed in the section on mediating processes.

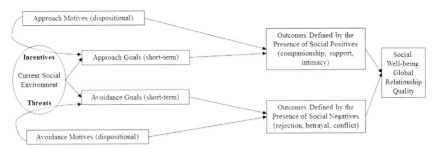

Figure 1 Model of approach and avoidance social motivation.

In addition to goals that people have for their social bonds broadly speaking (such as make friends or not be lonely), they also have goals for their specific relationships. The approach—avoidance model once again predicts that individual differences in the strength of approach—avoidance motives combine with signals of incentives and threats in the current social environment to predict to adoption of approach and avoidance relationship goals. In turn, approach relationship goals direct behavior in the service of realizing the potential rewards and minimizing the potential threats of specific relationships. For example, consider a man who has been married for 25 years. If he has strong approach motives and/or recently has had warm and loving interactions with his wife, then our hypothetical husband is likely to adopt approach goals for his marriage that are focused on obtaining or maintaining rewards, such as making his wife happy and growing closer or maintaining intimacy with her. Progress is defined as experiencing these rewards. On the other hand, if he has strong avoidance motivation and/or recently has had conflictual and hurtful interaction with his wife, then our hypothetical husband is likely to adopt avoidance goals aimed at minimizing future threats, such as not upsetting his wife and protecting himself from being hurt. Success is defined by avoiding these threats. Finally, his overall assessment of his relationship quality (i.e., marital satisfaction) is a combination of the presence of incentives and rewards, and the absence of threats and punishments. Again, both of our hypothetical husbands have similar goals in terms of their content, but the way in which the goals are framed diverges, as will be reviewed below, and has implications for both the husband adopting the goal and the relationship he has with his wife.

Gable (2006) tested the first tenet of this model, chronic motives predict short-term goals, in terms of its applicability to broader social motives and goals. First, as in work on achievement goals (e.g., Elliot & Church,

1997), across three studies, individual differences in approach social motivation, hope for affiliation, predicted the likelihood to adopt approach social goals, such as making new friends. On the other hand, those with strong avoidance motivation, specifically, fear of rejection, were more likely to adopt short-term avoidance social goals such as not wanting to be lonely than those with weaker avoidance motivation. Thus, there is good evidence that underlying social motivation influences the adoption of approach and avoidance social goals in a pattern consistent with the model outlined in Figure 1.

Examining the associations between motives and goals within a particular relationship, Impett and colleagues conducted a study of sacrifice in romantic relationships (Impett, Gable, & Peplau, 2005). Similar to work on broad social goals, people who were high on approach social motivation (hope for affiliation) were likely to cite approach goals, such as wanting to feel closer to their partners or making their partners happy, as reasons for making everyday sacrifices (e.g., foregoing a preferred activity). In addition, people with strong avoidance motives (fear of rejection) were likely to cite avoidance goals, such as not wanting to feel guilty or avoiding an argument, as reasons for their everyday sacrifices, providing evidence for the motivation to goal link predicted in the model on Figure 1.

5. APPROACH AND AVOIDANCE MOTIVATION AND OUTCOMES

There is ample evidence from diverse studies that individual differences in social approach and avoidance motives and goals are associated with indicators of well-being and the quality of social bonds. Consistent with hypotheses and consistent with prior work from other domains (e.g., Elliot & Sheldon, 1998; Elliot, Thrash, & Murayama, 2011), social approach and avoidance motives and goals showed distinct associations with indicators of well-being and relationship quality. For example, in a series of studies, Gable (2006) examined how the strength of the approach and avoidance social goals that people had for relationships with family, friends, romantic partner, and others in general predicted relationship quality. The results showed that approach motivation strength positively predicted positive feelings toward partners and overall satisfaction with close relationships, both concurrently and over time. Avoidance motivation strength positively predicted negative affect toward relationship partners and relationship insecurity, also concurrently and over time. Also as predicted by the model outlined in Figure 1, approach and avoidance goals and motives jointly predicted loneliness (loneliness was a function of both incentive-based outcomes such as positive feelings, and punishment-based outcomes such as insecurity). The links between social motivation and outcomes remained robust even after accounting for domain-general approach and avoidance motivation (BIS and BAS), highlighting the utility of the social motivation model. Elliot, Gable, and Mapes (2006) documented similar results in a study of approach and avoidance goals for friendships. Strong approach goals were associated with more satisfaction with social ties, greater overall well-being, and less loneliness, compared to weaker approach goals. In their studies of young adults and older adults making social transitions (moving out of the parental home in the former, moving into senior housing in the latter), Nikitin, Burgermeister, and Freund (2012) found that social approach goals were positively associated with well-being, and social avoidance goals were negatively associated with well-being.

Studies that examine outcomes associated with approach and avoidance goals that people have for specific relationships show similar, parallel results. In a series of studies with dating and married couples, Laurenceau and his colleagues found that stronger approach motivation strength was associated with greater positive affect following a laboratory discussion about loving aspects of their relationships (Laurenceau, Kleinman, Kaczynski, & Carver, 2010) However, avoidance motivation strength was positively associated with anxiety following a laboratory-based conflict discussion. In terms of overall global satisfaction, in a daily diary study Gable and Poore (2008) also found that individuals with strong approach goals were more satisfied with their relationships on a daily basis than those with weak approach goals, and those with strong avoidance goals were less satisfied with their relationships than those with weak avoidance goals at the end of the day.

Similarly, in series of studies, Impett et al. (2010) found that approach and avoidance goals in dating couples predicted relationship satisfaction both on a day-to-day basis and in global evaluations. Specifically, people with stronger approach goals for their relationships reported higher levels of daily relationship satisfaction and greater satisfaction over time than those with weaker approach goals for their relationships. In these studies, they also found that those with stronger avoidance goals for their relationships reported less satisfaction over time than those with weaker avoidance goals for their relationships. In addition, partners' approach goal strength was positively associated with one's own satisfaction, and partners' avoidance goals strength was negatively associated with one's own satisfaction.

Impett and her colleagues (2008) have also looked more carefully at the links between approach and avoidance motivation and sexual behavior and sexual desire in romantic relationships. In an initial study, approach goals (but not avoidance goals) were strongly positively related to sexual desire concurrently. Strong approach goals were associated with experiencing more desire and excitement during sexual interactions and also with greater maintenance of sexual desire over time. In a recent study, Muise, Impett, and Desmarais (2013) reported that when sex was engaged in for approach goals, such as to enhance intimacy and bring pleasure to a partner, greater sexual satisfaction was reported over time. On the other hand, engaging in sex for avoidance motives, such as not feeling guilty or not wanting to disappoint the partner, was associated with decreased sexual satisfaction over time.

Similarly, in their work on sacrifice in romantic relationships, Impett and her colleagues (2005) have found that having different goals for the same behavior has implications for relationship outcomes. For example, when participants' every day sacrifices for their partners were motivated by approach reasons, they reported greater positive affect and relationship satisfaction. However, when these behaviors were motivated by the avoidance of negative consequences, they had more conflict with the partner and less relationship satisfaction. These results were robust over time.

Summing up this work, several studies have shown that approach and avoidance motives and goals have an impact on important social, relational, and personal outcomes. The patterns of results have been highly consistent across studies that employ different methods. Moreover, the literature has documented that general social motives and goals are consistent and strong predictors of outcomes, and that the motives and goals that people have for specific relationships and behaviors within a relationship influences outcomes. Many of these studies examined outcomes that were comprised of both incentive-based and threat-based assessments, such as loneliness, well-being, and overall satisfaction. However, those that did measure outcomes defined by the presence of incentives (e.g., positive affect, sexual desire) found that approach goals were more strongly predictive of these outcomes than avoidance goals, which often were not related at all to these outcomes. Similar specificity has been documented for the association between avoidance goals and outcomes defined by the presence of threats, such as insecurity and negative affect. This overall pattern of findings is highly consistent with the model of social motives and goals depicted in Figure 1.

6. MEDIATING LINKS BETWEEN SOCIAL MOTIVATION AND OUTCOMES

Approach and avoidance social goals are quite similar in terms of their content. Both types of goals center on meeting the human need for relatedness. However, as the previous review demonstrates, meeting this need via incentive-based goals leads to a pattern of outcomes that is different than meeting this need via threat-based goals. Research has begun to tackle the question as to what processes might account for the links between relationship goals and outcomes. Gable and Berkman (2008) emphasized that approach and avoidance motivational systems are independent of one another and investigations of these processes should not a priori assume that the processes that link approach goals to outcomes are the same or even mirror images of the processes that link avoidance goals to outcomes. Data have largely supported this idea.

For example, research examining how motives and goals are linked to the incentives and threats to which they are oriented provided early evidence for these effects (e.g., Gable, 2006; Gable et al., 2000). Specifically, research has looked at patterns of experiences with day-to-day positive events (i.e., incentives) and negative events (i.e., threats). This work has shown that stronger approach social motives and goals are consistently associated with reporting the experience of a greater number of positive events, but not necessarily fewer negative events, than weaker approach goals. Moreover in these studies, the frequency of positive events accounted for part of the link between approach motives (or goals) and outcomes. On the other hand, compared to weaker avoidance social motives, stronger avoidance social motives and goals have been consistently associated with reporting increased emotional and cognitive reactivity (e.g., negative affect, importance ratings) to negative social events when they do occur (Elliot et al., 2006; Gable, 2006), but not necessarily more or less reactivity to positive social events. Again this reactivity to negative events accounts for at least part of the link between avoidance goals and outcomes.

Finally, consistent with the view that appetitive and aversive systems are independent, across these studies threat-based motives and goals are unrelated to, or only weakly related to how positive events are experienced, and incentive-based motive and goals are unrelated to, or only weakly related to how negative events are experienced. While understanding the experience of positive and negative events is useful, it does not tell us about more basic psychological processes that might be responsible for these differences in experience. More recent research has examined how social motivation is linked to outcomes through ways in which social information is processed, such as attention, cognitive biases, and interpretation of ambiguous information, and how different experiences are used to form global evaluations of relationship quality and overall well-being.

6.1 Attention

Motives and goals can have a profound and immediate effect on experience and outcomes by directing one's attention toward certain stimuli or away from other stimuli. There is a long history of research on the impact that approach and avoidance motives have on how easily people attend to, and how difficult it is to disengage from, positively and negatively valenced stimuli. For example, Avila and Parcet (2002) showed that participants higher in general incentive-based motivation (BAS) were quicker to attend to targets when they were primed with a positive incentive cue (relative to no cue) than those lower on BAS. Similarly, Derryberry and Reed (1994) reported that people with strong approach motivation had more trouble disengaging their attention from potential incentives, and those with strong avoidance motivation had more trouble disengaging from potential punishments. Similarly, people who have strong avoidance motivation of a particular class of stimuli, such as people who suffer from phobias, show heightened attention to threatening cues in tests that examine rapid attention deployment and capture (e.g., Mathews & MacLeod, 1994; Williams, Mathews, & MacLeaod, 1996).

Does social motivation direct attention in our social world in a similar way? For example, when encountering a group of people where does our attention fall, on the smiling face or the angry face? Results from recent direct tests of these attention patterns in the social domain have been consistent with these previous findings. In a basic gaze tracking task, Nikitin and Freund (2011) found that people with strong avoidance motivation were quicker to fix their gaze, and lingered longer, on angry faces than those with weaker avoidance motivation. In addition, avoidance motivation was negatively associated with attention to (both fixation and time spent on) happy faces. In an eye tracking study, researchers examined the amount of time people attended to social versus nonsocial aspects of an array after priming them with approach social or avoidance social goals (Krajewski, Sauerland, & Muessigmann, 2015). They found that when primed with social approach goals people spent more time attending to the social aspects of the array than those primed with avoidance social goals. In summary, initial evidence that social motivation directs attention early on in the perceptual process is consistent with theoretical expectations.

6.2 Cognitive Biases

Beyond basic perceptual processes, cognitive processes such as biases in expectancies for, and memory or recall of social information play a mediating role in the motivation to downstream effects link (e.g., Neuberg, 1996). Expectations are especially important in the social domain because repeated interactions with the same people over time form expectancies regarding the social partner or category of relationships (e.g., coworkers). Is the half-smiling friend pleasantly surprised or slightly annoyed that you stopped in unexpectedly? Approach and avoidance social motivations can influence expectations for the likelihood of the social environment presenting incentives or threats and thus bias the interpretation of ambiguous stimuli in either direction. Approach motivation can bias people to expect potential rewards and thus categorize ambiguous social stimuli as a potential reward. On the other hand, avoidance motivation may bias people to expect punishments and thus categorize ambiguous stimuli in their social environment as a potential threat. Similarly, motives can influence the type of information recalled from past social interactions. Again, the nature of the social domain with repeated interactions over time with the same people leave a bevy of experiences upon which to form memories, and motivation influences which experiences are relegated to memory (e.g., Kennedy, Mather, & Carstensen, 2004). Does one recall all of the lovely birthday gifts given by a spouse, or the time he forgot a wedding anniversary?

Strachman and Gable (2006) investigated the associations between social motivation and interpretation of ambiguous social information and memory of social information. They found that those with strong avoidance goals were more likely to interpret neutral and positive information from a social scenario more negatively that those with weaker avoidance goals. Individual differences in the strength of avoidance social goals were also positively associated with recalling more of the negative information from the scenario. In another study, participants who were randomly assigned to hold an avoidance goal remembered more negative information about a potential interaction partner than those who were randomly assigned to hold an approach goal. These study results are consistent with predictions from the approach—avoidance social motivation model, and previous work on motivation and cognitive biases more broadly.

6.3 Weight of Social Information

The formation of global assessments of well-being, loneliness, or satisfaction in a given relationships are combinations of many factors (e.g., Pavot & Diener, 2008). Some of these factors are defined by the presence—absence of rewards (e.g., positive emotions, fun, passion) and others are defined by the presence—absence of threats (e.g., negative emotions, conflict, security). In their work investigating how general approach and avoidance motives (BAS and BIS) influenced the weighting of positive and negative emotion in global assessments, Updegraff and colleagues found that those who had strong approach motivation based their overall satisfaction more strongly on positive emotions than those low in approach (Updegraff, Gable, & Taylor, 2004). This was found in a laboratory study in which participants evaluated their overall experience as participants in the lab, and in field study in which participants rated their overall life satisfaction on a daily basis over the course of weeks.

Similarly in the social domain, motivation not only influences how different aspects of social life (e.g., companionship, betrayal) are experienced, as reviewed above, but motives also influence how these aspects are weighed in global evaluations of social well-being and satisfaction with particular relationships. For example, how much does having three semester-long friendships in the dorm compare to not being accepted into a fraternity when forming feelings of current loneliness? Gable and Poore (2008) examined these processes in the context of satisfaction with romantic relationships in a signal-contingent daily experience study. Participants provided ratings of how passionate and how secure they felt about their partners at randomly timed intervals throughout the day. Then at the end of the day, they reported their overall satisfaction with their relationships. People with strong approach goals weighed passion more heavily than those low in approach goals in their end of day reports of relationship satisfaction, while those with strong avoidance social goals weighed security more heavily than those with weaker avoidance social goals in their end of day reports of satisfaction. Thus, while everyone's feelings of security and passion fluctuated throughout the day and from day-to-day, for some people their overall satisfaction was primarily a function of the incentives their relationships did or did not provide and for some people their satisfaction was primarily a function of the threats their relationship did or did not provide. In short, prior motives determined, to some degree, the actual definition of satisfaction and well-being.

7. MODERATORS OF APPROACH AND AVOIDANCE SOCIAL MOTIVATION PROCESSES

As the previous review and model in Figure 1 outline, approach and avoidance motivation and the current social environment influence the strength of short-term approach and avoidance goals, and both motives and goals are associated with outcomes via several processes. However, recent work has suggested that other individual difference factors may also moderate these processes. It is not surprising that an individual difference that has previously been shown to be highly influential in the social and relationship domain—attachment—has emerged as a moderator of approach and avoidance social motivation processes. For example, Impett and colleagues have found that attachment anxiety influences the strength of both approach and avoidance social goals. In particular, people who were highly anxious had stronger goals that are focused on obtaining positive outcomes *and* stronger goals focused on avoiding negative outcomes that those who are low on anxiety (Impett & Gordon, 2010; Impett, Gordon, & Strachman, 2008).

In other work, insecure attachment predicted the strength of goals that individuals adopted toward commitment in relationships (Dandurand, Bouaziz, & Lafontaine, 2013). Again, anxious attachment was positively associated with approach *and* avoidance commitment goals. In this study, avoidant attachment (discomfort with closeness) was negatively linked with approach commitment goals. In a study of goals for interactions with a partner in daily life, Locke (2008) also found that higher avoidant attachment predicted weaker approach goals for interactions with partners; anxious attachment predicted stronger goals of both approach and avoidance types and also more instability in goal adoption across interactions. The pattern of findings across these studies is consistent with what is known about attachment. Anxiously, attached individuals are often highly fearful of rejection and abandonment but also very much desire intimacy and closeness. In fact, an early term used in the attachment literature to describe this attachment pattern was ambivalence. Thus, these anxiously attached individuals have strong approach and strong avoidance social goals. On the other hand, individuals high on avoidant attachment value their own independence and place a low value on relationships in general. That is, they are not likely to be motivated by the incentives that relationships can provide so they are likely to have weak approach goals.

Other researchers have suggested that self-esteem and other personal resources moderate the adoption of approach and avoidance goals (Law, Elliot, & Murayama, 2012; Murray, Derrick, Leder, & Holmes, 2008). For example, Park (2010) outlined a model predicting that following a threat to the self, high self-esteem people should adopt approach-motivated social goals that are focused on gaining incentives. On the other hand, following a threat to the self, individuals with low self-esteem decrease approach motivation or increase avoidance motivation to minimize further threats. There is empirical evidence from work on interpersonal and achievement goal pursuit that supports the notion that self-esteem and personal resources influence goal adoption.

Heimpel, Elliot, and Wood (2006) found that self-esteem was negatively related to avoidance personal goals; high self-esteem people were less likely to adopt avoidance goals than low self-esteem individuals. Schnelle, Brandstätter, and Knöpfel (2010) found similar results, and also found that manipulating the perception of resources affected goal adoption such that lower perceptions of resources led to more avoidance goal adoption compared to perceiving more resources. In the relationship domain, Murray and colleagues have proposed the risk-regulation model, which holds as a central tenet that when one feels confident in their worth they are more likely to pursue goals aimed at connectedness (Murray, Holmes, & Collins, 2006). Murray and her colleagues have found evidence in support in this prediction in the context of responding to feelings of threat to the relationship (e.g., Murray, Griffin, Rose, & Bellavia, 2003). Taken in whole, these studies suggest that the strength of approach and avoidance goals are influenced by both chronic (e.g., self-esteem) and situationally activated perceptions of personal resources.

8. FUTURE DIRECTIONS

Given the long history of research on appetitive and aversive motivation and the sustained empirical interest in the fundamental need for social connection, it is somewhat surprising that only recently has there been systematic research on social approach and avoidance motives and goals. However, what is hopefully apparent in the current review is that the approach—avoidance framework can account for the simultaneous regulation of the inherent incentives and threats necessary for the formation and maintenance of social bonds. There are of course many gaps in the current literature that also suggest fruitful avenues for future research.

First, something that has not been explicitly addressed thus far in this review is that interpersonal relationships are dyadic. This simple truth makes the social domain different from much of the past motivation research that considers only the individual as the unit of analysis. In order for models of social motivation to truly advance, they must go beyond the person and account for the other half of the dyad. Therefore, in the context of social bonds it may be important to investigate not only the goals of one individual and his or her outcomes, but also how those goals influence the interaction partner's outcomes, and how the two partner's goals interact. This is likely even more important as social bonds become long-term relationships (e.g., friendships, family ties, romantic relationships).

Initial evidence for the importance of this dyadic perspective is emerging in the literature. For example, Bohns et al. (2013) found that romantic couples whose style of goal pursuit was complementary (for example, one pursued goals with a vigilant style, the other with an eager style) also reported high-quality relationships. In addition, Impett et al. (2010) conducted studies investigating the role positive emotions played in the link between goals and satisfaction in dating couples. Consistent with prior work (e.g. Gable et al., 2000), they found that the strength of participants' approach goals was positively associated with general daily positive affect and relationship-specific positive emotions such as gratitude, love, and compassion. More importantly for the present discussion, they found that the strength of participants' approach goals also predicted partners' reports of positive emotions in the same direction. These studies illustrate that taking into account how relationship and interaction partners' goals "fit" together and how they influence one another's outcomes is critical. Future research should focus on these issues.

Another gap in the literature centers on the fact that many social bonds exist over time. Indeed, our most important relationships unfold over the course of long periods of time. These relationships involve repeated interactions, and in the case of interdependent relationships, the expectation of future interactions. As such, goals likely fluctuate dynamically over time. These fluctuations might be responses to progress assessments or changes in the dyadic partner's behavior and the overall relationship environment. However, to date there is little work on how approach and avoidance goals and motivational processes change and unfold over time in relationships. One area where the examination of shifts in goal processes may yield especially interesting results is in the investigation of the well-known decline in marital satisfaction that occurs in newlywed couples (Karney & Bradbury, 1997).

9. CONCLUDING COMMENTS

Imagine two hypothetical women, Marilyn and Hillary, moving to New York City after college graduation for their first jobs on Wall Street. Both women will be challenged with many logistical tasks such as learning the subway system, finding out which are the good restaurants in their neighborhood, setting up a new apartment. On the social side, the tasks are also big. While of course Marilyn is sad to leave many of her friends behind, she wants to form a new social network, create a bond with her new roommate, and maybe even go out on a few dates if her work schedule allows. It is hard to meet new people, so whenever Marilyn meets someone new she tries to strike up a conversation under any circumstance, and in a few months she has made a few new friends. She also feels that she gets along pretty well with her new roommate, despite the occasional disagreements that come with sharing small spaces, and overall feels pretty good about her social life. Hillary is also sad to leave many of her friends behind and determined not to be lonely in her new city. She also wants to make sure she does not have a bad relationship with her new roommate or be single for any longer than necessary. Hillary does not want to be rejected so she only talks to people with whom she thinks she can be friends. She is worried that her roommate does not like her because despite the fact that they get along well most of the time, they occasionally disagree about shared space. Hillary is feeling lonely in New York.

The approach–avoidance motivation model sheds light on how Marilyn and Hillary's social motives and goals have an impact on their well-being and interpersonal relationships. It outlines how their goals might influences what they pay attention to in their social environments, how they interpret and remember social information, and even how they define loneliness and relationship satisfaction. Future work on social motivation will continue to illuminate their different paths.

ACKNOWLEDGMENTS

This work was supported by the National Science Foundation under Grant No. BCS 1050875 awarded to the author. Any opinions, findings, and conclusions or recommendations expressed in this material are those of the author(s) and do not necessarily reflect the views of the National Science Foundation.

REFERENCES

Akerlind, I., Hörnquist, J. O., & Hansson, B. (1987). Loneliness correlates in advanced alcohol abusers. I. Social factors and needs. *Scandinavian Journal of Social Medicine, 15*(3), 175–183.

Amodio, D. M., Master, S. L., Yee, C. M., & Taylor, S. E. (2008). Neurocognitive components of the behavioral inhibition and activation systems: implications for theories of self-regulation. *Psychophysiology, 45*(1), 11−19.

Aron, A., & Aron, E. N. (1997). Self-expansion motivation and including other in the self. In S. Duck (Ed.), *Handbook of personal relationships: Theory, research, and interventions* (2nd ed., pp. 251−270). Chichester, England: John Wiley & Sons.

Atkinson, J. W., Heyns, R. W., & Veroff, J. (1954). The effects of experimental arousal of the affiliation motive on thematic apperception. *Journal of Abnormal and Social Psychology, 49,* 405−410.

Avila, C., & Parcet, M. A. (2002). Individual differences in reward sensitivity and attentional focus. *Personality and Individual Differences, 33,* 979−996.

Ayduk, O., Downey, G., Testa, A., Yen, Y., & Shoda, Y. (1999). Does rejection elicit hostility in rejection sensitive women? *Social Cognition Special Issue: Social cognition and relationships, 17*(2), 245−271.

Baron, K. G., Smith, T. W., Butner, J., Nealey-Moore, J., Hawkins, M. W., & Uchino, B. N. (2007). Hostility, anger, and marital adjustment: concurrent and prospective associations with psychosocial vulnerability. *Journal of Behavioral Medicine, 30*(1), 1−10. http://dx.doi.org/10.1007/s10865-006-9086-z.

Baumeister, R. F., & Leary, M. R. (1995). The need to belong: desire for interpersonal attachments as a fundamental human motivation. *Psychological Bulletin, 117,* 497−529.

Beckes, L., & Coan, J. A. (2011). Social baseline theory: the role of social proximity in emotion and economy of action. *Social and Personality Psychology Compass, 5*(12), 976−988. http://dx.doi.org/10.1111/j.1751-9004.2011.00400.x.

Berntson, G. G., & Cacioppo, J. T. (2008). *The functional neuroarchitecture of evaluative processes. Handbook of approach and avoidance motivation.* New York, NY: Psychology Press.

Bohns, V. K., Lucas, G. M., Molden, D. C., Finkel, E. J., Coolsen, M. K., Kumashiro, M., et al. (2013). Opposites fit: regulatory focus complementarity and relationship well-being. *Social Cognition, 31*(1), 1−14.

Bowlby. (1982). Attachment and loss. In *Attachment* (Vol. 1). New York: Basic Books (Original work published 1969).

Boyatzis, R. E. (1973). Affiliation motivation. In D. C. McClelland, & R. S. Steele (Eds.), *Human motivation: A book of readings* (pp. 252−276). Morristown, NJ: General Learning Press.

Bradshaw, J., Hoelscher, P., & Richardson, D. (2007). An index of child well-being in the european union. *Social Indicators Research, 80*(1), 133−177.

Bugental, D. P. (2000). Acquisition of the algorithms of social life: a domain-based approach. *Psychological Bulletin, 126,* 187−219.

Cantor, N., & Malley, J. (1991). *Life tasks, personal needs, and close relationships. Cognition in close relationships.* Hillsdale, NJ: Lawrence Erlbaum Associates, Inc.

Carver, C. S., & Scheier, M. F. (1990). Origins and functions of positive and negative affect: a control-process view. *Psychological Review, 97,* 19−35.

Cavallo, J. V., Fitzsimons, G. M., & Holmes, J. G. (2009). Taking chances in the face of threat: romantic risk regulation and approach motivation. *Personality and Social Psychology Bulletin, 35,* 737−751.

Chen, Y., & Feeley, T. H. (2014). Social support, social strain, loneliness, and well-being among older adults: an analysis of the health and retirement study. *Journal of Social and Personal Relationships, 31*(2), 141−161.

Cheung, E. O., Gardner, W. L., & Anderson, J. F. (2015). Emotionships: examining people's emotion-regulation relationships and their consequences for well-being. *Social Psychological and Personality Science, 6,* 407−414. http://dx.doi.org/10.1177/1948550614564223.

Cohen, S., Doyle, W. J., Skoner, D. P., Rabin, B. S., & Gwaltney, J. M. (1997). Social ties and susceptibility to the common cold. *JAMA, 277*(24), 1940−1944.

Cohen, S., & Willis, T. A. (1985). Stress, social support, and the buffering hypothesis. *Psychological Bulletin, 98*, 310−357.

Corr, P. J. (Ed.). (2008). *The reinforcement sensitivity theory of personality.* Cambridge University Press.

Cutrona, C., Russell, D., & Rose, J. (1986). Social support and adaptation to stress by the elderly. *Psychology and Aging, 1*(1), 47−54. http://dx.doi.org/10.1037/0882-7974.1.1.47.

Dandurand, C., Bouaziz, A. R., & Lafontaine, M. F. (2013). Attachment and couple satisfaction: the mediating effect of approach and avoidance commitment. *Journal of Relationships Research, 4*, e3.

Davila, J., Bradbury, T. N., Cohan, C. L., & Tochluk, S. (1997). Marital functioning and depressive symptoms: evidence for a stress generation model. *Journal of personality and social psychology, 73*(4), 849.

DeCharms, R. C. (1957). Affiliation motivation and productivity in small groups. *Journal of Abnormal and Social Psychology, 55*, 222−226.

Deci, E. L., & Ryan, R. M. (2000). The "what" and "why" of goal pursuits: human needs and the self-determination of behavior. *Psychological Inquiry, 11*, 227−268.

Derryberry, D., & Reed, M. A. (1994). Temperament and attention: orienting toward and away from positive and negative signals. *Journal of personality and social psychology, 66*(6), 1128.

Diener, E. (2000). Subjective well-being: the science of happiness and a proposal for a national index. *American Psychological Association, 55*(1), 34.

Downey, G., Feldman, S., & Ayduk, O. (2000). Rejection sensitivity and male violence in romantic relationships. *Personal Relationships, 7*(1), 45−61.

Downey, G., Freitas, B. L., Michaelis, B., & Khouri, H. (1998). The self-fulfilling prophecy in close relationships: rejection sensitivity and rejection by romantic partners. *Journal of Personality and Social Psychology, 75*, 545−560.

Dunkel-Schetter, C., & Bennett, T. (1990). Differentiating the cognitive and behavioral aspects of social support. In B. R. Sarason, I. G. Sarason, & G. Pierce (Eds.), *Social support: An interactional view* (pp. 267−296). New York: Wiley.

Durkheim, E. (1897/1951). *Suicide.* New York, NY: Free Press.

Eaker, E. D., Sullivan, L. M., Kelly-Hayes, M., D'Agostino, R. B., & Benjamin, E. J. (2007). Marital status, marital strain, and risk of coronary heart disease or total mortality: the framingham offspring study. *Psychosomatic Medicine, 69*(6), 509−513. http://dx.doi.org/10.1097/PSY.0b013e3180f62357.

Eisenberger, N. I., Lieberman, M. D., & Williams, K. D. (2003). Does rejection hurt? an fMRI study of social exclusion. *Science, 302*(5643), 290−292.

Elliot, A. J. (1997). Integrating the "classic" and "contemporary" approaches to achievement motivation: a hierarchical model of approach and avoidance achievement motivation. In M. Maehr, & P. Pintrich (Eds.), *Advances in motivation and achievement* (Vol. 10, pp. 243−279). Greenwich, CT: JAI Press.

Elliot, A. J. (2006). A hierarchical model of approach and avoidance motivation. *Motivation and Emotion, 30*, 111−116.

Elliot, A. J., & Church, M. A. (1997). A hierarchical model of approach and avoidance achievement motivation. *Journal of Personality and Social Psychology, 72*, 218−232.

Elliot, A. J., Gable, S. L., & Mapes, R. R. (2006). Approach and avoidance motivation in the social domain. *Personality and Social Psychology Bulletin, 32*(3), 378−391.

Elliot, A. J., & Sheldon, K. M. (1998). Avoidance personal goals and the personality-illness relationship. *Journal of Personality and Social Psychology, 75*, 1282−1299.

Elliot, A. J., Thrash, T. M., & Murayama, K. (2011). A longitudinal analysis of self-regulation and well-being: avoidance personal goals, avoidance coping, stress generation, and subjective well-being. *Journal of Personality, 79*(3), 643−674.

Ellsberg, M., Jansen, H. A. F. M., Heise, L., Watts, C. H., & García-Moreno, C. (2008). Intimate partner violence and women's physical and mental health in the WHO multi-country study on women's health and domestic violence: an observational study. *The Lancet, 371*(9619), 1165–1172.

Emmons, R. A. (1999). *The psychology of ultimate concerns: Motivation and spirituality in personality.* New York, NY: Guilford Press.

Epley, N., Akalis, S., Waytz, A., & Cacioppo, J. T. (2008). Creating social connection through inferential reproduction: loneliness and perceived agency in gadgets, gods, and greyhounds. *Psychological Science, 19*(2), 114–120.

Epley, N., Waytz, A., Akalis, S., & Cacioppo, J. T. (2008). When we need a human: motivational determinants of anthropomorphism. *Social Cognition, 26*(2), 143–155.

Ernst, J. M., & Cacioppo, J. T. (1999). Lonely hearts: psychological perspectives on loneliness. *Applied and Preventive Psychology, 8*(1), 1–22.

Feeney, B. C., & Collins, N. L. (2015). A new look at social support: a theoretical perspective on thriving through relationships. *Personality and Social Psychology Review, 19*, 113–147.

Feeney, J. A. (2000). Implications of attachment style for patterns of health and illness. *Child: Care, Health and Development, 26*, 277–288. http://dx.doi.org/10.1046/j.1365-2214.2000.00146.

Fincham, F. D., & Beach, S. R. (2010). Of memes and marriage: toward a positive relationship science. *Journal of Family Theory and Review, 2*(1), 4–24.

Fiske, A. P. (1992). The four elementary forms of sociality: framework for a unified theory of social relations. *Psychological Review, 99*(4), 689–723. http://dx.doi.org/10.1037/0033-295X.99.4.689.

Gable, S. L. (2006). Approach and avoidance social motives and goals. *Journal of Personality, 71*, 175–222.

Gable, S. L., & Berkman, E. T. (2008). Making connections and avoiding loneliness: approach and avoidance social motives. In A. J. Elliot (Ed.), *Handbook of approach and avoidance motivation* (pp. 203–216). Lawrence Erlbaum Associates.

Gable, S. L., Gosnell, C. G., Maisel, N., & Strachman, A. N. (2012). Safely testing the alarm: responses to personal events. *Journal of Personality and Social Psychology, 103*(6), 949–962.

Gable, S. L., & Impett, E. A. (2012). Approach and avoidance motivation in close relationships. *Personality and Social Psychology Compass, 6*(1), 95–108.

Gable, S. L., & Poore, J. (2008). Which thoughts count? Algorithms for evaluating satisfaction in relationships. *Psychological Science, 19*, 1030–1036.

Gable, S. L., Reis, H. T., & Elliot, A. J. (2000). Behavioral activation and inhibition in everyday life. *Journal of Personality and Social Psychology, 78*, 1135–1149.

Gable, S. L., Reis, H. T., Impett, E., & Asher, E. R. (2004). What do you do when things go right? the intrapersonal and interpersonal benefits of sharing positive events. *Journal of Personality and Social Psychology, 87*, 228–245.

Gere, J., & MacDonald, G. (2010). An update of the empirical case for the need to belong. *The Journal of Individual Psychology, 66*(1), 93–115.

Gray, J. A. (1987). *The psychology of fear and stress* (2nd ed.). New York: Cambridge University Press.

Gray, J. A. (1990). Brain systems that mediate both emotion and cognition. *Cognition and Emotion, 4*, 269–288.

Heimpel, S. A., Elliot, A. J., & Wood, J. V. (2006). Basic personality dispositions, self-esteem, and personal goals: an approach–avoidance analysis. *Journal of Personality, 74*, 1293–1320.

Helliwell, J. F., & Putnam, R. D. (2005). *The social context of well-being. The science of well-being.* New York, NY: Oxford University Press.

Higgins, E. T. (1998). Promotion and prevention: regulatory focus as a motivational principle. *Advances in Experimental Social Psychology, 30*, 1–46.

Higgins, E. T., Shah, J., & Friedman, R. (1997). Emotional responses to goal attainment: strength of regulatory focus as moderator. *Journal of personality and social psychology, 72*(3), 515.

Hoebel, B. G., Avena, N. M., & Rada, P. (2008). *An accumbens dopamine-acetylcholine system for approach and avoidance. Handbook of approach and avoidance motivation.*

Holt-Lunstad, J., Smith, T. B., & Layton, J. B. (2010). Social relationships and mortality risk: a meta-analytic review. *PLoS Medicine, 7*(7), e1000316. http://dx.doi.org/10.1371/journal.pmed.1000316.

Impett, E. A., & Gordon, A. (2010). Why do people sacrifice to approach rewards versus to avoid costs? Insights from attachment theory. *Personal Relationships, 17,* 299–315.

Impett, E. A., Gordon, A., Kogan, A., Oveis, C., Gable, S. L., & Keltner, D. (2010). Moving toward more perfect unions: daily and long-term consequences of approach and avoidance goals in romantic relationships. *Journal of Personality and Social Psychology, 99,* 948–963.

Impett, E. A., Gordon, A., & Strachman, A. (2008). Attachment and daily sexual goals: a study of dating couples. *Personal Relationships, 15,* 375–390.

Impett, E. A., Peplau, L. A., & Gable, S. L. (2005). Approach and avoidance sexual motivation: implications for personal and interpersonal well-being. *Personal Relationships, 12,* 465–482.

Karney, B. R., & Bradbury, T. N. (1997). Neuroticism, marital interaction, and the trajectory of marital satisfaction. *Journal of personality and social psychology, 72*(5), 1075.

Kasser, T., & Ryan, R. M. (1996). Further examining the American dream: differential correlates of intrinsic and extrinsic goals. *Personality and Social Psychology Bulletin, 22*(3), 280–287.

Kennedy, Q., Mather, M., & Carstensen, L. L. (2004). The role of motivation in the age-related positivity effect in autobiographical memory. *Psychological Science, 15,* 208–214. http://dx.doi.org/10.1111/j.0956-7976.2004.01503011.

Keyes, C. L. M. (1998). Social well-being. *Social Psychology Quarterly, 61*(2), 121–140.

Kiecolt-Glaser, J. K. (1999). Stress, personal relationships, and immune function: health implications. *Brain, Behavior, and Immunity, 13*(1), 61–72.

Kiecolt-Glaser, J. K., & Newton, T. L. (2001). Marriage and health: his and hers. *Psychological bulletin, 127*(4), 472.

Klinger, E. (1977). *Meaning and void: Inner experiences and the incentives in people's lives.* Minneapolis: University of Minnesota Press.

Krajewski, J., Sauerland, M., & Muessigmann, M. (2015). The effects of priming-induced social approach and avoidance goals on the exploration of goal-relevant stimuli. *Social Psychology, 42,* 152–158.

Lakey, B., & Cassady, P. B. (1990). Cognitive processes in perceived social support. *Journal of Personality and Social Psychology, 59,* 337–343.

Lang, P. J., & Bradley, M. M. (2008). *Cortex-reflex connections appetitive and defensive motivation is the substrate of emotion. Handbook of approach and avoidance motivation.*

Laurenceau, J. P., Kleinman, B. M., Kaczynski, K. J., & Carver, C. S. (2010). Assessment of relationship-specific incentive and threat sensitivities: predicting satisfaction and affect in adult intimate relationships. *Psychological assessment, 22*(2), 407.

Law, W., Elliot, A. J., & Murayama, K. (2012). Perceived competence moderates the relation between performance-approach and performance-avoidance goals. *Journal of Educational Psychology, 104*(3), 806.

Lewin, K. (1935). *A dynamic theory of personality.* New York: McGraw-Hill.

Locke, K. D. (2008). Attachment styles and interpersonal approach and avoidance goals in everyday couple interactions. *Personal Relationships, 15*(3), 359–374.

Mathews, A., & MacLeod, C. (1994). Cognitive approaches to emotion and emotional disorders. *Annual Review of Psychology, 45,* 25–50.

McAdams, D. P. (1982). Intimacy motivation. In A. J. Stewart (Ed.), *Motivation and society* (pp. 133–171). San Francisco: Jossey-Bass Publishers.

Mehrabian, A. (1976). Questionnaire measures of affiliative tendency and sensitivity to rejection. *Psychological Reports, 38,* 199—209.

Mehrabian, A., & Ksionzky, S. (1974). *A theory of affiliation.* Lexington, MA: Lexington Books.

Mikulincer, M. (1998). Attachment working models and the sense of trust: an exploration of interaction goals and affect regulation. *Journal of Personality and Social Psychology, 74,* 1209—1224.

Miller, G., Rohleder, N., & Cole, S. W. (2009). Chronic interpersonal stress predicts activation of pro- and anti- inflammatory signaling pathways six months later. *Psychosomatic Medicine, 71*(1), 57—62. http://dx.doi.org/10.1097/PSY.0b013e318190d7de.

Miller, N. (1961). Acquisition of avoidance dispositions by social learning. *Journal of Abnormal and Social Psychology, 63,* 12—19.

Muise, A., Impett, E. A., & Desmarais, S. (2013). Getting it on versus getting it over with sexual motivation, desire, and satisfaction in intimate bonds. *Personality and Social Psychology Bulletin.* http://dx.doi.org/10.1177/0146167213490963.

Murray, S. L., Derrick, J. L., Leder, S., & Holmes, J. G. (2008). Balancing connectedness and self-protection goals in close relationships: a levels-of-processing perspective on risk regulation. *Journal of personality and social psychology, 94*(3), 429.

Murray, S. L., Griffin, D. W., Rose, P., & Bellavia, G. M. (2003). Calibrating the sociometer: the relational contingencies of self-esteem. *Journal of personality and social psychology, 85*(1), 63.

Murray, S. L., Holmes, J. G., & Collins, N. L. (2006). Optimizing assurance: the risk regulation system in relationships. *Psychological bulletin, 132*(5), 641.

Neeleman, J., & Power, M. J. (1994). Social support and depression in three groups of psychiatric patients and a group of medical controls. *Social Psychiatry and Psychiatric Epidemiology, 29*(1), 46—51.

Neuberg, S. L. (1996). Expectancy influences in social interaction: the moderating role of social goals. In P. M. Gollwitzer, & J. A. Bargh (Eds.), *The psychology of action: Linking cognition and motivation to behavior* (pp. 529—552). New York: Guilford Press.

Nikitin, J., Burgermeister, L. C., & Freund, A. M. (2012). The role of age and social motivation in developmental transitions in young and old adulthood. *Frontiers in psychology, 3.*

Nikitin, J., & Freund, A. M. (2011). Age and motivation predict gaze behavior for facial expressions. *Psychology and aging, 26*(3), 695.

Overholser, J. C. (1992). Interpersonal dependency and social loss. *Personality and Individual Differences, 13*(1), 17—23.

Park, L. E. (2010). Responses to self-threat: linking self and relational constructs with approach and avoidance motivation. *Social and Personality Psychology Compass, 4*(3), 201—221.

Pavlov, I. (1927). *Conditioned reflexes: An investigation into the physiological activity of the cortex (Translation by G. Anrep).* New York: Dover.

Pavot, W., & Diener, E. (2008). The satisfaction with life scale and the emerging construct of life satisfaction. *The Journal of Positive Psychology, 3*(2), 137—152.

Rafaeli, E., Cranford, J. A., Green, A. S., Shrout, P. E., & Bolger, N. (2008). The good and bad of relationships: how social hindrance and social support affect relationship feelings in daily life. *Personality and Social Psychology Bulletin, 34*(12), 1703—1718. http://dx.doi.org/10.1177/0146167208323742.

Reis, H. T., & Gable, S. L. (2003). Toward a positive psychology of relationships. In C. L. Keyes, & J. Haidt (Eds.), *Flourishing: The positive person and the good life* (pp. 129—159). Washington, D.C.: American Psychological Association.

Rönkä, A. R., Rautio, A., Koiranen, M., Sunnari, V., & Taanila, A. (2014). Experience of loneliness among adolescent girls and boys: Northern Finland birth cohort 1986 study. *Journal of Youth Studies, 17*(2), 183—203.

Rusbult, C. E., Kumashiro, M., Kubacka, K. E., & Finkel, E. J. (2009). "The part of me that you bring out": ideal similarity and the michelangelo phenomenon. *Journal of Personality and Social Psychology, 96*(1), 61–82. http://dx.doi.org/10.1037/a0014016.

Russell, J. A., & Mehrabian, A. (1978). Approach–avoidance and affiliation as functions of the emotion-eliciting quality of an environment. *Environment and Behavior, 10*, 355–387.

Ryff, C. D. (1995). Psychological well-being in adult life. *Current Directions in Psychological Science, 4*, 99–103.

Schneirla, T. C. (1959). An evolutionary and developmental theory of biphasic processes underlying approach and withdrawal. In *Nebraska symposium on motivation* (Vol. 7, pp. 1–43). Lincoln, Nebraska: University of Nebraska Press.

Schnelle, J., Brandstätter, V., & Knöpfel, A. (2010). The adoption of approach versus avoidance goals: the role of goal-relevant resources. *Motivation and Emotion, 34*(3), 215–229.

Segrin, C., & Flora, J. (2000). Poor social skills are a vulnerability factor in the development of psychosocial problems. *Human Communication Research, 26*(3), 489–514.

Shah, J. (2003). Automatic for the people: how representations of significant others implicitly affect goal pursuit. *Journal of Personality and Social Psychology, 84*, 661–681.

Shankar, A., McMunn, A., Banks, J., & Steptoe, A. (2011). Loneliness, social isolation, and behavioral and biological health indicators in older adults. *Health Psychology, 30*(4), 377–385.

Shaver, P. R., & Brennan, K. A. (1991). Measures of depression and loneliness. In J. P. Robeinson, P. R. Shaver, & L. S. WRightsman (Eds.), *Measrues of perosnaoiyt and social psychological attitudes* (Vol. 1, pp. 195–289). San Diego, CA: Academic Press.

Sherman, A. M., Lansford, J. E., & Volling, B. L. (2006). Sibling relationships and best friendships in young adulthood: warmth, conflict, and well-being. *Personal Relationships, 13*(2), 151–165.

Shipley, T. E., & Veroff, J. (1952). A projective measure of need for affiliation. *Journal of Experimental Psychology, 43*, 349–356.

Sobotka, S. S., Davidson, R. J., & Senulis, J. A. (1992). Anterior brain electrical asymmetries in response to reward and punishment. *Electroencephalography and Clinical Neurophysiology, 83*, 236–247.

Strachman, A., & Gable, S. L. (2006). What you want (and don't want) affects what you see (and don't see): avoidance social goals and social events. *Personality and Social Psychology Bulletin, 32*, 1446–1458.

Sutton, S. K., & Davidson, R. J. (1997). Prefrontal brain asymmetry: a biological substrate of the behavioral approach and inhibition systems. *Psychological Science, 8*, 204–210.

Uchino, B. N. (2013). Understanding the links between social ties and health: on building stronger bridges with relationship science. *Journal of Social and Personal Relationships, 30*(2), 155–162.

Uchino, B. N., Holt-Lunstad, J., Uno, D., & Flinders, J. B. (2001). Heterogeneity in the social networks of young and older adults: prediction of mental health and cardiovascular reactivity during acute stress. *Journal of behavioral medicine, 24*(4), 361–382.

Updegraff, J. A., Gable, S. L., & Taylor, S. E. (2004). What makes experiences satisfying? the interaction of approach-avoidance motivations and emotions in well-being. *Journal of Personality and Social Psychology, 86*, 496–504.

VanderWeele, T. J., Hawkley, L. C., Thisted, R. A., & Cacioppo, J. T. (2011). A marginal structural model analysis for loneliness: implications for intervention trials and clinical practice. *Journal of Consulting and Clinical Psychology, 79*(2), 225–235.

Veroff, J., Kulka, R. A., & Douvan, E. (1981). *Mental health in America: Patterns of help-seeking from 1957 to 1976.* New York: Basic Books.

Whisman, M. A. (2001). The association between depression and marital dissatisfaction. In S. R. H. Beach (Ed.), *Marital and family processes in depression: A scientific foundation for clinical practice* (pp. 3–24). Washington, DC, US: American Psychological Association.

Whisman, M. A., Uebelacker, L. A., & Settles, T. D. (2010). Marital distress and the metabolic syndrome: linking social functioning with physical health. *Journal of Family Psychology, 24*(3), 367.

Wilcox, V. L., Kasl, S. V., & Berkman, L. F. (1994). Social support and physical disability in older people after hospitalization: a prospective study. *Health Psychology, 13*(2), 170–179. http://dx.doi.org/10.1037/0278-6133.13.2.170.

Williams, J. M. G., Mathews, A., & MacLeaod, C. (1996). The emotional stroop task and psychopathology. *Psychological Bulletin, 120,* 3–24.

CHAPTER TWO

Between Persistence and Flexibility: The Yin and Yang of Action Control

Bernhard Hommel

Cognitive Psychology Unit & Leiden Institute for Brain and Cognition, Leiden University, Leiden, The Netherlands
E-mail: hommel@fsw.leidenuniv.nl

Contents

1. Introduction   34
2. The Will   35
3. The Ego   39
4. Control as Balance   43
5. The Metacontrol State Model   46
6. The Plasticity of Control States   49
7. Short-term Biases of Cognitive Control   50
8. The Impact of Learning, Experience, and Culture on Cognitive Control   54
9. Conclusions   60
Acknowledgments   61
References   61

Abstract

Traditional approaches to action control assume the existence of a more or less unitary control system that struggles with, and serves to overcome action tendencies induced by automatic processes. In this article, I point out that and why these approaches fail to capture the complexity and dynamics of cognitive control. I describe an alternative approach that assumes that control emerges from the interaction of at least two counteracting forces: one system promoting persistence and the maintenance of action goals and another promoting mental and behavioral flexibility. I describe how this interaction might be shaped by various factors, including genetic predisposition, learning, personal experience, and the cultural context, and suggest a simple functional model (the Metacontrol State Model, MSM) that explains how this shaping process works. Then I provide an overview of studies from various fields (including perception, attention, performance monitoring, conflict resolution, creativity, meditation, religion, and interpersonal perception and behavior) that successfully tested predictions from the MSM.

Advances in Motivation Science, Volume 2
ISSN 2215-0919
http://dx.doi.org/10.1016/bs.adms.2015.04.003

33

1. INTRODUCTION

Human action is often goal-oriented (to a degree that the existence of goals is often considered to be the defining aspect of human action), often initiated in the absence of action-related external stimulation, often spontaneous and nonhabitual, and can commonly be adjusted rapidly if no longer functional or not meeting situational challenges. The human capacity to achieve all of this is commonly ascribed to what we now call cognitive control or executive functions. The general idea is that the processes captured by these labels constitute a kind of second layer of information processing: while the first layer consists of basic processes to translate stimulation or input (the terms preferred by behavioristic and information-processing approaches, respectively)—such as sensory registration, identification, attentional selection, response decision, and motor execution—the second layer operates on the first by rewiring the respective processes in such a way that behavior is optimized and intended goals are reached (e.g., Verbruggen, McLaren, & Chambers, 2014).

Even though the terms cognitive control and executive function are relatively new (with Atkinson & Shiffrin, 1968; as one of the first proponents), the underlying concepts and the investigation of the underlying mechanisms are much older. In the following, I will discuss two predecessors and the related theoretical implications that have survived the terminological transition and that still dominate the discussion of human action control. Concepts that are used for such a long time and that have stimulated so much research are unlikely to be entirely incorrect, but I do think that they have limitations that need to be overcome in future research. I will thus present an alternative view of human action control, at least of some relevant aspects of it, that is also not without predecessors but has the advantage of providing a more dynamic, and thus probably more realistic, view of how humans keep their actions adaptive. I will begin by discussing two more traditional and popular views of action control—one assuming a *will* that is fighting against habits and another assuming an *ego* that mediates between societal requirements and personal urges—and point out a number of limitations of these views. Then I will synthesize the positive aspects of these two views and bring them together with more recent ideas from cognitive psychology and the cognitive neurosciences, to construct a more dynamic approach to human action control. Finally, I will sketch major determinants of the operation characteristics of control functions and provide some empirical examples to illustrate and justify my choices. However, I will not start without emphasizing that this chapter is a (empirical and theoretical) work in progress, a developing theoretical approach rather than a complete theory.

2. THE WILL

Approaches to human action control are older than the first psychological laboratory, which explains why they were commonly focusing on the conscious experience of control—the major empirical tool of nonexperimental researchers. The dominant view during the years in which the first laboratories were established was ideomotor theory, which has an even longer philosophical tradition (Stock & Stock, 2004). The approach focuses on the process of gaining control over one's body and its movements. It basically assumes that perceptual impressions of actively achieved changes in one's environment are automatically associated with whatever motor pattern was used to achieve them (for a review, see Hommel, 2009). Once these associations are created, the agent can reactivate the codes underlying the perceptual impressions at will and thereby automatically prime the associated motor patterns—the motor system thus becomes a slave of the will, as it were.

As the first experimental investigations of human cognition were focusing on perception, ideomotor theory and the will in general did not receive substantial empirical attention until the early 1900s. Around that time, experimental methods were developed to assess the time it takes to implement a particular action goal (e.g., Michotte & Prüm, 1911) and the impact of implementing a particular goal on information processing and conscious experience (Ach, 1910, 1935). Of particular interest, even the very first attempts to assess human will were using a scenario that survives to this day: Ach (1910) argued that the best and most objective way to measure the human will requires putting it in opposition to a counteracting force, which according to Ach was habit. Following this rationale, he developed methods to strengthen particular stimulus—response associations through repetition (e.g., by having participants produce rhyming responses to sequences of nonsense syllables) and then tested the degree of willpower by requiring the participant to produce a different response on old versus new items (for an overview, see Hommel, 2000a). As expected, items that were previously associated with a different action category were more difficult and took more time to respond to than new or familiar, but previously unassociated items. In numerous studies, Ach and colleagues demonstrated that the size of this interference effect varies systematically with the strength of the previously induced habit and/or the strength of the exerted or individually available willpower (for an overview, see Ach, 1935).

Note the similarity between this approach and the now popular rationale to assess the existence and efficiency of cognitive control functions by analyzing how much they are hampered by stimuli that are (or have been) associated with goal-incongruent responses—such as in Stroop, Simon, or flanker tasks (e.g., Hommel, 2000b). In fact, it is not only the experimental approach that is still heavily used, but the theoretical framework has remained in place as well. It comes in several flavors. The revival at the end of the 1960s along the lines of Atkinson and Shiffrin (1968) was basically replacing the apparently outdated terms "will" and "habit" by the more depersonalized terms "cognitive control" (or executive control, or executive function) and "automatic processes." As in the original framework, novel and unfamiliar actions were supposed to rely on control processes to configure the cognitive system while overlearned actions could rely on automatic processes and thus require little or no control. The basic idea was that learning is the mechanism that creates automaticity over time by building more or less direct associations between stimulus representations and response representations (e.g., Kornblum, Hasbroucq, & Osman, 1990; de Wit & Dickinson, 2009). There is a long-standing controversy with regard to the question how automatic processes or automaticity need to be characterized, and it is fair to say that no universal criterion has been found so far. Some authors have advocated nonintentionality as the key criterion while others have suggested the ballistic, nonsuppressible nature of automatic processes, and even others have favored the lack of (commonly not further defined) "cognitive" or "central" resources needed to run automatic processes or the immunity to interference from other processes (e.g., Bargh, 1994; Moors & De Houwer, 2006).

The major problem underlying discussions and theoretical considerations of that sort is that they are facing a classical Rylean category issue (Ryle, 1949). This problem is a bit more transparent when one refers to the original concept of the "will." Will is something that persons have but not a characteristic of a nervous system—much like there is nothing in a particular building that reflects its being part of a university, as in Ryle's famous example. Obviously, the willing person has a nervous system and (if we accept the functionalist stance underlying the rationale of cognitive psychology and the cognitive neurosciences) the process of willing must be reflected in the activities of that system. Accordingly, it certainly makes sense to try to capture the functional and/or neural reflection of the process of willing, but it makes little sense to characterize particular processes as carrying or not carrying the essence of will. In fact, the exact same process may very well subserve "will" in one situation and conflict with it in another. Translating the personalized concept of will into the depersonalized concept of control may sound more objective and scientific (Goschke, 2003) but it does not address the basic logical problem.

Consider, for instance, automaticity in the Stroop task (Stroop, 1935). In this task, participants are to name the color of color words, and they are known to be slower to do that if the to-be-named color is inconsistent with the meaning of the word. The standard explanation from control/automaticity approaches is that this is because people are used to reading words rather than naming their color, which has automatized the reading process that now interferes with the intentional color-naming response (for a review, see MacLeod, 1991). Note that, in this example, the reading process is not uncontrolled: it is actually triggered, and thus under the control of the word and its meaning. In that sense, the reading process is not automatic. One might object that it is inconsistent with the action goal, and should in that sense be considered automatic. But that does not hold as well. It is known that the Stroop effect is very small (less than 10% of its original size) or absent in task versions operating with keypresses rather than overt naming responses (McClain, 1983) and that the few demonstrations of reliable effects are likely to result from internal naming (Chmiel, 1984; Martin, 1978). This implies that the reading response is actually contingent on, and therefore controlled by the goal to utter color words, which undermines the assumption that the reading response is automatic. How about functionality, one might object: could not one say that it is not useful to activate the reading response related to the word meaning, and that the fact that we nevertheless find evidence for such activation demonstrates automaticity? Even that approach is not tenable, as studies on the so-called Gratton effect (Gratton, Coles, & Donchin, 1992) have revealed. What these studies show is that the interference related to the nominally irrelevant word meaning is drastically reduced (if not eliminated) after incompatible trials, that is, after trials in which the word meaning suggested the wrong response. In contrast, interference increases after compatible trials, that is, after trials in which the word meaning suggested the correct response (e.g., Egner, 2007). But this means that the tendency to react to the nominally irrelevant stimulus feature is closely depending on its informational value and, hence, on its functionality for action control. And as this functionality depends on the action goal, which again is reflected in control processes, we must conclude that what seems like the automatic activation of word meaning is actually the goal-contingent, adaptive use of stimulus information that has just (i.e., in the previous trial) proven to support action control.

These considerations suggest that it makes little sense to contrast control and automatic processes and consider them to compete for action control, as the particularly popular dual-process models in the field are doing (for an overview and a defense of the control/automaticity dichotomy, see Verbruggen et al., 2014). Moreover, there is increasing evidence that what is considered to be control processes actually shows many characteristics of what is considered to be automatic. For instance, one of the key paradigms to investigate operations of cognitive control is using task switching (for a review, see Kiesel et al., 2010). Participants are asked to respond to particular stimuli according to one set of rules in some trials and according to another set of rules in other trials. The standard finding is that performance is better if the set of rules (i.e., the task) remains the same than if the task changes, which is commonly taken to reflect the extra demands required to implement a different task set—a control process. Interestingly, however, there is ample evidence that the implementation of tasks sets can be triggered by external stimuli (e.g., Waszak, Hommel, & Allport, 2003), even if these stimuli are masked to render them unconscious (Reuss, Kiesel, Kunde, & Hommel, 2011). Hence, there are good reasons to assume that in a particular trial, "control/led" and "automatic" processes are both under stimulus control (i.e., automatic) and contingent on the current action goal (i.e., controlled by "the agent"). This is consistent with approaches suggesting that planned action consists in self-automatization. As suggested by Exner (1879), Bargh (1989) and others, planning and preparing for an action comprises the implementation of all sorts of goal-contingent stimulus–response links that delegate the triggering and eventual execution of the action to the environment as far as possible—a kind of prepared reflex (Hommel, 2000b).

To summarize, there is considerable evidence that automatic processes are under surprisingly tight cognitive control while cognitive control processes can be triggered automatically and even in the absence of conscious awareness. In principle, this makes it impossible to identify clear-cut criteria to categorize processes according to that dichotomy, which undermines its usefulness. The popularity of the dichotomy is likely to emerge from its intuitive plausibility. Take, for instance, the example of substance addiction.

Many will know from their own experience that breaking with one's habits can be extremely difficult, such as quitting to smoke. Subjectively, the conflict emerges between the urge to smoke, especially in the presence of smoke-compatible stimuli or situations, and the insight that leading a healthy life requires one to quit. It is easy to see that this experience can be nicely couched in terms of a struggle between will (the intention to quit) and habit (the overlearned urge to smoke). However, it is a far cry from this everyday example expressed in everyday language to a theoretical contrast between what dual-pathway theorists would consider the control process (suggesting to quit) and the automatic process (suggesting to smoke). After all, the smoking response meets all sorts of criteria of what in other circumstances would count as a control process: it is expected to result and actually results in pleasure, fits with previous experience, has shown to be functional in many earlier situations, fits with preferred personal stereotypes (like admired actors that also smoked), and so forth and so on. Hence, there are many reasons to smoke and it seems far-fetched to reduce the tendency to consider them a mere reflex—in fact, even for those who want to quit, smoking is a goal-directed, intentional action. It is just that the intention is inconsistent with other intentions—a classical goal conflict.

Taken altogether, a closer look reveals that the intuitive opposition of control and automaticity makes little sense and fails to provide much help in characterizing and categorizing the processes underlying human action control. The main difference between what is commonly considered control processes and what is commonly considered automatic processes lies in the familiarity with the stimulus—response relationship and the recency of acquisition of the stimulus driving the action: while the stimuli driving the apparently more "automatic" processes have commonly been acquired much earlier, the stimuli driving "control" processes (i.e., the "if" parts of the instructed "if-then" rules) have been acquired or instructed more recently. While this difference may allow for a relative categorization of one process or stimulus—response association as more "automatic" than the other, it remains unclear what benefits such a relative categorization brings theoretically.

3. THE EGO

Another approach to human action control is Freudian in nature. According to Freud's (1923) personality model, human action control is haunted by the continuous conflict between societal rules and expectations (the Superego) on the one hand and of personal needs and urges (the Id) on the other. To deal with this conflict, humans develop an ego that mediates between the two conflicting parties and tries to identify suitable compromises and solutions. In many cases, acceptable solutions will consist in the inhibition of personal needs and urges, which means that inhibition processes play a dominant role in this approach.

More modern versions of the ego model, such as the attentional approach of Kahneman (1973) and the ego-depletion model of Baumeister, Bratslavsky, Muraven, and Tice (1998), have focused on the assumed capacity requirements of cognitive control. The basic assumption is that control operations require cognitive resources that automatic operations do not. This allows for a number of empirical predictions that have been tested with some success. For instance, extensive and repeated reliance on control operations should tend to exhaust the hypothetical resource, which should impair subsequent control operations, but not automatic operations, until the resource is refilled. Along the same lines, allowing the resource to refill, or supporting and speeding up the refill process, should eliminate the reduced efficiency of control operations.

The most problematic aspect of all available versions of ego or capacity theories is the notorious under-definition of the most central concept—the resource. In the context of attention theory, this has clearly stood in the way of a broader impact of the approach (Navon, 1984), even though it is still used, often in a rather metaphorical way in applied fields (e.g., Wickens, 1984). The main problem is that the failure to characterize the resource invites circular reasoning (if some process unexpectedly fails to suffer from resource depletion it can be easily declared automatic), which strictly speaking renders the approaches untestable (Navon, 1984). A related problem refers to the nature of the capacity limitation. Straightforward predictions only hold to the degree that the individual capacity limitation is fixed, so that the refill will always reestablish the original or optimal level. However, some approaches have considered the possibility that the individual capacity might vary (Kahneman, 1973). This is motivationally not implausible and would be consistent with the "difficulty law of motivation" proposed by Hillgruber (1912; see Hommel, Fischer, Colzato, van den Wildenberg, & Cellini, 2012). According to this law, the difficulty of an action is the motive for investing more effort and devoting more cognitive control to reach the task goal. If so, increasing task difficulty should automatically ("drive-like," as Hillgruber says) increase cognitive control without conscious deliberation, an idea that has lived on in several disguises (e.g., Kahneman, 1973; Kukla,

1972; for a review, see Brehm & Self, 1989) and been confirmed empirically (e.g., Hommel et al., 2012). In a certain sense, the law can be considered a predecessor of the control approach of Botvinick, Braver, Barch, Carter, and Cohen (2001), who suggested that registering processing problems lead to a stronger focus on task-relevant information—a classical control operation. However, while the assumption that individual capacity limitations can vary is theoretically reasonable and empirically plausible, it basically renders ego-depletion and other capacity models untestable.

Another Freudian approach, or family of approaches, focuses more on inhibition. According to Freudian theorizing, socially inappropriate behavior would be prevented by having the ego suppress corresponding drive-induced tendencies. Along the same lines, numerous approaches have argued that, given the evidence that many stimuli can trigger unwanted behavioral tendencies in conflict tasks (such as the reading response in the Stroop task), there must be an inhibitory system suppressing these tendencies (e.g., Ridderinkhof, Forstmann, Wylie, Burle, & van den Wildenberg, 2010). In fact, many dual-pathway models of action control have suggested the existence of such an inhibitory system, and individual differences in the efficiency of the assumed inhibitory system have been taken to account for various behavioral problems including addiction (for overviews, see Wiers & Stacy, 2006). Behavioral studies investigating the efficiency of inhibition processes have often used conflict tasks—following the rationale introduced by Ach (1910), with the assumption that more evidence of conflict-induced interference from "automatic" processes indicates less efficiency—and tasks assessing how fast people can abort an already planned or ongoing action (e.g., Ridderinkhof et al., 2010).

Unfortunately, inhibitory approaches suffer from no less than three theoretical problems that are commonly overlooked. First, assuming an inhibitory system that is independent from the system representing the action goal doubles the "loans of intelligence" that theory building should seek to minimize. As described by McCauley (1987), explaining the intelligence of behavior by the intelligence of some assumed subsystem does not provide but merely postpones an explanation. But "intelligence loans ought to be repaid!" as McCauley rightly emphasizes. To clarify, consider again our Stroop example. To account for the observation that participants report the correct color name most of the time, even though they are more used to reading the word, requires the assumption that the actual task or goal is represented somewhere in the system and that it regulates information processing in such a way that the perceived color is somehow translated into the appropriate color-naming response. This representation need not be explicit but it must somehow incorporate the relevant stimulus—response rules and impact information processing so as to apply them. Let us now change perspective and consider the hypothetical inhibitory system. It may be easy to imagine that such a system can register the presence of multiple conflicting response tendencies, but how can it know which one to inhibit? To know that it would need to have access to a representation of the stimulus—response rules, the ability to apply them to identify the correct response, and then use that knowledge to inhibit all other response tendencies. In other words, the inhibitory system needs to be as intelligent and knowledgeable as the goal system, which doubles the hypothesized intelligence. But if nature has equipped us with one system that already knows what the right response should be—the goal system as I call it—why would it provide us with an exact copy of it for inhibition purposes? Why would it not leave the work to the first system, which already has all the necessary information? Hence, assuming a separate inhibitory system strongly violates Occam's razor principle.

Second, almost all approaches to human decision-making share two basic assumptions (for a review, see Bogacz, 2007): that decision-making is competitive (i.e., multiple representations of alternatives actively compete for selection) and that it is selective and/or capacity-limited (so that often one or few of the competing alternatives can be selected at one time). Biologically plausible models commonly reflect these basic principles by assuming that increasing the evidence for one alternative directly reduces the probability for the other alternatives to be selected. In winner-take-all models, this is commonly translated into mutually inhibitory relationships between representations of alternatives. Accordingly, increasing the activation of the representation of one alternative would lead to the reduction of the activation of alternative representations up to a point where the activation of one representation is at maximum and the activations of all other representations is at some minimum or at least sufficiently low. Note that this can be described as an inhibitory process: every gain for the eventual winner implies a relative suppression of all losers. And yet, systems of that sort do not require any independent inhibitor—inhibition is the necessary consequence of combining competition with capacity limitations, as in every neural system. If so, the assumption of an independent inhibitory system is entirely redundant and, thus, unnecessary.

Third, inhibitory approaches commonly jump from the observation of conflict-induced processing costs to assumptions about the efficiency of inhibition. The idea is that, once activated, incorrect response tendencies need to be suppressed, which takes time. As it is the inhibitory system that is responsible for the suppression, the more time it takes, the less efficient the inhibitory system must be. However, following the considerations just discussed, another, more parsimonious interpretation is possible, if not more likely. If we combine the assumption of competitive selection and capacity limitations, the time it takes to activate a correct response against competing alternatives should depend on two factors: the degree to which the action goal (or the representations embodying it) "supports" (provides top-down support) for the representation of the correct response and the degree to which competing responses were activated. Both of these factors are relatively well understood. Neuroimaging studies have provided evidence that the degree of top-down support can fluctuate from trial to trial but that it is strengthened whenever selection becomes more difficult (Egner & Hirsch, 2005). The registration of such difficulty has been shown to increase the focus on task-relevant representations in working memory (van Veen & Carter, 2002), which again results in increased facilitation of goal-consistent representations—but not in increased inhibition of irrelevant information (Egner & Hirsch, 2005). This suggests that the consideration of decision-making as competitive and capacity limited is sufficient to account for strategic adjustments in action control, but leaves no space or need for a dedicated inhibitory system.

Along the same lines, a recent genetic study of Miyake, Friedman, and colleagues has provided evidence that inhibition is an emergent property of cognitive processing rather than a separable factor. In earlier approaches, Miyake et al. (2000) have suggested the existence of three major systems underlying cognitive control: one responsible for information update, another for shifting between tasks, and a third for inhibition. While the first two systems were also indicated in the later genetic study (Friedman et al., 2008), the third, inhibitory system was found to be more of a general characteristic of action control rather than a separable factor equivalent to updating and shifting. This fits with the idea that inhibition is a necessary by-product of competitive, capacity-limited selection.

4. CONTROL AS BALANCE

An obvious commonality of many of the control approaches discussed so far is that they assume one unitary system to take care of control. More recently, a number of authors have argued for a more complex approach that considers multiple components or subsystems of control. One influential example is the just-mentioned approach of Friedman, Miyake, and colleagues. From a more functional point of view, Goschke and colleagues (Goschke, 2003; Dreisbach & Goschke, 2004) have pointed out that cognitive control often faces control dilemmas that are binary in nature, with the choice between maintenance (or persistence) and flexibility being a crucial one. While a strong maintenance of goals helps concentrating on relevant information and suppressing irrelevant information, it increases the probability that this renders a cognitive system too inflexible and insensitive to alternative possibilities and reasons to give up ineffective action plans. In turn, focusing on flexibility facilitates switching between alternative possibilities and actions but increases the possibility of distraction and dysfunctional cross talk between cognitive representations. The challenge for cognitive control or metacontrol (i.e., the control of cognitive control) would thus be to find the right balance between persistence and flexibility for a given task and situation. Indeed, Goschke and colleagues have shown how instructions and task conditions can systematically bias control characteristics toward persistence or flexibility, and that doing so creates the expected trade-offs. For instance, Dreisbach and Goschke (2004) found that the induction of positive affect increases flexibility at the cost of persistence and Müller et al. (2008) showed that prospective monetary gains have comparable effects. Given the link between positive affect, reward expectations, and dopamine (Cools, 2008), Goschke and colleagues argue that dopamine plays a crucial role in defining the control policy of executive functions and shifting control between the poles of persistence and flexibility in particular.

This possible link between dopamine and control policies was also strongly emphasized by Cools and D'Esposito (Cools, 2008, 2012; Cools & D'Esposito, 2010). According to their approach, it is important to distinguish between at least two dopaminergic pathways—a mesofrontal pathway targeting the prefrontal cortex and a nigrostriatal pathway targeting the striatum. Prefrontal cortex and striatum are assumed to play opposite roles in determining control policies, with the prefrontal component propagating persistence and the striatal component supporting flexibility. This is consistent with numerous findings suggesting a dominant role of the prefrontal cortex in behavior and cognitive skills requiring the maintenance of information, such as working memory, and a dominant role of the striatum in behavior and cognitive skills that require cognitive flexibility, such as in tasks calling for a frequent update of information. A particularly important implication of the approach relates to individual differences. As indicated by many pharmacological studies, neurotransmitters like dopamine do not have linear performance characteristics (i.e., more is not necessarily better), but follow an inverted U-shaped function, with best performance or efficiency related to medium levels (Cools & D'Esposito, 2011). This means that interventions that are affecting the current dopamine level are likely to have different implications for individuals with low versus high baseline levels, and there is indeed evidence that many dopamine-targeting interventions tend to "overdose" people with high dopamine levels. For instance, while positive mood is commonly assumed to improve creativity (for a review, see Baas, De Dreu, & Nijstad, 2008), this effect seems to be limited to individuals with low striatal dopamine levels (Akbari Chermahini & Hommel, 2012a).

With a stronger emphasis on dopaminergic receptor families, Durstewitz and Seamans (2008) have proposed a dual-state framework. These authors focus on prefrontal cortex and point out that the dopamine targeting this area is mainly processed by receptors from two families: D1- and D2-class receptors. They discuss empirical and modeling evidence that the prefrontal cortex can assume two different control states: One is characterized by the dominance of D1 receptors, which is accompanied by high performance in tasks requiring the maintenance of information. The other is characterized by the dominance of D2 receptors, which is accompanied by high performance in tasks requiring flexibility in the switching between options. The idea is that control policies are realized by shifting between D1- and D2-dominated states of the prefrontal cortex, which amounts to finding the right balance between persistence and flexibility.

Taken altogether, these available approaches differ in emphasis and level of analysis, but they provide a nicely converging picture. All approaches emphasize the existence of more than one executive control function, which goes beyond will- or ego-based unifactorial models. This does not necessarily render these more simple models incorrect, it just suggests that they underestimate the complexity and dynamical properties of cognitive control. Moreover, apart from the more conceptually oriented psychometric approach of Friedman, Miyake, and colleagues, all approaches emphasize the interactive, to a considerable degree even oppositional nature of the interactions between the components of cognitive control. This suggests that control emerges from the competition between at least two systems, one propagating persistence and the other propagating flexibility. The particular balance or imbalance between these two systems determines the (meta)control policy, that is, the performance characteristic of the control system. The more neuroscientifically interested approaches consider dopamine the crucial mediator that, in interaction with existing dopamine levels, control the relative impact of the two counteracting systems. One of these systems seems to be, or at least includes the prefrontal cortex, which is targeted by the mesofrontal dopaminergic pathway. The other system seems to be, or includes, the striatum targeted by the nigrostriatal dopaminergic pathway. Interestingly, dopaminergic receptors are not equally distributed over these two systems: While the prefrontal cortex is dominated by D1-family receptors, the striatum is dominated by D2 receptors (Beaulieu & Gainetdinov, 2011). This renders the approaches of Cools and D'Esposito (2010) and of Durstewitz and Seamans (2008) highly compatible, arguably even functionally equivalent, as D1 dominance would directly translate into a stronger relative contribution of the prefrontal cortex and D2 dominance into a stronger relative contribution of the striatum.

5. THE METACONTROL STATE MODEL

In the following, I will provide a brief overview of work led by Lorenza Colzato and myself that was guided by the idea that cognitive control may not be a unitary function but emerges from the interaction of two counteracting forces (or metacontrol states), which renders our approach a part of a broader family of control accounts that also includes the discussed approaches of Goschke and colleagues, Cools and D'Esposito, and Durstewitz and Seamans. Hence, even though most of our studies were targeting a coarser level of analysis and were thus less committed to particular brain areas and receptor families, we consider our general approach consistent and compatible with these other approaches and we were greatly inspired by them.

Given that we were interested in bringing together phenomena related to cognitive control from various levels of complexity, it was necessary to generalize and simplify the idea of (meta)control as balance, and to make it more concrete at the same time. To achieve that, we tried to relate this idea to existing models of human decision-making and considered how changes in balance—that is, changes in control style from more persistence to more flexibility, and vice versa—might affect decision-making processes. According to Bogacz (2007), there is a general modeling trend from earlier evidence collection models, which assume that representations of to-be-decided-upon alternatives collect internal and external stimulus information speaking in their favor, to more competitive models that reach decisions more quickly and that have greater biological plausibility. Figure 1(a) shows the minimal requirements for a competitive model: For one, the two or more alternative representations are competitive, which means that increases in activation of one reduce the activation of the other (until one of them reaches a certain threshold)—which in the figure is indicated by the mutually inhibitory links between the alternatives. Note that the resulting competition amounts to a capacity limitation along the lines discussed above, and that it leads to inhibition of less supported alternatives without the need of having a separate inhibiting system. As alternatives may receive some support from congruent internal or external sources, the dynamics of the interaction will have properties that random walk and diffusion models (e.g., Ratcliff & Rouder, 1998) are trying to capture. The second ingredient that biologically plausible competitive models need is some specific support from sources reflecting the current goal, which corresponds to what is considered top-down support in many modeling approaches (e.g., Desimone & Duncan, 1995). It is this input that makes sure that the "walk" is eventually not "random" but that the eventual decision is consistent with the current goal, at least in most of the cases.

How might a bias toward more persistence or more flexibility be integrated in such a minimal model? According to Hommel and Colzato (2010) and Hommel (2012) there are at least two, not necessarily mutually exclusive possibilities. One consists in increasing impact of the goal to increase persistence (as indicated in Figure 1(b)) and reduce it to achieve flexibility (Figure 1(d)). An increase will make it more likely that the most goal-consistent alternative will eventually be selected and it will make it easier to suppress less consistent or irrelevant alternatives, which would make decision-making more efficient, more selective, and more focused. In contrast, a reduced impact of the goal will increase the possibility that goal-inconsistent alternatives will be selected and lead to a stronger impact of irrelevant alternatives, but it facilitates the switch to other alternatives and the consideration of multiple alternatives in quick succession. The other possibility would be to strengthen (Figure 1(c)) or weaken (Figure 1(e)) the competitiveness between alternatives to achieve persistence and flexibility, respectively. The consequences would be more or less the same as for the modulation of goal impact, only that the modulation of competitiveness might introduce more goal-unrelated influences on the activation of alternatives. As these two possibilities have turned out to be difficult to disentangle empirically so far, and as they may very well be concurrently applied, I will not try to discriminate between them in what follows. Instead, I will assume, for the sake of simplicity, that changes of control styles affect both the impact of the goal and the competitiveness between

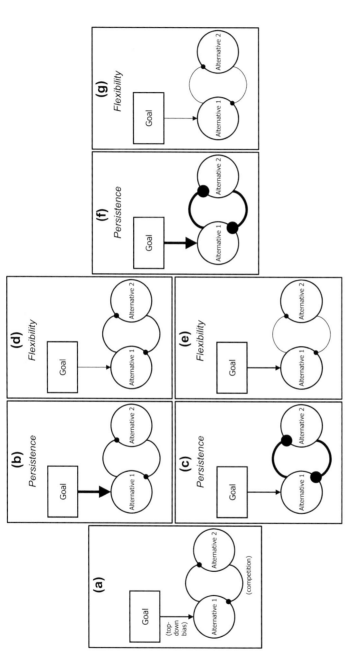

Figure 1 Possible mechanisms involved in competitive decision-making. The goal-related Alternative 1 is supported by the goal representation (which provides a "top-down bias"), but competes with choice Alternative 2 for selection through mutual inhibition ("competition"). Selection requires one alternative to pass a certain threshold (not shown), which given the mutual inhibition would result in the relative inhibition of the nonselected alternative. (a) shows the generic model; (b) and (d) show how strong persistence and pronounced flexibility might be achieved by modulating the strength of the top-down support from goal representations, respectively; (c) and (e) show how strong persistence and pronounced flexibility might be achieved by modulating the strength of mutual inhibition between alternatives, respectively; and (f) and (g) show the assumptions underlying the discussion in this chapter, which combine both possible mechanisms (goal modulation and the modulation of mutual inhibition).

alternatives, as indicated in Figure 1(f) and (g). In the following, I will use this model, which I will refer to as the *Metacontrol State Model* (or MSM), to explain how situational circumstances, experience, learning, and people's cultural context can bias cognitive control states, and the information-processing characteristics they control, in predictable ways and even create chronic biases that outlive the conditions for which they were originally created.

6. THE PLASTICITY OF CONTROL STATES

Task-switching studies have revealed that establishing a control state to orchestrate a new task takes quite some time, often in the neighborhood of half a second or a second (for a review, see Kiesel et al., 2010). Even though the duration of establishing a new control state has been considered to depend on the number of to-be-changed control parameters (Logan & Gordon, 2001) and the degree to which the new task set had been inhibited in earlier trials (Mayr & Keele, 2000), most approaches implicitly or explicitly assume that the remains of previous control states are fully eliminated before the new task will be executed. However, there are some indications that this scenario is not realistic. For one, the first systematic studies on task switching have already shown that previous control states can be sticky and affect later control even after a new state has been implemented (Allport, Styles, & Hsieh, 1994). For another, there are some indications in the literature that parameters of previously established states can systematically bias the characteristics of later states (Förster, 2012). These priming-like effects are particularly interesting from a MSM point of view, as I will elaborate in the next section.

While short-term transfer of control-state characteristics from one task to another supports the assumption that control states are inert, inertia by itself does not prevent random and radical changes in control-state policies—it just slows them down. However, there is considerable evidence that people do not choose control policies randomly or only according to external demands; rather, they seem to have individual preferences for particular control styles and default values that can be biased toward the persistence or the flexibility pole of the control dimension that I have suggested. Some of these preferences are likely to reflect genetic predispositions. There is considerable evidence that the genetic setup of individuals can have specific, selective effects on the efficiency of processing along the mesofrontal or nigrostriatal dopaminergic pathway, which has implications for people's abilities to engage in persistence or flexibility.

For instance, the COMT Val158Met polymorphism is known to affect frontal dopaminergic processing, which again has been assumed to shift the dominance in frontostriatal interactions toward the frontal system in some genotypes and toward the striatal system in others (e.g., Nolan, Bilder, Lachman, & Volavka, 2004). Indeed, individuals with a genotype favoring frontal dopaminergic processing were shown to have more difficulties switching from one task to another than individuals with a genotype favoring striatal dopaminergic processing (Colzato, Waszak, Nieuwenhuis, Posthuma, & Hommel, 2010). Interestingly, the same polymorphism also predicted the degree to which people benefit from playing video games: individuals with a genotype favoring striatal dopaminergic processing showed better transfer from a video game training to task switching (Colzato, van den Wildenberg, & Hommel, 2014). Other polymorphisms are known to affect striatal dopaminergic processing, which in turn is likely to shift the balance from or toward the striatal component of the frontostriatal interaction from the other side. For instance, genetic markers of striatal dopamine were shown to predict individual differences in the control of stimulus integration over time (Colzato, Slagter, de Rover, & Hommel, 2011), in the handling of integrated episodes (Colzato, Zmigrod, & Hommel, 2013), in attentional flexibility (Colzato, Pratt & Hommel, 2010) and functional impulsivity (Colzato, van den Wildenberg, van der Does, & Hommel, 2010).

While it remains to be seen whether and to what degree these genetic constraints and biases can be overcome, there is considerable evidence that personal experience, learning, and cultural embedding can affect and create apparently rather stable interindividual differences. In the following, I will first focus on short-lived biases of metacontrol states that not only provide evidence for the inertia of control parameters, but also demonstrate the usefulness of the MSM in accounting for intra- and interindividual differences in control policies under various circumstances. Then, before I close with a brief conclusion, I will turn to more durable biases and show that people can acquire particular personal metacontrol styles that predict important characteristics of their performance.

7. SHORT-TERM BIASES OF COGNITIVE CONTROL

One set of studies that have tested predictions from MSM with respect to short-term biases toward more maintaining or more flexible control states has used mood induction. The induction of positive mood has often be assumed to promote "loose thinking" and creative thought (Ashby, Isen,

& Turken, 1999), and there is considerable evidence that at least brain-storming-like divergent-thinking tasks benefit from positive mood (Baas et al., 2008; Isen, 1999). If so, one would expect that positive mood leads to a more "flexible" control state as indicated in Figure 1(d) and (e) (cf., Nijstad, De Dreu, Rietzschel, & Baas, 2010). Take, for instance, the Alternate Uses Task (AUT) often used to assess divergent thinking (Guilford, 1967). In this task, participants are presented with the description of a simple everyday item, like a pen, and are then asked to list as many uses they can think of within limited time. Such a task would require rather weak top-down support, as the search criterion is rather vague. Given that many answers are possible and correct, the competitiveness between alternatives should also be as weak as possible (i.e., just strong enough to select them sequentially). This means that performance in this task would strongly benefit from a control mode that is strongly biased toward flexibility. Accordingly, it makes sense that divergent-thinking benefits from positive-going mood.

These considerations are not limited to creativity tasks, so we can consider the implications of positive mood for other tasks as well. If positive mood would bias control toward more flexibility, it should increase the impact of goal-unrelated, irrelevant information and reduce the impact of top-down control. This is consistent with observations of Dreisbach and Goschke (2004), who found that the induction of positive mood is accompanied by less systematic attentional focusing and greater distractibility. Along the same lines, there is evidence that positive-mood induction reduces the degree to which task performance is monitored and adjusted in the face of internal conflict. It is known that, in tasks with conflicting stimuli, like Stroop or flanker tasks, the experience of conflict leads to a reduction of the impact of irrelevant information in the next trial—the Gratton effect (Gratton et al., 1992). According to Botvinick, Braver, Carter, Barch, and Cohen (2001), this is because the registration of multiple response activations (i.e., response conflict) is fed to frontal systems responsible for the maintenance of the action goal, and results in the reactivation/strengthening of the goal representation. This should increase the top-down control of information processing in the next trial, and thereby reduce possible conflict. Interestingly, the presentation of unexpected reward (van Steenbergen, Band, & Hommel, 2009, 2012) and the induction of positive mood (van Steenbergen, Band, & Hommel, 2010) effectively prevent this process of control adjustment, suggesting that positive mood indeed reduces the impact of top-down control. A recent neuroimaging study indicates that this reduction is caused by attenuating the response of the assumed conflict monitor (the anterior cingulate cortex) to stimulus-induced conflict (van Steenbergen, Band, Hommel, Rombouts, & Nieuwenhuis, in press). While positive mood reduces top-down control, negative mood leads to an increase: van Steenbergen, Booij, Band, Hommel, and van der Does (2012) tested the effect of dysphoria induced by acute tryptophan depletion in remitted depressed patients and observed a significant increase of control adjustment under these conditions.

Systematic mood effects were also obtained in dual-task contexts. For instance, Zwosta, Hommel, Goschke, and Fischer (2013) reported that the induction of negative mood led to a stronger shielding of the prioritized task (i.e., less cross talk) than the induction of positive mood, which fits with the idea that positive mood reduces top-down impact. Fischer and Hommel (2012) used a different rationale to investigate dual-task performance. They mixed the task with a creativity task that required either divergent thinking, as in the mentioned AUT, or convergent thinking, as in the Remote Associations Task (RAT; Mednick, 1968). This task provides more and rather tight top-down constraints, and there is only one possible answer per item (e.g., which word goes with "market," "man," and "glue"?), suggesting that the task calls for a control state with a strong impact of the goal—a bias toward persistence. If so, performing the RAT should increase top-down control and reduce cross talk in an overlapping dual-task, which is indeed what Fischer and Hommel observed.

So far, I have considered mood as an independent variable that biases cognitive control to a more persistence-supporting or a more flexibility-supporting state and task-related control-state configurations as the dependent variable. From a functional perspective, one might consider influence in the opposite direction as well. That is, adopting a control state close to the persistence pole of the control dimension might be associated with more negative mood than adopting a control state close to the flexibility pole. Akbari Chermahini and Hommel (2012b) tested this possibility by having participants perform convergent- or divergent-thinking tasks and assessing whether these tasks had an impact on mood. This was indeed the case: mood was improved by performing the divergent-thinking task and performing the convergent-thinking task had the opposite effect.

Another factor that has been found to have a systematic impact on cognitive control states is meditation. Meditation has been notoriously suspected to improve creativity, but systematic evidence regarding whether this is really the case is rare. We have pointed out that this is likely to be the case for two reasons (Lippelt, Hommel, & Colzato, 2014). For one, different kinds of meditation have different goals and use different techniques to achieve them. As pointed out by Lutz, Slagter, Dunne, and Davidson (2008), some techniques are coaching the meditator how to focus on one single thought while avoiding distraction (focused-attention meditation), while other techniques aim at teaching the meditator how to open up and to accept any thought that may come up at any time (open-monitoring meditation). It is unlikely that these two techniques are associated with the same cognitive control state; rather, it makes sense to assume that focused-attention meditation serves to bias cognitive control toward the persistence pole while open-monitoring meditation promotes flexibility (Lippelt et al., 2014). For another, creativity is not a unitary construct and comprises several components with partially opposite characteristics (Wallas, 1926; Guilford, 1967). In particular, some creativity tasks (like the RAT) are tapping more into convergent thinking while others (like the AUT) are tapping more into divergent thinking. If we consider the above reasons and evidence that convergent-thinking benefits from a persistence-heavy control state while divergent-thinking benefits from a flexibility-biased state, it makes little sense to assume that both kinds of thinking benefit from the same kind of meditation. Rather, focused-attention meditation should promote convergent thinking while open-monitoring meditation would be suspected to facilitate divergent thinking.

These predictions were indeed confirmed in studies that systematically compared the impact of focused-attention meditation and open-monitoring meditation on convergent and divergent thinking. In a study on meditation practitioners (Colzato, Ozturk, & Hommel, 2012) and a study comparing practitioners with meditation novices (Colzato, Szapora, Lippelt, & Hommel, in press), open-monitoring meditation led to a substantial improvement of divergent thinking without affecting convergent thinking. Focused-attention meditation in turn tended to improve convergent thinking without having any impact on divergent thinking. Why the impact of focused-attention meditation on convergent thinking was not statistically reliable is likely to due to the fact that most participants were students—who can be assumed to engage in convergent thinking on an everyday basis—so that their performance was probably at ceiling already.

A further line of research investigated whether control states might affect interpersonal processes. The rationale motivating this research is based on the assumption that people cognitively represent themselves and others like any other event (Hommel, Müsseler, Aschersleben, & Prinz, 2001; Hommel, 2004): as a network of codes that represent various perceptual and conceptual features characterizing the event (for further discussion, see Greenwald et al., 2002; Hommel, 2013; Hommel, Colzato, & van den Wildenberg, 2009; Kim & Hommel, 2015). If this is the case, one would assume that a control state close to the persistence pole of the dimension should lead to a more pronounced discrimination between "me" and "other," because this control state is associated with maximal competitiveness between alternative representations. In other words, the mutually inhibitory links between the "me" representation and the "other" representation should be particularly strong, so that activating one should tend to inhibit the other to a maximal degree. In contrast, a control state close to the flexibility pole should lead to minimal discrimination, that is, to maximal interpersonal integration. In other words, this control state would propagate a view of me and other as one unit while a persistence-heavy control state would induce a more "individualistic" representation.

Along these lines, one would expect that engaging in activities that are likely to drive the control state toward persistence would reduce self-other integration, while engaging in flexibility-heavy tasks should have the opposite effect. This pattern of results was indeed observed by Colzato, van den Wildenberg, and Hommel (2013): Performing a divergent-thinking task was associated with a substantial increase in the joint Simon effect (Sebanz, Knoblich, & Prinz, 2003; for an overview, see Dolk et al., 2014), which indicates the degree to which participants are affected by the presence of another person working on the same task. The same effect was obtained by having participants to circle either personal pronouns (such as "I," "my," or "me") or relational pronouns (such as "we," "our," or "us") in a text (Colzato, de Bruijn & Hommel, 2012). In another study, engaging in divergent thinking was reported to increase interpersonal trust (Sellaro, Hommel, de Kwaadsteniet, & Colzato, 2014), and the same effect was obtained by exposing participants to the scent of lavender, which is assumed to induce a more flexibility-heavy control state (Sellaro, van Dijk, Rossi Paccani, Hommel & Colzato, 2014).

8. THE IMPACT OF LEARNING, EXPERIENCE, AND CULTURE ON COGNITIVE CONTROL

The evidence I have discussed so far shows that particular metacontrol states have a specific impact on internal representations and information processing. This impact was restricted to a temporal scale of seconds or minutes, and this is indeed a scale that is particularly likely to show such effects. As it is known from task-switching studies (see above), changing control states takes quite a bit of time and just-implemented states tend to be sticky to some degree, so that it makes sense to look for state-related aftereffects and cross talk in the range of minutes or seconds. And yet, it also makes sense to assume that longer-term effects and biases are possible. Consider the hypothesized metacontrol dimension ranging from extreme persistence and top-down impact to extreme flexibility and openness. There are certainly tasks and situations in life that call for control states that are more biased toward one than the other pole, but it is unlikely that there is a particular optimal value for each task or situation. As emphasized by Goschke (2003), some degree of goal-orientation/top-down control and some degree of flexibility will be necessary under almost all circumstances, which still leaves quite some range of possible values on the hypothetical dimension—not unlike the case of choosing between speed and accuracy. The existence of a range of possibilities creates uncertainty, which is commonly assumed to be aversive. This suggests that people seek ways to reduce uncertainty regarding metacontrol parameters. One way to reduce it is to adopt a particular default value, which an individual can use in all situations that do not require deviations from that value. Where do individual default values come from? Several options are possible and they are not mutually exclusive. In the following, I will discuss a few options that colleagues and I have addressed empirically.

One relates to personal conditions that are more compatible with one than with the other pole of the hypothetical metacontrol dimension. Engaging in a loving relationship is such a condition, as it is likely to promote positive feelings and general positive mood. If so, MSM would predict that passionate lovers are less efficient in maintaining tight action control. Indeed, van Steenbergen, Langeslag, Band, and Hommel (2014) observed that the intensity of passionate love as assessed by the Passionate Love Scale predicted the individual efficiency in cognitive control as measured in Stroop and flanker-task performance—with greater passion leading to less control.

Another way to influence cognitive control is learning. Colzato, van Leeuwen, van den Wildenberg, and Hommel (2010) considered that the new generation of "First Person Shooter" games may require players to develop a more flexible mind-set that allows them to engage in complex scenarios, to rapidly react to moving visual and sudden acoustic events, and to switch back and forth between different subtasks. If so, one would expect that extensive experience with such games should enhance cognitive flexibility and, indeed, players of such video games were found to be superior to nonplayers in a task-switching paradigm. While this study does not reveal whether and how performance in persistence-heavy tasks was affected, it does suggest that the flexibility part of control can be systematically trained. However, it must be noted that the study was correlational in nature, which leaves the possibility that players are a self-selected group with superior flexibility skills. It is also important to point out that task-switching paradigms are rather complex, and that task-switching performance arguably comprises both persistence and flexibility components.

Another example of learning-related changes in metacontrol abilities relates to bilingualism. There is considerable evidence that bilinguals not only outperform monolinguals in various language tasks (even though bilinguals can show poorer performance early in learning), but they show superior performance in a number of nonlingual tasks as well (for an overview, see Bialystok & Craik, 2010). These observations have motivated the view that acquiring a new language goes hand in hand with learning how to suppress conflicting information. In the learning process, this information will be mainly linguistic, such as the words and grammatical structures of one's native language. However, if we assume that discriminating between, and holding in check conflicting languages is a metacontrol process, it is very well possible that training and improving this process generalizes to the control of the processing of nonlinguistic material.

In a systematic comparison of tasks tapping into direct, "active" suppression (like the stop-signal task: Logan & Cowan, 1984) and tasks involving the inhibition of alternatives through the process of competitive selection, as discussed above, Colzato, Bajo et al. (2008) were able to show that it is only the latter, not the former process that bilinguals excel in. For instance, while bilinguals and monolinguals showed no difference whatsoever in the stop-signal task, bilinguals performed more poorly in the attentional blink task. In the attentional blink task, participants report the presence and identity of two targets presented in close succession. The term "attentional blink" refers to the common observation that both targets can be accurately reported with longer lags between them while the second target is often missed when the lag is short. This has been attributed to the processing of the first target, which seems to be so demanding that a second target cannot be considered before processing the first is completed (for an overview, see Hommel et al., 2006). Interestingly, however, there are considerable interindividual differences in the size of the effect (e.g., Martens, Munneke, Smid, & Johnson, 2006) and situational circumstances under which the "blink" of the second target can be avoided altogether (e.g., Olivers & Nieuwenhuis, 2006). Moreover, trials in which the second target is missed are characterized by a particularly large allocation of attentional resources to processing the first target (Shapiro, Schmitz, Martens, Hommel, & Schnitzler, 2006), which suggests that the attentional blink phenomenon is due to too much top-down control (Olivers & Nieuwenhuis, 2006). If so, it makes sense that bilinguals, who have been claimed to acquire stronger top-down control (e.g., Bialystok, Craik, Klein & Viswanathan, 2004), exhibit a more pronounced attentional blink. It also makes sense that bilinguals outperform monolinguals in convergent thinking, but show poorer performance than monolinguals in divergent thinking (Hommel, Colzato, Fischer, & Christoffels, 2011).

Becoming and remaining a bilingual is certainly a long-term learning experience, but the learning process and the exercise are commonly much more socially embedded than mastering a video game. Given that the learning experience seems to affect people's personal control styles, we can hypothesize that societal practice and culture might contribute to the development and persistence of metacontrol styles. We pursued this possibility in a recent line of research that looked into the impact of religion on cognitive control. There is some evidence from cultural studies that metacontrol styles might be sensitive to the cultural environment in which people grow up. For instance, people growing up in North America have been shown to be less sensitive to contextual cues and show a more analytic cognitive style (i.e., to pay more attention to local features of objects and events) than people growing up in Asia, who exhibit a more holistic style (i.e., pay more attention to global features) (Nisbett & Miyamoto, 2005). The concept of culture is very hard to define, however, so that one, for instance, can argue whether all citizens of the United States really share the same culture and whether one can speak of a homogeneous Asian (or even "Eastern") culture. A similar concept that is easier to define is religion, and here I do not mean religiousness as such, but adopting a particular religious faith. Even though not all faiths are based on available holy scripts and rules, and even though the degree to which members of a religious community follow religious rules and regulations varies, some basic and widely shared rules and values can often be identified for at least some variants of religious conviction.

How might religion shape metacontrol? Hommel and Colzato (2010) have argued that many kinds of religious faith have characteristics that are likely to require a particular metacontrol style, so that adopting a particular faith is likely to lead to the establishment of metacontrol parameter defaults that are compatible with the required style. For instance, Dutch neo-Calvinism is built upon the concept of sphere sovereignty, which emphasizes

that each sphere or sector of society has its own responsibilities and author-
ities, and stands equal to other spheres (e.g., Boesak, 1984). This implies that
active Dutch Calvinists have been often socially rewarded for adopting a
metacontrol style that emphasizes a rather independent view of the self. According to my reasoning, this should require a pronounced bias toward the
persistence pole of the control dimension, which again implies strong reliance on top-down control, good shielding against irrelevant information
and little distractibility, but also comparably less self-other integration and
global attention.

In a first test of these ideas, we (Colzato, van den Wildenberg, &
Hommel, 2008) compared Dutch Calvinists with Dutch atheists that were
brought up in the same country and culture and were matched with respect
to race, intelligence, sex, and age, in the global—local task developed by
Navon (1977). This task assesses how fast people can process global and local
characteristics of hierarchically constructed visual stimuli (e.g., larger symbols
made of smaller symbols). Typically, this task gives rise to the "global precedence" effect, which demonstrates that global features can be processed
faster than local features—presumably due to a mixture of physiological
and attentional factors. We were particularly interested in the size of this precedence effect. If Calvinists would be more oriented toward local details,
their precedence effect should be small, meaning that they should not be
much slower to report local than global stimulus characteristics. In comparison, atheists should show a larger precedence effect, that is, a more pronounced delay in reporting local as compared to global characteristics.
This is indeed what we observed. A follow-up study replicated the effect
and showed that the attentional control characteristics of baptized atheists
(i.e., individuals raised as Calvinists, but no longer believing or engaging
in religious practices) are indistinguishable from that of practicing Calvinists
(Colzato, van Beest et al., 2010). This suggests that early practice in living a
particular faith is more important than continued practice—chronic metacontrol parameters seem sticky. The same study also demonstrated that
Italian Roman Catholics and Israeli Orthodox Jews (i.e., members of reli-
gions that emphasize social responsibility and interrelatedness of all societal
aspects) show the opposite effect than Calvinists do (i.e., the global precedence effect was more pronounced in the religious groups than in matched
atheist groups), as our approach would predict. Along the same lines,
Colzato, Hommel, van den Wildenberg, and Hsieh (2010) reported a
more pronounced global precedence effect in Taiwanese Buddhists (i.e.,
members of a religion that also emphasizes social interrelatedness) than in

matched Taiwanese atheists. Taken together, these observations rule out that religiousness as such, or some correlated behavioral or personality feature accounts for our findings. Instead, it seems to be the particular religious practice that creates chronic metacontrol parameter values (Hommel & Colzato, 2010).

A further study showed that religious faith not only affects attentional control, but the sensitivity to task-irrelevant information as well. According to the MSM, Calvinists would be expected to show particularly low sensitivity to task-irrelevant information while Catholics should show particularly high sensitivity. Hommel, Colzato, Scorolli, Borghi, and van den Wildenberg (2011) tested this prediction in a Simon task that assesses the degree to which response selection is affected by irrelevant stimulus information. While Dutch Calvinists showed a less pronounced Simon effect than matched Dutch atheists, Italian Catholics showed a more pronounced Simon effect than Italian atheists—which confirms expectations. A further study tested the prediction that Calvinists would show a particularly large attentional blink. Recall that the attentional blink has been attributed to too much top-down control, suggesting that religious practice that emphasizes top-down control, as Dutch Calvinism does, should increase the effect. This is indeed what Colzato, Hommel, and Shapiro (2010) demonstrated. Finally, Colzato et al. (2012) investigated the impact of Buddhism on self-other integration. As explained in the previous section, self-other integration can be expected to increase to the degree that control states approach the flexibility pole. If so, practicing Buddhists would be expected to show more pronounced self-other integration than atheists, and one major aim of Buddhist practices is indeed to overcome the separation of self and other (Dogen, 1976). Colzato et al. tested this hypothesis by comparing Taiwanese Buddhists with matched Taiwanese atheists in a joint Simon task. As predicted, Buddhists showed a more pronounced effect, suggesting stronger self-other integration.

As pointed out already, religious practice is an example of a relatively well-defined social activity that is likely to shape the behavior of the involved individual. But it is not the only example. Another is membership in a relatively coherent minority group. To investigate whether such membership can also have a long-lasting impact on cognitive control, we compared homosexual and heterosexual individuals in a global–local task (Colzato et al., 2010). Our theoretical vantage point was speculation about the possible existence of some kind of "gaydar" (Reuter, 2002), an assumed special skill of homosexual individuals to detect the sexual orientation of others. Previous studies have revealed that homosexual participants are indeed better than heterosexuals in detecting the sexual orientation of strangers shown on photographs or in short movie clips, but this advantage disappears with slightly longer movie clips (Ambady, Hallahan, & Conner, 1999). We took this outcome pattern to rule out differences in knowledge about visible cues signaling sexual orientation, such as clothing, hair dress, or gesture. Instead, homosexuals might check for such cues more actively, as they rely more on them to identify possible partners. If so, the default control setting of homosexuals might be more biased toward local aspects of stimulus events, as this is the setting they are using more often than heterosexuals—at least for the purpose of partner identification. We tested this possibility by presenting homosexuals and heterosexuals with the global–local task. As expected, homosexuals had a smaller global preference effect than heterosexuals, which indicates that they have a relative preference for the processing of local stimulus aspects.

9. CONCLUSIONS

The main aim of this article is to point out that action control is unlikely to be a unitary function, but rather emerges from the interaction of two counteracting forces, one propagating a strong top-down control of information processing and the other opening up the system for alternative options and novel information. As I have argued, this more dynamic metacontrol approach has functional and neural plausibility, and is consistent with recent functional and neuroscientific insights. In this article, I did not focus on the neuroscientific evidence, but rather tried to show that a relatively simple functional model is sufficient to account for various phenomena indicating the existence of short-term biases of cognitive control styles and long-term chronic biases associated with particular kinds of experience and cultural context.

Even though the MSM I proposed has two components, these components are different from those considered by traditional dual-pathway models. The latter assume that the two alternative or conflicting pathways differ with respect to their reliance on familiarity and previous experience, their controllability, and their mechanisms. The MSM does not assume any of those differences and it in particular does not consider a stronger contribution of the nonfrontal component reflecting less control. Nor does it consider control configurations that leave space for other than goal-related top-down information necessarily inefficient or dysfunctional. The idea that more top-down control is better, as implicit or even explicit in many dual-pathway approaches, is in fact not particularly realistic outside of the psychological laboratory. In the absence of an experimenter who has already limited the available possibilities to exactly one task, one or two stimuli, and one or two predefined responses mapped upon them, a human agent is always facing the possibility that the current task is not the most important, most appropriate, most efficient, and most successful, which requires the continuous monitoring for interesting alternatives. Switching off processing channels busy with these considerations might buy a few milliseconds, but could have fatal consequences.

MSM can also do without an ego or agent and without a dedicated inhibitory system. Inhibition emerges through competition and, thus, does not require loans of intelligence to explain how inhibitory systems know which representations to target. The main intelligence in the control system that calls for explanation is the choice of metacontrol styles: why does control sometimes lean toward persistence and sometimes toward flexibility, and what are the criteria for changing this policy? I have tried to reduce this loan of intelligence as well by considering genetic reasons for individual differences and by showing that individuals can acquire chronic default values through cultural learning and other kinds of personal experience. The remaining flexibility that people do seem to have might be explained by considering situational cues and immediate feedback, but certainly more research will be necessary to unravel the details of these processes. Moreover, it is fair to say that the MSM is currently more of a heuristic tool rather than a formalized theoretical framework, and making progress on this will require much more fine-tuning. Nevertheless, I am convinced that considering the dynamic, interactive nature of cognitive control will deepen our insight into the mechanisms underlying the emergence of human behavior.

ACKNOWLEDGMENTS

This research was supported by a grant of the Netherlands Research Organization (NWO) to the author (433-09-243).

REFERENCES

Ach, N. (1910). *Über den Willensakt und das Temperament [on act of will and temperament]*. Leipzig: Quelle & Meyer.
Ach, N. (1935). Analyse des Willens [analysis of the will]. In E. Aberhalden (Ed.), *Handbuch der biologischen Arbeitsmethoden* (Vol. VI). Berlin: Urban & Schwarzenberg.

Akbari Chermahini, S., & Hommel, B. (2012a). More creative through positive mood? Not everyone! *Frontiers in Human Neuroscience, 6*, 319.

Akbari Chermahini, S., & Hommel, B. (2012b). Creative mood swings: divergent and convergent thinking affect mood in opposite ways. *Psychological Research, 76*, 634–640.

Allport, D. A., Styles, E. A., & Hsieh, S. (1994). Shifting intentional set: exploring the dynamic control of tasks. In C. Umilta, & M. Moscovitch (Eds.), *Attention and performance* (Vol. XV, pp. 421–452). Cambridge: MIT Press.

Ambady, N., Hallahan, M., & Conner, B. (1999). Accuracy of judgments of sexual orientation from thin slices of behavior. *Journal of Personality and Social Psychology, 77*, 538–547.

Ashby, F. G., Isen, A. M., & Turken, A. U. (1999). A neuro-psychological theory of positive affect and its influence on cognition. *Psychological Review, 106*, 529–550.

Atkinson, R. C., & Shiffrin, R. M. (1968). Human memory: a proposed system and its control processes. In K. W. Spence, & J. T. Spence (Eds.), *The psychology of learning and motivation* (Vol. 2, pp. 89–195). New York: Academic Press.

Baas, M., De Dreu, C. K. W., & Nijstad, B. A. (2008). A meta-analysis of 25 years of research on mood and creativity: hedonic tone, activation, or regulatory focus? *Psychological Bulletin, 134*, 779–806.

Bargh, J. A. (1989). Conditional automaticity: varieties of automatic influence in social perception and cognition. In J. S. Uleman, & J. A. Bargh (Eds.), *Unintended thought* (pp. 3–51). New York: Guilford Press.

Bargh, J. A. (1994). The four horsemen of automaticity: awareness, efficiency, intention, and control in social cognition. In R. S. Wyer, Jr., & T. K. Srull (Eds.), *Handbook of social cognition* (2nd ed.). (pp. 1–40). Hillsdale, NJ: Erlbaum.

Baumeister, R. F., Bratslavsky, E., Muraven, M., & Tice, D. M. (1998). Ego depletion: is the active self a limited resource? *Journal of Personality and Social Psychology, 74*, 1252–1265.

Beaulieu, J.-M., & Gainetdinov, R. R. (2011). The physiology, signaling, and pharmacology of dopamine receptors. *Pharmacological Reviews, 63*, 182–217.

Bialystok, E., & Craik, F. I. M. (2010). Cognitive and linguistic processing in the bilingual mind. *Current Directions in Psychological Sciences, 19*, 19–23.

Bialystok, E., Craik, F. I. M., Klein, R., & Viswanathan, M. (2004). Bilingualism, aging, and cognitive control: evidence from the Simon task. *Psychology and Aging, 19*, 290–303.

Boesak, A. (1984). *Apartheid, liberation and the Calvinist tradition*. Johannesburg: Skotaville Publications.

Bogacz, R. (2007). Optimal decision-making theories: linking neurobiology with behavior. *Trends in Cognitive Sciences, 11*, 118–125.

Botvinick, M. M., Braver, T. S., Carter, C. S., Barch, D. M., & Cohen, J. D. (2001). Conflict monitoring and cognitive control. *Psychological Review, 108*, 624–652.

Brehm, J. W., & Self, E. A. (1989). The intensity of motivation. *Annual Review of Psychology, 40*, 109–131.

Chmiel, N. (1984). Phonological encoding for reading: the effect of concurrent articulation in a Stroop task. *British Journal of Psychology, 75*, 213–220.

Colzato, L. S., Bajo, M. T., van den Wildenberg, W. P. M., Paolieri, D., Nieuwenhuis, S. T., La Heij, W., et al. (2008). How does bilingualism improve executive control? A comparison of active and reactive inhibition mechanisms. *Journal of Experimental Psychology: Learning, Memory, and Cognition, 34*, 302–312.

Colzato, L. S., van Beest, I., van den Wildenberg, W. P. M., Scorolli, C., Dorchin, S., Meiran, N., et al. (2010). God: do I have your attention? *Cognition, 117*, 87–94.

Colzato, L. S., de Bruijn, E., & Hommel, B. (2012). Up to "me" or up to "us"? The impact of self-construal priming on cognitive self-other integration. *Frontiers in Psychology, 3*, 341.

Colzato, L. S., Hommel, B., & Shapiro, K. (2010). Religion and the attentional blink: depth of faith predicts depth of the blink. *Frontiers in Psychology, 1*, 147.

Colzato, L. S., Hommel, B., van den Wildenberg, W., & Hsieh, S. (2010). Buddha as an eye opener: a link between prosocial attitude and attentional control. *Frontiers in Psychology, 1*, 156.

Colzato, L. S., van Hooidonk, L., van den Wildenberg, W. P. M., Harinck, F., & Hommel, B. (2010). Sexual orientation biases attentional control: a possible gaydar mechanism. *Frontiers in Psychology, 1*, 13.

Colzato, L. S., van Leeuwen, P. J. A., van den Wildenberg, W., & Hommel, B. (2010). DOOM'd to switch: superior cognitive flexibility in players of first person shooter games. *Frontiers in Psychology, 1*, 8.

Colzato, L. S., Ozturk, A., & Hommel, B. (2012). Meditate to create: the impact of focused-attention and open-monitoring training on convergent and divergent thinking. *Frontiers in Psychology, 3*, 116.

Colzato, L. S., Pratt, J., & Hommel, B. (2010). Dopaminergic control of attentional flexibility: inhibition of return is associated with the dopamine transporter gene (DAT1). *Frontiers in Neuroscience, 4*, 53.

Colzato, L. S., Slagter, H., de Rover, M., & Hommel, B. (2011). Dopamine and the management of attentional resources: genetic markers of striatal D2 dopamine predict individual differences in the attentional blink. *Journal of Cognitive Neuroscience, 23*, 3576–3585.

Colzato, L. S., Szapora, A., Lippelt, D., & Hommel, B. Prior meditation practice modulates performance and strategy use in convergent- and divergent-thinking problems. *Mindfulness*, in press.

Colzato, L. S., Waszak, F., Nieuwenhuis, S., Posthuma, D., & Hommel, B. (2010). The flexible mind is associated with the Catechol-O-methyltransferase (COMT) Val158Met polymorphism: evidence for a role of dopamine in the control of task switching. *Neuropsychologia, 48*, 2764–2768.

Colzato, L. S., van den Wildenberg, W. P. M., van der Does, W., & Hommel, B. (2010). Genetic markers of striatal dopamine predict individual differences in dysfunctional, but not functional impulsivity. *Neuroscience, 170*, 782–788.

Colzato, L. S., van den Wildenberg, W. P. M., & Hommel, B. (2008). Losing the big picture: how religion may control visual attention. *PLoS One, 3*(11), e3679.

Colzato, L. S., van den Wildenberg, W. P. M., & Hommel, B. (2013). Increasing self-other integration through divergent thinking. *Psychonomic Bulletin & Review, 20*, 1011–1016.

Colzato, L. S., van den Wildenberg, W. P. M., & Hommel, B. (2014). Cognitive control and the COMT Val158Met polymorphism: genetic modulation of videogame training and transfer to task-switching efficiency. *Psychological Research, 78*, 670–678.

Colzato, L. S., Zech, H., Hommel, B., Verdonschot, R., van den Wildenberg, W., & Hsieh, S. (2012). Loving-kindness brings loving-kindness: the impact of Buddhism on cognitive self-other integration. *Psychonomic Bulletin & Review, 19*, 541–545.

Colzato, L. S., Zmigrod, S., & Hommel, B. (2013). Dopamine, norepinephrine, and the management of sensorimotor bindings: individual differences in updating of stimulus-response episodes are predicted by DAT1, but not DBH5′-ins/del. *Experimental Brain Research, 228*, 213–220.

Cools, R. (2008). Role of dopamine in the motivational and cognitive control of behaviour. *Neuroscientist, 14*, 381–395.

Cools, R. (2012). Chemical neuromodulation of goal-directed behavior. In P. M. Todd, T. T. Hills, & T. W. Robbins (Eds.), *Cognitive search: Evolution, algorithms, and the brain: Strüngmann forum report*. Cambridge, MA: MIT Press.

Cools, R., & D'Esposito, M. (2010). Dopaminergic modulation of flexible cognitive control in humans. In A. Björklund, S. Dunnett, L. Iversen, & S. Iversen (Eds.), *Dopamine handbook* (pp. 249–260). Oxford: Oxford University Press.

Cools, R., & D'Esposito, M. (2011). Inverted U-shaped dopamine actions on human working memory and cognitive control. *Biological Psychiatry, 69*, e113–e125.

Desimone, R., & Duncan, J. (1995). Neural mechanism of selective visual attention. *Annual Review of Neuroscience, 18*, 193−222.

Dogen, I. (1976). *Shobogenzo (Y. Yokai, trans.)*. New York: Weatherhill.

Dolk, T., Hommel, B., Colzato, L. S., Schütz-Bosbach, S., Prinz, W., & Liepelt, R. (2014). The joint Simon effect: a review and theoretical integration. *Frontiers in Psychology, 5*, 974.

Dreisbach, G., & Goschke, T. (2004). How positive affect modulates cognitive control: reduced perseveration at the cost of increased distractibility. *Journal of Experimental Psychology: Learning, Memory, and Cognition, 30*, 343−353.

Durstewitz, D., & Seamans, J. K. (2008). The dual-state theory of prefrontal cortex dopamine function with relevance to catechol-o-methyltransferase genotypes and schizophrenia. *Biological Psychiatry, 64*, 739−749.

Egner, T. (2007). Congruency sequence effects and cognitive control. *Cognitive, Affective, & Behavioral Neuroscience, 7*, 380−390.

Egner, T., & Hirsch, J. (2005). Cognitive control mechanisms resolve conflict through cortical amplification of task-relevant information. *Nature Neuroscience, 8*, 1784−1790.

Exner, S. (1879). Physiologie der Grosshirnrinde. In L. Hermann (Ed.), *Handbuch der Physiologie, 2. Band, 2. Theil* (pp. 189−350). Leipzig: Vogel.

Fischer, R., & Hommel, B. (2012). Deep thinking increases task-set shielding and reduces shifting flexibility in dual-task performance. *Cognition, 123*, 303−307.

Förster, J. (2012). GLOMOsys: the how and why of global and local processing. *Current Directions in Psychological Science, 21*, 15−19.

Freud, S. (1923). *Das Ich und das Es. Leipzig etc.: Internationaler Psycho-analytischer Verlag. English translation: The Ego and the Id, Joan Riviere (trans.)*. London: Hogarth Press and Institute of Psycho-analysis.

Friedman, N. P., Miyake, A., Young, S. E., DeFries, J. C., Corley, R. P., & Hewitt, J. K. (2008). Individual differences in executive functions are almost entirely genetic in origin. *Journal of Experimental Psychology: General, 137*, 201−225.

Goschke, T. (2003). Voluntary action and cognitive control from a cognitive neuroscience perspective. In S. Maasen, W. Prinz, & G. Roth (Eds.), *Voluntary action: Brains, minds, and sociality* (pp. 49−85). Oxford: Oxford University Press.

Gratton, G., Coles, M. G. H., & Donchin, E. (1992). Optimizing the use of information: strategic control of activation of responses. *Journal of Experimental Psychology. General, 121*, 480−506.

Greenwald, A. G., Banaji, M. R., Rudman, L. A., Farnham, S. D., Nosek, B. A., & Mellott, D. S. (2002). A unified theory of implicit attitudes, stereotypes, self-esteem, and self-concept. *Psychological Review, 109*, 3−25.

Guilford, J. P. (1967). *The nature of human intelligence*. New York: McGraw-Hill.

Hillgruber, A. (1912). Fortlaufende Arbeit und Willensbetätigung [Continuous work and will performance]. *Untersuchungen zur Psychologie und Philosophie, 1*.

Hommel, B. (2000a). Intentional control of automatic stimulus-response translation. In Y. Rossetti, & A. Revonsuo (Eds.), *Interaction between dissociable conscious and nonconscious processes* (pp. 223−244). Amsterdam: John Benjamins Publishing Company.

Hommel, B. (2000b). The prepared reflex: automaticity and control in stimulus-response translation. In S. Monsell, & J. Driver (Eds.), *Control of cognitive processes: Attention and performance XVIII* (pp. 247−273). Cambridge, MA: MIT Press.

Hommel, B. (2004). Event files: Feature binding in and across perception and action. *Trends in Cognitive Sciences, 8*, 494−500.

Hommel, B. (2009). Action control according to TEC (theory of event coding). *Psychological Research, 73*, 512−526.

Hommel, B. (2012). Convergent and divergent operations in cognitive search. In P. M. Todd, T. T. Hills, & T. W. Robbins (Eds.), *Cognitive search: Evolution, algorithms, and the brain* (pp. 221−235). Cambridge, MA: MIT Press.

Hommel, B. (2013). Ideomotor action control: on the perceptual grounding of voluntary actions and agents. In W. Prinz, M. Beisert, & A. Herwig (Eds.), *Action science: Foundations of an emerging discipline* (pp. 113—136). Cambridge, MA: MIT Press.

Hommel, B., & Colzato, L. S. (2010). Religion as a control guide: on the impact of religion on cognition. *Zygon: Journal of Religion & Science, 45,* 596—604.

Hommel, B., Colzato, L. S., Fischer, R., & Christoffels, I. (2011). Bilingualism and creativity: benefits in convergent thinking come with losses in divergent thinking. *Frontiers in Psychology, 2,* 273.

Hommel, B., Colzato, L. S., Scorolli, C., Borghi, A. M., & van den Wildenberg, W. P. M. (2011). Religion and action control: faith-specific modulation of the Simon effect but not stop-signal performance. *Cognition, 120,* 177—185.

Hommel, B., Colzato, L. S., & van den Wildenberg, W. P. M. (2009). How social are task representations? *Psychological Science, 20,* 794—798.

Hommel, B., Fischer, R., Colzato, L. S., van den Wildenberg, W. P. M., & Cellini, C. (2012). The effect of fMRI (noise) on cognitive control. *Journal of Experimental Psychology: Human Perception and Performance, 38,* 290—301.

Hommel, B., Kessler, K., Schmitz, F., Gross, J., Akyürek, E., Shapiro, K., et al. (2006). How the brain blinks: towards a neurocognitive model of the attentional blink. *Psychological Research, 70,* 425—435.

Hommel, B., Müsseler, J., Aschersleben, G., & Prinz, W. (2001). The theory of event coding (TEC): a framework for perception and action planning. *Behavioral and Brain Sciences, 24,* 849—878.

Isen, A. M. (1999). On the relationship between affect and creative problem solving. In S. Russ (Ed.), *Affect, creative experience, and psychological adjustment* (pp. 3—17). London: Taylor & Francis.

Kahneman, D. (1973). *Attention and effort.* Englewood Cliffs, NJ: Prentice-Hall.

Kim, D., & Hommel, B. (2015). An event-based account of conformity. *Psychological Science, 26,* 484—489.

Kiesel, A., Steinhauser, M., Wendt, M., Falkenstein, M., Jost, K., Philipp, A. M., et al. (2010). Control and interference in task switching—a review. *Psychological Bulletin, 136,* 849—874.

Kornblum, S., Hasbroucq, T., & Osman, A. (1990). Dimensional overlap: cognitive basis for stimulus-response compatibility—a model and taxonomy. *Psychological Review, 97,* 253—270.

Kukla, A. (1972). Foundations of an attributional theory of performance. *Psychological Review, 79,* 454—470.

Lippelt, D. P., Hommel, B., & Colzato, L. S. (2014). Focused attention, open monitoring and loving kindness meditation: effects on attention, conflict monitoring and creativity. *Frontiers in Psychology, 5,* 1083.

Logan, G. D., & Cowan, W. B. (1984). On the ability to inhibit thought and action: a theory of an act of control. *Psychological Review, 91,* 295—327.

Logan, G. D., & Gordon, R. D. (2001). Executive control of visual attention in dual-task situations. *Psychological Review, 108,* 393—434.

Lutz, A., Slagter, H. A., Dunne, J. D., & Davidson, R. J. (2008). Attention regulation and monitoring in meditation. *Trends in Cognitive Sciences, 12,* 163—169.

MacLeod, C. M. (1991). Half a century of research on the Stroop effect: an integrative review. *Psychological Review, 109,* 163—203.

Martens, S., Munneke, J., Smid, H., & Johnson, A. (2006). Quick minds don't blink: electrophysiological correlates of individual differences in attentional selection. *Journal of Cognitive Neuroscience, 18,* 1423—1438.

Martin, M. (1978). Speech recoding in silent reading. *Memory & Cognition, 30,* 187—200.

Mayr, U., & Keele, S. W. (2000). Changing internal constraints on action: the role of backward inhibition. *Journal of Experimental Psychology: General, 129,* 4—26.

McCauley, R. N. (1987). The role of cognitive explanations in psychology. *Behaviorism, 15,* 27—40.

McClain, L. (1983). Effects of response type and set size on Stroop color-word performance. *Perceptual & Motor Skills, 56,* 735—743.

Mednick, S. A. (1968). The remote associates test. *The Journal of Creative Behavior, 2,* 213—214.

Michotte, A., & Prüm, E. (1911). Etude experimental sur la choix volontaire. *Archives de Psychologie, 10,* 113—320.

Miyake, A., Friedman, N. P., Emerson, M. J., Witzki, A. H., Howerter, A., & Wager, T. (2000). The unity and diversity of executive functions and their contributions to complex "frontal lobe" tasks: a latent variable analysis. *Cognitive Psychology, 41,* 49—100.

Moors, A., & De Houwer, J. (2006). Automaticity: a theoretical and conceptual analysis. *Psychological Bulletin, 132,* 297—326.

Müller, J., Dreisbach, G., Goschke, T., Hensch, T., Lesch, K.-P., & Brocke, B. (2008). Dopamine and cognitive control: the prospect of monetary gains influences the balance between flexibility and stability in a set-shifting paradigm. *European Journal of Neuroscience, 26,* 3661—3668.

Navon, D. (1977). Forest before trees: the precedence of global features in visual perception. *Cognitive Psychology, 9,* 353—383.

Navon, D. (1984). Resources—a theoretical soup stone? *Psychological Review, 91,* 216—234.

Nijstad, B. A., De Dreu, C. K. W., Rietzschel, E. F., & Baas, M. (2010). The dual pathway to creativity model: creative ideation as a function of flexibility and persistence. *European Review of Social Psychology, 21,* 34—77.

Nisbett, R. E., & Miyamoto, Y. (2005). The influence of culture: holistic versus analytic perception. *Trends in Cognitive Sciences, 9,* 467—473.

Nolan, K., Bilder, R., Lachman, H., & Volavka, K. (2004). Catechol-O-methyltransferase Val158Met polymorphism in schizophrenia: differential effects of Val and Met alleles on cognitive stability and flexibility. *American Journal of Psychiatry, 161,* 359—361.

Olivers, C. N. L., & Nieuwenhuis, S. (2006). The beneficial effects of additional task load, positive affect, and instruction on the attentional blink. *Journal of Experimental Psychology: Human Perception and Performance, 32,* 364—379.

Ratcliff, R., & Rouder, J. N. (1998). Modeling response times for two-choice decisions. *Psychological Science, 9,* 347—356.

Reuss, H., Kiesel, A., Kunde, W., & Hommel, B. (2011). Unconscious activation of task sets. *Consciousness and Cognition, 20,* 556—567.

Reuter, D. F. (2002). *Gaydar: The ultimate insider guide to the gay sixth sense.* New York: Crown.

Ridderinkhof, K. R., Forstmann, B. U., Wylie, S., Burle, B., & van den Wildenberg, W. P. M. (2010). Neurocognitive mechanisms of action control: resisting the call of Sirens. *Wylie Interdisciplinary Reviews (WIREs) Cognitive Science, 2,* 174—192.

Ryle, G. (1949). *The concept of mind.* Chicago: The University of Chicago Press.

Sebanz, N., Knoblich, G., & Prinz, W. (2003). Representing others' actions: just like one's own? *Cognition, 88,* B11—B21.

Sellaro, R., van Dijk, W. W., Rossi Paccani, C., Hommel, B., & Colzato, L. S. (2014). A question of scent: lavender aroma promotes interpersonal trust. *Frontiers in Psychology, 5,* 1486.

Sellaro, R., Hommel, B., de Kwaadsteniet, E. W., & Colzato, L. S. (2014). Increasing interpersonal trust through divergent thinking. *Frontiers in Psychology, 5,* 561.

Shapiro, K., Schmitz, F., Martens, S., Hommel, B., & Schnitzler, A. (2006). Resource sharing in the attentional blink. *Neuroreport, 17,* 163—166.

van Steenbergen, H., Band, G. P. H., & Hommel, B. (2009). Reward counteracts conflict adaptation: evidence for a role of affect in executive control. *Psychological Science, 20,* 1473—1477.

van Steenbergen, H., Band, G. P. H., & Hommel, B. (2010). In the mood for adaptation: how affect regulates conflict-driven control. *Psychological Science, 21*, 1629–1634.

van Steenbergen, H., Band, G. P. H., & Hommel, B. (2012). Reward valence modulates conflict-driven attentional adaptation: Electrophysiological evidence. *Biological Psychology, 90*, 234–241.

van Steenbergen, H., Band, G. P. H., Hommel, B., Rombouts, S. A., & Nieuwenhuis, S. Hedonic hotspots regulate cingulate-driven adaptation to cognitive demands. *Cerebral Cortex*, in press.

van Steenbergen, H., Booij, L., Band, G. P. H., Hommel, B., & van der Does, A. J. W. (2012). Affective regulation of conflict-driven control in remitted depressive patients after acute tryptophan depletion. *Cognitive, Affective, & Behavioral Neuroscience, 12*, 280–286.

van Steenbergen, H., Langeslag, S. J. E., Band, G. P. H., & Hommel, B. (2014). Reduced cognitive control in passionate lovers. *Motivation and Emotion, 38*, 444–450.

Stock, A., & Stock, C. (2004). A short history of ideo-motor action. *Psychological Research, 68*, 176–188.

Stroop, J. R. (1935). Studies of interference in serial verbal reactions. *Journal of Experimental Psychology, 28*, 643–662.

van Veen, V., & Carter, C. S. (2002). Conflict and cognitive control in the brain. *Current Directions in Psychological Science, 15*, 237–240.

Verbruggen, F., McLaren, I. P. L., & Chambers, C. D. (2014). Banishing the control homunculi in studies of action control and behavior change. *Perspectives on Psychological Science, 9*, 497–524.

Wallas, G. (1926). *The art of thought*. New York: Harcourt Brace.

Waszak, F., Hommel, B., & Allport, A. (2003). Task-switching and long-term priming: role of episodic stimulus-task bindings in task-shift costs. *Cognitive Psychology, 46*, 361–413.

Wickens, C. D. (1984). Processing resources in attention. In R. Parasuraman, & R. Davies (Eds.), *Varieties of attention* (pp. 63–101). New York: Academic Press.

Wiers, R. W., & Stacy, A. W. (Eds.). (2006). *Handbook of implicit cognition and addiction*. Thousand Oaks, CA: Sage.

de Wit, S., & Dickinson, A. (2009). Associative theories of goal-directed behaviour. A case for animal-human translational models. *Psychological Research, 73*, 463–476.

Zwosta, K., Hommel, B., Goschke, T., & Fischer, R. (2013). Mood states determine the degree of task shielding in dual-task performance. *Cognition & Emotion, 27*, 1142–1152.

CHAPTER THREE

The Architecture of Goal Systems: Multifinality, Equifinality, and Counterfinality in Means—End Relations

Arie W. Kruglanski[*,1], Marina Chernikova[*], Maxim Babush[*], Michelle Dugas[*] and Birga M. Schumpe[§]
*University of Maryland, College Park, MD, USA
[§]Helmut-Schmidt University, Hamburg, Germany
[1]Corresponding author: E-mail: kruglanski@gmail.com

Contents

1. Introduction	70
2. Multifinality	71
2.1 Empirical Research on Multifinality	72
2.1.1 The Dilution Effect	*72*
2.1.2 Multifinality Constraint Effect	*74*
2.1.3 Multifinality in Unconscious Choice	*75*
2.1.4 Regulatory Mode Effects	*76*
2.2 Multifinality Discussion	77
3. Equifinality	78
3.1 Empirical Research on Equifinality	78
3.1.1 Substitutability	*78*
3.1.2 Commitment to Goals and Means	*79*
3.1.3 Dilution Effects in Equifinality Contexts	*80*
3.1.4 Dilution Effects in Social Identification	*82*
3.1.5 Means Variety	*85*
3.2 Equifinality Discussion	87
4. Counterfinality	88
4.1 Empirical Research on Counterfinality	88
4.1.1 Goal Magnitude	*90*
4.1.2 Attainment Expectancy	*92*
4.1.3 Addiction to Counterfinal Means	*93*
4.2 Counterfinality Discussion	93
5. Recapitulation and Conclusion	94
5.1 Domains of Applicability	95
5.2 Underlying Mechanisms	95
References	96

Advances in Motivation Science, Volume 2
ISSN 2215-0919
http://dx.doi.org/10.1016/bs.adms.2015.04.001

Abstract

In this chapter, we will describe several means—goal configurations within goal systems theory: *multifinality*, *equifinality*, and *counterfinality*. In the multifinality configuration, one means serves several goals; in the equifinality configuration, one goal is served by several substitutable means; and in the counterfinality configuration, one goal is served by a single means that simultaneously undermines another goal. We will discuss recent advances in motivation research that have focused on each of these means—goal configurations, as well as the implications and potential future directions of such research.

1. INTRODUCTION

Much of human motivation is decidedly cognitive. Our goals, wishes, and desires are mentally represented, and so are their presumed means of attainment. The common notion of *planning* refers to the construction of relations between activities and the desirable states of affairs they are presumed to bring about, that is, between means and goals. In carrying out such a construction, individuals map out the motivational space they intend to navigate and chart the trajectory that best suits their intentions. The mental map thus created contains a representation of the various goals salient for individuals in the situation in which they find themselves; it also contains the representation of possible means to the goals in question as well as obstacles that may interfere with the attainment of these goals. Ultimately, individuals' motivationally relevant mental map consists of interlocking configurations of goals and means, creating a conceptual network individuals are contemplating and taking into account when making their choices and carrying out their actions.

In the present article, we describe three major configurations whereby relations between means and goals may be represented. These are the configurations of *multifinality*, *equifinality*, and *counterfinality* (see Figure 1(a—c)). The *multifinality* configuration refers to a situation wherein a single means is seen as serving more than one goal, thus affording the attainment of several objectives via a single activity (i.e., "several birds with one stone"). Though the multifinality configuration maximizes value (that accumulates across the different goals the multifinal means may attain), it may sacrifice the perceived instrumentality of each means because of a "dilution effect," related to the number of links between the means and the goals.

In contrast to the *multifinality* configuration, that of *equifinality* depicts a situation wherein each of a different means leads to a single goal (as captured

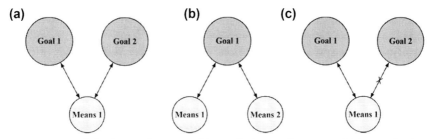

Figure 1 (a) Multifinality configuration. (b) Equifinality configuration. (c) Counterfinality configuration.

in the "all roads leading to Rome" aphorism). This pattern of means—goal relations implies the need to exercise choice between the different means; it also extends the possibility of substituting, if need be, each of the means for any of the others. For instance, if a given means failed to deliver progress, a different means to the same goal could be taken instead, thus preserving the expectancy that the goal in question will be attained after all.

Though the possibility of substitution could be helpful, it has a downside as well. Once again, this stems from the dilution effect that multiple links between means and goals can produce. As a consequence, perceived instrumentality of each means to a goal should vary inversely with the number of means to that goal, that is, with size of the equifinal set of means.

Finally, the *counterfinality* configuration depicts a pattern of goals-means relations wherein a means seen to serve a given focal goal is at the same time believed to undermine another goal (as captured in the "no pain no gain" adage). In what follows, we elaborate on each of the three configurations and describe empirical research that bears on their various properties.

2. MULTIFINALITY

People rarely pursue only one goal at a time; typically, several goals are simultaneously salient to them and guide their choices and decisions. In some cases, the multiple active goals may be antithetical to each other, ushering in goal conflict. For instance, one may be interested in a vacation on a beach, but also possibly in a holiday in the mountains. Obviously, doing both at the same time is impossible, hence prompting the need to choose one of the competing alternatives over the other.

Often, however, the presence of several simultaneous goals need not signify conflict. For instance, in choosing a vehicle, one may have in mind the goals of attaining high gas mileage, low price, and ample comfort. In choosing a college to attend, one may entertain the goals of having superb faculty, small class size, and a pleasant campus environment. These various requirements or preferences are not necessarily in conflict with each other. Indeed, it is possible to think of situations where they are all met. One might find a car that gives one good gas mileage, is relatively inexpensive, and is also comfortable. Similarly, one might find a college with distinguished faculty, a good student to faculty ratio, and an attractive campus. In those cases, one may have at one's disposal multifinal options that afford the attainment of all the active goals in the situation.

To reiterate, in goal systems theory, *multifinal* means are defined as means which are capable of attaining more than one goal at the same time (Kruglanski, Kopetz, et al., 2013; Kruglanski et al., 2002). For example, taking a dance class may serve both the goal of fitness and the goal of meeting new people; riding a bicycle can serve both the goal of using convenient transportation and the goal of reducing one's carbon footprint (for an illustration of the multifinality configuration within goal systems theory, see Figure 1(a)). Multifinality in goal systems is contrasted with the unifinality configuration, in which one goal is served by a single means; the equifinality configuration, in which one goal is served by multiple means (see Figure 1(b)); and the counterfinality configuration, in which a means that serves one goal undermines another goal (Figure 1(c)).

2.1 Empirical Research on Multifinality

2.1.1 The Dilution Effect

Because a multifinal means allows one to attain other goals in addition to a focal goal, it is perceived to deliver greater value, or a bigger "bang for the buck," than a unifinal means (Chun, Kruglanski, Sleeth-Keppler, & Friedman, 2011; Kruglanski, Kopetz, et al., 2013). However, a multifinal means is also perceived to be less instrumental (i.e., effective toward goal pursuit) than a unifinal means. This is because, due to its linkages with multiple goals, its strength of association to any *single* one of those goals is diluted. Such a dilution effect (Zhang, Fishbach, & Kruglanski, 2007) reflects Anderson's (1983) "fan effect" principle, whereby the activation potential of any cognitive node is inversely related to the number of connections it has to other nodes. In the present context, the more goals are connected to a given means, the weaker will be each individual means–goal association. Because the strength of association between means and goals is psychologically interpreted as instrumentality of the means to the goal (Kruglanski, 1996; Zhang et al., 2007), a means that is associated with only one goal (i.e., a unifinal means) is perceived to be more instrumental than a means associated with multiple goals (i.e., a multifinal means).

These notions were supported in six experiments by Zhang et al. (2007). Specifically, this research demonstrated that increasing the number of goals a means can serve reduces the association strength—and, in turn, perceptions of instrumentality—between that means and each individual goal. As a consequence, means that are linked to several goals (as opposed to a single goal) are less likely to be chosen and pursued when only one of the goals is active. In one study, Zhang et al. (2007) found that associating a means (e.g., "eating tomatoes") with one goal (e.g., "preventing heart cancer" or "preventing eye disease") versus two goals (e.g., "preventing heart cancer" *and* "preventing eye disease") changed the means' perceived instrumentality toward each goal. Participants who read about a means that served one goal only perceived it to be more instrumental to that goal than participants who read about a means that served two goals. Similar dilution effects on instrumentality were observed when participants themselves had to generate a means that served either one goal or multiple goals (Zhang et al., 2007).

In another study, Zhang et al. (2007) manipulated perceived goal distinctiveness by asking participants to write about either the similarity or dissimilarity of two goals. They found that means–goal association strength was diluted the most when the additional goal served by the multifinal means was dissimilar (vs being similar) to the focal goal. That is, when two goals served by the means were perceived as different, the multifinal means had a weaker association with each goal than it did when the two goals were perceived as similar. Presumably, when goals are similar they may activate each other; this may add activation over and above the activation by the means, thus reducing the dilution effect.

In yet another study, Zhang et al. (2007) manipulated the association strength between a multifinal means ("jogging") and one of the goals it served (i.e., either "increasing oxygen in the blood" or "strengthening muscles"). Interestingly, the strengthening of one means–goal link (e.g., jogging-oxygen) led the other means–goal link (e.g., jogging-muscles) to actually grow *weaker*; this suggests that means–goal association strength is influenced by the other linkages in that means–goal configuration, as predicted by goal systems theory (Kruglanski et al., 2002). In other words, the association strength between a given node in the network and other nodes appears to be a constant sum, so that increasing the strength of a link between two nodes reduces the strength of remaining connections involving these nodes.

Importantly, Zhang et al. (2007) also showed that means—goal association strength (as measured by reaction time) mediates the effect of number of goals on perceived means instrumentality. The means—goal association becomes weaker when another goal is added to the list of goals a means serves, and that weakened means—goal association predicts the lowered instrumentality of the means in regard to serving the focal goal. Lastly, the authors found that when a means (an office pen) was described as serving only one goal ("writing") versus two goals ("writing" and "working as a laser pointer"), participants whose goal of writing was activated were more likely to use the pen for writing when it was described as serving *only* the goal of writing (i.e., unifinal; Zhang et al., 2007). Thus, Zhang et al. (2007) studies suggest that although multifinal means may offer more value by serving more goals at the same time, if one cares about a single goal more than the others, multifinal means may be perceived as less instrumental than unifinal means and would ultimately fail to be chosen when pursuing that particular goal.

2.1.2 Multifinality Constraint Effect

There are times when an individual has multiple coactivated goals (e.g., to get to work quickly as well as to avoid harming the environment), and multifinal means (e.g., riding the bus) may be preferable in these situations because they help avoid goal conflict. Thus, in cases when multiple goals are activated, individuals may limit their set of acceptable means to those that benefit (or at least do not harm) the entire set of active goals—this is known as the multifinality constraints effect (Kopetz, Faber, Fishbach, & Kruglanski, 2011). Kopetz et al. (2011) found that a reminder of daily tasks that participants wished to accomplish narrowed their set of foods at a cafeteria for the focal goal of having lunch to only those means that would serve their dual goals of lunch and save time for other errands. Kopetz et al. (2011) also demonstrated that when the feasibility of finding a multifinal means is high (because the multiple goals in question, "being healthy" and "being in shape," share many means), participants do not restrict their number of acceptable means. However, when the feasibility of finding a multifinal means is moderate (because the two goals in question, "being healthy" and "doing well in school," share only some means), a substantial reduction in the number of acceptable means occurs, and participants list only those means that are multifinal. Finally, when the feasibility of finding a multifinal means is extremely low (e.g., because the two goals in question, "being healthy" and "drinking alcohol," have almost no means in common), participants do not restrict their means choice to those means which could be multifinal—presumably because they recognize the impossibility of selecting multifinal means in such a situation.

In several additional studies, Kopetz et al. (2011) found that when a focal and an alternative goal are equally important, participants restrict their choice of means to those that serve both goals. On the other hand, when the focal goal is manipulated to become relatively more important than the alternative goal, participants expand their means set size to include *all* means that are instrumental to the focal goal. Taken together, Kopetz et al. (2011) studies provide consistent evidence that multifinality constraints can influence means choice when an individual has multiple simultaneously activated goals.

2.1.3 Multifinality in Unconscious Choice

The broad tendency to search for and select multifinal means when multiple goals are activated has also been shown to apply when some of the activated goals are implicit, that is, unconscious. In this vein, Chun et al. (2011) investigated whether individuals' choices in the service of an explicit focal goal also reflect a tendency to fulfill implicit background goals. The authors predicted that individuals' choices are often guided by the multifinal pursuit of both implicit and explicit goals, and they examined this prediction across five studies. Chun et al. (2011) found that Wilson and Nisbett's classic (1978) results—in which participants frequently chose the rightmost pair of socks without realizing why they did so—could be explained in terms of multifinality. More specifically, in Chun et al.'s (2011) study, participants tended to choose the rightmost pair of socks more often when the socks served two goals (the explicit goal of choosing the best pair of socks and the implicit goal of making a decision quickly). This occurred even though participants were not aware of the influence of the implicit goal on their sock selections. In a subsequent study, Chun et al. (2011) discovered that individuals tended to judge fabric as being of higher quality when it satisfied both participants' explicit goal (to select the best fabric) and an implicitly primed goal (either identifying or disidentifying with their university).

Interestingly, Chun et al. (2011) found that the power of implicit goals to direct behavior was limited to cases in which the multifinal and unifinal means options were equally instrumental to individuals' explicit goals. When a unifinal means was found to be more instrumental to the focal goal than the multifinal means, the unifinal option was actually preferred more often. Thus, it seems that explicit goal considerations take precedence over implicit multifinality effects. Furthermore, Chun et al. (2011) also showed that individuals tend to choose multifinal means *less* if the implicit goal the multifinal means served (self-enhancement) had already been satisfied with an alternative means (a self-affirmation manipulation). Lastly, Chun et al. (2011) showed that the existence of only a single goal (whether implicit or explicit) prompted the choice of means that were instrumental to whichever goal was activated; this was contrasted with a condition in which both an implicit and explicit goal were present, which prompted the choice of multifinal means. Together, Chun et al.'s (2011) studies provide support for the notion that a goal need not be explicit to influence means choice. They also indicate that unconscious goal pursuit is not mechanical or automatic but rather is rational in the sense of leading to the selection of the best means to the goal, and devaluating a means after a goal it served was attained.

2.1.4 Regulatory Mode Effects

There can also be individual differences and situational factors that predict the preference for multifinal versus unifinal means. Orehek, Mauro, Kruglanski, and van der Bles (2012) found that individuals high on the *locomotion* tendency (the self-regulatory orientation that constitutes a desire for movement and change) prefer unifinal means, whereas those high on the *assessment* tendency (the self-regulatory orientation that involves a desire to critically evaluate alternatives) prefer multifinal means. This was the case whether locomotion and assessment were measured as an individual difference (in Study 1) or manipulated situationally (in Studies 2–5). In one study, participants' locomotion and assessment levels were measured with the regulatory mode scale (Kruglanski et al., 2000). Then, participants were randomly assigned to reading about a means ("consuming tomatoes") that satisfied one goal ("preventing cancer" or "preventing eye disease") or two goals (both "preventing cancer" *and* "preventing eye disease"). The predominance of a locomotion (vs assessment) tendency was positively correlated with preference for unifinal means, but was negatively correlated with preference for multifinal means. Orehek et al. (2012) replicated this study with manipulations that induced in participants the states of locomotion and assessment and found similar results: participants in the locomotion condition preferred a unifinal means over a multifinal one, whereas those in the assessment condition preferred a multifinal means over a unifinal one. Orehek et al. (2012) also found that locomotors' preference for unifinal means (and assessors' preference for multifinal means) holds even when the number of goals the means serves is increased from two to three.

In another study, Orehek et al. (2012) told all participants that a single means ("drinking water") served two goals ("having clear skin" and "having more energy"). Furthermore, in this study, the association strength between the means and the goals was manipulated, such that in one condition the means of drinking water served both goals equally, and in the other condition the means of drinking water was more strongly associated with one goal than the other. Orehek et al. (2012) found that participants in the locomotion condition were *more* thirsty, and participants in the assessment condition were *less* thirsty, when the association between the means and one of the goals was strengthened. This study provides evidence that locomotors prefer unifinal means because of the stronger means—goal association that unifinal means suggest. Because locomotors desire goal-related movement, they are more likely to choose means which presumably will allow them to achieve smooth and uninterrupted goal progress (which is afforded by means with a stronger association to the goal). Lastly, in a paradigm that allowed participants to make a behavioral choice between a unifinal means (writing with a regular pen fit for writing) and a multifinal means (a pen that served also as a laser pointer), locomotors were more likely to select the unifinal means, whereas assessors were more likely to select the multifinal means (Orehek et al., 2012). Orehek et al. (2012) studies show that the choice between multifinal and unifinal means is not always clear-cut, as individuals will sometimes have preexisting preferences for one or the other type of means.

2.2 Multifinality Discussion

People are often interested in pursuing more than one goal, but limited time and energy make it difficult to pursue more than a handful of goals on a given day. Means that can serve multiple goals at once—that is, multifinal means—increase the number of goals people can pursue concurrently. Several intriguing features of such multifinal means have been uncovered in recent years. First, such means can be subject to the *dilution effect*, in which a multifinal means to a goal will be perceived as less instrumental to a given goal than a unifinal means to that same goal (Zhang et al., 2007). In addition, if a person's several goals are activated at the same time, the *multifinality constraints effect* may come into play: that is, one's suitable set of means may be restricted to those that benefit all of the currently active goals (Kopetz et al., 2011). Implicit background goals can also lead to a preference for multifinal means that serve both an explicit focal goal and an implicit alternative goal (Chun et al., 2011). However, when a goal has been deactivated (due to either goal attainment or goal unattainability), multifinal means will no longer be more desirable than unifinal means (Schultz, 2010). Lastly, individual differences and situationally induced factors can come into play during means choice: individuals high on the *locomotion* self-regulatory orientation (whether measured or situationally induced) tend to prefer unifinal means, whereas those high on the *assessment* orientation (whether measured or situationally induced) tend to prefer multifinal means (Orehek et al., 2012).

Research thus far has focused on the consequences of multifinality for means choice (e.g., the preference for multifinal versus unifinal means as it interacts with locomotion vs assessment tendencies). Subsequent work could investigate the antecedents multifinality, that is, the kind of personality or situational factors that prompt individuals to seek out or creatively generate means that are capable of accomplish multiple objectives at the same time and those that lead them to seek out single-ended means.

3. EQUIFINALITY

Often people consider multiple possible ways of pursuing a given goal. An individual with the goal of attaining or improving her or his fitness might attempt to do so by running, cycling, and/or attending yoga classes; all of these exemplify means for attaining the same goal (of fitness). Such means are often referred to as equifinal (Heider, 1958), and the totality of equifinal means to a given goal constitutes, therefore, the *equifinality set*. As noted earlier, the *equifinality configuration* (see Figure 1(b)) raises the possibility of substituting one means for another, and it poses the problem of choosing a given means from the set of those available. Recent research on the equifinality configuration is described below.

3.1 Empirical Research on Equifinality

3.1.1 Substitutability

Substitutability signifies the opportunity to switch to an alternative means if goal progress through a given means is blocked (Kruglanski et al., 2002). The notion of substitutability has been alluded to in several major psychological theories such as psychoanalysis (in which symptom substitution was discussed in reference to neurosis; Freud, 1920) and cognitive dissonance theory (in which it was suggested that people can reduce dissonance through multiple substitutable means; Festinger, 1957). In the same vein, Lewin (1935) discussed the problem of task substitutability, whereas more recently researchers have discussed contexts wherein multiple means afford substitutability in the service of the maintenance of self-esteem (e.g., Steele & Liu, 1983; Tesser, 2000).

3.1.2 Commitment to Goals and Means

Prior discussions of substitutability rarely progressed beyond the mere mention of its possible occurrence in a given context. However, substitutability has potentially important consequences for a number of psychological phenomena. One of these concerns the degree of commitment to goals and to means. Specifically, Kruglanski, Pierro, and Sheveland (2011) argued that an individual's commitment to a goal is likely to be augmented when multiple means are available for goal attainment. First, the availability of multiple means should bolster an individual's confidence in her or his ability to attain the goal—that is, increase the *expectancy* of goal attainment. After all, if one means fails, alternate means offer an opportunity to try again. Secondly, the availability of multiple means might suggest that the focal goal they are attached to is of higher *value* due to a process similar to the availability heuristic, whereby information that is easier to retrieve from memory is inferred to be more important than information that is difficult to retrieve (Schwarz et al., 1991; Tversky & Kahneman, 1974). Together, inferences about the greater *expectancy* and *value* of a goal when multiple (vs fewer) means are available should increase commitment to the goal (Kruglanski, Chernikova, Rosenzweig, & Kopetz, 2014).

Although a greater number of available means can strengthen goal commitment, it can have a weakening effect on means commitment. Specifically, Kruglanski et al. (2011) reasoned that as the number of means available to achieve a goal increases, one's dependence on any given means should decrease because there are suitable alternatives available in the case of failure or thwarting of goal progress via the original means. This argument echoes findings in interdependence theory research, wherein commitment to one's relationship partner depends on the comparison level for alternative partners (e.g., Rusbult, 1980; Van Lange, De Cremer, Van Dijk, & Van Vugt, 2007). In goal systemic terms, one's current partner represents a single means to the goal of a satisfying relationship; however, if other individuals are perceived as suitable alternative means to this goal, commitment to the current partner decreases as the equifinality set associated with the relationship goal increases.

Kruglanski et al. (2011) tested the hypothesized effect of increasing equifinality set size on goal and means commitment across four studies and found consistent support for their predictions. In Studies 1 and 2, participants freely generated either any type of means (Study 1) or a specifically social means (Study 2) to one of two work goals. Following the means generation task, participants completed measures of commitment, goal expectancy, and goal importance. As expected, the number of means generated was negatively associated with commitment to a particular means and positively associated with goal commitment. Furthermore, perceptions of likelihood of goal attainment (i.e., expectancies) and of goal importance (i.e., value) mediated the effect of means number on goal commitment.

To more stringently assess causality, Kruglanski et al. (2011) conducted two additional studies in which the number of means was experimentally manipulated. Specifically, in a within-subjects design, Study 3 instructed participants to list two goals, then generate a single means to one of the goals and three means to the other goal, or vice versa. The results of this study replicated the earlier findings of the larger means sets being associated with a greater commitment to the goal and a lesser commitment to any given means. Study 4 replicated the findings of Study 3 with a between-subjects design; it also found further support for the mediating roles of the expectancy of goal attainment and of goal value on the relationship between goal commitment and means set size.

3.1.3 Dilution Effects in Equifinality Contexts

As discussed earlier, attachment of a single means to multiple goals dilutes, or weakens, the strength of the association between that means and a given goal—which in turn reduces the perceived instrumentality of that means to each of the goals. Drawing on the same underlying logic, additional research has investigated whether a similar dilution of instrumentality also occurs when multiple means are attached to a single goal.

There are good reasons to believe that the dilution effect would occur not only in multifinality configurations, but in equifinality configurations as well. Specifically, the concept of spreading activation (Anderson, 1983), which underlies the dilution effect, suggests that as the number of associations attached to a mental construct increases, each individual association becomes weaker. Accordingly, the strength of association between two concepts (means and goals in our case) should be positively associated with the uniqueness of the interconnection *regardless* of the direction of connections, that is, whether we refer to linking a given means with multiple goals or vice versa, linking a given goal with multiple means.

Bélanger, Schori-Eyal, Pica, Kruglanski, and Lafrenière (unpublished manuscript) investigated this hypothesis across five studies, and obtained consistent evidence for the dilution effect in the equifinality configuration. Specifically, Bélanger, Schori-Eyal et al. (unpublished manuscript) found that when participants were given multiple (vs a single) means to a goal, they perceived each of the multiple means to be less effective in reaching the goal than the single means. The same pattern held true when the individuals generated multiple (vs a single) means to a goal themselves. As in the multifinality configuration, here as well, the dilution effect was amplified when means within the equifinality set were perceived to be distinct from (vs similar to) one another.

To further explore the parallels of the dilution effect in multifinality and equifinality settings, Bélanger, Schori-Eyal et al. (unpublished manuscript, Study 4) investigated the hypothesis that the overall association strength of links to a given goal is fixed and that it is distributed over the number of links in the goal structure. Accordingly, these researchers examined whether increasing the strength of the association between a given means and a goal would strengthen the perceived instrumentality of that particular means to the goal while at the same time weakening the strength of association and perceived instrumentality of *other* means to the same goal. In the study designed to examine these notions, participants were presented with the goal of health served by two means: *eating olives* and *eating fish*. The strength of the means—goal association between *eating olives* and health was then enhanced via a sequential priming task. After the priming procedure, participants rated their perceived instrumentality of both eating olives and eating fish as means to achieving good health. Consistent with predictions, as the association between eating olives and health increased, the strength of the association between eating fish and health decreased; perceptions of instrumentality followed the same pattern. Overall, the results of the Bélanger, Schori-Eyal et al. (unpublished manuscript) studies demonstrate that the same mechanism underlies the dilution effect in both multifinal means—goal configurations (as revealed in Zhang et al., 2007) and equifinal ones.

In an interesting extension of the previous findings, Bélanger, Schori-Eyal et al. (unpublished manuscript, Study 5) examined the consequences of dilution on intrinsic motivation for an activity. Intrinsic motivation is described as one in which the activity is desired because of the inherent satisfaction and pleasure of its performance (Deci & Ryan, 1985). Drawing on goal systems theory, Shah and Kruglanski (2000) argued that the strength of association between a means and a goal should be positively associated with intrinsic motivation because the stronger the association, the greater the experience of fusion between the means and the goal. Though Shah and Kruglanski

(2000) found correlational evidence in support of this hypothesis, Bélanger, Schori-Eyal et al. (unpublished manuscript, Study 5) sought to test it experimentally by connecting either one or several means to a goal. Specifically, the goal of *relatedness* was made salient and participants were presented with either one means ("hanging out with others") or two means ("hanging out with others" and "helping others") to this particular goal. Participants then rated the effectiveness of "hanging out with others" as a means to relatedness, as well as their intrinsic motivation to use this means. Consistent with previous studies, the means of "hanging out with others" was perceived to be less instrumental in the two means condition. Furthermore, perceptions of means instrumentality predicted participants' intrinsic motivation to use that means.

3.1.4 Dilution Effects in Social Identification

To illustrate the possible social implications of the dilution effect, Dugas and Kruglanski (unpublished manuscript) applied a goal systemic framework to the topic of group identification. Conceptualizing groups as means to goals (cf. Yzerbyt & Demoulin, 2010), the authors set out to test the hypothesis that if membership in a given group is a means to a goal of self-identity which is served also by other means, then the fewer those other means, the greater the identification with the group. In other words, the greater the number of the additional means, the stronger the dilution effect, and the less pronounced the experience that the group is instrumental to the goal of self-identity.

Across four studies, Dugas and Kruglanski (unpublished manuscript) obtained supportive evidence for the foregoing notions. Specifically, it was found that the presence of multiple (vs a single) means to a goal lessened individuals' identification toward a wide range of groups, including intimacy groups (Study 1), social categories (Study 2), nominal groups (Study 3), and campus groups (Study 4). The results of these studies are reviewed in further detail below.

Adopting a similar paradigm as used in Zhang et al. (2007), Studies 1 and 2 manipulated equifinality set sizes with short essays presenting different means–goals relationships. Study 1 assigned participants to read about either two or one means to achieving either intimacy or identity goals. If they read about achieving intimacy goals, participants in the two means condition were presented with a close group of friends and family as two groups that can serve as means to these goals. For those assigned to read about achieving a distinct identity, gender and national group (i.e., being

American) were presented as means to achieving this goal. In the two means conditions, order of the groups was counterbalanced, with the first group presented in the text considered the target group. In the single means conditions, the target groups presented to participants were also counterbalanced. Consistent with expectations, participants identified less with the target group when presented with two means to a goal than when presented with a single means.

Study 2 replicated this finding with a similar paradigm which investigated how much participants identified with a target group when presented with either two goal-relevant groups (multiple means condition) or one goal-relevant group and a second goal-irrelevant group (single means condition). Even when controlling for the number of groups merely mentioned in the essay, participants exhibited less identification with the target group when presented with multiple means to the salient goal.

Studies 1 and 2 examined dilution of identification with existing group memberships. Study 3 explored the effect in the context of nominal groups within a paradigm used in optimal distinctiveness research on group identification, which posits that individuals should be motivated to identify with groups that achieve a balance between competing needs for assimilation and differentiation (Brewer, 1991). Previous research on optimal distinctiveness found that participants identify to a greater extent with minority (vs majority) groups because they achieve an optimal level of inclusion with a group and differentiation from other (Leonardelli & Brewer, 2001). Extending these findings, Dugas and Kruglanski (unpublished manuscript, Study 3) sought to test whether identification with minority, and to a lesser extent, majority groups would be diluted when presented with alternative means to achieve optimal distinctiveness. Following the procedure of Leonardelli and Brewer (2001) to create the nominal groups, Dugas and Kruglanski (unpublished manuscript) presented participants with a series of images with a large number of dots, asking participants to estimate the number of dots depicted in each image. Participants then received false feedback about whether they were overestimators or underestimators, and were informed that their group formed a majority (75—80%) or minority (20—25%) of the population. Following this procedure, participants were told that the researchers wanted to learn more about overestimators and underestimators, and were asked to complete several filler scales assessing personality traits before being presented with the manipulation for equifinality set size. To manipulate equifinality set size, participants were asked to write about two groups to which they belong that fulfill a sense of optimal distinctiveness (multiple means condition) or the first 15 min of their day (single means condition). It was hypothesized that thinking of other groups that fulfill a sense of optimal distinctiveness would dilute identification with minority groups to a greater extent than identification with majority groups because only minority groups are associated with the goal of optimal distinctiveness. Consistent with these expectations, participants identified less with the minority group in the multiple means (vs single means) condition; however, there were no significant differences in identification with a majority group.

Together, the findings from these studies suggest that memberships in groups serve as means to goals and hence are susceptible to dilution effects in the same way as are other means to other goals, but the mechanisms underlying dilution have not yet been examined. To examine the potential underlying mechanism, Dugas and Kruglanski (unpublished manuscript, Study 4) investigated the mediating role of perceptions of instrumentality on the dilution effect, using a paradigm common in uncertainty–identity research. Uncertainty–identity theory posits that individuals identify with groups as means of reducing uncertainty, and extreme groups provide an especially effective means to that end because of their strict and well-defined norms (Hogg, 2007; Hogg, Meehan, & Farquharson, 2010). Study 4 sought to test further whether providing alternative means to reduce uncertainty would attenuate the positive relationship between uncertainty and identification with extreme groups.

Following the procedure used by Hogg et al. (2010), Dugas and Kruglanski (unpublished manuscript) induced in their participants the experience of uncertainty by asking them how having to pay tuition made them feel either *uncertain* or *certain* about their futures. Following this manipulation, participants in the multiple means condition read an article about an extreme campus group whose objective was to reduce tuition fees, as well two other articles describing alternative methods for reducing tuition. Those in the single means condition read an article about the extreme campus group and two neutral articles. Consistent with expectations, participants in the uncertainty condition who read about several alternative means to reducing uncertainty regarding tuition rated the campus group as less instrumental to the end of uncertainty reduction and identified less with the group than those who only read about the campus group. Furthermore, perceptions of group instrumentality mediated the effect of equifinality set size (i.e., the number of means) on group identification. In the context of uncertainty reduction, these findings underscore an important implication of the dilution effect. More specifically, they suggest that when an individual is presented with several alternative means that serve the same goal, extreme means are likely to be perceived as less instrumental and less desirable, even under conditions of uncertainty known to engender extremism (Kruglanski, 2014).

The evidence reviewed above provides a compelling case for the existence of the dilution effect in equifinality contexts. As the number of available means to a goal increases, preference for those means and perceptions of their instrumentality tend to decrease. Thus far, we have reviewed research on equifinality that focuses on static contexts in which goal progress does not come into play. However, goal systems are dynamic, as individuals are continuously investing effort toward achieving one goal or another. Whether an individual has made progress toward their goal could have important effects on phenomena observed in equifinal means—goal configurations. We will now address equifinality-related phenomena in such dynamic contexts.

3.1.5 Means Variety

As we have seen, the number of means available for a given goal can have an effect on motivational constructs such as commitment, intrinsic motivation, and group identification. However, it is possible that additional features of equifinal configurations determine perceptions of goals and means as well. Just as individuals exhibit preferences for either multifinal or unifinal means configurations (Kruglanski et al., 2014; Orehek et al., 2012), those additional features of equifinal configurations might be differentially motivating to people. For example, means sets can differ not only in the number of means available but also in the variety, or similarity, among the means in a given set. A set of similar, low variety, means to pursue the goal of fitness could include running, walking, and speed walking. In contrast, a means set high in variety could include running, kayaking, and yoga. In research described below, Etkin and Ratner (2012, 2013) examined how such differences among means may affect the motivation of people in different stages of goal pursuit.

Specifically, Etkin and Ratner (2012) hypothesized that individuals' preference for means sets that are high versus low in variety depends on their subjective perceptions of *goal progress*. Individuals who perceive themselves as having made little goal progress are likely to experience uncertainty about their future means preferences (Simonson, 1990), and a means set that is high in variety offers a measure of reassurance that these future preferences can be met. Accordingly, Etkin and Ratner (2012) hypothesized that participants low in perceived goal progress would be more motivated by equifinal sets that are high in variety. In contrast, individuals who are high in perceived goal progress should experience greater certainty about goal attainment, and be rather disinclined to spend time on difficult choices among highly dissimilar (high variety) means.

Etkin and Ratner (2012) found support for these hypotheses in a series of studies. Whether goal progress was measured (Study 1B) or manipulated (Studies 1A and 2), individuals in the low progress conditions reported greater motivation toward a fitness goal when the provided means set was high (vs low) in variety; those in the high progress conditions showed the opposite tendency. Study 3 replicated the same pattern of findings with persistence and performance on difficult anagram tasks as objective measures of motivation.

Etkin and Ratner (2012, Study 4) also investigated whether means–set variety would influence individuals' preferences for different means sets. Toward this end, Study 4 manipulated means–set variety and subjective progress toward the goal of fitness. Consistent with predictions, when participants perceived themselves to be making low progress on their fitness goal, they were willing to pay more for the means (a pack of protein bars) after thinking about how the bars were different (vs similar). On the other hand, when participants perceived themselves to be making low goal progress, they were willing to pay more for the pack of protein bars after thinking about how the bars were similar (vs different). It is evident from these findings that even when number of means is held constant, the degree of variety within a means set can strongly influence individuals' motivation toward a goal. Of particular interest to consumer psychologists, Etkin and Ratner's (2012) studies demonstrate that equifinal configurations can have implications for real-world consumer behavior (i.e., the willingness to pay more or less for various products).

Etkin and Ratner (2013) further extended their research program on variety within means sets by examining how different levels of variety interact with temporal construals of goal pursuit. The authors argued that planning for goal pursuit in the near future should elicit concrete construals, while planning for goal pursuit in the distant future should elicit abstract construals. Notably, previous research has found that concrete construals lead to seeking out *differences* among sets of objects, whereas abstract construals lead to seeking out *similarities* among sets of objects (Förster, 2009). As such, individuals who are planning to carry out goal pursuit in the near future should experience greater "fit" between their goal and a means set that is high (vs low) in variety, whereas the opposite should hold for individuals who are planning for goal pursuit in the distant future. Such fit should lead to an increase in motivation (e.g., Higgins, 2005). Therefore, the authors hypothesized that individuals planning for goal pursuit in the near future would be more motivated by a set of means which is high in variety, whereas those planning for goal pursuit in the distant future would be more motivated by a set of means which is low in variety.

Etkin and Ratner (2013) found evidence to support these predictions in a series of studies that spanned several domains of goal pursuit, including health fitness, finance, and academic performance. In one example, participants were willing to pay more for high (vs low) variety personal training sessions when the sessions were going to take place in the near future, but were willing to pay less for high (vs low) variety training sessions when these were about to take place in the distant future. Etkin and Ratner (2013, Study 6) also hypothesized that means variety could affect the timing of goal pursuit whereby people may be motivated to actively "fit" their current goal pursuit to their available means set. In support of this prediction, the authors found that participants who read a description of similar (vs different) means to their goal of exercise exhibited a greater preference for delaying their goal pursuit.

Taken as a body, Etkin and Ratner's (2012, 2013) findings illustrate the importance of investigating various features of equifinality configurations. Evidently, both the number of means and the differences between those means can have implications for goal pursuit and consumer behavior. Furthermore, the findings from this research serve as a reminder that the dynamics of goal pursuit cannot be ignored when discussing the implications of equifinality and other goal system configurations.

3.2 Equifinality Discussion

The recent advances in research on features of the equifinality configurations have revealed considerable influences on individuals' motivation. Importantly, these findings underscore the trade-offs inherent in having multiple means available for a given goal. For example, Kruglanski et al.'s (2011) studies demonstrate the motivational benefits of having numerous attainment means to individuals' goals—in particular, greater commitment and willingness to invest effort in the pursuit of those goals. However, stronger commitment to the focal goal comes with its own downside, as it brings about a weaker commitment to any given means.

Experimental research on the dilution effect in equifinal configurations empirically highlights the potentially detrimental effects of numerous (vs fewer) means being linked to a given goal. In particular, Bélanger, Schori-Eyal et al. (unpublished manuscript) revealed that a greater means set size decreased intrinsic motivation toward a given means, and Dugas and Kruglanski (unpublished manuscript) illustrated that a greater size of the means set can lead to decreases in group identification. Finally, the work of Etkin and Ratner (2012, 2013) demonstrates that specific features of equifinality sets can differentially affect motivation depending on moderating factors such as subjective goal progress and temporal construal of goal pursuit.

Notwithstanding the current body of findings on equifinality, there remain intriguing further directions for exploring this particular motivational configuration. For example, research on regulatory mode (locomotion and assessment) and multifinality has yielded interesting moderated relationships in means preferences (Orehek et al., 2012), but this kind of work has yet to be extended to contexts of substitution and equifinality. It would also be of interest to explore the features of means which make them more or less substitutable for one another, and the factors that determine what individual difference and situational factors influence whether under means failure persons would choose to switch means to a goal versus abandon that goal altogether. These topics could be profitably explored in future research.

4. COUNTERFINALITY

A critical aspect of goal pursuit is the selection of the best means with which to accomplish a goal. How is such a selection accomplished? "Rational" criteria for it may have to do with evidence that the means appears to have a higher *expectancy* of goal attainment than other means and/or that it delivers greater *value*, by dint of serving other goals as well, thus exhibiting multifinality (Kruglanski, Kopetz, et al., 2013). An intriguing and less "rational" possible factor affecting means preference and choice, however, is *counterfinality*, defined as the case wherein a means that serves a focal goal also undermines an alternative goal (see Figure 1(c)). We propose that a counterfinal means may be perceived as particularly *instrumental* to the focal goal precisely because of its detrimental effect on other goals. That may be because under those conditions, the means may be perceived as uniquely, and hence particularly strongly, attached to the focal goal (Kruglanski, 1996; Zhang et al., 2007), and also because its use despite its costs implies its efficacy (the "cost heuristic").

4.1 Empirical Research on Counterfinality

Research suggests that under certain conditions people rely on counterfinality cues, such as difficulty, to infer means instrumentality. For example,

Kruger, Wirtz, Van Boven, and Altermatt (2004) found that participants gave works of art higher ratings of quality, value, and liking when they thought the work took more time and effort to produce. Other researchers have found that the use of counterfinality cues may be particularly prevalent when people are pursuing a goal. For example, Labroo and Kim (2009) found that while ease of processing (i.e., fluency) is generally liked, people prefer metacognitive difficulty (i.e., disfluency) when evaluating a means to a goal. That is, during goal pursuit, people evaluate means that involve effort as more instrumental. Thus, when primed with a pleasure goal, participants evaluated chocolate (a means to the experience of pleasure) that was presented in a disfluent ad more favorably and expressed a greater willingness to pay for it as compared to chocolate presented in a more fluent ad (Labroo & Kim, 2009).

Several recent lines of research provide specific support for counterfinality effects. In one set of studies, Hennecke, Freund, and Clore (unpublished manuscript) found that less enjoyable means (i.e., those that were less instrumental to the goal of enjoyment) were perceived to be generally less instrumental to their goals. In Study 1, participants were asked to provide examples of activities that were either not enjoyable (low intrinsic enjoyment), somewhat enjoyable (medium intrinsic enjoyment), or very enjoyable (high intrinsic enjoyment). Then, participants rated how "instrumental or useful" each of the three activities were. As predicted, activities low in intrinsic enjoyment were described as more instrumental to their goals than activities medium or high in intrinsic enjoyment.

In Study 2, participants listed two exercise goals (e.g., to stay healthy, to lose weight), and two means of exercise (e.g., running, lifting weights). Participants were asked either to mentally simulate the means (i.e., provide a detailed description of the steps involved in using one of the means) or to list the positive consequences of exercise in the control condition. To manipulate enjoyment, participants completed the mental simulation while listening to either happy or sad music. It was expected that in the latter condition the sad music would lead to the means being perceived as less enjoyable and therefore more instrumental, and the results confirmed this prediction.

In Study 3, participants rated the instrumentality of two hypothetical analgesics which were described as either sweet or bitter. As predicted, participants rated the bitter pill as more instrumental to pain reduction. In Study 4, participants ingested either a bitter, sweet, or neutral-tasting substance while keeping their arm in cold water for as long as possible.

Participants provided ratings of the analgesic effectiveness of the substance several times during the task. There were no differences in experienced pain across conditions. However, at the 150-second mark, although the subjective pain decreased in both conditions—only participants in the bitter (i.e., counterfinal) condition attributed this decrease to the instrumentality of the ingested substance toward the goal of decreasing pain.

4.1.1 Goal Magnitude

In a similar vein, Schumpe and Kruglanski (submitted for publication) found evidence that a counterfinal goal—means constellation is associated with the means being perceived as more instrumental. In a laboratory experiment, undergraduate students either evaluated a mouthwash that was described as causing a burning sensation (counterfinal) or as causing no burning sensation (unifinal). In line with predictions, the mouthwash was perceived as more instrumental to the goal of killing germs when it was also detrimental—that is, counterfinal—to participants' alternative goal of avoiding unpleasant experiences. Most interestingly, this effect was specific to the perceived instrumentality of the mouthwash, as the overall attitude toward the mouthwash did not differ across conditions (see Figure 2).

Further, goal magnitude was found to be an important moderator of the counterfinality effect. Schumpe and Kruglanski (submitted for publication) hypothesized that especially when individuals are highly committed to a

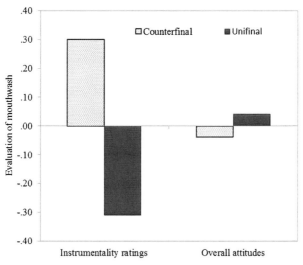

Figure 2 Instrumentality ratings and overall attitudes for counterfinal and unifinal mouthwashes.

goal, they would perceive any means as highly instrumental. Phenomena like the *myside bias* (Stanovich, West, & Toplak, 2013), *motivational biases* (Bruner & Goodman, 1947), and *wishful thinking* (Balcetis & Dunning, 2009; Bélanger, Kruglanski, Chen, & Orehek, 2014; Bélanger, Kruglanski, Chen, Orehek, & Johnson, 2015) lend support to the notion that human perception and cognition is subject to motivational forces, and hence, is influenced by goal magnitude. Consistent with this reasoning, Schumpe and Kruglanski (submitted for publication) found that individuals with higher goal magnitude perceived a product as highly instrumental regardless of whether the product was unifinal or counterfinal. However, individuals with lower goal magnitude exhibited the counterfinality effect, that is, they viewed the counterfinal means as more instrumental as compared to the unifinal means (see Figure 3).

In another study, participants were asked to rate the effectiveness of a fitness program based on testimonials describing the program as either causing muscle soreness or not. Participants who were highly committed to the goal of fitness rated the fitness program as highly effective independent of how painful they thought it was. When goal magnitude was low, however, the program was rated as more effective when participants believed it to be more painful (Schumpe & Kruglanski, submitted for publication).

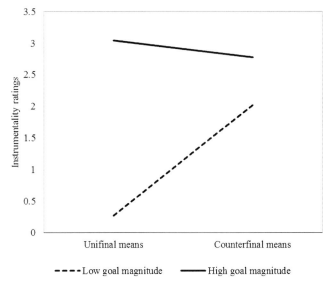

Figure 3 Instrumentality ratings for unifinal and counterfinal means in participants with low and high goal magnitude.

The weakened impact of counterfinality on perceived instrumentality for individuals who are highly committed to a focal goal can be explained by the discounting of alternative goals. Individuals have been found to suppress alternative goals that are in conflict with a pursued focal goal (Shah, Friedman, & Kruglanski, 2002). In other words, when a cause is very important to an individual, the possibly detrimental effects of a chosen means would be of minor concern. Accordingly, Schumpe and Kruglanski (submitted for publication) asked tattooed individuals with varying degrees of commitment toward tattooing to indicate the main goal they wanted to achieve by getting tattooed. The amount of pain they experienced while getting tattooed, as well as the level of commitment, predicted the perceived instrumentality of tattooing as a means to their goal. Most interestingly, the authors found the expected interaction—that is, the counterfinality effect for low (vs high) levels of commitment. Thus, the counterfinality effect and the moderating role of commitment were found in an applied setting as well.

4.1.2 Attainment Expectancy

The perceived likelihood of being able to attain a goal (i.e., goal expectancy) is also an important predictor of whether counterfinal means will be perceived as instrumental. Specifically, Bélanger, Lafrenière, Giacomantonio, Brizi, and Nathaniel (Unpublished manuscript) found that counterfinal means were perceived as more instrumental when participants believed that the expectancy of fulfilling their goals was low. Several individual differences associated with different levels of general goal expectancy were also related to the perceived instrumentality of counterfinal means. Specifically, individuals high on depression and anxiety (traits associated with *lower* expectations of being able to accomplish goals) perceived *counterfinal* means to be more instrumental, whereas those who were high on hope of success, pathways thinking, self-esteem, and belonging support (traits associated with *higher* expectations of being able to accomplish goals) perceived *multifinal* means to be more instrumental (Bélanger, Lafrenière et al., Unpublished manuscript).

Other research further attests to the influence of goal expectancy (i.e., the perceived likelihood of attaining the goal) on the selection of counterfinal means. For example, Klein (2013) presented participants with a goal that was either difficult to attain (obtaining a vaccine for the swine flu) or easy to attain (obtaining a vaccine for the common cold). Klein (2013) found that people considered a counterfinal means (an H1N1 vaccine that was expensive and difficult to obtain) as more instrumental to treating a severe illness (the swine flu) than a unifinal means (one that was cheap and easy to obtain). Importantly, however, no differential preference between the means appeared in reference to a vaccine for the less severe illness, a common cold, since the goal of finding a vaccine for the common cold was easier to obtain.

4.1.3 Addiction to Counterfinal Means

The dynamics of counterfinality have been recently examined in the domain of addiction. Specifically, Connor, Gullo, Feeney, and Young (2011) measured drug users' expectancies of the positive and negative consequences of cannabis use with two expectancy scales. The positive expectancy scale included items such as "smoking cannabis makes me laugh," and the negative expectancy scale included items such as "smoking cannabis makes me feel insecure." In this study they found that negative expectancy was generally associated with *greater* cannabis dependence. That is, the more counterfinal participants perceived cannabis to be to their goal of having good outcomes, the more likely they were to be addicted to it. The authors also found an interaction, such that individuals with high scores on the negative *and* positive expectancy scales were most likely to be addicted to cannabis. Thus, the more individuals believed that cannabis was counterfinal to one goal (i.e., feeling secure) and instrumental to another goal (i.e., laughing), the more likely they were to be addicted to it.

And in the domain of alcohol dependence, Li and Dingle (2012), using survey data, found that beliefs about the negative consequences of alcohol consumption (e.g., being hung-over) were actually positively related to risky alcohol consumption such as binge drinking. Relatedly, alcohol-dependent individuals believed that alcohol consumption had negative consequences to a greater extent than students, even though the alcohol-dependent respondents consume more alcohol—according to the survey data, to alleviate anxiety. In other words, these findings suggest that alcohol-dependent participants might perceive alcohol as an effective means of reducing anxiety particularly if they perceive it to be detrimental (i.e., counterfinal) to other goals such as the possession of good health.

4.2 Counterfinality Discussion

While selecting a means to a goal, people often have to rely on certain attributes that may signal instrumentality in order to infer whether a means is instrumental to a goal. Empirical evidence reviewed above suggests that when selecting a means to a goal, people often infer attributes such as instrumentality based on how detrimental, or *counterfinal*, that means is to an alternative goal. Research also shows that counterfinal means are perceived to be more instrumental, particularly when goal importance and expectancy are low.

Though the counterfinality effects are intriguing, their exact nature requires further probing. Increased perceived instrumentality to a focal goal could be mediated by its perceived stronger positive association to such a goal in light of the fact that its association to the alternative goals is negative. Alternatively, or in addition, one might infer that the means is particularly instrumental to the focal goal if one is willing to pay the price of undermining alternative goals. Such an analysis implies that the alternative goals should be sufficiently salient so that their undermining would register and have an effect, yet they should not be so dominant as to override the positive effect of the means with respect to the focal goal. More insight into the relation between the focal and the alternative goals in their joint impact on the counterfinal means should provide a fruitful avenue for further theorizing and research.

Finally, it is possible that the choice of counterfinal means is particularly likely where an individual wishes to signal commitment to the focal cause and she/he communicates this by exhibiting the willingness to sacrifice alternative goals. For instance, individuals may signal their commitment to a political or religious cause by exhibiting a readiness to undertake risky activities including the readiness to die on behalf of that cause (Bélanger, Caouette, Sharvit, & Dugas, 2014; Kruglanski, Bélanger, et al., 2013; Kruglanski et al., 2014).

5. RECAPITULATION AND CONCLUSION

In carrying out their various activities, people have goals that are cognitively represented, and their behaviors are carried out in the service of those goals. The relations between means and outcomes are also mentally represented. One knows, or at least surmises, that pursuing a given course of action would lead to a given consequence, hence one directs one actions to consequences one deems desirable—that is, to a state of affairs one wishes to achieve that is more desirable than the present or potential future state of affairs.

In the present chapter we explored three different patterns of means—goals relations and considered their implications for motivational phenomena. The *multifinality* configuration offers enhanced value derived from the attainment of multiple goals through a single activity. As we have seen, however, such enhancement comes at a price, in the form of reduced expectancy of goal attainment mediated by the dilution effect. The *equifinality* configuration affords increased overall expectancy of goal attainment while diluting the specific expectancy via any of the several means attached to a given goal. Finally, the *counterfinality* configuration enhances the expectancy that a means which undermines a different goal is particularly likely to bring about the attainment of the focal goal it serves.

Though appreciable empirical research to date attests to the configurational phenomena associated with the multifinality, equifinality, and counterfinality patterns of means—goals relations, considerable further work on these phenomena could be profitably carried out. Two general research directions appear especially promising in this regard: (1) Tracking down the manifestations of the different configurations across different domains of psychological phenomena, and (2) exploring in greater depth the mediating mechanisms of the various configurational effects. We briefly consider these in turn.

5.1 Domains of Applicability

The structural, content-free, nature of the means—goals configurations implies their applicability across broad swathes of psychological contents. As we have seen already, effects associated with the equifinality pattern mediated feelings of social identity (Dugas & Kruglanski, unpublished manuscript) and those related to the counterfinality configuration were manifest in the domain of addictions to drugs and alcohol (Connor et al., 2011; Li & Dingle, 2012). Additional insights into various phenomena could be potentially gained from the present configurational perspective. To mention one example, provision of alternative equifinal means to a goal of personal significance, which arguably underlies engagement in terrorism and political violence (Kruglanski, Bélanger, et al., 2013; Kruglanski et al., 2014), might reduce the inclination to pursue these destructive activities by (1) diluting their perceived efficacy, and (2) providing a different, prosocial, path to a sense of mattering and significance.

5.2 Underlying Mechanisms

The various configurational effects of means—goals relations described in the preceding pages assume a construal process wherein structural linkages between motivationally relevant constructs are interpreted in specific ways to yield the appropriate psychological experiences. For instance, multiple linkages between a means and several goals in a multifinality configuration, and/or between a goal and several means in an equifinality configuration, are construed to signify lessened instrumentality of the means in question. Similarly, an undermining relation of a counterfinal means to an alternative goal has been shown to be construed as greater effectiveness of that means to the focal goal. Whereas research thus far has consistently demonstrated the occurrence of such construals, one might wonder about their inevitability and/or about conditions that might affect their likelihood of occurrence. For instance, it would be of interest to explore whether similar construals are made across different cultures and whether conditions that situationally prime the construals in question augment their effects. The foregoing questions could be profitably explored in future research.

In summary, the various means—goal configurations described in goal systems theory have led to fruitful research in a variety of domains, including those of unconscious choice, group processes, and substance abuse. More broadly, the research described in this article shows that the structural relationships between means and goals can have significant implications for motivation and goal pursuit. Further implications of the structure of means—goal relations ought to be explored in future research guided by the present notions concerning the architecture of goal systems.

REFERENCES

Anderson, J. R. (1983). *The architecture of cognition*. Cambridge, MA: Harvard University Press.
Balcetis, E., & Dunning, D. (2009). Wishful seeing: more desired objects are seen as closer. *Psychological Science, 21*, 147–152.
Bélanger, J. J., Caouette, J., Sharvit, K., & Dugas, M. (2014). The psychology of martyrdom: making the ultimate sacrifice in the name of a cause. *Journal of Personality and Social Psychology, 107*, 494–515.
Bélanger, J. J., Kruglanski, A. W., Chen, X., & Orehek, E. (2014). Bending perception to desire: Effects of task demands, motivation, and cognitive resources. *Motivation and Emotion, 38*(6), 802–814.
Bélanger, J. J., Kruglanski, A. W., Chen, X., Orehek, E., & Johnson, D. J. (2015). When Mona Lisa smiled and love was in the air: on the cognitive energetics of motivated judgments. *Social Cognition, 33*(2), 104–119.
Bélanger, J. J., Lafrenière, M.-A., Giacomantonio, M., Brizi, A., & Nathaniel, L. (2015). *Beyond goal-commitment: How expectancy shapes means instrumentality*. Unpublished manuscript.
Bélanger, J. J., Schori-Eyal, N., Pica, G., Kruglanski, A. W., & Lafreniere, M.-A. *The "more is less" effect in equifinal structures: A further test of the dilution model*. Unpublished manuscript.
Brewer, M. B. (1991). The social self: on being the same and different at the same time. *Personality and Social Psychology Bulletin, 17*, 475–482.
Bruner, J. S., & Goodman, C. C. (1947). Value and need as organizing factors in perception. *The Journal of Abnormal and Social Psychology, 42*, 33–44.
Chun, W. Y., Kruglanski, A. W., Sleeth-Keppler, D., & Friedman, R. S. (2011). Multifinality in implicit choice. *Journal of Personality and Social Psychology, 101*, 1124–1137.

Connor, J. P., Gullo, M. J., Feeney, G. F., & Young, R. M. (2011). Validation of the Cannabis Expectancy Questionnaire (CEQ) in adult cannabis users in treatment. *Drug and Alcohol Dependence, 115*(3), 167−174.

Deci, E. L., & Ryan, R. M. (1985). *Intrinsic motivation and self-determination in human behavior.* New York, NY: Plenum.

Dugas, M., & Kruglanski, A. W. (2015). *Diluting identity: A goal systemic theory of group identification.* Unpublished manuscript.

Etkin, J., & Ratner, R. K. (2012). The dynamic impact of variety among means on motivation. *Journal of Consumer Research, 38*, 1076−1092.

Etkin, J., & Ratner, R. K. (2013). Goal pursuit, now and later: temporal compatibility of different versus similar means. *Journal of Consumer Research, 39*, 1085−1099.

Festinger, L. (1957). *A theory of cognitive dissonance.* Oxford, England: Row, Peterson.

Förster, J. (2009). Relations between perceptual and conceptual scope: how global versus local processing fits a focus on similarity versus dissimilarity. *Journal of Experimental Psychology: General, 138*, 88−111.

Freud, S. (1920). *A general introduction to psychoanalysis.* New York, NY: Washington Square Press.

Heider, F. (1958). *The psychology of interpersonal relations.* New York: Wiley.

Hennecke, M., Freund, A. M., & Clore, G. L. (2015). *No pain, no gain: Intrinsically enjoyable means are perceived as less instrumental.* Unpublished manuscript.

Higgins, E. T. (2005). Value from regulatory fit. *Current Directions in Psychological Science, 14*, 209−213.

Hogg, M. A. (2007). Uncertainty-identity theory. In M. P. Zanna (Ed.), *Advances in experimental social psychology* (pp. 69−126). San Diego, CA: Academic Press.

Hogg, M. A., Meehan, C., & Farquharson, J. (2010). The solace of radicalism: self-uncertainty and group identification in the face of threat. *Journal of Experimental Social Psychology, 46*, 1061−1066.

Klein, K. M. (2013). *Tracking the cost heuristic: A rule of thumb in choice of counterfinal means* (Doctoral dissertation). Retrieved from http://hdl.handle.net/1903/14890; http://www.google.com/url?q=http%3A%2F%2Fhdl.handle.net%2F1903%2F14890&sa=D&sntz=1&usg=AFQjCNGoaQJuCj7nA9a4dO5bf-KcJ7Gdkw.

Kopetz, C., Faber, T., Fishbach, A., & Kruglanski, A. W. (2011). The multifinality constraints effect: how goal multiplicity narrows the means set to a focal end. *Journal of Personality and Social Psychology, 100*, 810−826.

Kruger, J., Wirtz, D., Van Boven, L., & Altermatt, T. W. (2004). The effort heuristic. *Journal of Experimental Social Psychology, 40*, 91−98.

Kruglanski, A. W. (1996). Motivated social cognition: principles of the Interface. In E. T. Higgins, & A. W. Kruglanski (Eds.), *Social psychology: Handbook of basic principles* (pp. 493−520). New York, NY: Guilford.

Kruglanski, A. W. (October 28, 2014). Psychology not theology: overcoming ISIS' secret appeal. *E-International Relations.* Retrieved from http://www.e-ir.info/2014/10/28/psychology-not-theology-overcoming-isis-secret-appeal/.

Kruglanski, A. W., Bélanger, J., Gelfand, M. G., Gunaratna, R., Hetiarrachchi, M., Reinares, F., et al. (2013). Terrorism, a (Self) love story: redirecting the significance-quest can end violence. *American Psychologist, 68*, 559−575.

Kruglanski, A. W., Chernikova, M., Rosenzweig, E., & Kopetz, C. (2014). On motivational readiness. *Psychological Review, 121*, 367−388.

Kruglanski, A. W., Gelfand, M. J., Bélanger, J. J., Sheveland, A., Herriarachchi, M., & Gunaratna, R. (2014). The psychology of radicalization and deradicalization: How significance quest impacts violent extremism. *Advances in Political Psychology, 35*(S1), 69−93.

Kruglanski, A. W., Kopetz, C., Bélanger, J. J., Chun, W. Y., Orehek, E., & Fishbach, A. (2013). Features of multifinality. *Personality and Social Psychology Review, 17*, 22−39.

Kruglanski, A. W., Pierro, A., & Sheveland, A. (2011). How many roads lead to Rome? Equifinality set-size and commitment to goals and means. *European Journal of Social Psychology, 41*, 344–352.

Kruglanski, A. W., Shah, J. Y., Fishbach, A., Friedman, R., Chun, W. Y., & Sleeth-Keppler, D. (2002). A theory of goal systems. *Advances in Experimental Social Psychology, 34*, 331–378.

Kruglanski, A. W., Thompson, E. P., Higgins, E. T., Atash, M., Pierro, A., Shah, J. Y., et al. (2000). To "do the right thing" or to "just do it": locomotion and assessment as distinct self-regulatory imperatives. *Journal of Personality and Social Psychology, 79*, 793–815.

Labroo, A. A., & Kim, S. (2009). The "instrumentality" heuristic: why metacognitive difficulty is desirable during goal pursuit. *Psychological Science, 20*, 127–134.

Leonardelli, G. J., & Brewer, M. B. (2001). Minority and majority discrimination: when and why. *Journal of Experimental Social Psychology, 37*, 468–485.

Lewin, K. (1935). *A dynamic theory of personality*. New York: Mc Graw-Hill.

Li, H. K., & Dingle, G. A. (2012). Using the Drinking Expectancy Questionnaire (revised scoring method) in clinical practice. *Addictive Behaviors, 37*(2), 198–204.

Orehek, E., Mauro, R., Kruglanski, A. W., & van der Bles, A. M. (2012). Prioritizing association strength versus value: the influence of self-regulatory modes on means evaluation in single goal and multigoal contexts. *Journal of Personality and Social Psychology, 102*, 22–31.

Rusbult, C. E. (1980). Commitment and satisfaction in romantic associations: a test of the investment model. *Journal of Experimental Social Psychology, 16*, 172–186.

Schultz, J. (2010). *Multifinal no more: Deactivation of the background goal causes (price) devaluation of multifinal means* (Unpublished Doctoral dissertation). College Park: University of Maryland.

Schumpe, B. M., & Kruglanski, A. W. (2015). *Counterfinality: on the positive impact of negative information*. Manuscript submitted for publication.

Schwarz, N., Bless, H., Strack, F., Klumpp, G., Rittenauer-Schatka, H., & Simons, A. (1991). Ease of retrieval as information: another look at the availability heuristic. *Journal of Personality and Social Psychology, 61*(2), 195–202.

Shah, J. Y., Friedman, R., & Kruglanski, A. W. (2002). Forgetting all else: on the antecedents and consequences of goal shielding. *Journal of Personality and Social Psychology, 83*, 1261–1280.

Shah, J. Y., & Kruglanski, A. W. (2000). Aspects of goal networks. In M. Boekaerts, P. R. Pintrich, & M. Zeidener (Eds.), *Handbook of self-regulation* (pp. 85–110). San Diego, CA: Academic Press.

Simonson, I. (1990). The effect of purchase quantity and timing on variety-seeking behavior. *Journal of Marketing Research, 27*, 150–162.

Stanovich, K. E., West, R. F., & Toplak, M. E. (2013). Myside bias, rational thinking, and intelligence. *Current Directions in Psychological Science, 22*, 259–264.

Steele, C. M., & Liu, T. J. (1983). Dissonance processes as self-affirmation. *Journal of Personality and Social Psychology, 45*, 5–19.

Tesser, A. (2000). On the confluence of self-esteem maintenance mechanism. *Personality and Social Psychology Review, 4*, 290–299.

Tversky, A., & Kahneman, D. (1974). Judgment under uncertainty: Heuristics and biases. *Science, 185*, 1124–1130.

Van Lange, P. A. M., De Cremer, D., Van Dijk, E., & Van Vugt, M. (2007). Self-interest and beyond: Basic principles of social interaction. In A. W. Kruglanski, & E. T. Higgings (Eds.), *Social Psychology: Handbook of basic principles* (pp. 540–561). New York: Guilford.

Wilson, D., & Nisbett, R. E. (1978). The accuracy of verbal reports about the effects of stimuli on evaluations and behavior. *Social Psychology, 41*, 118–131.

Yzerbyt, V. Y., & Demoulin, S. (2010). Intergroup relations. In S. T. Fiske, D. T. Gilbert, & G. Lindzey (Eds.), *Handbook of social psychology* (pp. 1024–1083). Hoboken, NJ: Wiley.

Zhang, Y., Fishbach, A., & Kruglanski, A. W. (2007). The dilution model: how additional goals undermine the perceived instrumentality of a shared path. *Journal of Personality and Social Psychology, 92*, 389–401.

CHAPTER FOUR

Breaking the Rules: A Historical Overview of Goal-Setting Theory

Edwin A. Locke*, [1] and Gary P. Latham[§]
*R.H. Smith School of Business, University of Maryland (Emeritus), College Park, MD, USA
[§]Rotman School of Management, University of Toronto, Toronto, ON, Canada
[1]Corresponding author: E-mail: elocke@rhsmith.umd.edu

Contents

1. Early Development: Laying the Groundwork for Goal-Setting Theory	100
1.1 Defying Behaviorism: Locke	100
2. An Inductive Approach to Theory Building	103
3. Empirical Findings	105
3.1 Goals	105
3.2 Feedback	105
3.3 Self-set Goals	106
3.4 Expectancy and Self-efficacy	106
3.5 Commitment	107
3.6 Affect	107
4. Learning from Field Experiments: Latham	107
4.1 Assigned versus Participatively Set Goals	109
4.2 Goals and Self-management	111
5. Goal-Setting Studies by Others	111
6. The Theory: 1990	112
7. The Theory Expanded: 2013	115
8. Observations on Theory Building	118
9. Future Directions	119
10. Conclusions	120
References	121

Abstract

This paper describes the development of goal-setting theory starting from the 1960s when Locke saw but rejected behaviorism as the dominant paradigm in psychology. Locke began with laboratory experiments of goals while Latham pioneered field studies of goal setting. Because goals had reliable effects, many other researchers conducted goal-setting studies. This provided a large database from which the theory was developed inductively over a 25-year period. The theory was formulated in 1990, and research on the theory continues apace to this day; recent developments on the theory were published in 2013. We advocate (and seek to provide a model of) the inductive

Advances in Motivation Science, Volume 2
ISSN 2215-0919
http://dx.doi.org/10.1016/bs.adms.2015.05.001

approach to theory building, and end this article with suggested future directions for research on goal-setting theory.

1. EARLY DEVELOPMENT: LAYING THE GROUNDWORK FOR GOAL-SETTING THEORY

1.1 Defying Behaviorism: Locke

Theories are developed within a scientific context and goal-setting theory is no exception. However, the theory did not grow out of the dominant paradigm of the 1960s, when Locke entered graduate school. Then the field of psychology was dominated by the doctrine known as behaviorism. This doctrine asserted that one can understand human action without dealing with the idea that people are conscious, and direct their actions through thoughts (Skinner, 1953). The behaviorists argued that psychologists should only study observable behavior, and that environmental stimuli and the consequences of one's actions (reinforcements) control it. Psychology was to be the science of observable behavior without taking into account cognition or affect (Watson, 1925). Skinner (1971) argued that man has neither freedom nor dignity.

The behaviorists wanted to be "scientific." They accepted the then popular philosophy of logical positivism that, in essence, argued that all knowledge comes from sensory experience. Thus they dismissed the role of conceptual thought (Blanshard, 1962), including introspection. Since physical objects have observable attributes, such as size, weight, color, shape, and material components that can be readily observed and measured, and consciousness does not, it was rejected as outside the scientific domain.

There was still another reason why the behaviorists banished consciousness from psychology. They viewed consciousness as an epiphenomenon, an aspect of humans that has no causal power. An individual's mind, they said, is controlled solely by the environment. Free will is thus an illusion. Determinism is a fact. There is no such thing as free choice. People are the passive products of operant conditioning; behavior is controlled by its consequences (i.e., reinforcers).

Many psychologists had no philosophical defense against behaviorism. This led to a culture in which some people were unwilling to use the word consciousness even in conversation. A common insult during this era was to be called "mentalistic," namely a person who naively believes in the relevance of the conscious mind to one's actions. Behaviorism, however, collapsed as a dominant force in psychology in the late 1970s, partly due to its philosophical base, positivism, collapsing into incoherence (Blanshard, 1962), and partly due to the futility of ignoring the mind combined with the rise of eminent, pro-mind/cognitive psychologists such as Piaget (1973) in Europe and Bandura (1977, 1986) in North America.

What kept Locke from accepting the dogma of behaviorism was Ayn Rand's philosophy (see Peikoff, 1984; for a summary) which demonstrated that consciousness is an axiom, a self-evident philosophical primary that, though requiring a brain, is not reducible to physical matter and not deducible from anything else. Free will is a corollary of the axiom of consciousness. Determinism refutes itself in that if people have no choice about what they think or believe, then determinism itself cannot be validated. A determinist can only say, "I was compelled to believe it by forces outside of my control." And determinists cannot actually know even that, because how could they know that they were compelled? Determinism mitigates the very possibility of knowledge.

Knowing that behaviorism was wrong, however, did not tell Locke what to study. The idea for goal setting came from a study by Mace (1935) that was reported in Ryan and Smith's (1954, pp. 353–427) *Industrial Psychology* textbook and later in Ryan (1970). Mace studied the effects of several types of assigned performance goals on task performance. There was a graph in the textbook that compared the effects of telling participants to do their best versus giving them a specific performance standard to meet each day for several days. The graph showed that a group given a specific standard to attain greatly outperformed the group told to "do your best." However, no statistical tests were performed.

Locke concluded that conscious performance goals were both philosophically legitimate and scientifically sound. This was the beginning of his career-long interest in goal setting, starting with his doctoral dissertation. Hence, this was the breaking of the first rule: study only observable behavior. Goals are mental entities, the object or aim of an action, and a cause of action. As such, goals are at odds with behaviorism that, as noted, views consciousness as an epiphenomenon that plays no causal role.

Ryan (1970) argued that conscious, task-specific intentions (which he viewed as the same as goals) is a better place to start the study of motivation than to look at "reinforcers," as advocated by behaviorists. Further, he argued that looking at task-specific intentions is more fruitful than studying general, conscious traits (personality) because intentions are closer to action than traits.

In this same time period, projective tests were popular, especially for measuring McClelland's (1961) need for achievement (n ach) motive. However, their relationship to action was not always reliable. Ryan suggested that traits and motives likely affect action through their effect on conscious intentions. Locke agreed with Ryan's view that studying immediate determinants of action was the best strategy for predicting, understanding, and influencing motivation.

Behaviorism, as an application of its philosophy, had made major inroads within experimental psychology, learning theory, child psychology, psychotherapy, institutional management, and other specialty areas. However, it made only minor inroads within industrial–organizational psychology (e.g., Campbell, 1971; Nord, 1969). This may be because I-O psychologists have always been concerned with the world of work; hence their research did not involve rats, pigeons, dogs, or other animals. The *Journal of Applied Psychology* and management journals accepted goal-setting articles even during the heyday of behaviorism. In the mid and late 1970s, Locke (1977, 1978) wrote articles critiquing the intrusion of "Behavior Modification" (applied behaviorism) into work settings. He argued that those studies "smuggled" in conscious processes such as goal setting without acknowledging having done so. Furthermore, behavior modification ignored findings showing that feedback itself was not an automatic reinforcer of behavior (Locke, 1978).

Latham's experience with behaviorism differed from Locke's. As an undergraduate student, he entered a bastion of behaviorism in Canada, Dalhousie University, in 1963. There he took year-long laboratory courses on operant conditioning principles, particularly the differential effects of different schedules of reinforcement on the response rates of rats and pigeons. In addition, he took courses from faculty who were social psychologists, child psychologists, and neuroscientists. He was exposed to the theories and research of Festinger, Lewin, and Piaget, and most of all Hebb (1949).[1]

When Latham entered the doctoral program at the University of Akron, Yukl, his advisor, was dabbling with the effect of monetary incentives administered in a laboratory setting on different schedules of reinforcement (Yukl, Wexley, & Seymore, 1972). Skinner's (1953) work with animals showed that in the early stages of learning, animals learn faster on a

---

[1] Hebb, arguably the father of neuroscience, did his undergraduate work at Dalhousie in the 1930s.

continuous schedule of reinforcement (i.e., a pellet of food) than they do on a variable-ratio schedule where the food is given on a "seemingly" random schedule when an animal responds correctly. However, once learning occurs, the animals respond faster when the food is administered on a variable ratio than they do on a continuous schedule, a phenomenon that gambling casino owners have become well aware of.

Upon receiving his PhD and becoming the staff psychologist for the Weyerhaeuser Company (forest products), Latham tested the effects of different reinforcement schedules for administering monetary bonuses to tree planters (Yukl & Latham, 1975; Yukl, Latham, & Pursell, 1976) and mountain beaver trappers (Latham & Dossett, 1978), and in doing so replicated findings obtained with animals. Having read Dulany (1968) and Nagle (1961), these experiments were done with full knowledge that behavior is either caused or mediated by cognition and affect. Moreover, a follow-up experiment revealed that the employees self-set specific, high goals (Saari & Latham, 1982). Journal reviewers insisted on the removal of that statement from the manuscript. Latham conducted no more experiments on reinforcement schedules.

2. AN INDUCTIVE APPROACH TO THEORY BUILDING

By embracing induction for theory building, Locke and Latham broke two additional rules: theory building by deduction and rapid generalization.

Many people believe that the path to theory building is to identify a theory in advance, make deductions from it, and then test it. In recent decades, this has had unfortunate effects on science because it has retarded theory building. This is because it puts things in the wrong order. In science, successful theory building starts with induction (Harriman, 2010), not deduction that must come later. Science is a process of discovering the unknown. Much of what is discovered is unexpected. Premature theorizing readily leads people to look for verification, and thus ignores that which was not expected. It leads to "tunnel vision." For example, studies supporting a theory are cited and nonsupporting studies are either ignored or dismissed. Being viewed as right sometimes becomes a self-esteem issue for the individual or individuals who developed the theory deductively. When a few studies show support for the deduced theory, the theory-building process typically ceases because the theory has been allegedly "verified." But, a few studies are rarely sufficient to build a coherent theory.

The deductive approach to building a theory, encouraged by many journal editors, can also lead to post hoc hypothesizing by researchers, that is, formulating hypotheses and developing a theory to deduce after rather than before the data have been collected and analyzed. The deductions then appear "forced"—because they are. Some researchers even ignore results that are stronger than those they had hypothesized. This is another example of tunnel vision. Recently it has been recommended that researchers be required to file their theories and hypotheses on a Web site before they conduct their studies in order to prevent theorizing "after the fact." But, this will not fix the deeper problem. Neither a single study, an "exact" replication, nor deduction is the way to build a theory.

This brings us to the third rule that we broke. When a theory is supported by one or two studies, some researchers readily generalize—but almost always prematurely. A case in point is Herzberg's theory of job enrichment (Herzberg, Mausner, & Snyderman, 1959). The theory was initially based on only two studies that used the same methodology, the critical incident technique (CIT). The essence of the theory is that some job factors cause only job satisfaction and others only dissatisfaction. The methodology Herzberg and his colleagues used was originally designed for job analysis. This methodology was not suited for building a theory of job design or satisfaction as many critics pointed out (e.g., Vroom, 1967). Thus there were many failures to replicate the results predicted by the theory when a different methodology was used. Hence this theory did not stand the test of time, although it did call attention to the importance of the work itself for job satisfaction (e.g., task variety, autonomy).

As an aside, job enrichment theory emphasizes the importance of providing employees feedback on their performance. But, to influence an employee's behavior, feedback typically needs to be tied to goal setting. Umstot, Bell, and Mitchell (1976), using a simulation, found that job enrichment increases job satisfaction, but it is goal setting that increases job performance.

In defiance of the status quo, we did not start with a theory of goal setting. This is because we were aware of the dangers of premature deduction and overgeneralization. Thus we held back in declaring that we had a theory—for 25 years! We gradually learned how to build a theory by induction (Locke, 2007).

3. EMPIRICAL FINDINGS

As noted earlier, Locke began his research on goal setting with his doctoral dissertation, assigning various types of performance goals on laboratory tasks. This worked so well that he kept going. The studies were not done in any particular order—it was just an issue of "trying stuff." The importance of "trying stuff" in science has never been properly acknowledged. If you already believe you know what is true, you do not need to conduct experiments. But Locke did not do exact replications. To build a theory, you need replication with variation (Locke, 2015), as will be explained shortly.

3.1 Goals

Do your best goals were compared to specific, challenging goals in line with Mace's (1935) findings. Statistical tests verified that specific, challenging goals are a better way than vague goals to increase performance on laboratory tasks. Different levels of goal difficulty were studied. The more difficult goals seemed to work better than easier goals to increase performance. Goal effects were studied using different laboratory tasks to ensure that the effects were not task specific. Locke found that specificity alone affects (reduces) the variability of performance, providing the goal is attainable, that is, performance is controllable by the individual. If a goal exceeds an individual's ability, then variance increases and becomes simply a function of individual differences (Locke, Chah, Harrison, & Lustgarten, 1989). That a specific, difficult goal leads to higher performance than a vague, do your best goal or no goal at all would become the core of goal-setting theory (e.g., Mento, Steel, & Karren, 1987).

3.2 Feedback

The behaviorists claimed that performance feedback is a reinforcer that affects performance automatically. In disagreement with this assertion, Locke undertook a series of studies, as well as a literature review, to see if conscious goals mediate feedback effects. They do (Locke & Bryan, 1968a, 1969; Locke, Cartledge, & Koeppel, 1968). Previous studies claiming that feedback has causal effects on performance had routinely smuggled conscious goals into their procedure, but did not bother to measure or acknowledge them (Locke, 1980). Feedback is only information that does not influence an individual unless it is evaluated as relevant to some goal of value. Action is based on a combination of cognition (knowledge, strategy) and motivation (choice, effort, persistence). Feedback is mediated by the goal that is set (Locke & Latham, 1990).

Several years later, Erez (1977) showed that feedback moderates the goal–performance relationship. People need feedback to assess their progress in pursuing a goal, and to determine whether they need to exert more, or the same, effort and/or change their task strategy to attain it. Feedback would become a moderator in goal-setting theory.

3.3 Self-set Goals

Although Locke conducted few field studies, he did find that self-set goals were significantly related to student grades (Locke & Bryan, 1968b). Later it was recognized that assigned goals affect self-set goals, and that the latter mediate the former (Locke & Latham, 2002). Assigned goals are well accepted in laboratory experiments due to demand characteristics. Thus main effects are almost always found without measuring self-set goals. But, self-set goals are still the most immediate cause of goal-directed action.

Studying the effect of self-set goals led to questions about the best way to measure them. In the above study, Locke and Bryan (1968b) found that the best measure is the lowest score an individual would be satisfied with attaining. Asking people what they hope to attain, or what they will actually try to attain often leads to overoptimistic estimates that seem to be closer to an individual's wish rather than reality.

3.4 Expectancy and Self-efficacy

Expectancy theory (Vroom, 1964) was popular in the fields of organizational psychology/behavior in the 1960–1970s. The theory views choice (motivation) as the multiplicative function of expectancy of success, valence (value or reward), and instrumentality (the probability that effort leads to reward). The problem is that high goals have lower expectancies than easier goals, and yet it is high goals that lead to high performance. This paradox is due to the fact that expectancy was routinely measured in relation to different outcomes. Thus the difficulty level of attaining the outcomes was not held constant. The solution to the paradox is to measure self-efficacy (Locke, Motowidlo, & Bobko, 1986). Self-efficacy is measured by having participants rate their confidence in being able to attain a range of performance outcomes and then summing the ratings. This measure is positively related to performance, and it also affects the level at which people set their goals.

3.5 Commitment

A goal that one is not committed to attaining has little or no influence on performance. Commitment is positively related to performance (Locke, Frederick, Buckner, & Bobko, 1984; Locke & Shaw, 1984). Commitment is most important when goals are difficult (Erez & Zidon, 1984). This is because people have little trouble pursuing easy goals, but may not be confident in attaining high goals that require a great deal of effort. Commitment would become a moderator in goal-setting theory.

3.6 Affect

Locke conducted a number of experiments on goals and affect. Goals are not only outcomes to aim for, they are at the same time standards by which to judge one's performance. People are more satisfied when they reach their goals than when they do not (e.g., Locke, Cartledge, & Knerr, 1970). This is because goals are based on or tied to values, namely that which one considers good or beneficial. In this research endeavor, there was an unexpected finding, one in hindsight that we should have expected. While more difficult goals lead to higher performance than easy goals, easy goals, other things being equal, lead to higher satisfaction because there are more successes (Mento, Locke, & Klein, 1992). This is the clue as to why more difficult goals work better than easy goals in bringing about high performance: to get satisfaction with difficult goals an individual has to do better, that is, achieve more.

This leads to the question of why people pursue difficult goals. The answer is that in the real world, more benefits come to those who make progress toward the attainment of difficult goals (Mento et al., 1992). Consider the benefits of a student studying and getting high grades in school: it affects what career opportunities become open to that person. To become a psychologist, a student has to get into a university and subsequently get good grades in difficult subjects, and then get accepted into a graduate school.

4. LEARNING FROM FIELD EXPERIMENTS: LATHAM

Whereas Locke was primarily concerned with conducting experiments with internal validity, Latham was primarily concerned with conducting studies with external validity. Skeptics were questioning whether something so simple as goal–performance effects obtained in a laboratory would prove effective in the workplace (e.g., Heneman & Schwab, 1972; Hinrichs, 1970).

After graduating from Dalhousie University, Latham entered the psychology department at Georgia Tech (1967–1969). There he was immersed in what Cronbach (1957) labeled the "other" discipline in psychology, namely, correlational methods as opposed to empirical experiments. In addition, the faculty stressed the necessity of overcoming "the criterion problem," that is, the development and measurement of a dependent variable with sufficient reliability to test the significance of a predictor or the effectiveness of an independent variable.

Two incidents in that time period affected Latham's academic career. First, "the criterion problem" and the necessity of finding solutions to problems in work settings led him to learn all he could about Flanagan's (1954) CIT, an *inductive* methodology for developing a criterion with interobserver reliability and relevance (content validity) in the workplace. Induction, as noted earlier, became the method of choice for developing goal-setting theory.

Second, Latham's master's thesis was on the development of job performance criteria for pulpwood producers (i.e., loggers) in the southeastern United States. The CIT revealed that a critical behavior that differentiates an effective from an ineffective logger is the setting of a specific goal as to the number of trees to cut in a day/week. A factor analysis of a survey that he and his major professor conducted revealed that goal setting and supervisory presence loaded on the only factor that contained an objective measure of a crew's productivity, cords per man-hour (Ronan, Latham, & Kinne, 1973).

Upon completing his master's thesis, Latham, was hired by the American Pulpwood Association where his focus was on productivity improvement. Following up on the results of a factor analysis (Ronan et al., 1973), he matched logging crews on their size, terrain, level of mechanization, and productivity before randomly assigning them to one of two conditions, namely, one where the crews were given a specific, challenging goal to attain in terms of number of trees to cut down, or to a control condition where the crews were urged to do their best to cut as many trees as possible. The exhortation to do your best was highly relevant to the employees because each of the crews in both conditions were paid on a piece-rate basis: the more trees they cut down, the more money they made. Within the very first week of this 3-month field experiment, the productivity of the goal-setting crews soared as did job attendance (Latham & Kinne,

1974). Goal setting had provided these crews a sense of purpose, challenge, and meaning in what had been previously perceived by them as tedious, repetitive work.

When their wood supply was too high, logging companies restricted the number of days they would buy logs from five to three. In a reverse of Parkinson's Law (work expands to fill the time available), the pulpwood crews, again paid on a piece-rate basis, harvested as much wood or more during those restricted days as they did in a normal workweek. To the dismay of the forest products companies who wanted to reduce their wood inventory, the restricted number of days they would buy logs became a high-performance goal for the logging crews that in turn led to a significant increase in their effort to cut the same amount of wood in 3 days as they typically did in 5 days (Latham & Locke, 1975). These field experiments suggest that money and deadlines increase performance to the extent that people set, and exert effort to pursue, a high goal. Effort would become a mediator in goal-setting theory.

Would goal setting increase the productivity of loggers who are unionized and paid by the hour? The answer is yes. Goal attainment enabled them to feel a sense of accomplishment. Logging truck drivers strategized ways of increasing the load of logs they could carry without exceeding a truck's legal net weight (Latham & Baldes, 1975; Latham & Saari, 1982). Strategy would become a mediator in goal-setting theory.

All of the above field experiments provided further evidence for what would become the core of goal-setting theory: a specific, high goal increases task performance. A question of importance for the workplace had to do with the optimal method of setting a goal.

4.1 Assigned versus Participatively Set Goals

Weyerhaeuser's senior management, where Latham was employed as a staff psychologist following the receipt of his PhD, wanted to know whether something so straightforward as goal setting could be improved upon to increase an employee's productivity. Influenced by Likert's (1967) theory of leadership, Latham's doctoral dissertation, as was the case with Locke, was on goal setting, specifically the relative effectiveness of assigned versus participatively set goals for hourly paid unionized logging crews. The results showed that those in the participative condition set higher goals than those who were assigned goals. And consistent with the theory, those in the former condition had significantly higher productivity than those in the assigned goal condition (Latham & Yukl, 1975a).

Would goal setting improve the performance of high-level employees, senior management asked? Doesn't everyone set goals, skeptics in the company queried? A 3 (assigned, participatively set goals, do your best) × 3 (praise, public recognition, monetary bonus) factorial design plus a true control condition involving master's level and PhD engineers/scientists was conducted. Those who received praise, public recognition, or the bonus had performed no better 6 months later than those in the control condition. As the theory states, feedback only increases performance if it leads to the setting of a specific, high goal. Those who participated in the goal-setting process performed better than those in the assigned goal, do-best, or control conditions. Goal commitment, however, was the same between the two specific, high goal conditions. But, goal difficulty level was higher in the participative than in the assigned goal condition (Latham, Mitchell, & Dossett, 1978). As was the case with Locke's laboratory findings, and the findings with the loggers, higher goals led to higher performance than easier goals.

Subsequent laboratory experiments revealed that when goal difficulty is held constant, performance does not differ significantly between the two goal conditions; both methods of setting a goal lead to higher performance than urging people to do their best (Latham & Saari, 1979). When the assigned goal is significantly higher than the goal that is set participatively, the assigned goal leads to the higher performance (Latham, Steele, & Saari, 1982). In short, it is the goal difficulty level rather than the method by which the goal is set that influences productivity.

Field experiments conducted by Erez in Israel obtained findings that contradicted the above findings. Her research consistently showed that participatively set goals lead to higher performance than goals that are assigned. Consequently, she, Latham, and Locke conducted a series of experiments to discover the reason for the contradictory findings. The results revealed that goals assigned in a curt manner do in fact lead to performance that is significantly lower than goals where employees participate in setting them. But, assigned goals that are accompanied by a rationale lead to the same high level of performance as participatively set goals (Latham, Erez, & Locke, 1988).

Subsequent research shed further light on this issue. Participation affects performance when it increases self-efficacy to perform the task, and leads to the development of an appropriate strategy. Strategy and self-efficacy have a reciprocal effect on one another, and both were shown to mediate the participative goal—performance relationship (Latham, Winters, & Locke, 1994).

As to the question of whether everyone sets specific goals, anecdotal information suggests that this is not the case. For example, everyone in the do-best conditions in the field experiment involving engineers/scientists were aware that their colleagues in the other conditions had specific, high goals. Yet, they did not do likewise. The goals of most people are typically vague such as to do one's best on the job rather than to increase their performance in specific ways. The problem with a goal that is not specific is that it does not provide a referent for self-evaluation. Thus it allows for a wide range of performance levels that are personally acceptable. A goal that is specific, on the other hand, makes explicit for each individual what it is that the person or team is striving to attain.

4.2 Goals and Self-management

The answer to the question of whether it is better to assign or set goals participatively was answered. A remaining question that had yet to be addressed in the workplace was whether self-regulation through goal setting is effective. The opportunity to examine that issue arose in a state government setting where the job attendance of unionized employees was low. A self-management program of eight weekly 1-hour group sessions was developed followed by eight 30-minute one-on-one sessions. The sessions included goal setting for job attendance, self-monitoring attendance through the use of charts, writing a behavioral contract specifying rewards (e.g., drinking a beer) and punishers (e.g., cleaning out the attic) for attaining/not attaining the weekly goal.[2]

Three months later, those who self-set goals had significantly higher attendance than those who had been randomly assigned to the control group, and their self-efficacy for coming to work was higher as well. Self-efficacy measured at the end of this intervention predicted job attendance 9 months later (Frayne & Latham, 1987). At the end of this 9-month interval, the employees in the control condition were given this same training program in self-management. Within 3 months, job attendance rose to the same level as the employees in the initially trained condition (Latham & Frayne, 1989).

5. GOAL-SETTING STUDIES BY OTHERS

The inductive development of goal-setting theory was facilitated by the fact that many people conducted goal-setting studies. Locke and Latham

---

[2] Azrin (1977) as well as Rousseau and Fried (2001) have argued that a set of factors, when considered together, often provide a more theoretically interesting pattern than any of the variables would show in isolation.

conducted approximately 25% of the studies used to formulate their theory (see Locke & Latham, 1990 Appendix F for Locke and Latham's totals). There are many reasons why so many researchers studied goal setting. The main reason was that goal setting works; goal effects are something that can be counted on, in contrast to many other approaches to motivation that had led to inconsistent or null results. For example, Howard (2013) found that goals predicted managers' job promotions in AT&T over a 25-year period. Consequently, goal setting came to be seen as the most valid and practical theory of motivation (Lee & Earley, 1992; Miner, 1984, 2003; Pinder, 1984) in the field of organizational psychology. These successes encouraged hundreds of further studies by others.

6. THE THEORY: 1990

In the late 1980s, we realized that a large number of goal-setting studies had been done and concluded that it was now time to integrate them into a theory. The inductive process began by simply categorizing the studies.

First, we wrote a background chapter that tied goal setting not only to Mace's work, but to other historical developments including Ryan's (1970) book on intentions. Lewin, Dembo, Festinger, and Sears (1944) had done a series of goal-setting studies in the 1940s, but they had used goals as a dependent rather than an independent variable. A number of academic theories make reference to goals in work settings. For example, there is the work of Frederick Taylor (1911) which helped lead to versions of Management by Objectives at DuPont, General Motors, and General Electric. Likert (1967) also advocated high-performance goals as part of his System 4 model of leadership. These developments did not prompt our goal-setting studies, but they helped us put our research and theory into a historical context.

In this regard, it should be noted that our theory of goal setting is at variance in important respects with a cybernetically based goal model, namely, control theory (Carver & Scheier, 1981). This is because control theorists tried to translate goal concepts into machine concepts (e.g., the goal is a "comparator"). Cognitive concepts do not mean the same thing as concepts pertaining to machines/equipment (e.g., a thermostat does not have its own goals). More importantly, control theory states that motivation is based solely on discrepancy reduction between the goal set and one's current performance. This is only half true. Goal setting is first and foremost a process of discrepancy creation.

Because poor conceptualization is often a cause of poor research, our first chapter in Locke and Latham (1990) is conceptual. We formulated a clear definition of a goal: the object or aim of an action. Aim means that people want something that they do not yet possess. The cause of action is the idea or desire for the state or object not present. Such a formulation cannot be applied to inanimate matter. Again, it cannot be overemphasized that goal setting is first a discrepancy production process and only then a discrepancy reduction process.

Categorizing approximately 400 goal-setting studies was relatively straightforward. Ten major categories emerged:

- Studies of main effects
- The relation of goals to expectancies and valence
- Goal mechanisms (causal mediators)
- Determinants of choice of self-set goals
- Goal commitment
- Goals and feedback
- Moderators in addition to commitment and feedback
- Goals and affect
- Applications to human resource management
- Integration: The high performance cycle

The next step involved integration within each category. For example, there were *meta*-analyses of the main effects of setting a goal, cited earlier. Furthermore, we did something that is seldom, if ever, done. We analyzed every published failure of goal setting. In doing so, we suggested testable hypotheses as to the reasons for a null finding, based on what we knew about goals, as we built our theory. The reason for this analysis was the law of contradiction. A failure had to mean either that the method was not used properly, or that our theory was lacking in some respect.

With respect to goal commitment, we looked at how it had been measured. Was it relevant to all goals or only certain types? As noted earlier, another issue was resolving contradictory findings in the literature such as the importance of employee participation in the setting of goals.

With respect to goal mediators, we were faced with integrating motivation (goals) and cognition (task knowledge or strategies). Was task knowledge a mediator, a moderator, or both?

With feedback, we had to differentiate between its function as a mediator and its function as a moderator.

In relation to expectancy, we had to figure out how to reconcile expectancy theory with goal-setting theory since they seemed to make opposite predictions of an individual's performance. As noted earlier, the resolution required the use of Bandura's (1977, 1997) concept of self-efficacy.

In reference to satisfaction, we had to determine why hard goals lead to higher performance but don't lead to higher satisfaction than easy goals.

By 1989 (Locke & Latham, 1990), approximately 400 studies had been conducted on goal setting as a predictor or a cause of performance on more than 88 different tasks, involving close to 40,000 participants in eight countries. Thus there was strong evidence for generalization. The time spans of these studies ranged from 1 min to 3 years. Both assigned and self-set goals were shown to affect performance, though the latter mediate the former. Many different dependent (behavioral, outcome) variables were used. In fact, any type of performance that can be controlled can serve as a dependent variable for accessing the causal effect of setting a specific, high goal. The internal and external validity of the findings had been attested to by *meta*-analyses (e.g., Tubbs, 1986; Wood, Mento, & Locke, 1987), enumerative reviews (e.g., Latham & Yukl, 1975b; Locke, Shaw, Saari, & Latham, 1981), peer evaluations (e.g., Lee & Earley, 1992; Miner, 1984; Pinder, 1984), and comparative assessments of goal setting with other theories (e.g., Locke et al., 1986). The positive relationship of goal setting with, or its causal effect on, performance had been found in 90% of these studies (Locke & Latham, 1990). The laboratory experiments on goal setting had been found to generalize to field settings (Latham & Lee, 1986).

The data now existed to inductively develop the causal relations in the theory of goal setting along with four moderators or boundary conditions (i.e., conditional variables), as well as identify the four mediators that explain the causal relationships.

Goal-setting theory is parsimonious. The theory states that a specific, high goal leads to higher performance than the setting of a vague goal such as to do one's best, or the setting of no goal at all. The higher the goal, the higher the performance given the following conditions (moderators): (1) ability, knowledge, or skill to perform the task, (2) commitment to the goal, (3) feedback on goal progress, and (4) situational resources; lack of situational constraints. The four mediators that explain the beneficial effect of a specific, high goal on performance are (1) the choice to (2) exert effort in a certain direction or on a certain task, and to (3) persist in doing so until the goal is attained. These three mediators are motivational. The fourth mediator (and also a moderator as noted above) is task strategy, a cognitive factor. Degree of goal attainment determines affect (satisfaction).

Goal-setting theory is well integrated with Bandura's (1977, 1997) self-efficacy theory. Self-efficacy is affected positively by the level of the assigned goal and affects the level of self-set goals. It facilitates goal commitment and the choice of effective task strategies. Self-efficacy can have main effects as well as effects through the level of a self-set goal.

There were a number of applications of goal setting to human resource management over and above increasing productivity. One example is the situational interview; asking applicants to indicate how they intend to act under various workplace situations proved to have predictive validity and did not pose legal problems (Latham, Saari, Pursell, & Campion, 1980). The underlying assumption of this procedure is that intentions predict behavior. Other human resource management areas where goal setting lies at the core are performance management (Latham et al., 1978) and training in self-management (Latham & Frayne, 1989).

We put together the results of goal-setting experiments to create a model, the high-performance cycle: specific, high goals with their moderators and mediators, lead to high performance, which typically lead to high rewards that in turn lead to commitment to the organization and thereby the setting of high goals. Thus this is a recursive model (Locke & Latham, 1990).

7. THE THEORY EXPANDED: 2013

After goal setting became a formal theory, deductions could readily be made from it—deductions based on inductive observations and integration. However, as advocates of induction, we never claimed that goal-setting theory was a closed system—quite the opposite. New discoveries are continually being made, allowing the theory to expand. That is how science should work.

In the last 20+ years, goal-setting research has exploded. From the 1960s to the present, over 1000 goal-setting studies have been conducted (Mitchell & Daniels, 2003). This means some 600 studies have been published since our 1990 book appeared. In 2013, we decided that the theory needed to be updated to take into account these discoveries. However, the amount of new material was too large for us to summarize and integrate. Consequently, we asked researchers who had expanded goal theory to write chapters for an edited book; we ended up with 72 authors/co-authors who wrote 37 original chapters (Locke & Latham, 2013).

The core tenets of goal-setting theory have stood up well, yet we now know much more than we did in 1990 of both theoretical and practical significance.

Ten highlights from our 2013 book are the following:

1. Arguably the most important finding subsequent to 1990 is the distinction between a performance and a learning goal. No sooner had Locke and Latham submitted their book to the publisher than Kanfer and Ackerman (1989) published an experiment showing that in the early stage of learning, urging people to do their best results in higher performance than the setting of a specific high goal.

   In a subsequent experiment, Winters and Latham (1996) defined a learning goal as a desired number of strategies, processes, or procedures to be developed in order to master a task; they defined a performance goal as the desired level of performance to attain. Consistent with Kanfer and Ackerman, they too found that on a task that people lacked the knowledge to perform, the do-best condition resulted in higher performance than the setting of a specific high-performance goal. Remember that ability is a moderator variable of the goal—performance relationship. But, performance on a task that people initially lack the ability to perform was highest when a specific high-learning goal was set (Winters & Latham, 1996). Subsequent research has shown that a learning goal has the same properties as a performance goal: it should be both challenging and specific in order to improve performance whether in the laboratory (Seijts & Latham, 2005, 2011; Seijts, Latham, Tasa, & Latham, 2004) or in field settings (Latham & Brown, 2006; Porter & Latham, 2013). Thus a rule of thumb is to set a learning goal when an individual lacks the ability to perform the task; set a performance (outcome) goal when the person has the ability to attain a desired level of performance. One experiment has shown that in some contexts the two may be set simultaneously (Masuda, Locke, & Williams, in press).

   2. Locke and Latham (1984) noted that a limitation of goal-setting theory is that it ignores the subconscious. Drawing on Bargh's (Bargh & Ferguson, 2000) automaticity model, both laboratory (Chen & Latham, 2014; Stajkovic, Locke, & Blair, 2006) and field experiments (Latham & Piccolo, 2012; Shantz & Latham, 2009, 2011) have revealed that goals can be primed in the subconscious to increase task/job performance. Moreover, the effects on performance of the primed goal and the consciously set goal are additive (e.g., Shantz & Latham, 2009).

Consistent with goal–setting theory, a context-specific prime leads to higher performance than a "general" prime (Latham & Piccolo, 2012).

3. On dynamic tasks, proximal goals (i.e., subgoals) should be set (Latham & Seijts, 1999). Proximal goals are motivational; they increase persistence for the distal goal. Arguably more important for a dynamic task is that proximal goals are informational in that they provide feedback on whether an individual must do something different in order to attain the distal goal.

4. With regard to goal difficulty level, stretch (hard and usually unreachable) goals have been successfully used in General Electric, in combination with challenging yet attainable goals. They are used to promote creative thinking. Failure to attain them is not punished (Kerr & Lerelley, 2013).

5. As for enduring effects, Howard (2013) found, as noted earlier, that self-set goals for job promotions at AT&T were shown to predict the managerial level an employee attained 25 years later. To date, the effect of a primed goal on job performance has been shown to endure for a 4-day workweek (Latham & Piccolo, 2012).

6. Goals, along with self-efficacy, mediate or partly mediate the effects of many other variables, including self-report measures of personality, leadership, job design, monetary incentives, and participation in decision making (Bandura, 2013; Heslin & Caprar, 2013).

7. Goal setting works in teams and at the macro level in small organizations to increase performance (Kramer, Thayer, & Salas, 2013; Porter & Latham, 2013; Young & Smith, 2013).

8. Goal setting has proven applications not only for human resource management, but also for sports, negotiations, health regulation, entrepreneurship, creativity, psychotherapy, and academic performance (e.g., Shilts, Townsend, & Dishman, 2013).

9. Similar to #8, goal-setting programs can also be used to promote personal development of students in a university; these programs involve a number of steps including writing essays, filling out questionnaires, tying goals to one's personal life, and tracking one's progress (Travers, 2013).

10. Possible problems and pitfalls of goal setting are well known and can be avoided if proper procedures are followed (Latham & Locke, 2006, 2013, in press). For example, organizations should have a core set of articulated values, ethical guidelines based on those values, and systems to ensure adherence to the guidelines by their employees.

A few researchers have misinterpreted the theory as advocating the setting of a high goal for employees that a pilot study shows only 10% of them can attain. This erroneous conclusion comes from misreading Appendix C of Locke and Latham (1990). Their recommendation was made solely for laboratory experiments in order to ensure variance in performance. Practitioners of goal setting typically adhere to the acronym SMART when setting goals in an organizational setting: that is, the goal set should be Specific, Measurable, Attainable, Relevant with a Time-frame for attainment (Mealiea & Latham, 1996). Recall that ability and situational resources/constraints are two of the four moderators in goal-setting theory. There is a positive relationship between supervisory perceptions that the goals they have been assigned exceed their ability and the requisite resources to attain them, and their abuse of their subordinates (Mawritz, Folger, & Latham, 2014).

8. OBSERVATIONS ON THEORY BUILDING

As noted earlier, we developed goal theory through induction. What did we discover?

First, conceptual clarity is needed, starting with a clear definition of the core concepts.

Second, there needs to be reliable measures of the key concepts.

Third, there needs to be evidence of generality; this may include generality across tasks, life domains, countries, settings (laboratory, simulations, field), outcomes (unless only one outcome is of interest), levels (individuals, group, organizations), time spans (these need to be specified), and countries/cultures. There is as yet an unresolved problem here. Induction is a basis for generalization; thus one should not attempt total enumeration. But, how does one know how far to go before generalization is possible? We do not have an answer. We do believe that confidence can be placed on generalizations if point 4 below is stressed.

Fourth, humans and societal actions involve chains of causation leading to sundry outcomes. To fully understand causal relationships, we need to understand causal mechanisms (mediators)—in the case of goals, how they have their effects (e.g., choice of direction, effort, persistence, strategy). There can be many layers of causality; the more layers we understand, the more confidence we can have in predicting and controlling cause–effect relationships. This involves discovering "if-then connections" (Gollwitzer, 1999; Oettingen, Wittchen, & Gollwitzer, 2013).

Fifth, scientific discoveries are contextual. For example, Newton's laws were an earth-shattering discovery and work brilliantly, but only for objects of a certain size and within a certain degree of precision. Thus theories need to identify boundary conditions (i.e., moderators or interactions). These become "if-then" laws.

Sixth, all available, relevant information needs to be integrated. If there are contradictions, the theory cannot be valid unless the null studies were not conducted properly.

Seventh, a theory should be connected to other relevant, valid theories, in order to further eliminate contradictions and ensure a wider scope for the theory. For example, there is a close connection between social cognitive theory (Bandura, 1977, 1986, 1997) and goal-setting theory.

The above list is not the last word on inductive theory building with regard to goal-setting theory. For us the list was an emergent process. We believe that this process leads to successful theory building.

9. FUTURE DIRECTIONS

Because human action is characteristically goal-directed, there is no specific limit to the types of actions goal setting can regulate, so long as the individual or team has some control over the outcome. Our 2013 book gives many examples of the use of goal setting in domains other than work tasks.

Especially important is to do more studies of the ways in which conscious and subconscious goals work together. We believe that the conscious mind is the active part of one's psychological make-up, yet it can only hold about seven disconnected items in awareness at the same time (Miller, 1956). We believe that the conscious mind not only regulates what goes into the subconscious, but it routinely affects what comes out, based on one's purpose. The subconscious is more passive yet it holds millions of items of information; the subconscious is potential awareness and is activated based on purpose and association. Although goal-setting studies have shown that conscious goals and the priming of the subconscious can have independent effects, in the end both are aspects of the individual and both are "at work" during one's waking life.

The issue of learning goals also needs research, including the effects of different learning goal instructions and learning strategies. More needs to be discovered regarding how learning and performance goals can be combined and/or ordered (e.g., see Masuda, Locke, & Williams, in press).

This ties into the field of cognitive psychology in that action, broadly speaking, is jointly glued by both cognition and motivation.

Another need is to study how goals are committed to over long time spans. The "marshmallow studies" (Mischel, 2014) show that being able to postpone gratification has many beneficial effects on life success. Certainly it should be possible to teach people to lengthen their time perspective by using proximal (i.e., short-term goals) as a pathway to more distal/long-term goals.

The research by Travers (2013) has opened a new domain, namely, using goals to promote self-development. What is striking about her research is that university students who set self-development goals (combined with mental work such as written diaries) may improve ancillary outcomes that were not specifically listed as goals. Goal-setting theory has always stressed the idea that goals and outcomes must be matched. Perhaps this is not necessarily so. Maybe goals generalize to dependent variables in ways that have not yet been discovered.

Today goal setting continues to lie at the core of many human resource management applications (Latham & Arshoff, 2013). The high-performance cycle that, as explained earlier, shows the relationship among goals, self-efficacy, job satisfaction, organizational commitment, and job performance has been updated and supported in an enumerative review of the literature (Latham, Locke, & Fassina, 2002). Empirical support for the high-performance cycle has been obtained by the U.S. Office of Personnel Management (Selden & Brewer, 2000) and in the private sector in Italy (Borgogni & Dello Russo, 2013).

10. CONCLUSIONS

In summary, the theory of goal setting came about as a result of breaking three rules, namely, eschewing (1) behaviorism, (2) premature generalizations, and (3) deduction as a method for theory development. Among the limitations of behaviorism is that it is reactive. Behavior is said to be solely a function of its consequences. It is the environment alone that shapes behaviors. This premise is a half-truth in that it ignores the fact that people are capable of forethought. Thus they can think about, plan, and act upon their environment to create a future state they desire. Goal-setting theory provides a framework that explains how people do so.

Among the problems of overgeneralizing a theory in the absence of empirically derived data is that doing so ignores the fact that grand theories in the behavioral sciences seldom endure. This is because they fail to acknowledge boundary conditions.

Using deduction as the method for developing a theory typically leads to what Kahneman (2011) called "theory blindness." This in turn leads to a closed rather than an open theory in that empirical research that contradicts the theory is ignored. Goal-setting theory, developed inductively, is an open theory. Goal-setting theory is a cognitive theory in that it explicitly acknowledges that human beings have the ability to voluntarily, and thoughtfully, engage in behavior that is goal directed.

REFERENCES

Azrin, N. H. (1977). A strategy for applied research: learning based but outcome oriented. *American Psychologist, 32*(2), 140–149.

Bandura, A. (1977). Self-efficacy: toward a unifying theory of behavioral change. *Psychological Review, 84,* 191–215.

Bandura, A. (1986). *Social foundations of thought and action: A social cognitive theory.* Englewood Cliffs, New Jersey: Prentice Hall.

Bandura, A. (1997). *Self-efficacy: The exercise of control.* Stanford, NY: W.H. Freeman.

Bandura, A. (2013). The role of self-efficacy in goal-based motivation. In E. A. Locke, & G. P. Latham (Eds.), *New developments in goal setting and task performance* (pp. 147–157). New York: Routledge.

Bargh, J. A., & Ferguson, M. J. (2000). Beyond behaviorism: on the automaticity of higher mental processes. *Psychological Bulletin, 126,* 925–945.

Blanshard, B. (1962). *Reason and analysis.* La Salle, IL: Open Court.

Borgogni, L., & Dello Russo, S. (2013). A quantitative analysis of the high performance goals. In E. A. Locke, & G. P. Latham (Eds.), *New developments in goal setting and task performance.* New York: Routledge.

Campbell, J. P. (1971). Personnel training and development. *Annual Review of Psychology, 22,* 565–602.

Carver, C. S., & Scheier, M. F. (1981). *Attention and self-regulation: A control-theory approach to human behavior.* New York: Springer-Verlag.

Chen, X. E., & Latham, G. P. (2014). The effect of priming learning vs performance goals on a complex task. *Organizational Behavior and Human Decision Processes, 125,* 88–97.

Cronbach, L. J. (1957). The two disciplines of scientific psychology. *American Psychologist, 12,* 671–684.

Dulany, D. E. (1968). Awareness, rules and propositional control: a confrontation with S-R behavior theory. In D. Horton, & T. Dixon (Eds.), *Verbal behavior and S-R behavior theory* (pp. 340–387). New York: Prentice Hall.

Erez, M. (1977). Feedback: a necessary condition for the goal setting-performance relationship. *Journal of Applied Psychology, 62,* 624–627.

Erez, M., & Zidon, I. (1984). Effect of goal acceptance on the relationship of goal difficulty to performance. *Journal of Applied Psychology, 69,* 69–78.

Flanagan, J. C. (1954). The critical incident technique. *Psychological Bulletin, 51,* 327–358.

Frayne, C. A., & Latham, G. P. (1987). The application of social learning theory to employee self-management of attendance. *Journal of Applied Psychology, 72,* 387–392.

Gollwitzer, P. M. (1999). Implementation intentions and effective goal pursuit: strong effects of simple plans. *American Psychologist, 54,* 493–503.

Harriman, D. (2010). *The logical leap.* New York: New American Library.

Hebb, D. O. (1949). *The organization of behavior: A neuropsychological theory.* Oxford: Wiley.

Heneman, H. G., & Schwab, D. P. (1972). Evaluation of research on expectancy theory predictions of employee performance. *Psychological Bulletin, 78,* 1—9.

Herzberg, F., Mausner, B., & Snyderman, B. B. (1959). *The motivation to work.* New York: Wiley.

Heslin, P. A., & Caprar, D. V. (2013). Goals and self-efficacy as mediators. In E. A. Locke, & G. P. Latham (Eds.), *New developments in goal setting and task performance.* New York: Routledge.

Hinrichs, J. R. (1970). Psychology of men at work. *Annual Review of Psychology, 21,* 519—554.

Howard, A. (2013). The predictive validity of conscious and subconscious motives on career advancement. In E. Locke, & G. Latham (Eds.), *New developments in goal setting and task performance.* New York: Routledge.

Kahneman, D. (2011). *Thinking, fast and slow.* New York: Farrar, Straus and Giroux.

Kanfer, R., & Ackerman, P. L. (1989). Motivation and cognitive abilities: an integrative/aptitude-treatment interaction approach to skill acquisition. *Journal of Applied Psychology Monograph, 74,* 657—690.

Kerr, S., & Lerelley, D. (2013). Stretch goals: risks, possibilities, and best practices. In E. A. Locke, & G. P. Latham (Eds.), *New developments in goal setting and task performance.* New York: Routledge.

Kramer, W. S., Thayer, A. L., & Salas, E. (2013). Goal setting in teams. In E. A. Locke, & G. P. Latham (Eds.), *New developments in goal setting and task performance.* New York: Routledge.

Latham, G. P., & Arshoff, A. S. (2013). The relevance of goal setting theory for human resource management. In E. A. Locke, & G. P. Latham (Eds.), *New developments in goal and task performance* (pp. 331—342). New York, NY: Routledge.

Latham, G. P., & Baldes, J. J. (1975). The "practical significance" of Locke's theory of goal setting. *Journal of Applied Psychology, 60,* 122—124.

Latham, G. P., & Brown, T. C. (2006). The effect of learning vs. outcome goals on self-efficacy, satisfaction and performance in an MBA Program. *Applied Psychology, 55,* 606—623.

Latham, G. P., & Dossett, D. L. (1978). Designing incentive plans for unionized employees: a comparison of continuous and variable ratio reinforcement schedules. *Personnel Psychology, 31,* 47—61.

Latham, G. P., Erez, M., & Locke, E. A. (1988). Resolving scientific disputes by the joint design of crucial experiments by the antagonists: application of the Erez-Latham dispute regarding participation in goal setting. *Journal of Applied Psychology Monograph, 73,* 753—772.

Latham, G. P., & Frayne, C. A. (1989). Self management training for increasing job attendance: a follow-up and a replication. *Journal of Applied Psychology, 74,* 411—416.

Latham, G. P., & Kinne, S. B. (1974). Improving job performance through training in goal setting. *Journal of Applied Psychology, 59,* 187—191.

Latham, G. P., & Lee, T. W. (1986). Goal setting. In E. A. Locke (Ed.), *Generalizing from laboratory to field settings.* Lexington, MA: Health.

Latham, G. P., & Locke, E. A. (1975). Increasing productivity with decreasing time limits: a field replication of Parkinson's law. *Journal of Applied Psychology, 60,* 524—526.

Latham, G. P., & Locke, E. A. (2006). Enhancing the benefits and overcoming the pitfalls of goal setting. *Organizational Dynamics, 35,* 332—340.

Latham, G. P., & Locke, E. A. (2013). Potential pitfalls in goal setting and how to avoid them. In E. A. Locke, & G. P. Latham (Eds.), *New developments in goal setting and task performance* (pp. 569—579). New York, NY: Routledge.

Latham, G. P., & Locke, E. A. Goal setting theory: controversies and resolutions. In D. Ones, N. Anderson, C. Viswesvaran, & H. Sinangil (Eds). *Handbook of industrial, work & organizational psychology:* Vol. 1, in press.

Latham, G. P., Locke, E. A., & Fassina, N. E. (2002). The high performance cycle: standing the test of time. In S. Sonnentag (Ed.), *The psychological management of individual performance: A handbook in the psychology of management in organizations* (pp. 201–228). Chichester: Wiley.

Latham, G. P., Mitchell, T. R., & Dossett, D. L. (1978). The importance of participative goal setting and anticipated rewards on goal difficulty and job performance. *Journal of Applied Psychology, 63*, 163–171.

Latham, G. P., & Piccolo, R. F. (2012). The effect of context specific versus non-specific subconscious goals on employee performance. *Human Resource Management, 51*, 535–538.

Latham, G. P., & Saari, L. M. (1979). The effects of holding goal difficulty constant on assigned and participatively set goals. *Academy of Management Journal, 22*, 163–168.

Latham, G. P., & Saari, L. M. (1982). The importance of union acceptance for productivity improvement through goal setting. *Personnel Psychology, 35*, 781–787.

Latham, G. P., Saari, L. M., Pursell, E. D., & Campion, M. (1980). The situational interview. *Journal of Applied Psychology, 65*, 422–427.

Latham, G. P., & Seijts, G. H. (1999). The effects of proximal and distal goals on performance on a moderately complex task. *Journal of Organizational Behavior, 20*, 421–429.

Latham, G. P., Steele, T. P., & Saari, L. M. (1982). The effects of participation and goal difficulty on performance. *Personnel Psychology, 35*, 677–686.

Latham, G. P., Winters, D. C., & Locke, E. A. (1994). Cognitive and motivational effects of participation: a mediator study. *Journal of Organizational Behavior, 15*, 49–63.

Latham, G. P., & Yukl, G. A. (1975a). Assigned versus participative goal setting with educated and uneducated woods workers. *Journal of Applied Psychology, 60*, 299–302.

Latham, G. P., & Yukl, G. A. (1975b). A review of research on the application of goal setting in organizations. *Academy of Management Journal, 18*, 824–845.

Lee, C., & Earley, P. C. (1992). Comparative peer evaluations of organizational behavior theories. *Organizational Development Journal, 10*, 37–42.

Lewin, K., Dembo, T., Festinger, L., & Sears, P. S. (1944). Level of aspiration. In J. McV. Hunt (Ed.), *Personality and the behavior disorders* (Vol. 1, pp. 333–378). New York: Ronald Press.

Likert, R. (1967). *The human organization: Its management and values.* New York: McGraw-Hill.

Locke, E. A. (1977). The myths of behavior mod in organizations. *Academy of Management Review, 2*, 543–553.

Locke, E. A. (1978). The ubiquity of the technique of goal setting in theories of and approaches to employee motivation. *Academy of Management Review, 3*, 594–601.

Locke, E. A. (1980). Latham versus Komaki: a tale of two paradigms. *Journal of Applied Psychology, 65*, 16–23.

Locke, E. A. (2007). The case of inductive theory building. *Journal of Management, 33*, 867–890.

Locke, E. A. (2015). Theory building, replication, and behavioral priming: where do we go from here? *Perspectives in Psychological Science, 10*(3), 408–414.

Locke, E. A., & Bryan, J. F. (1968a). Goal-setting as a determinant of the effect of knowledge of score on performance. *American Journal of Psychology, 81*, 398–407.

Locke, E. A., & Bryan, J. F. (1968b). Grade goals as determinants of academic achievement. *Journal of General Psychology, 79*, 217–228.

Locke, E. A., & Bryan, J. F. (1969). The directing function of goals in task performance. *Organizational Behavior and Human Performance, 4*, 35–42.

Locke, E. A., Cartledge, N., & Knerr, C. (1970). Studies of the relationship between satisfaction, goal-setting and performance. *Organizational Behavior and Human Performance, 5*, 135–158.

Locke, E. A., Cartledge, N., & Koeppel, J. (1968). Motivation effects of knowledge of results: a goal setting phenomenon? *Psychological Bulletin, 70*, 474–485.

Locke, E. A., Chah, D. O., Harrison, S., & Lustgarten, N. (1989). Separating the effects of goal specificity from goal level. *Organizational Behavior and Human Decision Processes, 43*, 270–287.

Locke, E. A., Frederick, E., Buckner, E., & Bobko, P. (1984). Effects of previously assigned goals on self-set goals and performance. *Journal of Applied Psychology, 69*, 694–699.

Locke, E. A., & Latham, G. P. (1984). *Goal setting: A motivational technique that works.* Englewood Cliffs, NJ: Prentice Hall.

Locke, E. A., & Latham, G. P. (1990). *A theory of goal setting and task performance.* Englewood Cliffs, NJ: Prentice Hall.

Locke, E. A., & Latham, G. P. (2002). Building a practically useful theory of goal setting and task motivation: a 35-year old odyssey. *American Psychologist, 57*, 705–717.

Locke, E. A., & Latham, G. P. (2013). *New developments on goal setting and task performance.* New York: Routledge.

Locke, E. A., Motowidlo, S. J., & Bobko, P. (1986). Using self-efficacy theory to resolve the conflict between goal theory and expectancy theory in organizational behavior and industrial/organizational psychology. *Journal of Social and Clinical Psychology, 4*, 328–338.

Locke, E. A., & Shaw, K. N. (1984). Atkinson's inverse-U curve and the missing cognitive variables. *Psychological Reports, 55*, 403–412.

Locke, E. A., Shaw, K. N., Saari, L. M., & Latham, G. P. (1981). Goal setting and task performance. *Psychological Bulletin, 90*, 125–152.

Mace, C. A. (1935). *Incentives: Some experimental studies. Industrial Health Research Board Report (Great Britain), No. 72.*

Masuda, A., Locke, E. A., & Williams, K. J. The effects of simultaneous learning and performance goals on performance: an inductive exploration. *Journal of Cognitive Psychology*, in press.

Mawritz, M., Folger, R., & Latham, G. P. (2014). Supervisors' exceedingly difficult goals and abusive supervision: the mediating effects of hindrance stress, anger, and anxiety. *Journal of Organizational Behavior, 35*, 358–372.

McClelland, D. C. (1961). *The achieving society.* Princeton, NJ: Van Nostrand.

Mealiea, L. W., & Latham, G. P. (1996). *Skills for managerial success: Theory, experience, and practice.* Chicago: Irwin.

Mento, A. J., Locke, E. A., & Klein, H. J. (1992). Relationship of goal level to valence and instrumentality. *Journal of Applied Psychology, 77*, 395–405.

Mento, A. J., Steel, R. P., & Karren, R. J. (1987). A meta-analytic study of the effects of goal setting on task performance. *Organizational Behavior and Human Decision Processes, 39*, 52–83.

Miller, G. A. (1956). The magical number seven, plus or minus two: some limits on our capacity for pursuing information. *Psychological Review, 63*, 89–97.

Miner, J. B. (1984). The validity and usefulness of theories in emerging organizational science. *Academy of Management Review, 9*, 296–306.

Miner, J. B. (2003). The rated importance, scientific validity, and practical usefulness of organizational behavior theories: a quantitative review. *Academy of Management: Learning and Education, 2*, 250–268.

Mischel, W. (2014). *The marshmallow test: Mastering self control.* New York: Little, Brown.

Mitchell, T. R., & Daniels, D. (2003). Motivation. In *Handbook of psychology. Two* (Vol. 10). pp. 223–254.

Nagle, E. (1961). *The structure of science.* New York: Harcourt, Brace, and World.

Nord, W. R. (1969). Beyond the teaching machine: the neglected area of operant conditioning in the theory and practice of management. *Organizational Behavior and Human Performance, 4*, 375–401.

Oettingen, G., Wittchen, M., & Gollwitzer, P. (2013). Regulating goal pursuit through mental contrasting with implementation intentions. In E. A. Locke, & G. P. Latham (Eds.), *New developments in goal setting and task performance*. New York: Routledge.

Peikoff, L. (1984). *Objectivism: The philosophy of Ayn Rand*. New York: Dutton.

Piaget, J. (1973). *Main trends in psychology*. London: George Allen & Unwin.

Pinder, C. C. (1984). *Work motivation: Theory, issues, and applications*. Glenview, IL: Scott Foresman.

Porter, R. L., & Latham, G. P. (2013). The effect of employee learning goals and goal commitment on departmental performance. *Journal of Leadership and Organizational Studies, 20*, 62−68.

Ronan, W. W., Latham, G. P., & Kinne, S. B. (1973). The effects of goal setting and supervision on worker behavior in an industrial situation. *Journal of Applied Psychology, 58*, 302−307.

Rousseau, D. M., & Fried, Y. (2001). Location, location, location: contextualizing organizational research. *Journal of Organizational Behavior, 22*, 1−13.

Ryan, T. A. (1970). *Intentional behavior*. New York: Ronald Press.

Ryan, T. A., & Smith, P. C. (1954). *Principles of industrial psychology*. New York: Ronald Press.

Saari, L. M., & Latham, G. P. (1982). Employee reactions to continuous and variable ratio reinforcement schedules involving a monetary incentive. *Journal of Applied Psychology, 67*, 506−508.

Seijts, G. H., & Latham, G. P. (2005). Learning versus performance goals: when should each be used? *Academy of Management Executive, 19*, 124−131.

Seijts, G. H., & Latham, G. P. (2011). The effect of commitment to a learning goal, self-efficacy, and the interaction between learning goal difficulty and commitment on performance in a business simulation. *Human Performance, 24*, 189−204.

Seijts, G. H., Latham, G. P., Tasa, K., & Latham, B. W. (2004). Goal setting and goal orientation: An integration of two different yet related literatures. *Academy of Management Journal, 47*, 227−239.

Selden, S. C., & Brewer, G. A. (2000). Work motivation in the senior executive service: testing the high performance cycle theory. *Journal of Public Administration Research and Theory, 10*, 531−550.

Shantz, A., & Latham, G. P. (2009). An exploratory field experiment of the effect of subconscious and conscious goals on employee performance. *Organizational Behavior and Human Decision Processes, 109*, 9−17.

Shantz, A., & Latham, G. P. (2011). The effect of primed goals on employee performance: implications for human resource management. *Human Resource Management, 50*, 289−299.

Shilts, M. K., Townsend, M. S., & Dishman, R. K. (2013). Using goal setting to promote health behavior changes: diet and physical activity. In E. A. Locke, & G. P. Latham (Eds.), *New developments in goal setting and task performance*. New York: Routledge.

Skinner, B. F. (1953). *Science and human behavior*. New York: Macmillan.

Skinner, B. F. (1971). *Beyond freedom and dignity*. New York: Knopf.

Stajkovic, A. D., Locke, E. A., & Blair, E. S. (2006). A first examination of the relationships between primed subconscious goals, assigned conscious goals, and task performance. *Journal of Applied Psychology, 91*, 1172−1180.

Taylor, F. W. (1911). *Principles of scientific management*. New York: Harper.

Travers, C. (2013). Using goal setting theory to promote personal development. In E. A. Locke, & G. P. Latham (Eds.), *New developments in goal setting and task performance*. New York: Routledge.

Tubbs, M. E. (1986). Goal setting: a meta-analytic examination of the empirical evidence. *Journal of Applied Psychology, 71*(3), 474−483.

Umstot, D. D., Bell, C. H., & Mitchell, T. R. (1976). Effects of job enrichment and task goals on satisfaction and productivity: implications for job design. *Journal of Applied Psychology, 61*, 379–394.

Vroom, V. H. (1964). *Work motivation*. New York: John Wiley & Sons.

Vroom, V. H. (1967). Some observations on Herzberg's two-factor theory. In *Paper presented at the meeting of American Psychological Association, Washington DC*.

Watson, J. B. (1925). *Behaviorism*. New York, NY: W.W. Norton & Company, Inc.

Winters, D., & Latham, G. P. (1996). The effect of learning versus outcome goals on a simple versus a complex task. *Group and Organization Management, 21*, 236–250.

Wood, R. E., Mento, A. J., & Locke, E. A. (1987). Task complexity as a moderator of goal effects: a meta-analysis. *Journal of Applied Psychology, 72*, 416–425.

Young, G., & Smith, K. G. (2013). Units, divisions, and organizations: macro-level goal setting. In E. A. Locke, & G. P. Latham (Eds.), *New developments in goal setting and task performance*. New York: Routledge.

Yukl, G. A., & Latham, G. P. (1975). Consequences of reinforcement schedules and incentive magnitudes for employee performance: problems encountered in an industrial setting. *Journal of Applied Psychology, 60*, 294–298.

Yukl, G. A., Latham, G. P., & Pursell, E. D. (1976). The effectiveness of performance incentives under continuous and variable ratio schedules of reinforcement. *Personnel Psychology, 29*, 221–231.

Yukl, G. A., Wexley, K. N., & Seymore, J. D. (1972). Effectiveness of pay incentives under variable ratio and continuous reinforcement schedules. *Journal of Applied Psychology, 56*, 13–23.

CHAPTER FIVE

The Big-Fish—Little-Pond Effect, Competence Self-perceptions, and Relativity: Substantive Advances and Methodological Innovation

Herbert W. Marsh*,§,¶,[1] and Marjorie Seaton*

*Australian Catholic University, Stratfield, NSW, Australia
§King Saud University, Riyadh, Saudi Arabia
¶University of Oxford, Oxford, UK
[1]Corresponding author: E-mail: herb.marsh@acu.edu.au

Contents

1. Introduction	128
2. The Importance of Self-concept	130
3. A Historical Perspective on Self-concept	132
4. The BFLPE Model	134
4.1 Early Theoretical Perspectives	135
4.2 Early Empirical Studies	138
4.2.1 What are the Methodological Requirements for a BFLPE Study?	*140*
5. Extended Empirical Support for BFLPE Generalizability	141
5.1 Is the BFLPE Nothing More than an Ephemeral Effect? Generalizability over Time	141
5.2 Is the BFLPE Evident in Different Countries and Cultures? Cross-Cultural Generalizability	142
5.2.1 PISA Studies of the BFLPE	*142*
5.2.2 TIMSS Studies of the BFLPE	*143*
5.3 Individual Differences: Generalizability and Potential Moderators of the BFLPE	145
5.3.1 Moderation and Generalizability: Two Sides of the Same Coin	*145*
5.3.2 Academic Goal Theory	*146*
5.3.3 Personality	*147*
5.3.4 Individual-Student Ability	*147*
5.3.5 Age	*148*
5.3.6 Teaching Style	*149*
5.4 Generalizability of BFLPEs to Other Constructs	149
5.4.1 So What if Students Have Lower ASCs in Academically Selective Schools?	*149*
5.4.2 Generalizability of the BFLPE to Other (Nonacademic) Domains	*151*

Advances in Motivation Science, Volume 2
ISSN 2215-0919
http://dx.doi.org/10.1016/bs.adms.2015.05.002

5.5 Explicit Tracking: BFLPEs for Gifted and Academically Disadvantaged Students 152
    5.5.1 The BFLPE and Academically Gifted Students   153
    5.5.2 The BFLPE and Academically Disadvantaged Students   154
6. New Theoretical Directions: Integrating the BFLPE with Alternative Theoretical 155
Perspectives
  6.1 Local Dominance Effects: Class versus School Social Comparison Processes 155
  6.2 SCT: Juxtaposition with the BFLPE   156
    6.2.1 Social Comparison Theory   156
    6.2.2 SCT Challenges of the BFLPE and BFLPE Challenges of SCT   157
    6.2.3 Integration of SCT and BFLPE   161
    6.2.4 School Grades, Grading-on-a-Curve and the BFLPE   162
7. Methodological Innovation and the BFLPE   163
  7.1 Early Research: Manifest, Single-Level Models   164
  7.2 Latent, Single-Level Models   165
  7.3 Manifest, Multilevel Models   165
  7.4 Latent, Multilevel Models   167
  7.5 Alternative Experimental Designs   169
8. Substantive Implications for Policy Practice   170
9. Limitations and Directions for Future Research   173
Acknowledgments   175
References   176

Abstract

Enhancing the academic self-concept (ASC) is an important goal in its own right and facilitates the accomplishment of a wide variety of educational outcomes. The big-fish—little-pond effect (BFLPE), based on an integration of theoretical models, posits that high-ability students will have lower ASCs when placed in high-ability educational tracks with other high-ability students, while lower-ability students will have higher ASCs when placed in low-ability tracks with other lower-ability students. Thus, in terms of ASC, highly segregated educational systems are expected to disadvantage the brightest students and advantage the least able students in terms of ASC. Here we re-view the BFLPE literature over the 30 years since the first BFLPE study, with a focus on ongoing empirical issues, new theoretical perspectives, increasingly sophisticated methodological approaches, and policy/practice implications. We conclude with an overview of methodological issues pertaining to the BFLPE and the ways in which BFLPE methodology has changed and progressed over the last 30 years to take advan-tage of advances in statistical methodology.

1. INTRODUCTION

In his preface to the 2008 Handbook of Motivation Science, James Shah (2008) discussed the pivotal role of motivational relativity as one of the 3 Rs of motivational science (along with regulation and reactivity). As noted by Shah, this focus was highlighted in the Handbook chapters by Lockwood and Pinkus (social comparison in motivation) and by Dweck (self-theories), and the central role of competence self-beliefs and the motive to be competent (White, 1959) emphasized in many chapters. Indeed, psychologists from the time of William James (1890/1963) have recognized that objective accomplishments are evaluated in relation to frames of reference, noting that "we have the paradox of a man shamed to death because he is only the second pugilist or the second oarsman in the world" (p. 310). Here we focus on the relativity of competence self-perceptions in academic settings, operationalized as academic self-concept (ASC). More specifically we outline theory, research, methodology, and implications of the widely studied big-fish—little-pond effect (BFLPE) model (Figure 1). According to the BFLPE, individual achievement and accomplishments are positively related to ASC (the brighter I am, the higher my ASC), but school- or class-average ability has a negative effect on ASC (the brighter my classmates, the lower my ASC). It is this latter negative effect of school–average ability which characterizes the BFLPE, demonstrating the relativity of self-perceptions of competence and the importance of frames of reference. In this chapter, we review theory, methodology, and research providing extensive support for the generalizability of the BFLPE across diverse samples, ages, instruments, and designs (Marsh, Seaton, et al., 2008; Nagengast & Marsh, 2012, 2013), offering support for it being one of the most robust findings in motivational science and educational psychology research.

The broad interest in the BFLPE and its relevance to motivational science, social comparison, and competence self-perceptions is encapsulated

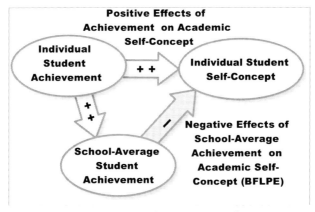

Figure 1 The big-fish-little-pond-effect.

in Gladwell's (2013) best-selling popular culture book, *David and Goliath: Underdogs, Misfits, and the Art of Battling Giants*, where he notes

> We compare ourselves those in the same situation as ourselves, which means that students in an elite school—except, perhaps, those at the very top of the class— are going to face a burden that they would not face in a less competitive atmo- sphere. Citizens of happy countries have higher suicide rates than citizens of unhappy countries, because they look at the smiling faces around them and the contrast is too great. Students at "great" schools look at the brilliant students around them, and how do you think they feel? The phenomenon of relative depri- vation applied to education is called—appropriately enough—the "Big Fish–Little Pond Effect." The more elite an educational institution is, the worse students feel about their own academic abilities. Students who would be at the top of their class at a good school can easily fall to the bottom of a really good school. Stu- dents who would feel that they have mastered a subject at a good school can have the feeling that they are falling farther and farther behind in a really good school. And that feeling—as subjective and ridiculous and irrational as it may be—**matters**. How you feel about your academic abilities—your 'academic self-concept'—in the context of your classroom shapes your willingness to tackle challenges and finish difficult tasks. It's a crucial element in your motivation and confidence. The Big Fish-Little Pond theory was pioneered by psychologist Herbert Marsh, and to Marsh, most parents and students make their school choice for the wrong reason. (pp. 79–80)

In our review of BFLPE research, we emphasize that solutions to unre- solved old and emerging new issues of substantive and theoretical impor- tance are stimulated by new and evolving research methodology—a methodological-substantive synergy (Marsh & Hau, 2007). We set the stage by highlighting the importance of self-concept, the focus of BFLPE research, the basic BFLPE paradigm and its theoretical underpinning, the early history of BFLPE research, and a summary of recent developments. We conclude with an overview of methodological issues pertaining to the BFLPE and the ways in which BFLPE methodology has changed and pro- gressed over the last 30 years to take advantage of advances in statistical methodology. Indeed, methodological developments stimulated by the BFLPE have also stimulated the development of new statistical tools now being used across the social sciences.

2. THE IMPORTANCE OF SELF-CONCEPT

Self-concept is widely acknowledged as a critical construct that is asso- ciated with the social and personal adjustment of children and adolescents

(Harter, 1990, 2012), academic achievement (Delugach, Bracken, Bracken, & Schicke, 1992; Marsh & Craven, 2006; Marsh & Yeung, 1997a, 1997b), approaches to learning (Burnett, Pillay, & Dart, 2003), emotional adjustment and socialization (Donahue, Robins, Roberts, & John, 1993), bullying (Marsh, Parada, Craven, & Finger, 2004), elite athlete success (Marsh & Perry, 2005), and parent—adolescent relations (Barber, Hall, & Armistead, 2003).

In his review of personality, motivation, and social psychological research, Greenwald emphasized the central importance of self "because it is a major (perhaps the major) structure of personality" (1988, p. 30). In support of this claim, he asserted, "(a) that the search for self-worth is one of the strongest motivating forces in the adolescent and adult human behavior, and (b) that differences between persons in their manner of, and effectiveness in, establishing self-worth are fundamental to personality" (1988, p. 37). Self-concept is also central to the positive psychology movement, which focuses on how healthy, normal, and exceptional individuals can get the most from life (e.g., Diener, 2000; Marsh & Craven, 2006; Seligman & Csikszentmihalyi, 2000). Self-concept also facilitates other important aspects of psychological well-being including happiness, motivation, anxiety, depression, and academic striving behaviors.

Self-concept has mutually reinforcing relations with achievement and accomplishments such that prior self-concept influences subsequent accomplishments beyond what can be explained by prior accomplishments, and prior accomplishments influence subsequent self-concept beyond what can be explained by prior self-concepts (Haney & Durlak, 1998; Marsh & Craven, 2006; Valentine, DuBois, & Cooper, 2004). Thus, Guo, Marsh, Parker, and Morin (2015) found that ASC in high school had stronger effects on long-term occupational aspirations and educational attainment 5 years after high school graduation than did IQ or intrinsic and utility-value motivation. Implicit in this research showing the reciprocal effects between self-concept and accomplishments is the assumption that self-concept's effect on subsequent behavior is mediated by processes such as how individuals invest their effort, persistence in the face of difficulty, and choice behavior. Thus, for example, Marsh and Yeung (1997b) showed that self-concepts in specific school subjects are better predictors of subsequent coursework selection than prior achievement in the same school subjects. Particularly in education settings, a positive ASC is both a desirable goal and a means of facilitating subsequent learning and other academic accomplishments.

3. A HISTORICAL PERSPECTIVE ON SELF-CONCEPT

Self-concept has a long, controversial history that captured the imagination of philosophers and great thinkers for centuries, and long predates the science of psychology. Hattie (1992) traced the roots of theorizing about the self from Socrates and Plato in the fourth century BC, through Descartes, James, and Freud, and, more recently, to Bandura, Rogers, and others. Socrates saw the self as the soul of a person; Descartes separated the mind from the body, with his famous quotation "I think, therefore I am"; James contended that the self entails a stream of consciousness; and Rogers argued that "the self is an awareness of being" (Hattie, 1992, p. 34).

William James could reasonably be considered the father of the psychological study of self-concept. In the first introductory textbook in psychology, James's *The Principles of Psychology* (1890/1963), the longest chapter was devoted to the self. In this chapter, James laid a foundation for the study of self and introduced many issues still of relevance today. Thus, for example, James introduced the distinction between I (i.e., self as knower, or active agent) and me (self as known, or the content of experience) as well as the multifaceted, hierarchical nature of self-concept "with the bodily Self at the bottom, the spiritual Self at the top, and the extracorporeal material selves and the various social selves between" (p. 313). Of particular relevance to this chapter, James highlighted the role of feedback from peers or significant others on the formation of self-perceptions, anticipating symbolic interactionists (e.g., Cooley, 1902) in sociology and subsequent social comparison theory (SCT) in psychology (e.g., Festinger, 1954).

However, despite the rich beginning provided by James, advances in theory, research, and measurement of self-concept were slow, particularly during the heyday of behaviorism. Reviewers in that era noted the poor quality both of theoretical models and self-concept measurement instruments (e.g., Shavelson, Hubner, & Stanton, 1976; Wells & Marwell, 1976; Wylie, 1979), leading Hattie (1992) to describe this period as one of "dust bowl empiricism" in which the predominant research design in self-concept studies was "throw it in and see what happens." Thus, in her review of past, present, and future self-concept research, Byrne concluded

Without question, the most profound happening in self-concept research during the past century was the wake-up call sounded regarding the sorry state of its reported findings, which was followed by a conscious effort on the part of methodologically oriented researchers to rectify the situation.

2002, p. 898

During the last 30 years there has been substantial growth in the quality of self-concept research due largely to the heuristic synergy between better measurement instruments, theoretical models, quantitative methodology, and research design. A key to this resurgence was the classic review article by Shavelson et al. (1976). They noted critical problems in self-concept research, including deficient definitions of the self-concept construct, weak measurement instruments, and little emphasis on rigorous tests of counterinterpretations. However, unlike many other reviews of that period that only criticized self-concept research, Shavelson et al. developed a constructive approach in which they reviewed existing definitions of self-concept, developed a construct definition of self-concept on the basis of this theoretical work, and proposed a structural model of self-concept that profoundly influenced subsequent research (see Marsh & Hattie, 1996). Based on an integration of 17 different conceptual definitions of self-concept identified in their review, Shavelson et al. broadly defined self-concept as a person's self-perceptions formed through experience with, and interpretations of, one's environment. These self-perceptions are influenced especially by evaluations by significant others, reinforcements, and attributions for one's own behavior. Self-concept is not an entity within the person, but a hypothetical construct that is potentially useful in explaining and predicting how a person acts. Shavelson et al. emphasized that self-concept is important both as an outcome and as a mediating variable that helps the understanding of other outcomes. Self-concepts influence the way one acts and behaves, which in turn influence one's self-perceptions.

Although a multidimensional conception of self-concept was already evident in William James' (1890/1963) pioneering work, early self-concept research was dominated by a unidimensional perspective in which self-concept was typically represented by a single score (e.g., Coopersmith, 1967), variously referred to as general self-concept, global self-worth, or self-esteem. In their classic review of self-concept research, Shavelson et al. (1976) developed a multidimensional, hierarchical model of self-concept, represented pictorially as a hierarchical organization in which general self-concept at the apex is divided into academic and nonacademic components of self-concept. The academic component is divided into self-concepts specific to general school subjects and non-ASC is divided into physical, social, and emotional components. This multidimensional model integrates the unidimensional perspective, which focuses on the global component of the self-concept hierarchy, and the multidimensional perspective, which focuses on the increasingly domain-specific components of self-concept near the base of the hierarchy. At the time, Shavelson et al. (1976) were unable to test the multiple facets of self-concept posited by their model as appropriate multidimensional measurement instruments had not yet been developed.

Remarkably, when Shavelson et al. (1976) proposed their model, the resistance to the multidimensional aspect of the model was so strong that leading researchers of that period (e.g., Coopersmith, 1967; Marx & Winne, 1978) argued that self-concept was either a unidimensional construct or that the facets of self-concept were dominated so heavily by a general factor that they could not be differentiated adequately. Subsequently, Byrne (1984, pp. 449–450; also see Marsh, Byrne, & Shavelson, 1988) noted "Many consider this inability to attain discriminant validity among the dimensions of SC to be one of the major complexities facing SC researchers today." However, the basic assumption of this model asserted that self-concept was a multidimensional construct and provided a blueprint for a new generation of self-concept instruments model that provided overwhelming support for the multidimensionality of self-concept and fundamentally impacted self-concept theory, research, and practice. Thus, Marsh and Craven (1997) argued

> If the role of self-concept research is to better understand the complexity of self in different contexts, to predict a wide variety of behaviors, to provide outcome measures for diverse interventions, and to relate self-concept to other constructs, then the specific domains of self-concept are more useful than a general domain. (p. 191)

4. THE BFLPE MODEL

As noted earlier, psychologists from the time of William James (1890/1963) have recognized that objective accomplishments are evaluated in relation to frames of reference. More recently, Shavelson et al. (1976) emphasized that individuals have multiple frames of reference against which to evaluate their accomplishments in formulating their self-concepts. These include (1) an absolute ideal (e.g., running a 5-min mile); (2) a personal, internal standard (e.g., a personal best); (3) the expectations of significant others; or (4) a relative standard based on comparisons with peers. The focus of the present chapter is the widely studied BFLPE model that emphasizes the frame of reference based on the relative performance of classmates and the negative effect of school- or class-average achievement on ASC (Figure 1).

A hypothetical example may help to make this model more concrete. Imagine two students who both have similar above-average academic ability. At the end of primary school, one student (Anna) applies for and is selected to attend an academically selective school. This school performs exceptionally well academically and so the average ability level of this school is higher than the average of all other schools in the area. The other student (Becky) decides to go to the local high school. This school is not an academically selective school; its average ability level is similar to the average of all other schools in the area. Becky, the student in the average-ability school, is achieving extremely well compared to her classmates, and as such, she feels very competent academically. She is a big fish in a small pond. Conversely, in Anna's school there are many high achievers and her performance is average compared with her classmates. As such, Anna does not feel very competent academically. She is a little fish in a big pond. So, although both Anna and Becky are of similar ability levels, Anna's ASC is lower than that of Becky's because of differing frames of reference. The selective school has had a negative effect on Anna's ASC (the BFLPE). Hence, in high-ability environments, equally able students tend to have lower ASCs than students who are educated in settings where the average ability of classmates is lower. This hypothetical example closely follows an actual case study (Marsh, 2007) of Jane who was attending an academically selective Australian high school, but was doing poorly and not attending school regularly. A change in employment forced her parents to move to another city so Jane had to attend a new high school that was not a selective school. Due to her poor progress at her last school, Jane was initially placed in a class with the least able students in the new school. It quickly became evident, however, that she was a very able student and she soon worked her way into the most advanced classes in the new school. Her parents found that she was taking school more seriously and spending more time on her homework. Jane herself indicated that at the old (selective) school she had to work really hard to get just average marks which was not worth the effort. However, if she worked hard in her new school she could be one of the best, which was apparently worth the effort.

4.1 Early Theoretical Perspectives

The initial inspiration for the BFLPE model (Marsh, 1974) came from psychophysical research based on perceptual stimuli (e.g., the loudness or frequencies of sound, the size or color of objects, the heaviness of lifted weights, perceptual illusions). In psychophysical research, it is well established that the judgment of any particular stimulus will vary with the context against which it is viewed (Helson, 1964; Marsh, 1974). Thus, for example, a gray object will appear to be darker in relation to a white background and lighter in relation to a black background—a contrast effect. Frame of reference effects were also noted by Festinger (1954) in his classic paper "Theory of social comparison processes," in which he introduced the term *social comparison*, noting that individuals tend to evaluate themselves by comparing their own opinions and abilities with those of others, and argued that this behavior is an essential aspect of human nature.

Emphasizing ASC in educational contexts, Marsh (1984b; see also Marsh & Parker, 1984; Marsh, Seaton, et al., 2008) proposed the BFLPE to capture frame of reference effects based on an integration of theoretical models and empirical research from diverse disciplines: relative deprivation theory (Davis, 1966; Stouffer, Suchman, DeVinney, Star, & Williams, 1949), sociology (Alwin & Otto, 1977; Hyman, 1942), psychophysical judgment (e.g., Helson, 1964; Marsh, 1974; Parducci, 1995; Wedell & Parducci, 2000), social judgment (e.g., Morse & Gergen, 1970; Sherif & Sherif, 1969; Upshaw, 1969), and SCT (Festinger, 1954). In this BFLPE model, Marsh hypothesized that students compare their abilities with the abilities of their classmates and use this social comparison impression as one basis for forming their own self-concept (Figure 1). The BFLPE is negative when equally able students have lower ASCs when they compare themselves with more able classmates, and higher ASCs when they compare themselves with less-able classmates. According to BFLPE predictions, ASC is positively affected by individual achievement (i.e., brighter students have higher self-concepts) and the path leading from individual ability to individual self-concept is substantial and positive (++ in Figure 1). However, ASC is negatively affected by school- or class-average achievement (i.e., the same student will have a lower ASC when class-average ability is high) and so the path from school- or class-average ability is negative. Hence, ASC is influenced by, not only the student's own academic accomplishments, but also the accomplishments of the student's classmates. Consistent with theoretical predictions and an increasing emphasis on the multidimensionality of self-concept (Marsh & Craven, 2006), the BFLPE in academic settings is specific to ASC; school- and class-average achievement has little positive or negative effect on nonacademic components of self-concept or on global self-esteem (e.g., Marsh, 1987; Marsh, Chessor, Craven, & Roche, 1995; Marsh & Parker, 1984; for a review, see Marsh, Seaton, et al. (2008)).

A series of predictions—some of which appeared to be paradoxical at the time (Marsh, 1984b; also see Marsh, Seaton, et al., 2008)—can be generated from this model. In particular the model predicts that:

1. ASC will be positively related to academic ability, which, of course, is not surprising;
2. school-average ASC will be similar in high-ability and low-ability schools;
3. school-average ability will be negatively related to ASC after controlling for individual ability;
4. ASC will be more highly correlated with individual ability after controlling for school-average ability;
5. ASC can be more accurately predicted from individual- and school-level ability than from either of these predictors considered separately;
6. the negative effect of school-average ability is specific to ASC and does not generalize to nonacademic components of self-concept (e.g., physical self-concept) and self-esteem; and
7. the frame of reference is established by school-average ability, so all students in a high-ability school are predicted to have lower ASCs than would the same students if they attended a low-ability school; thus, interactions between school-average and individual ability will be small or nonsignificant.

Although Marsh (1984b) provided at least preliminary support for each of these predictions, other aspects of the Marsh (1984b) results were not captured by this model. Expanding on this theoretical model, Marsh (1987) noted the negative effect of school-average ability is not the only plausible outcome. For example, being an average-ability student in a high-ability group of classmates may affect ASC such that it is (1) below average because the frame of reference is established by the performance of above-average students (i.e., a BFLPE or contrast effect), (2) above average as a consequence of membership in the high-ability grouping (i.e., a reflected glory, group identification, or assimilation effect), or (3) average because it is unaffected by the immediate context of the other students, or because (1) and (2) both occur and cancel each other. In this respect, the negative BFLPE actually observed could be the combined effects of a large negative (contrast) effect consistent with the social comparison emphasis of the model and a smaller positive (assimilation) effect.

Placing the model within a broader historical context, the BFLPE is a specific example of more general frame of reference effects that have a long history in psychology (see Sherif & Sherif, 1969). In BFLPE studies, the standard of comparison is operationalized to be the school-average ability level, consistent with more general models of frame of reference effects in psychophysics (e.g., Helson, 1964) and social psychology (e.g., Upshaw, 1969). Hence, within a single school (or a sample of schools that are homogeneous in relation to school-average ability), students evaluate themselves according to the same standard of comparison (i.e., school-average ability is constant). Nevertheless, this model does not incorporate the multiple frames of reference established by the school and by classes within schools—particularly in schools with ability streaming such that there might be competing frames of reference due to the school (school-average ability) and the class (class-average ability). Although it is easy to generalize the BFLPE model to classes instead of schools, the original model made no predictions about the relative importance of the school and the class (see subsequent discussion of Marsh, Kuyper, Morin, Parker, and Seaton (2014)).

Davis (1966) proposed a similar model to explain career aspirations of college men; why the academic quality of a college had so little effect on career aspirations. He proposed that attending a high-ability college would result in a lower school grades independent of individual academic ability, and that school grades influenced self-evaluations and, subsequently, career decisions. On the basis of his research, Davis concluded, "The aphorism 'It is better to be a big frog in a small pond than a small frog in a big pond' is not perfect advice, but it is not trivial" (p. 31). However, Davis could not fully test his model because he had no individual measures of academic ability and his main focus was on the influence of university grades on career aspirations. Also, it is unclear whether the critical mechanism in Davis' research was a frame of reference effect in which students compare their self-perceived academic ability with their perceptions of other students in their university—as posited in the BFLPE—or a grading-on-a-curve phenomenon such that teachers and schools assign grades to any one student relative to the accomplishments of other students with the same class or school (a focus of subsequent BFLPE research better suited to disentangling these competing interpretations).

4.2 Early Empirical Studies

Marsh and Parker (1984; Marsh, 1984b) first coined the phrase BFLPE and established the foundation for subsequent BFLPE research. Marsh (1984b; Marsh & Parker, 1984) initially reviewed studies of the relations between self-concept, academic achievement, and socioeconomic status (SES). Wylie (1979) had concluded that most studies of relations between global self-esteem and SES found weak positive relations, but noted two studies that reported paradoxical negative relations (Soares & Soares, 1969; Trowbridge, 1972). However, Marsh (1984b) noted that both these studies were based on school-average measures of SES rather than individual family SES, suggesting that the unit of analysis may be a critical issue.

Marsh and Parker (1984) found that when the effects of family SES and individual-student achievement were included in the same path model, there was a substantial negative effect of school-average SES on ASC. Marsh (1984b) argued that this was a more appropriate analysis in that for a given child, family SES and individual-student ability are controlled (i.e., held constant). Results indicated a pattern of results now known as the BFLPE: individual academic ability and ASC were positively related; and controlling for individual academic ability, the relation between school-average ability and ASC was negative. In other words, students of equal ability had lower ASCs in high-ability/high-SES schools than those in low-ability/low-SES schools. Although their initial focus was on school-average SES rather than school-average ability, these two school-average variables were so highly correlated (due in part to the small number of schools and the way in which schools were sampled) that their respective effects could not be differentiated. However, in subsequent research, Marsh (1987) was able to differentiate the effects with a much larger database (the Youth in Transition Study), showing that negative effects of school-average ability on ASC were substantially stronger than those based on school-average SES.

In related research, Jerusalem (1984) examined the self-concepts of German students who moved from nonselective primary schools to secondary schools that were streamed on the basis of academic achievement. At the transition point, students who would subsequently enter the high-ability schools had substantially higher ASCs than students who would subsequently enter the low-ability schools. However, by the end of the first year in the new schools there were no differences in ASCs for the two groups. In path analyses of these data, the direct influence of school type on ASC was negative.

However, apparently calling into question the finding of this early BFLPE research, Kulik and Kulik (1982) performed a meta-analysis to examine how ability grouping affected a range of issues for high school students. This study was not designed to evaluate the BFLPE or even frame of reference effects. Indeed, although their major focus was on academic achievement, for ASC they concluded that ability grouping had no effect. However, Marsh (1984a) proposed an alternative perspective based on his initial BFLPE research, arguing that their meta-analysis confounded the negative effects for students in high-ability groupings with the positive effects for students in low-ability groupings. Subsequently, Kulik (1985) reanalyzed their original results and considered the effects of high-ability and low-ability students separately, confirming Marsh's predictions. Hattie (2002; also see Trautwein, Lüdtke, Marsh, Köller, & Baumert, 2006; Trautwein, Lüdtke, Marsh, & Nagy, 2009) reviewed meta-analyses of ability-grouping research (including the Kulik and Kulik meta-analysis) and confirmed this pattern of results—a counterbalancing of positive effects in low-ability settings with negative effects in high-ability settings as predicted by BFLPE theory. Over the last three decades since these first BFLPE studies, there has been a large number of empirical studies in support of the broad generalizability of these findings, suggesting that the BFLPE is one of the most robust results in motivation science, educational psychology, and, perhaps, psychology more generally.

4.2.1 What are the Methodological Requirements for a BFLPE Study?

Following from this early theoretical and empirical research, the basic requirements for BFLPE studies are (see further discussion by Marsh, Seaton, et al. (2008) and Seaton and Marsh (2013))

- a multilevel design with many schools (or classes) and a substantial (representative or total) sample of students from each school;
- an objective measure of achievement for each individual student that is directly comparable over different schools and an appropriate measure of ASC, both of which are psychometrically strong; and
- tests of the effects of school-average achievement on ASC after controlling for effects of individual-student achievement

As the methodological sophistication of BFLPE research grew, these requirements expanded to include (1) latent-variable models that controlled measurement error with the use of multiple indicators of each construct, (2) multilevel models that controlled for the clustering effect of the hierarchical models (i.e., students nested within schools or classes), (3) models that controlled for sampling error (treating students within a school as a sample rather than a population), and (4) models that better disentangled the positive effects of achievement at the student level from the negative effects of achievement at the school- and class-level. Thus, a particularly important area of growth in BFLPE research has been the design of appropriate multilevel studies and the development of multilevel latent statistical models for evaluating BFLPEs.

5. EXTENDED EMPIRICAL SUPPORT FOR BFLPE GENERALIZABILITY

5.1 Is the BFLPE Nothing More than an Ephemeral Effect? Generalizability over Time

Some researchers have claimed that the BFLPE, particularly when based on cross-sectional data, is a short-term ephemeral effect, claiming that the lack of evidence of long-term stability of the BFLPE questions its very validity (Dai, 2004; Dai & Rinn, 2008). Marsh, Seaton, et al. (2008) reviewed a number of studies suggesting that the size of the BFLPE actually increased in size over time for students who remained in the same selective school setting. In the Marsh, Kong, and Hau (2000) longitudinal study, measures were taken prior to the start of high school and for the first three years of high school. Even after controlling the negative BFLPE from prior years, there were additional negative effects on school-average ability in each year of the study. Similarly, in the large U.S. High School and Beyond Study, Marsh (1991) demonstrated that for many outcomes there were new negative effects of school-average achievement at the end of high school even after controlling for those already experienced earlier in high school. Extending this work, two German studies (Marsh, Trautwein, Lüdtke, Baumert, & Köller, 2007) showed that the substantial BFLPE at the end of high school showed little or no diminution 2 years (Study 1) or 4 years (Study 2) after graduation from high school. Hence, the BFLPE is stable and persistent over time.

Particularly important in demonstrating the temporal development of the BFLPE is a study of the reunification of the East and West German school systems following the fall of the Berlin Wall (Marsh, Köller, & Baumert, 2001). Before unification, high-ability students in West Germany were educated in academically selective schools, but there was no ability grouping in East German schools. After unification, all students were segregated according to ability. At the beginning of the first school year following reunification, the BFLPE was not evident for the East German students and was significantly larger for the West German students. By the middle of the school year, the BFLPE had grown larger for the East German students, but was still not as large as that of the West German students. However, by the end of the year there was no difference between the East and West German students with the BFLPE being evident in both groups of students. Hence, as it took at least half a school year to take hold, it appears that the developmental trajectory of the BFLPE is a gradual, but a stable and insidious one.

5.2 Is the BFLPE Evident in Different Countries and Cultures? Cross-Cultural Generalizability

The answer to this question has important implications for BFLPE theory. One of the goals of cross-cultural research is to test the replicability of existing theories in other cultures, investigate new findings in diverse cultural contexts, and propose universal, pan-human theories (Segall, Lonner, & Berry, 1998). Research in different countries and cultures can reveal whether or not psychological constructs can be universally applied (Matsumoto, 2001) and, if they can, then their validity is greatly strengthened. As Schwartz and Bilsky (1990) noted, "Theories that aspire to universality…must be tested in numerous, culturally diverse samples" (p. 878). Cross-cultural support for the BFLPE would support its external validity and generalizability.

BFLPE studies have been conducted in an impressive array of countries and cultures, including Australia (e.g., Craven, Marsh, & Print, 2000; Marsh et al., 1995; Marsh & Parker, 1984; Seaton, Marsh, Yeung, & Craven, 2011), the USA (e.g., Marsh, 1987, 1991; Mulkey, Catsambis, Steelman, & Crain, 2005), Israel (Zeidner & Schleyer, 1998), Germany (Marsh et al., 2001, 2007), Hong Kong (Marsh et al., 2000), Singapore (Liem, Marsh, Martin, McInerney, & Yeung, 2013), France (Huguet et al., 2009), and Saudi Arabia (Marsh et al., 2013). However, Marsh, Seaton, et al. (2008) noted the need to pursue more carefully constructed cross-national comparisons in order to evaluate more fully the generalizability of support for the BFLPE. Strong cross-cultural studies of the BFLPE require the comparison of at least two—and preferably many—countries based on comparable samples, the same ASC instrument, and the same measures of achievement. Otherwise, apparent cross-cultural differences in BFLPEs based on separate studies conducted in single countries are likely to confound potential differences in the composition of samples being compared and, perhaps, the appropriateness of materials. Although these demanding standards for strong cross-cultural research are difficult to achieve, their achievement is greatly facilitated by studies based on the Program for International Student Assessment (PISA) and Trends in Math and Science Survey (TIMSS) databases.

5.2.1 PISA Studies of the BFLPE

There now exists very strong support for the cross-cultural generalizability of the BFLPE for high school students, based on successive data collections of the Organisation for Economic Cooperation and Development (OECD) PISA data. Marsh and Hau (2003) used the PISA 2000 data based on 103,558 15-year-old students from 26 predominantly industrialized

Western countries (Marsh, Hau, Artelt, Baumert, & Peschar, 2006). Using multilevel modeling, they found support for the BFLPE (positive effects of individual-student achievement on ASC, but negative effects of school-average achievement on ASC) for the total sample and in 24 of the 26 countries considered separately. Although there were significant differences between countries, the country-level variation in the negative effect of school-average achievement was small, thus supporting the cross-cultural generalizability of the BFLPE. However, the Marsh and Hau study contained mostly Western countries, so to address this limitation, Seaton, Marsh, and Craven (2009, 2010) used PISA 2003 (265,180 students, 10,221 schools, 41 countries), which included more collectivist and developing economies than PISA 2000. Of the 41 countries, 38 displayed a BFLPE. The three countries that did not display a BFLPE (Ireland, Korea, Iceland) were all economically developed and only one could be regarded as collectivist (Korea; Iceland could not be classified). Moreover, neither the country's cultural orientation, nor its stage of economic development moderated the BFLPE. Nagengast and Marsh (2012, 2013) used the PISA 2006 database in the largest cross-cultural study of the BFLPE undertaken to date, based on a larger sample of culturally and economically diverse countries than the previous two PISA studies. They showed that the BFLPE was evident in 50 of the 56 countries examined. Moreover, echoing Davis' (1996) study, they demonstrated a BFLPE for career aspirations, in that there was a negative relation between school-average achievement and future career intentions.

Summarizing the three BFLPE-PISA studies, Nagengast and Marsh (2012) reported that the effect of school-average achievement was negative in all but one of the 123 samples considered across the three studies, and significantly so in 114 samples. Taken together, these cross-cultural studies attest to the generalizability of the BFLPE. Hence, it is easy to see why Seaton et al. (2009) concluded that the BFLPE was a pan-human theory as it "is not only a symptom of developed countries and individualist societies, but it is also evident in developing nations and collectivist countries of the world" (p. 414).

5.2.2 TIMSS Studies of the BFLPE

Even though PISA is widely praised as perhaps the best database for making cross-national educational comparisons (e.g., Marsh, Hau, et al., 2006), it also has critics. For example, in their monograph on concerns related to PISA, Hopmann, Brinek, and Retzl (2007; also see Ertl, 2006) summarized a range of substantive, methodological, and policy-related concerns. These included the inappropriateness of the PISA model in respect of what is actually taught in many school systems, technical issues related to translation and scaling, problems with the sampling design, and PISA's focus on literacy in testing mathematics and science. Potential concerns such as these dictate that cross-cultural BFLPE research based almost exclusively on PISA data should be cross-validated with data from different sources. Hence, it was surprising that studies by Marsh and colleagues (Marsh, Abduljabbar, et al., 2014; Marsh et al., 2015) were apparently the first cross-cultural BFLPE studies based on the TIMSS data—the major competitor of PISA in terms of international comparisons in mathematics and science. Although there are many similarities between the two databases, PISA focuses more on the application of knowledge to "real-life" problems (Wu, 2009), while TIMSS focuses on achievement more closely linked to school curriculums which apparently explains why Western countries tended to perform better on PISA than TIMSS, while Eastern European and Asian countries tended to perform better on TIMSS than PISA.

In the first of these TIMSS BFLPE studies, Marsh, Abduljabbar, et al. (2014) considered samples of 8th-grade boys and girls from the US and Saudi Arabia. For standardized achievement test scores, there were substantial differences favoring US students. However, there were almost no gender differences in achievement for US students (in largely coed schools) but in the single-sex Saudi schools, girls outperformed boys. Nevertheless, consistent with previous cross-cultural research based primarily on PISA data (but not previously evaluated with TIMSS), in each of the four (2 gender × 2 country) groups, ASCs were positively influenced by individual-student achievement but negatively influenced by class-average achievement (the BFLPE). BFLPEs were similar in size for boys and girls in coeducational (United States) and in single-sex (Saudi) classrooms.

In the second of the TIMSS BFLPE studies, Marsh et al. (2015) considered nationally representative samples of 4th- and 8th-grade boys and girls (117,321 students from 6499 classes) from 6 Western countries (Australia, England, Italy, Norway, Scotland, and USA), 4 Asian countries (Hong Kong, Japan, Singapore, and Taiwan), and 3 Middle Eastern Islamic countries (Iran, Kuwait, Tunisia). This study is apparently the first TIMSS study to compare BFLPEs for matched samples of primary (4th grade) and secondary (8th grade) students, and the first to specifically compare BFLPE results in Middle Eastern Islamic countries with those from Asian and Western countries that have been the basis of most BFLPE research. Furthermore, although there have been some studies showing BFLPEs in primary schools (e.g., Jerusalem, 1984; Marsh et al., 1995; Marsh & Parker, 1984; Tymms, 2001), most large-scale studies are based on secondary schools and there has apparently been no previous rigorous research comparing BFLPEs in primary and secondary schools.

In support of the cross-cultural generalizability of the BFLPE, positive effects of individual-student achievement and negative effects of class-average achievement on ASC were significant for each of the 26 (13 countries × 2 age cohorts). Consistent with earlier research in Arab and Islamic countries (Marsh et al., 2013), Marsh et al. (2015) also found that individual-student achievement was less correlated with ASC in Middle Eastern Islamic countries, particularly for the younger age cohort. This is consistent with previous suggestions by these authors that students from these countries do not receive as much evaluative feedback about their achievement as Western and Asian students, and are not socialized in such a way as to critically evaluate their academic skills in relation to classmates. Indeed, there was also support for earlier speculations that ASC formation and its relation with achievement in Middle Eastern Islamic middle school students was similar to that found in younger students from Western countries. Thus, support for the BFLPE for 8th-grade Middle Eastern Islamic students was similar to that found for the 4th-grade cohort in the Western and Asian countries.

5.3 Individual Differences: Generalizability and Potential Moderators of the BFLPE

5.3.1 Moderation and Generalizability: Two Sides of the Same Coin

One approach to testing the generalizability of the BFLPE is to evaluate potential moderators—particularly those of sufficient strength to eliminate the BFLPE or even to change its direction (i.e., positive effects of school-average achievement for those with certain characteristics). Moderation is of course, a double-edged sword. Significant moderators contribute to understanding the nature of the BFLPE and are potentially heuristic in terms of reducing the negative consequences. However, the failure to find substantial moderators argues for the broad generalizability and robustness of the effects.

Seaton et al. (2010) examined the extent to which the BFLPE was moderated by each of 16 individual difference variables based on PISA 2003 data (41 countries, 10,221 schools, 265,180 students), including SES (parental occupation, parental education, home educational resources, and cultural possessions), individual ability, intrinsic and extrinsic motivation, self-efficacy, study methods (elaboration, memorization, and control strategies), anxiety, competitive and cooperative learning orientations, sense of school belonging, and student—teacher relationships. Results indicated that the BFLPE had small interactions with a number of these constructs. However, as the sample size was particularly large and many of the effects were small, most of the significant effects were not considered to be of practical importance, with the exception of three constructs. The BFLPE was more pronounced for highly anxious students, for those who used surface learning (memorization) as a learning strategy, and for those students who preferred to work cooperatively. However, the BFLPE was not moderated by individual-student ability, SES, intrinsic and extrinsic motivation, self-efficacy, elaboration and control learning strategies, competitive orientation, a sense of belonging to school, or relationship with teachers. Furthermore, none of the interactions was sufficiently large to eliminate the BFLPE (e.g., low-anxious students still suffered the BFLPE, but to a lesser extent than high-anxious students). The authors concluded the results attested to the broad generalizability of the BFLPE and suggested "students are more similar than different in relation to the BFLPE" (p. 36).

5.3.2 Academic Goal Theory

Wouters, Colpin, Van Damme, and Verschueren (2013) evaluated the extent to which the BFLPE varied as a function of individual-student and class-average constructs from achievement goal theory (mastery, performance-approach, and performance-avoidance goals; see Elliot & Church, 1997) for a large sample of Flemish Belgium students (N = 2987 grade 6 students from 174 elementary school classes). There was clear support for the BFLPE (class-average ES = −0.34). However, there were also small moderating effects of each of the individual achievement goal constructs such that students who more strongly endorsed any of these goals experienced larger BFLPEs (ESs of interactions = −0.07 to −0.10, indicating the negative effect of class-average ability became more negative when achievement goal constructs were higher). The authors suggested that students who are more academically engaged are more susceptible to BFLPEs, regardless of their purposes for being engaged. However, somewhat surprisingly, when all three achievement goals were included in the same model, mastery goals were the only goal that significantly interacted with class-average ability (ESs = −0.07). Nevertheless, whether considered individually or in combination, the moderator effects were small relative to the substantial BFLPE; on average, students high or low in relation to each of the achievement goals all experienced BFLPEs. In contrast to the individual-student goal constructs, interactions between each of the three corresponding class-average values of these constructs and class-average achievement were all statistically nonsignificant. Importantly, however, these class-level constructs reflected contextual variables (the average value of students in each class) rather than climate variables (student perceptions of the classroom climate, representing, perhaps, individual differences in teaching styles; see discussion by Marsh et al. (2012)).

Cheng, McInerney, and Mok (2014) also evaluated whether the BFLPE was moderated by any of seven goal orientations (intrinsic: task, effort, social concern, affiliation; extrinsic: competition, social power, praise, and token) for a large sample of Hong Kong high school students (N = 7334 students from 201 math classes). Again they found a substantial BFLPE (ES = −0.62). Although all but one of the goal orientations (affiliation) interacted significantly with the negative effect of class-average ability, they concluded that the sizes of these moderating effects were very small (−0.06 to −0.09). However, they noted that they predicted that BFLPEs would be smaller, not larger, for students with a more intrinsic goal orientation. Similar to Wouters et al. (2013), they suggested "students who were more motivated in general, irrespective of the types of goal orientation, experienced stronger BFLPE" (pp. 575—576).

5.3.3 Personality

Of course, not all moderators are of practical significance. Thus, for example, Jonkmann, Becker, Marsh, Lüdtke, and Trautwein (2012) evaluated the extent to which the BFLPE is moderated by personality traits (i.e., Big Five personality traits and narcissism). Consistent with a priori predictions, highly narcissistic students (i.e., those with exaggerated feelings of superiority, self-importance, and grandiosity) experienced significantly smaller BFLPEs. However, even here the size of the interaction was small relative to the size of the BFLPE, such that highly narcissistic students still experienced the BFLPE—albeit to a lesser extent than nonnarcissistic students. Indeed, the results offer support for the construct validity of the theoretical model underlying the BFLPE, in that students predicted to be less affected by the relative performances of their classmates experienced significantly smaller BFLPEs. However, obviously the results do not translate into intervention programs to counter the BFLPE through fostering a counterproductive construct such as narcissism.

5.3.4 Individual-Student Ability

Perhaps the most extensive research on moderators of the BFLPE has focused on individual-student ability, exploring whether high ability is a protective factor. Indeed, the theoretical debate regarding this substantive issue of whether the BFLPE is moderated by individual-student achievement (e.g., Coleman & Fults, 1985; Marsh, Kuyper, et al., 2014; Marsh, Seaton, et al., 2008) has important policy/practice implications for gifted education research. For example, if the negative effects of the BFLPE are limited largely to less-able students, as suggested by Coleman and Fults, and more able students are actually benefited by selective schooling policies, then the results argue for a more careful screening of students, rather than problems with selective schooling per se. However, according to the theoretical model underpinning the BFLPE (Marsh, 1984b, 2007; also see Marsh, Seaton, et al., 2008) the frame of reference is largely determined by class/school-average achievement, which is necessarily the same for all students within a given school or class. This theoretical rationale is similar to that in classical psychophysical models such as Helson's (1964) adaptation level theory. Thus, the BFLPE should be similar for the brightest and the weakest students within a given class or school. Consistent with these theoretical predictions, a growing body of empirical research (Marsh, 1984b; Marsh, Kuyper, et al., 2014; Marsh, Seaton, et al., 2008) shows that interactions between school-average and individual-student achievement are consistently small or nonsignificant, and not even consistent in direction—that bright, average, and less-bright students experience negative BFLPEs to a similar extent.

5.3.5 Age

A majority of BFLPE studies, and the strongest support for the effect, come from studies at the secondary level—particularly the PISA and TIMSS studies reviewed earlier. However, even within secondary schools, longitudinal research reviewed earlier suggests that the size of the BFLPE grows larger the longer students remain in the same secondary school, and are stable in size 2 and 4 years after graduation from high school. Nevertheless, there are a number of studies showing the BFLPE in primary schools, including the original BFLPE studies by Marsh and Parker (1984; also see Craven et al., 2000) and Marsh et al. (1995). Indeed, Tymms (2001) found support for a small but significant BFLPE in UK students as young as 7 years of age. Nevertheless, the cross-cultural TIMSS study (Marsh et al., 2015) is apparently the strongest research showing that the BFLPE is evident in both primary (4th grade) and secondary (8th grade) students across Western, Asian, and Middle Eastern Islamic countries.

5.3.6 Teaching Style

Most studies of potential moderators of the BFLPE have focused on individual-student characteristics, but few have considered its generalizability in relation to individual differences in teachers or teaching styles. Although there is limited research addressing this issue, it has important relevance to designing interventions to counter the negative effects of the BFLPE. Addressing this issue, Lüdtke, Köller, Marsh, and Trautwein (2005) hypothesized that an individualized teacher frame of reference that emphasized feedback to students in terms of improvement in relation to prior achievement, effort, and learning would enhance self-concept and reduce the negative BFLPEs. Teacher frame of reference was independently assessed by student ratings of their teacher and ratings by two trained observers. Multilevel analyses confirmed the BFLPE. However, while teacher frame of reference effects were similar when based on student ratings and observations, and led to enhanced ASC at the individual-student level, it they did not moderate the negative BFLPE.

5.4 Generalizability of BFLPEs to Other Constructs

Other important educational outcomes have been the focus of BFLPE studies. For example, Craven et al. (2000) showed that primary students in gifted and talented classes had significantly lower motivation levels than those in streamed and mixed-ability classes. Xu (2012) demonstrated the existence of the BFLPE for importance, effort persistence, and rehearsal, elaboration, and control strategies. The negative BFLPE has also been found for academic interest (intrinsic value, personal importance, and attainment value; Trautwein et al., 2006). However, perhaps the most important study was the early Marsh (1991) study of the implications of the BFLPE for variables particularly selected to represent most of the important outcomes of education, addressing the question of "So what?"—So what if students have lower ASCs in academically selective schools?

5.4.1 So What if Students Have Lower ASCs in Academically Selective Schools?

The strong, consistent support for the BFLPE is of great interest to self-concept researchers in relation to understanding the formation of ASC and for testing frame of reference models. However, parents, classroom teachers, and policy makers might ask: So what? What are the consequences of attending high–ability schools on other academic outcomes and how are these related to ASC? In addressing these issues, Marsh (1991) evaluated the effect of school–average ability on the major outcomes of education and the role of ASC and educational aspirations formed early in high school as mediators of the effects of school–average ability on subsequent outcomes. The High School and Beyond database is well suited for this purpose because it is very large (more than 1000 randomly selected high schools with approximately 30 randomly selected students from each school), national representative of the United States, and longitudinal, consisting of responses by the same high school students when they were in year 10 (sophomores), year 12 (seniors), and 2 years after the normal graduation from high school. The major components of the path analysis (see Figure 2) in this research were (1) individual-student and school-average measures of academic ability (a standardized test battery) and SES; (2) ASC and self-esteem, academic choice behavior (advanced coursework selection), academic effort (class

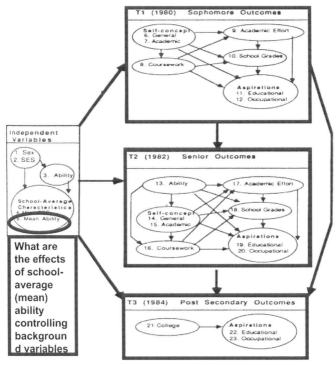

Figure 2 Testing the implications of the big-fish-little-pond-effect, the effect of school-average ability (mean ability), on a diverse range of educational outcomes collected in Year 10 (sophomore year of high school, Time 1), Year 12 (senior year of high school, Time 2), and 2 years after the normal graduation from high school (Time 3). *Adapted with permission from Marsh (2007).*

preparation, time spent on homework), school grades, educational aspirations, and occupational aspirations measured at T1 and T2, and (3) university attendance, educational aspirations, and occupational aspirations at T3.

The path model including all these outcome variables is complex, but the key findings are easy to summarize. The effects of school-average ability were negative for almost all of the year 10, year 12, and postsecondary outcomes; 15 of the 17 effects were significantly negative and 2 were not statistically significant. Even though it might be argued that most of the important outcome variables in educational research were included in the High School and Beyond database, the effect of school-average ability was not positive for a single outcome. School-average ability most negatively affected ASC as in the BFLPE studies and educational aspirations as in the school-context studies.

In summary, equally able students attending high-ability high schools selected less-demanding coursework and had lower ASCs, lower school grades, lower educational aspirations, and lower occupational aspirations in both year 10 and year 12. Attending high-ability schools also had negative effects on standardized test scores in the final year of high school and on subsequent university attendance, although these effects were smaller. For many year 10 and postsecondary outcomes, there were statistically significant negative effects of school-average ability even after controlling the substantial negative effects in year 10 outcomes; and new, additional negative effects of school-average ability during the last 2 years of high school beyond the already substantial negative effects found early in high school. These results are consistent with previous research but are more compelling because of the High School and Beyond's large sample size, diversity of academic outcomes, and longitudinal nature.

5.4.2 Generalizability of the BFLPE to Other (Nonacademic) Domains

Importantly, the BFLPE has been extended beyond the academic domain to the physical sphere (Beasley, 2013; Marsh & Cheng, 2012; Trautwein, Gerlach, & Lüdtke, 2008). Noting an absence of BFLPE studies in relation to elite athletes, Marsh and Perry (2005) speculated that there might be a BFLPE affecting the physical self-concept (PSC) of elite athletes participating in selective sport programs but recognized "Tests of this suggestion and an evaluation of implications if support is found are clearly beyond the scope of the present chapter, but provide an important area for further research" (Marsh & Perry, 2005, p. 80). Subsequently, several studies evaluated the BFLPE with nonelite athletes. In support of the BFLPE based on responses by 405 students in 20 gymnastics classes, Chanal, Marsh, Sarrazin, and Bois (2005) found the gymnastics self-concept was positively predicted by individual gymnastics skills, but was negatively predicted by class-average gymnastics skills. The size of this BFLPE (i.e., the negative impact of the class-average skills) grew more negative during the 10-week training program (as participants had more exposure to the relative performances of others in their class), but did not vary as a function of gender, age, or initial gymnastics skills. Beasley (2013) demonstrated that class-average physical ability in physical education classes had a negative effect on PSC. Girls had lower PSCs than boys, but, contrary to her predictions, class type (single-sex vs coeducational) did not moderate the BFLPE. Trautwein et al. (2008) likewise demonstrated that class-average physical ability had negative effects on PSC for a large sample of primary school children of 9 and 10 years of age. Furthermore, the negative effect of class-average physical ability led to subsequent declines in out-of-school physical activity that was substantially mediated by the declines in PSC. In apparently the only study actually based on elite athletes, Marsh, Morin, and Parker (in press) used a novel longitudinal cohort-sequence design to evaluate PSCs of elite athletes and nonathletes attending a selective sports high school. Consistent with the BFLPE, PSCs at the start of high school were much higher for elite athletes than for nonathlete classmates, but the differences declined gradually over time so that by the end of high school there were no differences in the two groups.

5.5 Explicit Tracking: BFLPEs for Gifted and Academically Disadvantaged Students

Much of the support for the BFLPE is based on de facto selection processes that result in naturally occurring differences between schools and classes in terms of school- or class-average achievement. However, a number of studies have also considered explicit tracking in which students are specifically selected to attend special schools, classes, or programs for academically gifted or disadvantaged students. Hence, a critical issue with important theoretical, substantive, and policy implications is whether these results based on de facto selection generalize to settings in which students are specifically selected to be in classes and schools with other students of similar abilities—as in the case of ability grouping, streamed classes, and academically selective schools. Importantly, the results have important implications at both ends of the ability continuum as ASC has been a critical variable in research on the effects of tracking and ability grouping for both academically gifted and academically disadvantaged students. Indeed, following Marsh's (1984b) critique of the

Kulik and Kulik (1982) meta-analysis on the effects of streaming, the Kulik (1985) reanalysis confirmed Marsh's predictions based on the BFLPE: bright students tended to have lower self-concepts when in streamed classes with other bright students (compared with equally able students in unstreamed classes); and less-able students had higher self-concepts when placed in streamed classes with other less-able students.

In a unique, quasi-experimental approach to the effect of track on the BFLPE, Wouters, De Fraine, Colpin, Van Damme, and Verschueren (2012) evaluated the effects of changing tracks in a multilevel longitudinal growth study over high school (grades 7—12) in a large sample of Belgian students (N = 2747, 50 high schools). Consistent with BFLPE predictions, students who changed from a higher track to a lower track had higher ASCs that were stable over time. The effect did not vary as of function of individual achievement levels, but was somewhat larger when the change occurred later in high school.

5.5.1 The BFLPE and Academically Gifted Students

As noted earlier, the Kulik (1985) reanalysis of their meta-analysis of ability streaming for high-ability and gifted students showed that this strategy had a negative effect on ASC, confirming Marsh's (1984b) predictions based on the BFLPE. Extending this research based on two BFLPE studies of gifted and talented primary school classes, Marsh et al. (1995) used pretest data (age, sex, IQ) collected prior to the intervention to match students who subsequently moved to gifted and talented classes with students from mixed-ability classes. In both studies, students in the gifted program experienced significant declines in all three domains of ASC over time and in relation to matched comparison students. In both studies, this general pattern of results was reasonably consistent across gender, age, and initial ability. Also consistent with a priori predictions, participation in gifted programs had little or no effect on non-ASC or global self-esteem.

In one of the studies, Marsh et al. (1995) collected self-concept measures on only two occasions so that there was no way to determine when the decline occurred within the time period. In the other study, however, measures were collected on three occasions. Here there was a decline between the first two occasions, but there were also new, additional declines between the last two occasions. Hence, the BFLPE was not a short-term adjustment effect but continued to grow larger over the first year in the gifted and talented setting. The negative effect on ASC for students participating in special gifted and talented classes was replicated in subsequent research by

Craven et al. (2000). In summary, these results replicate those based on the Kulik (1985) meta-analysis showing that participation in high-ability streams has a negative effect on ASCs.

5.5.2 The BFLPE and Academically Disadvantaged Students

BFLPE studies have mostly focused on the negative effects of ability grouping, tracking, and school/class-average achievement on ASC of high-ability students who attend high-ability schools and classes, but the BFLPE also has important theoretical and practical implications for less-able students in low-ability tracks or special schools/classes for academically disadvantaged students. Mainstreaming is an increasingly common practice of integrating academically disadvantaged students into regular, mixed-ability classes based loosely on implications of labeling theory. Labeling theory predicts that placing students with learning difficulties in special classes will undermine their self-concepts. However, Marsh, Tracey, & Craven (2006; see also Tracey, Marsh, & Craven, 2003) argued that there is little or no empirical support for these predictions. Importantly, BFLPE theory makes the opposite predictions that academically disadvantaged students will have higher self-concepts when grouped with other academically disadvantaged students (compared with similarly disadvantaged students in regular classroom settings). Indeed, in response to Marsh's (1984b) critique, the Kulik (1985) reanalysis of the Kulik and Kulik meta-analysis showed that streaming academically disadvantaged students into special classes and schools had positive effects on ASC compared with placing academically disadvantaged students into mainstream classes.

Marsh, Tracey, et al. (2006; see also Tracey et al., 2003) specifically tested predictions based on the BFLPE and labeling theory for 211 children in grades 2−6 with mild intellectual disabilities (IQs of 56−75). Compared with mainstreamed students, those in the special classes had significantly higher ASCs (consistent with BFLPE predictions) as well as higher peer self-concepts. Clearly, disadvantaged students in regular mixed-ability classes did not feel as included as proponents of the inclusion movement had hoped. There were no differences in the other non-ASC domains (parents, physical ability, and physical appearance). These Australian results were consistent with earlier German results by Rheinberg and Enstrup (1977). Based on a sample of 165 students with moderate learning disabilities (IQs of 70−85), students in the special schools had higher ASCs and achievement motivation, as well as lower test anxiety than those in mainstream classes. Similarly, in a UK study, Crabtree (2003) found support for BFLPE predictions in that integrating academically disadvantaged students into comprehensive classes resulted in lower ASCs. These findings are further supported by meta-analytic findings that academically disadvantaged students have substantially lower ASCs than other students, but such deficits are substantially reduced if disadvantaged students are placed in fully segregated classes with other disadvantaged students (Chapman, 1988; also see Hattie, 2002). In summary, mainstreaming has potentially negative consequences for the academic and social self-concepts of academically disadvantaged students, suggesting that integration policies should be reconsidered. Appropriate strategies are needed to counter these negative effects of inclusion on ASC rather than accepting the largely unsupported inference from labeling theory that the effects of inclusion on ASC are positive.

6. NEW THEORETICAL DIRECTIONS: INTEGRATING THE BFLPE WITH ALTERNATIVE THEORETICAL PERSPECTIVES

6.1 Local Dominance Effects: Class versus School Social Comparison Processes

Support for the BFLPE is based largely on studies of school-average achievement, but other studies also show a similar effect based on class-average achievement (Marsh, 2007; Marsh, Seaton, et al., 2008; Seaton & Marsh, 2013). However, there has been almost no research comparing the relative sizes of BFLPEs associated with class and school levels even though this distinction has important theoretical and policy/practice implications (Liem et al., 2013). Zell and Alicke (2009; see also Alicke, Zell, & Bloom, 2010) provided support for the BFLPE by experimentally manipulating the frame of reference in relation to feedback given to participants about their performances compared with others. Although support for frame of reference effects like those posited in the BFLPE based on random assignment to conditions is important in its own right, their focus was on the comparison standards used by students. When they pitted "local" against more "general" comparison standards, participants consistently used the most local comparison information available to them, even when they were told that the local comparison was not representative of the broader population and were provided with more appropriate normative comparison data.

Translating the local dominance effect into the BFLPE, because class-average achievement is a more proximally relevant frame of reference than the school-average achievement, class-average achievement should be more locally dominant. Indeed, a complete local dominance effect would predict that there would be little or no effect of school-average ability once the effects of class-average ability were controlled. Marsh, Kuyper, et al. (2014; see subsequent discussion of this study) tested local dominance predictions in a large, nationally representative study of Dutch schools. Importantly, in the Dutch school system, there are substantial differences between schools in relation school-average ability, but there are also well-defined streams within each school. Support for the local dominance effect in BFLPE studies was found by Marsh, Kuyper, et al. in that BFLPEs were evident for both class-average and school-average achievement when each was considered separately, although class-average effects were substantially larger. However when both sources of social comparison information were included in the same model, the effect of school-average achievement on ASC was no longer significant, absorbed into the locally dominant effect of class-average achievement. Hence, these results support the integration of the local dominance effect into BFLPE theory.

6.2 SCT: Juxtaposition with the BFLPE

6.2.1 Social Comparison Theory

As noted earlier the BFLPE has a wide-ranging theoretical base which incorporates psychophysical judgment, social judgment, sociology, relative deprivation, as well as SCT. However, the role that social comparison plays in the BFLPE has been the subject of extensive debate (e.g., Dai & Rinn, 2008; Marsh, Seaton, et al., 2008) and subsequent research attempting to integrate these theoretical perspectives and juxtaposing apparently conflicting results.

The focus of many SCT studies has been on the specific individual comparison target (e.g., Aspinwall & Taylor, 1993; Lockwood & Kunda, 1997). There is evidence to suggest, however, that comparisons are not always made with a specific target in mind. Individuals can also compare their achievements with a generalized other (e.g., an average mark or a typical person; Marsh, Trautwein, Lüdtke, & Köller, 2008) in a way that is more in line with BFLPE theory. Diener and Fujita (1997) reviewed BFLPE research in relation to the broader SCT literature, largely based on social psychological research stemming from Festinger (1954; also see Suls, 1977; Suls & Wheeler, 2000). They emphasized that BFLPE studies provided the clearest support for predictions based on SCT in what they referred to as an imposed social comparison paradigm because "schools more nearly approximate 'total environments' (strongly controlling the information that the individual receives about the distribution of academic abilities, and also emphasizing feedback that has primarily a comparative meaning) than the environments examined in other comparison studies" (p. 351). Thus, their theoretical rationale was that the frame of reference, based on classmates within the same school setting, was more clearly defined in BFLPE research than in most SCT studies. Their review provides strong support for the generalizability of the BFLPE for ASC and its relevance to SCT.

A major distinction between most SCT in social psychological research and BFLPE studies in educational settings is on the source of social comparison information. In BFLPE studies, the standard of comparison is posited to be a generalized other, operationalized as school- or class-average achievement. The process is implicit in that students are not explicitly instructed to make comparisons with other students. In most SCT studies using some variation of the rank-order paradigm (Suls & Wheeler, 2000; Wheeler, 1966), the focus is on a specific target person whom the participant explicitly chooses (e.g., Blanton, Buunk, Gibbons, & Kuyper, 1999; Diener & Fujita, 1997; Huguet, Dumas, Monteil, & Genestoux, 2001; Wheeler, 1966). The process is explicit in that participants are instructed to choose a target comparison person. SCT researchers focus on the strategies used to select comparison targets: someone who is performing better (an upward comparison) or worse (a downward comparison). SCT research suggests that when people wish to evaluate their abilities accurately, they do so by comparing themselves with similar others who are performing slightly better than themselves (e.g., Collins, 2000; Wood, 1989). However, SCT researchers note that upward comparisons can be both inspiring and deflating, leading researchers to describe social comparisons as a "double-edged sword" (Major, Testa, & Bylsma, 1991, p. 238; see also Buunk, Collins, Taylor, VanYperen, & Dakof, 1990; Diener & Fujita, 1997; Taylor, Buunk, & Aspinwall, 1990).

6.2.2 SCT Challenges of the BFLPE and BFLPE Challenges of SCT

In school-based research, several studies suggest that upward comparisons are associated with better academic performance. For example, Blanton et al. (1999) asked Dutch high school students to nominate the student in each of seven academic subjects with whom they preferred to compare their grades. Performance and comparison direction were assessed using school grades at three points during the academic year. Students also completed a measure of comparative evaluation, whereby they compared their academic abilities with those of their classmates in all seven subjects. They found that students compared themselves with other students who slightly outperformed them academically, and that controlling for prior grades, these upward comparisons predicted higher subsequent grades. Although students' own grades predicted comparative evaluation in all seven subjects, choosing to compare themselves with a more able student, however, had no effect on self-evaluations. Consistently with Blanton et al. (1999), Huguet et al. (2001) also demonstrated that French students compared themselves with close friends who were slightly outperforming them academically, and that these upward comparisons were predictive of higher subsequent grades. With the exception of one academic subject, Huguet et al. also offered evidence that comparing with someone performing better had no effect on one's self-evaluations.

Herein lies an apparent discrepancy. According to the BFLPE, students in high-ability schools have lower ASCs because the school-average ability is high, unlike high-ability students in average- or low-ability schools. Thus, while implicit upward comparisons had negative effects on ASC in BFLPE studies, explicit upward comparisons in SCT studies (Blanton et al., 1999; Huguet et al., 2001) led to improve academic performance and had little or no effect on self-evaluations. This apparent conflict was first highlighted by Wheeler and Suls (2004) who challenged Marsh to explain these divergent findings (J. Suls, personal communication, September 11, 2003). In response to Suls (but also sent to Blanton et al. and to Huguet et al.), Marsh (personal communication, November 12, 2003) noted that the Blanton et al. (1999) and Huguet et al. (2001) studies did not specifically evaluate ASC at all, and in particular did not include a measure of class- or school-average achievement based on a common metric, which is central to tests of the BFLPE. In fact, neither study provided a test of the BFLPE nor how it related to social comparison processes which were evaluated in these two studies. Noting that class-average differences in school grades had been scaled away either by standardizing grades or by centering the effects separately within each class, Marsh suggested that a BFLPE might be evident for self-evaluations (the closest available approximation to ASC) if a suitable measure of class-average achievement were available. Marsh emphasized that these were not criticisms of the original studies in that they were not intended to test the BFLPE, but that it was not appropriate to argue that they contradicted the BFLPE findings.

Independently, each of these research teams contacted Marsh and suggested ways in which his proposed reanalyses might be undertaken. Based on a collaborative synergy involving all the players in this scenario, data from both these studies were reanalyzed using more sophisticated (multilevel latent variable) analyses in relation to predictions from the BFLPE proposed by Marsh in his original response to Wheeler and Suls (Seaton et al., 2008). Results confirmed previous findings in that selecting a more able student as a comparison target predicted improved subsequent performance. The selection of upward comparison targets had no effect on self-evaluations in the reanalysis of the Blanton et al. (1999) data, but had some small positive effects for the Huguet et al. (2001) data. However, as emphasized by the BFLPE, school-average ability (an implicit comparison based on a generalized other as represented by class- or school-average achievement) had a negative effect on self-evaluations. This led these authors to conclude that the positive effects of selecting individual upward comparisons on performance coexisted with the negative effects on self-evaluations of implicit comparisons with the class-average achievement—the BFLPE.

Marsh, Trautwein, et al. (2008) integrated the BFLPE with SCT, juxtaposing effects based on an implicit generalized other (operationalized as class-average achievement, consistent with BFLPE studies) and a specific explicit other (operationalized as direction of comparison with a freely chosen target person, consistent with SCT studies). Following from the BFLPE (but possibly not from SCT), they hypothesized both class-average achievement and upward comparison targets to have negative effects on ASC in this German study. However, they noted that the basis for predictions for the chosen target persons had less empirical support from previous research than that based on class-average achievement. After completing a standardized test, students nominated the student whose test booklet they would like to see and responded to the item asking whether the chosen target comparison person was "(1) better than you? (2) not as good as you? (3) similar achievement level?" There was support for both predictions negative effects on ASC of both class-average achievement and upward comparison targets considered separately and even when both were included in the same model. The results suggest that the individual comparison was not just a "noisy" reflection of the class-average based on all students and that individuals might simultaneously evaluate themselves in relation to both sources of comparison.

There still remained the question as to why the effect of upward comparisons on ASC was clearly negative in the Marsh, Trautwein, et al. (2008) study, but nonsignificant or even positive in the Blanton et al. (1999) and Huguet et al. (2001) studies. In both the French and Dutch studies, the direction of comparison was inferred on the basis of differences in school grades for the target and comparison students, whereas in the

German study the difference was based on the target student's perception of the difference. In the French and Dutch studies, it is unknown whether the target student's perception actually agreed with the differences in grades that were used to infer the direction of the comparison. However, given the typical optimistic bias in self-perceptions, it is likely that target students overestimate their own ability relative to that of other students (also see Seaton et al., 2008). In the German study, the researchers did not actually know whether target student self-perceptions about differences between them and comparison students were accurate in relation to objective measures of achievement. However, student self-perceptions—whether accurate or not—must be more important in determining their self-concepts than inferences about student self-perceptions based on objective measures. Clearly, there is need for further research that more fully explores this distinction between comparisons based on an implicit generalized other or school/class-average achievement, explicit target comparisons using objective measures to infer the direction of differences, and explicit target comparison using student self-perceptions to infer the direction of differences.

In further collaboration by this extended research team, Marsh et al. (2010) explored alternative explanations of the apparently positive effect of upward comparisons on subsequent academic achievement in the French (Huguet et al., 2001) and Dutch (Blanton et al., 1999) studies. To recap, both studies had found that students tended to choose comparison targets who slightly outperformed them (i.e., upward comparison choices) and that this had an apparently beneficial effect on subsequent performance: the performance levels of the comparison target had a positive effect on subsequent achievement after controlling for pretest achievement. The results were interpreted as support for SCT and only tangentially relevant to the BFLPE, although even predictions from SCT are actually ambiguous as upward comparisons in SCT is seen as a double-edged sword.

However, Marsh et al. (2010) hypothesized an alternative explanation for these findings. They showed that this apparently beneficial effect was due, at least in part, to the failure to control for unreliability in manifest variables (based on multiple regression) typically used in SCT research and how this bias can be controlled with appropriate latent-variable multilevel SEM models used in BFLPE research. In reanalyses of the Blanton et al. (1999) and Huguet et al. (2001) studies (Studies 1 and 2) Marsh et al. showed that introducing increasing amounts of random noise (measurement error) to pretest measures of achievement systematically increased the apparent size of the positive social comparison effect even though the results were necessarily due to the failure to correct for unreliability. In Study 3, based on simulated data in which the social comparison effect was known to be zero, they showed that manifest variable models all resulted in statistically significant positive effects of upward comparison that were as large or larger than those found in previous research, depending on the (simulated) unreliability of the measured variables. However, for all levels of simulated unreliability, latent-variable models appropriately identified the social comparison effect to be zero. In Studies 4 and 5, latent-variable models were applied to the Blanton et al. and Huguet et al. data, resulting in substantially smaller but still significantly positive effects. Although this set of studies could not establish under what conditions a positive social comparison effect might be expected and how much of the positive effects of upward comparisons found elsewhere could be explained by this statistical artifact (referred to as the phantom social comparison effect), the studies further established the need for latent-variable multilevel models in SCT studies like those in BFLPE research.

6.2.3 Integration of SCT and BFLPE

Following their earlier study, Huguet et al. (2009) extended their original French (Huguet et al., 2001) study and addressed limitations noted by Seaton et al. (2008; e.g., stronger statistical models, appropriate ASC measure, and standardized test scores as well as school grades). Also, following Marsh et al. (2007), they asked individual students to compare their ability with that of their comparison target. Once again, a BFLPE emerged. Addressing the concern that there was no direct evidence that social comparison underpins the BFLPE, Huguet et al. specifically asked students how they compared with other students—what we hereafter refer to as "me versus class" (meVclass) ratings. Huguet et al. demonstrated that the BFLPE largely disappeared when meVclass direct (or "pure") measures of social comparison were controlled, providing apparently the first direct evidence that social comparison underpins the BFLPE. As Huguet et al. concluded, the BFLPE "is rooted in how students compare with their class taken as a whole, a comparison which proved to be more invidious as class average ability increased" (p. 26).

Interestingly, Huguet et al. (2009) found that individual–chosen comparisons were positively associated with ASC, indicating that the BFLPE coexisted with these assimilative comparisons. However, consistent with Marsh et al. (2007), when students' comparative rating of their comparison target as better or worse than they were was included in the model, the effect of upward comparison was significantly negative. Consistent with the interpretation by Marsh, Trautwein, et al., these results suggest that positive assimilation effects in earlier SCT were based on the use of objective differences between students and their comparison target rather than subjective differences as actually perceived by students. However, alternative interpretations still exist. Because perceived differences seem more relevant than objective differences in terms of both SCT and BFLPE research, these results suggest that the earlier findings were an artifact of not using perceived differences. However, Huguet et al. (2009) suggested that the effect might be due to making the difference more salient by asking students to make comparison ratings, leading them to conclude "it seems that students can benefit from high comparison-level choices only when they do not think about their targets in a way that might make them feel worse by comparison…that contrast occurred only when students were forced to self-evaluate against their comparison targets" (p. 166). Clearly this is an area in need of further research.

Marsh, Kuyper, et al. (2014) extended the original Blanton et al. (1999) study, addressed limitations noted by Seaton et al. (2008), tackled new issues raised by Huguet et al. (2009), and integrated new theoretical and methodological perspectives into BFLPE theory. Consistent with previous research and prior predictions (see earlier discussion), Marsh, Kuyper et al. found that individual-student achievement did not moderate the BFLPE (high-achieving and low-achieving students experienced similar BFLPEs). A key finding of the Marsh, Kuyper study was support for predictions based on the local dominance effect (Zell & Alicke, 2009; see earlier discussion). Based on new (latent three-level) statistical models and theoretical predictions integrating BFLPEs and local dominance effects, significantly negative BFLPEs at the school level were largely eliminated, absorbed into even larger BFLPEs at the class level. Students accurately perceived large achievement differences between different classes within their school and across different schools. However, consistent with the local dominance effect, ASCs and the BFLPE were largely determined by comparisons with students in their own class, not objective or subjective comparisons with other classes or schools. Because the majority of BFLPE studies have been conducted at the school rather than the class level, these results suggest that many studies have underestimated the size of the BFLPE.

6.2.4 School Grades, Grading-on-a-Curve and the BFLPE
Marsh, Kuyper, et al. (2014) also made an important contribution to disentangling the effects of school marks from test scores in the BFLPE. The

requirement that the achievement in BFLPE studies varies along a common metric provides an important dilemma for applied researchers as typically class marks are the most readily available measures of achievement. Indeed, Marsh (1987, 2007) provided a theoretical rationale for why class marks, compared with standardized test scores, provides a more salient, local source of feedback to students about their accomplishments and tends to be substantially more correlated with ASCs. However, teachers tend to grade-on-a-curve such that the best and worst students in each class tend to get the highest and lowest grades independent of the average ability levels of students within each class and class marks tend to be somewhat idiosyncratic to particular subjects and individual teachers. Hence, class marks are typically not appropriate for evaluating the BFLPE.

Marsh, Kuyper, et al. (2014) considered both standardized test scores (providing a common metric across all students, classes, and schools) and class marks (providing a more proximal measure of achievement that is more strongly related to ASC than test scores), allowing them to juxtapose BFLPEs and grading-on-a-curve effects. Consistent with previous research (e.g., Marsh, 1987; Marsh & Rowe, 1996), the inclusion of class marks into BFLPE models contributed substantially to the prediction of ASCs, reduced the positive effects of test scores at the individual-student level, and reduced the negative effects of class-average test scores (the BFLPE), but the negative effect of school-average ability persisted even after controlling for class marks. Hence grading-on-a-curve contributes to, and is one of the processes leading to the BFLPE, but does not completely explain the BFLPE. However, effects of grading-on-a-curve in the formation of class marks is also another manifestation of social comparison effects in which students within the same class are ranked relative to each other. Thus, when asked to compare themselves with their classmates ("meVclass") and these ratings were included into the BFLPE models, the addition of class marks had substantially less effect on ASCs and no longer led to further reductions in the size of BFLPEs. Thus, class marks apparently act as relatively pure measures of social comparison in the formation of the BFLPE.

7. METHODOLOGICAL INNOVATION AND THE BFLPE

The focus of this chapter, the BFLPE, is a prime example of what Marsh and Hau (2007) have termed a methodological-substantive synergy: substantive theoretical questions about the BFLPE have fueled new statistical methodologies; new methodologies in turn have stimulated new theoretical questions or allowed better responses to existing questions. In this section, we document some of these advances and innovations.

It has been more than 30 years since the first BFLPE study (Marsh & Parker, 1984) and this period has been exciting times for applied quantitative psychologists. During this time, there have been enormous advances in statistical methodology, due to the need for better approaches to address substantive issues as well as rapidly increasing computing power. There now exists a bevy of new and evolving quantitative tools to address a range of substantive and policy-related questions, with statistical power and flexibility that was previously unimaginable. Not only have BFLPE researchers been quick to take advantage of these innovations, but the need to provide better answers to substantive BFLPE questions has also stimulated these new evolving methodologies. Methodological innovations include better approaches to measurement and sampling error as well as the inherently multi-level structure of BFLPE data. In many respects, BFLPE research has been at the cutting edge of both latest methodological developments and substantive issues—a methodological–substantive synergy.

7.1 Early Research: Manifest, Single-Level Models

The statistical analyses used by Marsh and Parker (1984) seem primitive in relation to current methodological standards. The basic analysis was an ANOVA in which the school-level variable was a dichotomous variable. At this crude level, there was no way to distinguish between school-average SES and school-average ability. Indeed, the number of different schools was probably too small to provide confidence in the generalizability of the results, and no attempt was made to correct standard errors associated with clustering effect (lack of independence among students from the same school). Marsh (1987) used stronger statistical analyses and recognized the value of secondary data analysis of existing databases that were often much stronger than was feasible for individual researchers to construct. The Youth in Transition database was a large, nationally representative sample of schools that provided a much stronger basis for generalizability. Using a multiple regression approach to ANOVA, in which school-level variables were treated more appropriately, he showed that school-average ability had much stronger effects on ASC than did school-average SES. Following the lead of Bachman and O'Malley (1986), Marsh (1987) used a crude correction for the clustering effect—reducing the nominal sample size to make the statistical tests more conservative. Because this was a longitudinal study, he used a variation of pairwise deletion for missing data that might not be considered acceptable by modern-day standards.

7.2 Latent, Single-Level Models

The Marsh (1994) study took advantage of new advances in the application of confirmatory factor analysis and structural equation modeling. Because there were multiple indicators of many of the constructs—particularly mathematics and verbal self-concepts—he was able to posit latent self-concept factors inferred on the basis of multiple indicators. This had the important advantage of correcting for measurement error. Recognizing problems associated with aggregating a single measure of individual-student achievement to the school-average level for each school, he randomly divided the sample of students from each school into thirds and computed separate estimates of school-average ability for each of these subsamples. In this way, he was able to construct three indicators of school-average achievement for each school such that each indicator was based on a different sample of students. Using these three indicators, he then posited a latent school-average ability factor that took into account sampling error (variation among students within the same school). Whereas this study was important in using multiple indicators of different constructs to infer latent constructs that controlled measurement error in the BFLPE and recognizing the relevance of within-school variability in inferring a latent school-average ability factor, it still relied on a single-level analysis. Subsequently, Marsh and O'Mara (2010) implemented the "complex design" option available in the Mplus statistical package in a BFLPE study with a particularly complex factor structure (19 constructs inferred from multiple indicators measured over an 8-year period). They discussed the appropriateness of using the complex design option in a single-level analysis instead of multilevel modeling to control the clustered nature of the data inherent in multilevel BFLPE data.

7.3 Manifest, Multilevel Models

Methodologically, a major limitation of BFLPE studies prior to Marsh and Rowe (1996) was a reliance on single-level analyses that failed to take into account the inherent multilevel structure of the data in BFLPE studies. In BFLPE studies—and most studies conducted in school settings—individual-student characteristics and those associated with groups (classrooms, schools, etc.) are confounded because groups are typically not established according to random assignment. Students within the same group are typically more similar to other students than they are to students in other groups—a clustering effect. Even when students are initially assigned at random, they tend to become more similar to each other over time. This clustering effect violates assumptions of independence underlying most single-level analyses and results in inflated type 1 error rates. Furthermore, the apparently same variable may have a very different meaning when measured at different levels. Indeed, the BFLPE provides a classic, widely cited example of this multilevel issue in that the effect of ability on ASC is positive at the individual-student level but negative at the group (school or class) level. More specifically a measure of ability at the student level provides an indicator of achievement at the individual-student level, while class- or school-average ability at the class or school level is a proxy measure of a school's normative environment. Hence, school- or class-average ability has an effect on ASC beyond the effect of the individual student's ability. Multilevel modeling resolves the confounding of these two effects by facilitating a decomposition of any observed relationship among variables into separate within-school and between-school components (see Goldstein, 1995; Raudenbush & Bryk, 2002; Snijders & Bosker, 1999).

Marsh and Rowe (1996) argued that multilevel modeling is important in BFLPE studies because the juxtaposition between the effects of individual achievement and class- or school-average achievement is inherently a multilevel problem so that any attempt to model the data at a single level is likely to cause problems. By simultaneously considering data from multiple levels, the researcher opens up new substantive issues related to group-level variables and their interaction with individual-level variables that are typically ignored in single-level studies. The Marsh and Rowe study was the first BFLPE study to formally use multilevel modeling in a methodologically oriented reanalysis of data from Marsh (1987). They used a two-level model that allowed them to more appropriately disentangle the effect of individual-student ability and school-average ability that is the critical feature of the BFLPE. This also allowed them to more appropriately test cross-level interactions between individual-student and school-average levels of achievement, demonstrating that the BFLPE generalized reasonably well across students with different initial ability levels. Following Marsh and Rowe (1996), most subsequent BFLPE studies (see review by Marsh, Seaton, et al. (2008)) have used multilevel models with two levels in which L2 was either school or class, depending on the design of the study. Marsh and Hau (2003; Seaton et al., 2009, 2010) subsequently applied a three-level model (level 1 = students, level 2 = schools, level 3 = countries) with OECD/PISA data to test the cross-national generalizability of the BFLPE.

7.4 Latent, Multilevel Models

Until recently BFLPE studies—like most applied social science research—relied on either single-level SEMs or multilevel manifest models, but did not integrate these two statistical approaches into a single analytic framework. In multilevel analyses that have dominated recent BFLPE research, ASC, achievement, and other constructs were based on manifest indicators (e.g., scale scores) even when there were multiple indicators of each construct. An implicit, unwarranted assumption in these analyses is that these student level (L1) constructs are measured without error, resulting in underestimation of their effects and complicating interpretations of the effects of school-level variables. Indeed, it was this sort of problem that was highlighted in the Marsh, Seaton, et al. (2010) study showing that apparent assimilation effects of upward comparison effects on achievement were based in part on a failure to control for measurement error.

Stimulated by BFLPE research, Lüdtke et al. (2011, 2008; Marsh et al., 2009) showed that for aggregations of L1 constructs to form L2 constructs (e.g., school- or class-average achievement), the unreliability of the school-average aggregate can lead to biased estimation of contextual effects—particularly when the number of observations per school is small and when the intraclass correlation (ICC) of the corresponding student observations is low. They introduced a latent covariate approach in which the unobserved school mean is a doubly latent variable—latent in relation to measurement error (based on variation among the multiple indicators as in confirmatory factor analysis and structural equation modeling) and latent in relation to sampling error (based on student-to-student variation within each school). To the extent that there is measurement or sampling error in the use of observed class-average achievement, existing BFLPE research is likely to underestimate the size of the BFLPE unless it is based on new methodological approaches that control unreliability in aggregated L2 constructs.

Based on Lüdtke et al. (2008), Marsh et al. (2009) proposed a 2×2 taxonomy of models (see Figure 3) that could be latent or manifest in relation to either sampling error or measurement error. Marsh, Lüdtke, et al. presented the first doubly latent BFLPE study in which there were multiple indicators of each latent construct at the individual-student level that took into account measurement error at L1, latent aggregation across students to form latent L2 indicators that controlled for sampling error, and multiple indicators of each L2 construct that controlled measurement error

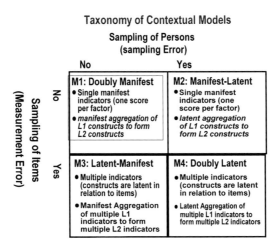

Figure 3 The 2 × 2 taxonomy of contextual models designed to control for measurement error (associated with sampling of items) and for sampling error (associated with sampling of people).

at L2. Variations in this basic model tested the extent to which the BFLPE was moderated by individual-student characteristics based on latent-variable interactions and set the stage for subsequent multilevel mediation models (Nagengast & Marsh, 2012). However, based on a large simulation study, Lüdtke, Marsh, Robitzsch, and Trautwein (2011) demonstrated that for models in this 2 × 2 taxonomy, there was a trade-off between bias, parsimony, and accuracy depending on the nature of the data. In particular, doubly latent models (i.e., latent in relation to both measurement error and sampling error) are very complex, and require large sample sizes and substantial ICCs. If samples sizes and ICCs are modest, the confidence intervals around estimates are likely to be large. Indeed, more parsimonious models that manifest in relation to either sampling error or measurement error might even prove to be more accurate (because of smaller confidence intervals) even thought they are biased. Fortunately, BFLPE studies are typically based on sufficiently large databases to warrant application of the doubly latent models. Marsh, Kuyper, et al. (2014), taking advantage of recent development of Mplus software that is used in most doubly latent BFLPE studies, extended this doubly latent two-level model to incorporate three levels (L1 = students, L2 = classes, L3 = schools). As described earlier in more details, they showed that separate two-level models based on either the school or the classroom both showed BFLPE results, but when both the school and classroom were incorporated into the three-level model, only the effect of class-average achievement was significant.

7.5 Alternative Experimental Designs

Many BFLPE studies are based on a single wave of data that makes problematic any interpretations of causality. Stronger designs are based on longitudinal data in which all or at least some of the same variables are collected in multiple waves. Fortunately, there is a substantial number of longitudinal studies that support interpretations of the BFLPE (e.g., Marsh, 1987, 1991; Marsh et al., 1995, 2001, 2000, 2009; Marsh & O'Mara, 2010; Marsh & Rowe, 1996; Marsh, Trautwein, et al., 2008; Trautwein et al., 2008). Indeed, as noted earlier, in a number of longitudinal studies of the BFLPE, the negative effects of school- or class-average achievement on ASC are evident in subsequent waves, even after controlling for BFLPEs in earlier waves. The Marsh et al. (2000; also see Marsh et al., 1995) longitudinal study was particularly strong in that pretest achievement measures from the end of primary school, that were a major basis of assignment of students to different school types, were available as a strong control for preexisting differences.

Several BFLPE studies have been described as quasi-experimental, providing additional control in relation to alternative interpretations. Thus, for example, the Marsh et al. (2001) study evaluated the BFLPE in connection with the reunification of East and West Germany, comparing results for East German students who had not previously experienced a selective school system with West German students who had been in selective schools during the two previous years. In two separate studies, Marsh et al. (1995) introduced a matching design that foreshadowed more powerful propensity matching approaches. Based on pretest data for a gifted and talented intervention, intervention students were matched to control students from the same schools providing stronger controls for preexisting differences.

Finally, although there have apparently been no large-scale BFLPE studies with true random assignment, Zell and Alicke (2009; see also Alicke et al., 2010) provided support for the processes underlying the BFLPE by experimentally manipulating the frame of reference in relation to feedback given to participants about how their performances compared with others. Consistent with BFLPE field studies, in a variety of different conditions they reported contrast effects in which higher frames of reference resulted in lower self-evaluations.

8. SUBSTANTIVE IMPLICATIONS FOR POLICY PRACTICE

BFLPE research provides an alternative perspective that is contradictory to educational policy in many countries concerning the placement of students in special education settings. Remarkably, despite the very different issues, this clash between our research and much existing policy exists at both ends of the achievement continuum (also see Robinson, Zigler, & Gallagher, 2000). At the high-ability end of the spectrum, there is an increasing trend toward the provision of highly segregated educational settings—special gifted and talented classes and academically selective schools for very bright students. This policy practice is typically based at least in part on a labeling theory perspective, suggesting that bright students will have higher self-concepts and experience other psychological benefits from being educated with other academically gifted students. Yet, the BFLPE and empirical evaluation of the effects of academically selective settings shows exactly the opposite effects. Placement of high-ability students in academically selective settings resulted in lower ASCs, not higher ASCs.

At the low-ability end of the spectrum for academically disadvantaged students, there is a worldwide inclusion movement to integrate these students into mainstream, regular classroom settings. Although prompted substantially by economic rationalist perspectives to reduce costs, the espoused rhetoric is again typically based on labeling theory. Labeling theory suggests that academically disadvantaged children are likely to be stigmatized and suffer lower self-concepts as a consequence of being in special classes with other academically disadvantaged students. Yet, theory underpinning the BFLPE and empirical evaluation of the effects of including academically disadvantaged students in regular mainstream classrooms showed exactly the opposite effects (Tracey et al., 2003). Inclusion of academically disadvantaged children into regular classrooms resulted in lower ASCs, not higher ASCs. Furthermore, the negative effects of this inclusion on peer self-concept reported by Tracey et al., suggested that academically disadvantaged children in regular classrooms actually felt socially excluded, not included.

We do not interpret BFLPE research to mean that educational policy makers should close academically selective schools and abandon plans to integrate students with intellectual disabilities into mainstream, comprehensive schools. We do not claim that all academically gifted students will suffer lower ASCs when attending academically high schools, but many will. We do not claim that all students with learning disadvantages will suffer lower ASCs when attending regular, mixed-ability classes, but many will. Rather, BFLPE research provides an important alternative perspective to existing policy directions being enacted in many countries throughout the world that have not been adequately evaluated in relation to current educational research.

In a democratic society, parents should have choice in schooling alternatives for their children and governments need to be responsive to these public demands. The role of educational researchers, in part, is to critically evaluate the implications of existing policy directions and to point out potentially negative, unintended consequences. Particularly when so many parents, teachers, and policy analysts uncritically assume that academic selective schools must automatically benefit the students who attend them, it is important to provide an alternative perspective based on strong theory and rigorous research. Hence, we urge parents to think carefully about the implications of school placements. Similarly, we urge policy makers and practitioners to reflect on potential negative side effects of current policy directions. A compromise position might be to more fully recognize the negative implications of the BFLPE and to pursue research to evaluate strategies designed to counter the negative effects of school-average ability. However, heeding the warning of many studies evaluating potential moderating effects of the BFLPE, moderating effects are typically small relative to the size of the BFLPE. It is also interesting to look at suggested strategies proposed to reduce the negative effects of the BFLPE (e.g., Craven et al., 2000; Marsh, 1993; Marsh & Craven, 1997, 2002; Marsh, Seaton, et al., 2008) in light of subsequent research. These suggestions include the following:

1. That highly independent participants who gain satisfaction from individual improvement, achieving personal bests, and mastery of new skills are likely to be less negatively affected by the BFLPE than participants who gain satisfaction from competing with and "beating" other participants and from being the "best" participant in their class. However, studies of the moderating effects of goal orientations (e.g., Cheng et al., 2014; Wouters et al., 2013) offer no support for this suggestion.

2. Developing assessment tasks that encourage individual participants to pursue their own goals that are of particular interest to them to reduce social comparison. To the extent that participants pursue their own unique goals (e.g., attainment of personal best performances) and feel positive about the results, they should be able to maintain a positive

self-concept even if other participants in selective settings are "more able" according to traditional performance measures.

3. Avoiding a highly competitive environment that encourages the social comparison processes underlying the BFLPE. Ironically, it seems that some selective programs intentionally foster a highly competitive environment (e.g., making known the test scores of everyone in the class) that is likely to exacerbate the BFLPE rather than to counteract it.

4. Providing participants with feedback in relation to criterion reference standards and personal improvement over time rather than comparisons based on the performances of other participants. To the extent that feedback emphasizes how each participant compares with other participants in the same setting, the BFLPE is likely to be exacerbated. However, although an experimental intervention by Lüdtke et al. (2005) based on this rationale did enhance ASC, it had no significant effect on the BFLPE.

5. Emphasizing to each student that she/he is a very able participant, providing internally focused feedback, attributional retraining, and valuing the unique accomplishments of each individual participant so that all participants can feel good about themselves. Although there is evidence that experimental intervention along these lines can enhance ASC (e.g., Craven, Marsh, & Debus, 1991), we know of no research testing whether it moderates the BFLPE.

6. Enhancing participants' feelings of connection, bonding, or identification with other participants in the selective setting and the group as a whole so that they develop a positive perspective from being associated with an elite group of participants (see Marsh et al., 2000). Although consistent with the theoretical underpinning of the BFLPE and some limited support that such positive reflected glory (assimilation) effects might counteract negative BFLPEs, interventions specifically designed to test such effects should be conducted before this can be recommended as a strategy to counter the BFLPE.

Although beyond the scope of the present chapter, Marsh and Craven (2002) also suggested that a particularly useful direction for further research is to consider intervention studies designed to alter motivational climates so as to undermine BFLPEs. Subsequent research (Marsh et al., 2012; Wouters et al., 2013) has emphasized the need to distinguish between classroom context (the average goal orientation of students within a class or school) and classroom climate (student ratings of a class-room climate common to all students in the class). However, based on limited research, there is little evidence that the BFLPE is moderated by either contextual goal orientations (e.g., Woulters et al., 2013) or key climate variables (e.g., teacher frame of reference; Lüdtke et al., 2005). However, neither of these studies was based on an intervention with random assignment to conditions that was designed to change classroom climate. Some support for these speculations come from the Marsh and Peart (1988) study in which a competitively oriented aerobics intervention, that emphasized social comparison, led to a decline in physical self-concept (relative to those in randomly assigned control groups) even though physical fitness levels increased. In contrast, in a cooperatively oriented group where exercises were done in pairs and emphasis was placed on personal improvement over time, there was an increase in both physical fitness levels and physical self-concept. The authors speculated that in terms of maintaining long-term physical activity levels, the effects on physical self-concept might be more important than the short-term effects on physical fitness resulting from the intervention.

In summary, for the most part, there is either insufficient research to support the heuristic suggestions offered by Marsh and Craven (2002) or, where there is some relevant research, it does not support the suggested strategies. Clearly this is an area where further research is needed, particularly experimental intervention studies designed to counter the BFLPE. However, as noted earlier, generalizability and moderation are two sides of the same coin in that strong support for the generalizability of the BFLPE means that there are unlikely to be variables or interventions that substantially moderate the effects.

9. LIMITATIONS AND DIRECTIONS FOR FUTURE RESEARCH

It is important to address potential limitations of BFLPE research in terms of the interpretation of results, policy implications, and directions for future research. BFLPE theory offers causal predictions about the effects of school- and class-average ability. In research reviewed here, the combination of sophisticated statistical analyses and longitudinal data provides strong tests of these causal predictions. However, causal interpretations should always be offered cautiously, particularly when based on nonexperimental designs. Although this limitation appears to be an inevitable consequence of the nature of BFLPE research, convergence of results based on an increasing number of studies, founded on alternative longitudinal and quasi-experimental designs and stronger statistical techniques, strengthen interpretation of the results. Nevertheless, other confounding variables not considered here (e.g., school expenditure levels, school policy variables, teaching-style of the teachers) are likely to have an impact upon academic performance and school climate, and warrant further study. However, it is worthwhile noting that the conditions typically considered conducive to effective learning, such as school resources, small class sizes, better-paid and more highly qualified teachers are likely to be better in higher-ability schools than in lower-ability schools (Marsh & Hau, 2003). Hence, controlling for such variables is likely to make more negative the negative effect of school- and class-average achievement on educational outcomes. As Marsh and Hau (2003) noted, these "potential biases are likely to be conservative in relation to the negative BFLPE." (p. 274)

There are important limitations in most studies seeking to evaluate the effects of special education settings at both ends of the achievement continuum. Thus, Goldring (1990, pp. 314−315) noted "researchers of gifted education programs can rarely assign students randomly to groups." A stronger research design might consist of actually matching gifted and talented students in selective settings with gifted and talented students from other settings (e.g., Marsh et al., 1995), but Marsh (1998) demonstrated that even this matching design is inherently biased in favor of students in selective settings under a variety of different matching strategies. He argued that alternative quasi-experimental designs such as the regression-discontinuity design should be considered. However, a problematic aspect of all correlational and quasi-experimental designs is that students selected to participate in gifted education programs are likely to be brighter than those who are not so that any residual variance in these preexisting differences is likely to bias results in favor of the gifted education intervention. However, interpretations of the BFLPE on ASC are conservative in relation to this potentially inherent bias; the negative effects are so strong that they overcome the likely positive bias in most BFLPE studies.

Although not a focus of this article, a similar bias is likely to be even stronger for the evaluation of gifted programs and school-average ability in relation to achievement. Thus, some or all of the apparent advantages sometimes demonstrated for gifted programs in relation to achievement is likely to be due to failure to fully control for preexisting differences. Highlighting this problem, Goldring (1990) emphasized that findings based on research in this area were questionable since the available research was predominated by methodologically weak studies. She found that apparent differences showing higher achievement for gifted education programs decreased monotonically with the number of pretest variables controlled, and that for the only study to use true random assignment the advantage disappeared altogether. Based on her meta-analysis, Goldring (1990) concluded that policy makers need to be aware of the limitations of the research literature on gifted and talented programs. Indeed, many of the statistical advances in BFLPE research could fruitfully be applied to the evaluation of gifted programs in relation to academic achievement. Thus, for example, based on a large representative sample of English primary schools Televantou et al. (2015; also see Marsh, Nagengast, Fletcher, & Televantou, 2011) showed that the effect of school-average ability on subsequent achievement was negative in one of the first applications of the doubly latent multilevel model applied to achievement data.

Although there has been less critical evaluation of BFLPE research in relation to the inclusion of academically disadvantaged students in regular classrooms (mainstreaming) compared with special classes, many of these concerns with gifted education programs are relevant here as well. In particular, whereas true random assignment is a desirable design strategy, it is very rare that it can be implemented in special education research. Here, however, some of the potential confounding factors are likely to be more worrisome. Thus, for example, whereas comparisons of nonequivalent groups are likely to be biased in favor of inclusion groups, resources, and student—teacher ratios are likely to be better in special classes for disadvantaged students. Hence, more research is needed to better evaluate the extent to which the negative effects of mainstreaming on ASC—the BFLPE—can be explained in terms of differential resourcing and whether stronger controls for preexisting differences result in even more negative effects associated with mainstreaming.

In summary, it is likely that researchers evaluating the effects of placement at both ends of the achievement continuum will continue to struggle with interpretation complications that are inherent in correlational and quasi-experimental research designs with nonequivalent groups. However, the results and methodological approaches used in BFLPE should have broad applicability to these issues.

ACKNOWLEDGMENTS

The authors would like to thank the many colleagues who have collaborated with us on BFLPE studies over the last quarter century, as well as many others who have contributed to this reresearch literature. This chapter is based in part on a keynote presentation at the 2011 SELF Conference held in Singapore.

REFERENCES

Alicke, M. D., Zell, E., & Bloom, D. L. (2010). Mere categorization and the frog-pond effect. *Psychological Science, 21*, 174–177. http://dx.doi.org/10.1177/0956797609357718.

Alwin, D. F., & Otto, L. B. (1977). High school context effects on aspirations. *Sociology of Education, 50*, 259–273. http://dx.doi.org/10.2307/2112499.

Aspinwall, L. G., & Taylor, S. E. (1993). Effects of social comparison direction, threat, and self-esteem on affect, self-evaluation, and expected success. *Journal of Personality & Social Psychology, 64*, 708–722.

Bachman, J. G., & O'Malley, P. M. (1986). Self-concepts, self-esteem, and educational experiences: the frog pond revisited (again). *Journal of Personality and Social Psychology, 50*, 33–46.

Barber, C. N., Hall, J., & Armistead, L. (2003). Parent-adolescent relationship and adolescent psychological functioning among African-American female adolescents: self-esteem as a mediator. *Journal of Child & Family Studies, 12*, 361–374.

Beasley, E. K. (2013). *Physical self-concept and gender: The role of frame of reference and social comparison among adolescent females* (Doctoral dissertation), Mississippi University for Women. http://etd.lsu.edu/docs/available/etd-07082013-100829/unrestricted/Beasley. Dissertation.Revisions.pdf.

Blanton, H., Buunk, B. P., Gibbons, F. X., & Kuyper, H. (1999). When better-than-others compare upward: choice of comparison and comparative evaluation as independent predictors of academic performance. *Journal of Personality and Social Psychology, 76*, 420–430.

Burnett, P. C., Pillay, H., & Dart, B. C. (2003). The influences of conceptions of learning and learner self-concept on high school students' approaches to learning. *School Psychology International, 24*, 54–66.

Buunk, B. P., Collins, R., Taylor, S. E., VanYperen, N. W., & Dakof, G. A. (1990). The affective consequences of social comparisons: either direction has its ups and downs. *Journal of Personality and Social Psychology, 59*(6), 1238–1249.

Byrne, B. M. (1984). The general/ASC nomological network: a review of construct validation research. *Review of Educational Research, 54*, 427–456.

Byrne, B. M. (2002). Validating the measurement and structure of self-concept: snapshots of past, present, and future research. *American Psychologist, 57*, 897–909. http://dx.doi.org/10.1037/0003-066X.57.11.897.

Chanal, J. P., Marsh, H. W., Sarrazin, P. G., & Bois, J. E. (2005). The big-fish-little-pond effect on gymnastics self-concept: generalizability of social comparison effects to a physical setting. *Journal of Sport & Exercise Psychology, 27*, 53–70.

Chapman, J. W. (1988). Learning disabled children's self-concepts. *Review of Educational Research, 58*, 347–371.

Cheng, C. R., McInerney, D. M., & Mok, M. M. C. (2014). Does big-fish–little-pond effect always exist? Investigation of goal orientations as moderators in the Hong Kong context. *Educational Psychology, 34*(5), 561–580. http://dx.doi.org/10.1080/01443410.2014.898740.

Coleman, J. M., & Fults, B. A. (1985). Special class placement, level of intelligence, and the self-concept of gifted children: a social comparison perspective. *Remedial and Special Education, 6*, 7–11.

Collins, R. (2000). Among the better ones. Upward assimilation in social comparison. In J. Suls, & L. Wheeler (Eds.), *Handbook of social comparison: Theory and research* (pp. 159–171). New York: Kluwer Academic/Plenum Publishers.

Cooley, C. H. (1902). *Human nature and the social order.* New York, NY: Scribner.

Coopersmith, S. A. (1967). *The antecedents of self-esteem.* San Francisco, CA: Freeman.

Crabtree, J. W. (2003). Maintaining positive self-concept: social comparisons in secondary school students with mild learning disabilities attending mainstream and special schools. In H. W. Marsh, R. G. Craven, & D. McInerney (Eds.), *International advances in self research* (Vol. 1, pp. 261—290). Greenwich, CT: Information Age.

Craven, R. G., Marsh, H. W., & Debus, R. (1991). Effects of internally focused feedback and attributional feedback on the enhancement of academic self-concept. *Journal of Educational Psychology, 83*, 17—26.

Craven, R. G., Marsh, H. W., & Print, M. (2000). Selective, streamed and mixed-ability programs for gifted students: impact on self-concept, motivation, and achievement. *Australian Journal of Education, 44*, 51—75.

Dai, D. Y. (2004). How universal is the big-fish-little-pond effect? *American Psychologist, 59*, 267—268. http://dx.doi.org/10.1037/0003-066X.59.4.267.

Dai, D. Y., & Rinn, A. N. (2008). The big-fish—little-pond effect: what do we know and where do we go from here? *Educational Psychology Review, 20*, 283—317. http://dx.doi.org/10.1007/s10648-008-9071-x.

Davis, J. A. (1966). The campus as a frog pond: an application of theory of relative deprivation to career decisions for college men. *American Journal of Sociology, 72*, 17—31. http://dx.doi.org/10.1086/224257.

Delugach, R. R., Bracken, B. A., Bracken, M. J., & Schicke, M. C. (1992). Self-concept: multidimensional construct exploration. *Psychology in the Schools, 29*, 213—223.

Diener, E. (2000). Subjective well-being: the science of happiness and a proposal for a national index. *American Psychologist, 55*(1), 34—43.

Diener, E., & Fujita, F. (1997). Social comparison and subjective well-being. In B. P. Buunk, & F. X. Gibbons (Eds.), *Health, coping, and well-being: Perspectives from social comparison theory* (pp. 329—357). Mahwah, NJ: Erlbaum.

Donahue, E. M., Robins, R. W., Roberts, B. W., & John, O. P. (1993). The divided self: concurrent and longitudinal effects of psychological adjustment and social roles on self-concept differentiation. *Journal of Personality and Social Psychology, 64*, 834—846.

Elliot, A. J., & Church, M. A. (1997). A hierarchical model of approach and avoidance achievement motivation. *Journal of Personality and Social Psychology, 72*, 218—232.

Ertl, H. (2006). Educational standards and the changing discourse on education: the reception and consequences of the PISA study in Germany. *Oxford Review of Education, 32*, 619—634.

Festinger, L. (1954). A theory of social comparison processes. *Human Relations, 7*, 117—140.

Gladwell, M. (2013). *David and goliath: Underdogs, misfits, and the art of battling giants.* Boston, MA: Little, Brown & Company.

Goldring, E. B. (1990). Assessing the status of information on classroom organizational frameworks for gifted students. *Journal of Educational Research, 83*, 313—326.

Goldstein, H. (1995). *Multilevel statistical models.* London, UK: Arnold.

Greenwald, A. G. (1988). A social-cognitive account of the self's development. In D. K. Lapsley, & F. C. Power (Eds.), *Self, ego and identity: Interpretative approaches* (pp. 30—42). New York: Springer-Verlag.

Guo, J., Marsh, H. W., Parker, P., & Morin, A. J. S. (2015). Directionality of the associations of high school expectancy-value, aspirations, and attainment a longitudinal study. *American Educational Research Journal* (on-line). http://dx.doi.org/10.3102/000283121456578.

Haney, P., & Durlak, J. A. (1998). Changing self-esteem in children and adolescents: a meta-analytic review. *Journal of Clinical Child Psychology, 27*, 423—433. http://dx.doi.org/10.1207/s15374424jccp2704_6.

Harter, S. (1990). Processes underlying adolescent self-concept formation. In R. Montemayor, G. Adams, & T. Gullotta (Eds.), *From childhood to adolescence.* CA: Sage Publications.

Harter, S. (2012). *The construction of the self: Developmental and sociocultural foundations.* Guilford Press.

Hattie, J. (1992). *Self-concept*. Hillsdale, NJ: Erlbaum.

Hattie, J. (2002). Classroom composition and peer effects. *International Journal of Educational Research, 37*, 449−481. http://dx.doi.org/10.1016/S0883-0355(03)00015-6.

Helson, H. (1964). *Adaptation-level theory*. New York: Harper & Row.

Hopmann, S., Brinek, G., & Retzl, M. (2007). *PISA according to PISA*. Vienna, Austria: Verlag.

Huguet, P., Dumas, F., Marsh, H. W., Regner, I., Wheeler, L., Suls, J., et al. (2009). Clarifying the role of social comparison in the big-fish-little-pond effect (BFLPE): an integrative study. *Journal of Personality and Social Psychology, 97*(1), 156−170.

Huguet, P., Dumas, F., Monteil, J. M., & Genestoux, N. (2001). Social comparison choices in the classroom: further evidence for students' upward comparison tendency and its beneficial impact on performance. *European Journal of Social Psychology, 31*, 557−578.

Hyman, H. (1942). The psychology of subjective status. *Psychological Bulletin, 39*, 473−474.

James, W. (1963). *The principles of psychology*. New York, NY: Holt, Rinehart & Winston (Original work published 1890).

Jerusalem, M. (1984). Reference group, learning environment and self-evaluations: a dynamic multi-level analysis with latent variables. In R. Schwarzer (Ed.), *The self in anxiety, stress and depression* (pp. 61−73). Amsterdam, The Netherlands: North-Holland.

Jonkmann, K., Becker, M., Marsh, H. W., Lüdtke, O., & Trautwein, U. (2012). Personality traits moderate the big-fish−little-pond effect of academic self-concept. *Learning and Individual Differences, 22*(6), 736−746. http://dx.doi.org/10.1016/j.lindif.2012.07.020.

Kulik, C. L. (1985). Effects of inter-class ability grouping on achievement and self-esteem. In *Paper presented at the 1985 annual meeting of the American Psychological Association, Los Angeles*.

Kulik, C. L., & Kulik, J. A. (1982). Effects of ability grouping on secondary school students: a meta-analysis of evaluation findings. *American Educational Research Journal, 21*, 799−806.

Liem, G. A. D., Marsh, H. W., Martin, A. J., McInerney, D. M., & Yeung, A. S. (2013). The big-fish-little-pond effect and a national policy of within-school ability streaming: alternative frames of reference. *American Educational Research Journal, 50*(2), 326−370. http://dx.doi.org/10.3102/0002831212464511.

Lockwood, P., & Kunda, Z. (1997). Superstars and me: predicting the impact of role models on the self. *Journal of Personality and Social Psychology, 73*, 91−103.

Lüdtke, O., Köller, O., Marsh, H., & Trautwein, U. (2005). Teacher frame of reference and the big-fish-little-pond effect. *Contemporary Educational Psychology, 30*, 263−285. http://dx.doi.org/10.1016/j.

Lüdtke, O., Marsh, H. W., Robitzsch, A., & Trautwein, U. (2011). A 2×2 taxonomy of multilevel latent contextual models: accuracy-bias trade-offs in full and partial error-correction models. *Psychological Methods, 16*(4), 444−467. http://dx.doi.org/10.1037/a0024376.

Lüdtke, O., Marsh, H. W., Robitzsch, A., Trautwein, U., Asparouhov, T., & Muthén, B. (2008). The multilevel latent covariate model: a new, more reliable approach to group-level effects in contextual studies. *Psychological Methods, 13*, 203−229.

Major, B., Testa, M., & Bylsma, W. H. (1991). Responses to upward and downward social comparisons: the impact of esteem-relevance and perceived control. In J. Suls, & T. A. Wills (Eds.), *Social comparison: Contemporary theory and research* (pp. 237−260). New Jersey: Lawrence Erlbaum Associates.

Marsh, H. W. (1974). *Judgmental anchoring: Stimulus and response variables* (Unpublished Doctoral dissertation). Los Angeles: University of California.

Marsh, H. W. (1984a). Self-concept, social comparison and ability grouping: a reply to Kulik and Kulik. *American Educational Research Journal, 21*, 799−806.

Marsh, H. W. (1984b). Self-concept: the application of a frame of reference model to explain paradoxical results. *Australian Journal of Education, 28*, 165−181.

Marsh, H. W. (1987). The big-fish-little-pond effect on ASC. *Journal of Educational Psychology, 79*, 280—295. http://dx.doi.org/10.1037/0022-0663.79.3.280.

Marsh, H. W. (1991). Failure of high-ability high schools to deliver academic benefits commensurate with their students' ability levels. *American Educational Research Journal, 28*, 445—480.

Marsh, H. W. (1993). ASC: theory, measurement and research. In J. Suls (Ed.), *Psychological perspectives on the self* (Vol. 4, pp. 59—98). Hillsdale, NJ: Erlbaum.

Marsh, H. W. (1994). Using the national educational longitudinal study of 1988 to evaluate theoretical models of self-concept: the self-description questionnaire. *Journal of Educational Psychology, 86*, 439—456. http://dx.doi.org/10.1037/0022-0663.86.3.439.

Marsh, H. W. (1998). Simulation study of nonequivalent group-matching and regression discontinuity designs: evaluations of gifted and talented programs. *Journal of Experimental Education, 66*, 163—192.

Marsh, H. W. (2007). *Self-concept theory, measurement and research into practice: The role of self-concept in educational psychology.* London, England: British Psychological Society.

Marsh, H. W., Abduljabbar, A. S., Abu-Hilal, M. M., Morin, A. J. S., Abdelfattah, F., Leung, K. C., et al. (2013). Factorial, convergent, and discriminant validity of TIMSS math and science motivation measures: a comparison of Arab and Anglo-Saxon countries. *Journal of Educational Psychology, 105*(1), 108—128. http://dx.doi.org/10.1037/a0029907.

Marsh, H. W., Abduljabbar, A. S., Parker, P. D., Morin, A. J. S., Abdelfattah, F., & Nagengast, B. (2014). The big-fish-little-pond effect in mathematics: a cross-cultural comparison of U.S. and Saudi Arabian TIMSS responses. *Journal of Cross-Cultural Psychology, 45*(5), 777—804. http://dx.doi.org/10.1177/0022022113519858.

Marsh, H. W., Abduljabbar, A. S., Morin, A. J. S., Parker, P., Abdelfattah, F., Nagengast, B., et al. (2015). The big-fish-little-pond effect: Generalizability of social comparison processes over two age cohorts from Western, Asian, and Middle Eastern Islamic countries. *Journal of Educational Psychology, 107*(1), 258—271. http://dx.doi.org/10.1037/a0037485.

Marsh, H. W., Byrne, B. M., & Shavelson, R. J. (1988). A multifaceted ASC: its hierarchical structure and its relation to academic achievement. *Journal of Educational Psychology, 80*, 366—380. http://dx.doi.org/10.1037/0022-0663.80.3.366.

Marsh, H. W., & Cheng, J. H. S. (2012). Physical self-concept. In G. Tenenbaum, R. C. Eklund, & A. Kamata (Eds.), *Measurement in sport and exercise psychology* (pp. 215—226). Champaign, IL: Human Kinetics.

Marsh, H. W., Chessor, D., Craven, R. G., & Roche, L. (1995). The effects of gifted and talented programs on ASC: the big fish strikes again. *American Educational Research Journal, 32*, 285—319.

Marsh, H. W., & Craven, R. G. (1997). Academic self-concept: beyond the dustbowl. In G. D. Phye (Ed.), *Handbook of classroom assessment: Learning, achievement, and adjustment* (pp. 131—198). San Diego, CA: Academic Press.

Marsh, H. W., & Craven, R. G. (2002). The pivotal role of frames of reference in academic self-concept formation: the big fish little pond effect. In F. Pajares, & T. Urdan (Eds.), *Adolescence and education* (Vol. II, pp. 83—123). Charlotte, NC: Information Age Publishing.

Marsh, H. W., & Craven, R. G. (2006). Reciprocal effects of self-concept and performance from a multidimensional perspective: beyond seductive pleasure and unidimensional perspectives. *Perspectives on Psychological Science, 1*, 133—163. http://dx.doi.org/10.1111/j.1745-6916.2006.00010.x.

Marsh, H. W., & Hattie, J. (1996). Theoretical perspectives on the structure of self-concept. In B. A. Bracken (Ed.), *Handbook of self-concept* (pp. 38—90). New York, NY: Wiley.

Marsh, H. W., & Hau, K.-T. (2003). Big-fish-little-pond effect on ASC: a cross-cultural (26-country) test of the negative effects of academically selective schools. *American Psychologist, 58*, 364—376. http://dx.doi.org/10.1037/0003-066X.58.5.364.

Marsh, H. W., & Hau, K.-T. (2007). Applications of latent-variable models in educational psychology: the need for methodological-substantive synergies. *Contemporary Educational Psychology, 32*, 151–170. http://dx.doi.org/10.1016/j.cedpsych.2006.10.008.

Marsh, H. W., Hau, K.-T., Artelt, C., Baumert, J., & Peschar, J. L. (2006). OECD's brief self-report measure of educational psychology's most useful affective constructs: cross-cultural, psychometric comparisons across 25 countries. *International Journal of Testing, 6*, 311–360. http://dx.doi.org/10.1207/s15327574ijt0604_1.

Marsh, H. W., Köller, O., & Baumert, J. (2001). Reunification of East and West German school systems: longitudinal multilevel modeling study of the big-fish-little-pond effect on ASC. *American Educational Research Journal, 38*, 321–350. http://dx.doi.org/10.3102/00028312038002321.

Marsh, H. W., Kong, C.-K., & Hau, K.-T. (2000). Longitudinal multilevel models of the big-fish-little-pond effect on ASC: counterbalancing contrast and reflected-glory effects in Hong Kong schools. *Journal of Personality and Social Psychology, 78*, 337–349. http://dx.doi.org/10.1037/0022-3514.78.2.337.

Marsh, H. W., Kuyper, H., Morin, A. J. S., Parker, P. D., & Seaton, M. (2014). Big-fish-little-pond social comparison and local dominance effects: integrating new statistical models, methodology, design, theory and substantive implications. *Learning and Instruction, 33*, 50–66. http://dx.doi.org/10.1016/j.learninstruc.2014.04.0020959-4752/.

Marsh, H. W., Lüdtke, O., Nagengast, B., Trautwein, U., Morin, A. J. S., Abduljabbar, A. S., et al. (2012). Classroom climate and contextual effects: conceptual and methodological issues in the evaluation of group-level effects. *Educational Psychologist, 47*(2), 106–124. http://dx.doi.org/10.1080/00461520.2012.670488.

Marsh, H. W., Lüdtke, O., Robitzsch, A., Trautwein, U., Asparouhov, T., Muthen, B., et al. (2009). Doubly-latent models of school contextual effects: integrating multilevel and structural equation approaches to control measurement and sampling error. *Multivariate Behavioral Research, 44*, 764–802.

Marsh, H. W., Morin, A. J. S., & Parker, P. D. Physical self-concept changes in a selective sport high school: a longitudinal cohort-sequence analysis of the big-fish-little-pond effect. *Journal of Sport and Exercise Psychology*, in press.

Marsh, H. W., Nagengast, B., Fletcher, J., & Televantou, I. (2011). Assessing educational effectiveness: policy implications from diverse areas of research. *Fiscal Studies, 32*, 279–295.

Marsh, H. W., & O'Mara, A. J. (2010). Long-term total negative effects of school-average ability on diverse educational outcomes: direct and indirect effects of the big-fish-little-pond effect. *German Journal of Educational Psychology, 24*, 51–72.

Marsh, H. W., Parada, R. H., Craven, R. G., & Finger, L. (2004). In the looking glass: a reciprocal effect model elucidating the complex nature of bullying, psychological determinants, and the central role of self-concept. In C. E. Sanders, & G. D. Phye (Eds.), *Bullying: Implications for the classroom* (pp. 63–109). San Diego: Academic Press.

Marsh, H. W., & Parker, J. W. (1984). Determinants of student self-concept: Is it better to be a relatively large fish in a small pond even if you don't learn to swim as well? *Journal of Personality and Social Psychology, 47*, 213–231. http://dx.doi.org/10.1037/0022-3514.47.1.213.

Marsh, H. W., & Peart, N. (1988). Competitive and cooperative physical fitness training programs for girls: effects on physical fitness and on multidimensional self-concepts. *Journal of Sport & Exercise Psychology, 10*, 390–407.

Marsh, H. W., & Perry, C. (2005). Does a positive self-concept contribute to winning gold medals in elite swimming? The causal ordering of elite athlete self-concept and championship performances. *Journal of Sport & Exercise Psychology, 27*, 71–91.

Marsh, H. W., & Rowe, K. J. (1996). The negative effects of school-average ability on ASC: an application of multilevel modelling. *Australian Journal of Education, 40*, 65–87.

Marsh, H. W., Seaton, M., Kuyper, H., Dumas, F., Huguet, P., Regner, I., et al. (2010). Phantom behavioral assimilation effects: systematic biases in social comparison choice studies. *Journal of Personality, 78*, 671—710. http://dx.doi.org/10.1111/j.1467-6494.2010.00630.x.

Marsh, H. W., Seaton, M., Trautwein, U., Lüdtke, O., Hau, K. T., O'Mara, A. J., et al. (2008). The big-fish-little-pond-effect stands up to critical scrutiny: implications for theory, methodology, and future research. *Educational Psychology Review, 20*, 319—350. http://dx.doi.org/10.1007/s10648-008-9075-6.

Marsh, H. W., Tracey, D. K., & Craven, R. G. (2006). Multidimensional self-concept structure for preadolescents with mild intellectual disabilities: a hybrid multigroup—MIMC approach to factorial invariance and latent mean differences. *Educational and Psychological Measurement, 66*, 795—818. http://dx.doi.org/10.1177/0013164405285910.

Marsh, H. W., Trautwein, U., Lüdtke, O., Baumert, J., & Köller, O. (2007). The big-fish-little-pond effect: persistent negative effects of selective high schools on self-concept after graduation. *American Educational Research Journal, 44*, 631—669. http://dx.doi.org/10.3102/0002831207306728.

Marsh, H. W., Trautwein, U., Lüdtke, O., & Köller, O. (2008). Social comparison and big-fish-little-pond effects on self-concept and efficacy perceptions: role of generalized and specific others. *Journal of Educational Psychology, 100*, 510—524. http://dx.doi.org/10.1037/0022-0663.100.3.510.

Marsh, H. W., & Yeung, A. S. (1997a). Causal effects of ASC on academic achievement: structural equation models of longitudinal data. *Journal of Educational Psychology, 89*, 41—54. http://dx.doi.org/10.1037/0022-0663.89.1.41.

Marsh, H. W., & Yeung, A. S. (1997b). Coursework selection: relations to ASC and achievement. *American Educational Research Journal, 34*, 691—720.

Marx, R. W., & Winne, P. H. (1978). Construct interpretations of three self-concept inventories. *American Educational Research Journal, 15*(1), 99—109.

Matsumoto, D. (2001). Cross-cultural psychology in the 21st century. In J. S. Halonen, & S. F. Davis (Eds.), *The many faces of psychological research in the 21st century (Chap. 5)*. Retrieved December 18, 2001 from the Teaching of Psychology Web site: http://teachpsych.lemoyne.edu/teachpsych/faces/script/ch05.htm.

Morse, S., & Gergen, K. J. (1970). Social comparison, self-consistency, and the concept of self. *Journal of Personality & Social Psychology, 16*, 148—156.

Mulkey, L. M., Catsambis, S., Steelman, L. C., & Crain, R. L. (2005). The long-term effects of ability grouping in mathematics: a national investigation. *Social Psychology of Education, 8*, 137—177.

Nagengast, B., & Marsh, H. W. (2012). Big fish in little ponds aspire more: mediation and cross-cultural generalizability of school-average ability effects on self-concept and career aspirations in science. *Journal of Educational Psychology, 104*(4), 1033—1053. http://dx.doi.org/10.1037/a0027697.

Nagengast, B., & Marsh, H. W. (2013). Motivation and engagement in science around the globe: testing measurement invariance with multigroup SEMs across 57 countries using PISA 2006. In L. Rutkowski, M. von Davier, & D. Rutkowski (Eds.), *A handbook of international large-scale assessment data analysis* (pp. 317—344). Chapman & Hall, CRC Press.

Parducci, A. (1995). *Happiness, pleasure, and judgment: The contextual theory and its applications*. Mahwah, NJ: Erlbaum.

Raudenbush, S. W., & Bryk, A. S. (2002). *Hierarchical linear models: Applications and data analysis methods* (2nd ed.). Thousand Oaks, CA: Sage.

Rheinberg, F., & Enstrup, B. (1977). Self-concept of intelligence with pupils in special and normal schools: a group effect. *Zeitschrift für Entwicklungspsychologie und Pädagogische Psychologie (Journal of Developmental Psychology and Educational Psychology), 9*, 171—180.

Robinson, N. M., Zigler, E., & Gallagher, J. J. (2000). Two tails of the normal curve: similarities and differences in the study of mental retardation and giftedness. *American Psychologist, 55*, 1413−1424. http://dx.doi.org/10.1037/0003-066X.55.12.1413.

Schwartz, S. H., & Bilsky, W. (1990). Toward a theory of the universal content and structure of values: extensions and cross-cultural replications. *Journal of Personality and Social Psychology, 58*(5), 878−891.

Seaton, M., & Marsh, H. W. (2013). Methodological innovation in big-fish-little-pond effect research: methodological-substantive synergy at work. In H. W. Marsh, R. G. Craven, & D. McInerney (Eds.), *International advances in self research* (Vol. 4, pp. 161−181). Charlotte, NC: Information Age Publishing.

Seaton, M., Marsh, H. W., & Craven, R. G. (2009). Earning its place as a pan-human theory: universality of the big-fish-little-pond effect across 41 culturally and economically diverse countries. *Journal of Educational Psychology, 101*, 403−419.

Seaton, M., Marsh, H. W., & Craven, R. G. (2010). Big-fish-little-pond-effect: generalizability and moderation - two sides of the same coin. *American Educational Research Journal, 47*, 390−434. http://dx.doi.org/10.3102/0002831209350493.

Seaton, M., Marsh, H. W., Dumas, F., Huguet, P., Monteil, J., Regner, I., et al. (2008). In search of the big fish: investigating the coexistence of the big-fish-little-pond effect with the positive effects of upward comparisons. *British Journal of Social Psychology, 47*, 73−103.

Seaton, M., Marsh, H. W., Yeung, A. S., & Craven, R. G. (2011). The big fish down under: examining moderators of the 'Big-Fish-Little-Pond-Effect' for Australia's high achievers. *Australian Journal of Education, 55*(2), 93−114.

Segall, M. H., Lonner, W. J., & Berry, J. W. (1998). Cross-cultural psychology as a scholarly discipline: on the flowering of culture in behavioral research. *American Psychologist, 53*, 1101−1110. http://dx.doi.org/10.1037/0003-066X.53.10.1101.

Seligman, M. E. P., & Csikszentmihalyi, M. (2000). Positive psychology: an introduction. *American Psychologist, 55*, 5−14. http://dx.doi.org/10.1037/0003-066X.55.1.5.

Shah, J. Y. (2008). Preface. In J. Y. Shah, & W. L. Garner (Eds.), *Handbook of motivational science*. New York: Guilford Press.

Shavelson, R. J., Hubner, J. J., & Stanton, G. C. (1976). Self-concept: validation of construct interpretations. *Review of Educational Research, 46*, 407−441.

Sherif, M., & Sherif, C. W. (1969). *Social psychology*. New York: Harper & Row.

Snijders, T. A. B., & Bosker, R. J. (1999). *Multilevel analysis: An introduction to basic and advanced multilevel modeling*. London: Sage.

Soares, A. T., & Soares, L. M. (1969). Self-perceptions of culturally disadvantaged children. *American Educational Research Journal, 6*, 31−45.

Stouffer, S. A., Suchman, E. A., DeVinney, L. C., Star, S. A., & Williams, R. M. (1949). *The American soldier: Adjustments during army life* (Vol. 1). Princeton: Princeton University Press.

Suls, J. M. (1977). Social comparison theory and research: an overview from 1954. In J. M. Suls, & R. L. Miller (Eds.), *Social comparison processes: Theoretical and empirical perspectives* (pp. 1−20). Washington, DC: Hemisphere.

Suls, J. M., & Wheeler, L. (2000). A selective history of classic and neo-social comparison theory. In J. M. Suls, & L. Wheeler (Eds.), *Handbook of social comparison: Theory and research* (pp. 3−22). Dordrecht, Netherlands: Kluwer Academic Publishers.

Taylor, S. E., Buunk, B. P., & Aspinwall, L. G. (1990). Social comparisons, stress, and coping. *Personality and Social Psychology Bulletin, 16*(1), 74−89.

Televantou, I., Marsh, H. W., Kyriakides, L., Nagengast, B., Fletcher, J., & Malmberg, L.-E. (2015). Phantom effects in school composition research: Consequences of failure to control biases due to measurement error in traditional multilevel models. *School Effectiveness and School Improvement, 26*(1), 75−101. http://dx.doi.org/10.1080/09243453.2013.871302.

Tracey, D. K., Marsh, H. W., & Craven, R. G. (2003). Self-concepts of preadolescent students with mild intellectual disabilities: issues of measurement and educational placement. In H. W. Marsh, R. G. Craven, & D. M. McInerney (Eds.), *International advances in self research* (Vol. 1, pp. 203—230). Greenwich, CT: Information Age.

Trautwein, U., Gerlach, E., & Lüdtke, O. (2008). Athletic classmates, physical self-concept, and free-time physical activity: a longitudinal study of frame of reference effects. *Journal of Educational Psychology, 100,* 988—1001.

Trautwein, U., Lüdtke, O., Marsh, H. W., Köller, O., & Baumert, J. (2006). Tracking, grading, and student motivation: using group composition and status to predict self-concept and interest in ninth-grade mathematics. *Journal of Educational Psychology, 98,* 788—806.

Trautwein, U., Lüdtke, O., Marsh, H. W., & Nagy, G. (2009). Within-school social comparison: how students perceive the standing of their class predicts academic self-concept. *Journal of Educational Psychology, 101,* 853—866. http://dx.doi.org/10.1037/a0016306.

Trowbridge, N. (1972). Self-concept and socio-economic status in elementary school children. *American Educational Research Journal, 9,* 525—537.

Tymms, P. (2001). A test of the big fish in a little pond hypothesis: an investigation into the feelings of seven-year-old pupils in school. *School Effectiveness and School Improvement, 12,* 161—181. http://dx.doi.org/10.1076/sesi.12.2.161.3452.

Upshaw, H. S. (1969). The personal reference scale: an approach to social judgment. In L. Berkowitz (Ed.), *Advances in experimental social psychology* (Vol. 4, pp. 315—370).

Valentine, J. C., DuBois, D. L., & Cooper, H. (2004). The relation between self-beliefs and academic achievement: a meta-analytic review. *Educational Psychologist, 39,* 111—133. http://dx.doi.org/10.1207/s15326985ep3902_3. APA-HARRIS_V1-11-0301-015.indd 455 4/25/11.

Wedell, D. H., & Parducci, A. (2000). Social comparison: lessons from basic research on judgment. In J. Suls, & L. Wheeler (Eds.), *Handbook of social comparison: Theory and research. The Plenum series in social/clinical psychology* (pp. 223—252). Dordrecht, Netherlands: Kluwer Academic Publishers.

Wells, L. E., & Marwell, G. (1976). *Self-esteem: Its conceptualization and measurement.* Beverly Hills, CA: Sage.

Wheeler, L. (1966). Motivation as a determinant of upward comparison. *Journal of Experimental Social Psychology, 2*(Suppl. 1), 27—31.

Wheeler, L., & Suls, J. (2004). Social comparison and self-evaluations of competence. In A. Elliot, & C. Dweck (Eds.), *Handbook of competence and motivation.* New York: Guilford Publications.

White, R. W. (1959). Motivation reconsidered: the concept of competence. *Psychological Review, 66,* 297—333.

Wood, J. V. (1989). Theory and research concerning social comparisons of personal attributes. *Psychological Bulletin, 106*(2), 231—248.

Wouters, S., Colpin, H., Van Damme, J., & Verschueren, K. (2013). Endorsing achievement goals exacerbates the big-fish-little-pond effect on academic self-concept. *Educational Psychology.* http://dx.doi.org/10.1080/01443410.2013.822963.

Wouters, S., De Fraine, B., Colpin, H., Van Damme, J., & Verschueren, K. (2012). The effect of track changes on the development of academic self-concept in high school: a dynamic test of the big-fish—little-pond effect. *Journal of Educational Psychology, 104*(3), 793—805. http://dx.doi.org/10.1037/a0027732.

Wu, M. (2009). A comparison of PISA and TIMSS 2003 achievement results in mathematics. *Prospects, 39,* 33—46. http://dx.doi.org/10.1007/s11125-009-9109-y.

Wylie, R. C. (1979). *The self-concept* (Vol. 2). Lincoln: University of Nebraska Press.

Xu, M. K. (2012). *Frame of reference effects in academic self-concept: An examination of the big-fish-little-pond effect and the internal/external frame of reference model for Hong Kong adolescents* (Unpublished Ph.D. thesis). Oxford University.

Zeidner, M., & Schleyer, E. J. (1998). The big-fish-little-pond effect for ASC, test anxiety, and school grades in gifted children. *Contemporary Educational Psychology, 24*, 305–329. http://dx.doi.org/10.1006/ceps.1998.0985.

Zell, E., & Alicke, M. D. (2009). Contextual neglect, self-evaluation, and the frog-pond effect. *Journal of Personality and Social Psychology, 97*, 467–482. http://dx.doi.org/10.1037/a0015453.

CHAPTER SIX

On the Panculturality of Self-enhancement and Self-protection Motivation: The Case for the Universality of Self-esteem

Constantine Sedikides*[,1], Lowell Gaertner[§] and Huajian Cai[¶]
*School of Psychology, University of Southampton, Southampton, UK
[§]Department of Psychology, University of Tennessee, Knoxville, TN, USA
[¶]Chinese Academy of Sciences, Beijing, China
[1]Corresponding author: E-mail: cs2@soton.ac.uk

Contents

1. Introduction 187
2. The Controversy 188
3. The Cultural Relativism Perspective 189
4. The Extended Self-enhancement Tactician Model (SCENT-R): Foundational Tenets 191
   4.1 Universal Valuation of the Individual Self over the Relational Self or Collective Self 191
   4.2 Universal Strength of the Self-enhancement and Self-protection Motives 193
   4.3 Universal Structure of Self-enhancement and Self-protection Strivings 195
   4.4 Universality of Desire for Self-esteem 198
   4.5 Summary and Conclusions 199
5. The Extended Self-enhancement Tactician (SCENT-R) Model: Key Postulates 200
   5.1 Self-centrality Breeds Self-enhancement: The Role of Domain Importance 200
      5.1.1 Self-esteem 201
      5.1.2 Self-enhancement and Self-protection 201
      5.1.3 The BTAE as an Index of Self-enhancement or Self-protection Motivation 204
      5.1.4 Self-enhancement and Self-protection Motivation in Socially Desirable Responding 206
   5.2 Constraints on Candid Self-enhancement: Modesty, Setting Orientation, and Other-Mediation 207
      5.2.1 Modesty 207
      5.2.2 Setting Orientation 209
      5.2.3 Other-Mediation 210
   5.3 Implicit Self-esteem: Manifestations and Motivational Significance 211
      5.3.1 Implicit Self-esteem in the East and the West 211
      5.3.2 Validity of the Self-esteem IAT 212

Advances in Motivation Science, Volume 2
ISSN 2215-0919
http://dx.doi.org/10.1016/bs.adms.2015.04.002

      5.3.3 Self-esteem IAT and the Motivational Dynamics of Self-evaluation   *213*
  5.4 Functionality of Self-esteem and Self-motives: Equivalence across East and   214
      West on Psychosocial Health
      5.4.1 The Relation between Self-esteem and Self-enhancement   *215*
      5.4.2 The Relation between Self-esteem and Psychosocial Health   *215*
      5.4.3 The Relation between Self-motives and Psychological Health   *216*
  5.5 Summary and Conclusions   218
6. Discussion   219
  6.1 Are the Self-motives and Self-esteem Universal or Culture Bound?   220
  6.2 Are the Self-motives or Self-esteem Necessarily Pursued or Valued at the   221
      Conscious Level?
  6.3 Are the Self-motives and Self-esteem Natural rather than Acquired?   221
7. Research Agenda   223
  7.1 Self-motive and Self-esteem Universalism   223
  7.2 Broader Issues   224
8. Coda   225
References   226

Abstract

Do self-enhancement/self-protection and self-esteem reflect fundamental human motivations or are they culturally bound occurrences? The debate on universalism versus cultural relativism of self-motives and self-esteem shows no sign of abatement. We advance the debate by proposing the extended self-enhancing tactician model. The model aspires to account for two seemingly contradictory phenomena: cross-cultural invariance (equivalence of self-motive strength and self-esteem desire across cultures) and cross-cultural variability (differential manifestations of self-motives and self-esteem across cultures). The model's four foundational tenets address cross-cultural invariance: (1) The individual self is panculturally valued, and it is so over the relational or collective self; (2) The self-enhancement/self-protection motives are equally potent in East and West; (3) The structure of self-enhancement and self-protection strivings is similar across the cultural divide; and (4) the desire for self-esteem is pancultural. The SCENT-R model's four key postulates address cross-cultural variability. First, Easterners assign relative importance to, and report higher, liking-based self-esteem, as well as consider collectivistic attributes important and self-enhance on them, whereas Westerners assign relative importance to, and report higher, competence-based self-esteem, as well as consider individualistic attributes important and self-enhance on them. Second, when constraints on candid self-enhancement are lifted, Easterners behave like Westerners: they report higher modesty and lower self-esteem than Westerners, but, controlling for modesty, differences in self-esteem disappear; they self-enhance in competitive, but self-efface in cooperative, settings; they profit from other-mediated than own-initiated self-enhancement. Third, implicit self-esteem is similarly high across cultures. Fourth, self-esteem and self-enhancement/self-protection confer parallel benefits in East—West, depending in part on domain relevance. Self-enhancement and self-protection, as well as self-esteem, reflect fundamental human motivation.

1. INTRODUCTION

The self is "…the totality of interrelated yet distinct psychological phenomena that either underlie, causally interact with, or depend upon reflexive consciousness" (Sedikides & Gregg, 2003, p. 110). This definition of the self appears cumbersome but has its merits. It emphasizes that the relevant properties and processes, as complex as they might be, can be conceptually defined and empirically addressed. It also embeds the self in the social world. Yet, this definition is unsatisfactory. This is the kind of self the rational android Data on *Star Trek* is likely to have, busily encoding, storing, and retrieving information in order to attain accurate knowledge or engage in effective action. Nonandroids have a different kind of self, visceral and dynamic, immersed in motivation and affect. We are concerned, in this chapter, with the motivated, affect-imbued self.

Psychologists have proposed several taxonomies of self-motives (Deci & Ryan, 2000; Epstein & Morling, 1995; Gregg, Sedikides, & Gebauer, 2011; Sedikides & Strube, 1997; Vignoles, Camillo, Manzi, Golledge, & Scabini, 2006). We focus on self-enhancement and self-protection, as these motives have had a prominent status in the field and are comparatively influential (Baumeister, 1998; Brown, 1998; Sedikides, 1993; Sedikides & Green, 2004). We define self-enhancement and self-protection as motivations to augment the positivity or diminish the negativity of the self, respectively (Alicke & Sedikides, 2009; Sedikides, 2012).[1] Psychologists have likewise proposed several taxonomies of self-related emotions or affect (Keltner & Beer, 1995; Sedikides et al., 2015; Tangney & Tracy, 2012; Zeigler-Hill, 2013). We focus on self-esteem, also a preeminent construct in the field and, importantly, the affective correlate (and potentially cause or effect) of self-enhancement and self-protection (Baumeister, 1998; Lönnqvist et al., 2009; Sedikides & Gregg, 2003; Tesser, 1988). We define self-esteem as an attitude toward oneself—an attitude that involves evaluative self-beliefs (e.g., being punctual is good) and that is associated with feelings about the self (e.g., I love it when I am useful to others) (Banaji & Prentice, 1994; Blascovich & Tomaka, 1991).

Given the potency of self-enhancement and self-protection, and the prevalence of self-esteem, one would expect them to be found universally: The

---

[1] This classification is a subset of a broader classification between approach and avoidance motivation (Elliot & Mapes, 2005).

self would be nurtured to positivity and shielded from negativity, as well as be prized, to a similar extent across cultures.[2] Going against the panculturality case, a cultural relativism argument states that self-enhancement and self-protection, as well as self-esteem, are found in some parts of the world (the West) but not necessarily in others (the East). The self is not promoted and protected, and is not equally treasured, across cultures.

Herein we reignite, summarize, and advance the textured debate surrounding the universalism versus cultural relativism of self-enhancement/self-protection and self-esteem. This is not a frivolous endeavor, as steps toward resolution of this debate can be generative and yield insight into the nature of motivation and the self. We begin by defining the controversy and describing the cultural relativism perspective. Then, we review the evidence in the context of the extended self-enhancement tactician (SCENT-R) Model. We conclude and draw implications.

2. THE CONTROVERSY

Western thinking has considered self-enhancement, self-protection, and self-esteem (or homologous constructs) as universal, since the time of Greek (Sophists; Kerferd, 1981) and Roman (Cicero; Wood, 1991) philosophers. This notion persisted, and indeed strengthened, with the Renaissance movement (Macfarlane, 1978), as well as by seventeenth century (Thomas Hobbes) and eighteenth to nineteenth century (Jeremy Bentham, John Stuart Mill) British philosophers (Allport, 1954), and was consolidated in the United States Constitution and legal system. The notion was introduced in psychology by William James (1907), was upheld by the writings of Gordon Allport (1937), by work on reinforcement principles (Dollard & Miller, 1950), and by the insights of Abraham Maslow (1943) and Carl Rogers (1961), and led to a salvo of theoretical and empirical contributions in the 1970s—1980s and beyond (Alicke & Sedikides, 2011; Baumeister, 1998; Becker, 1968; Brown, 2003; Deci & Ryan, 1995; Dunning, 1993; Greenwald, 1980; Paulhus & Reid, 1991; Pyszczynski, Greenberg, Solomon, Arndt, & Schimel, 2004; Schwartz, 1992; Sedikides & Strube, 1997; Sherman & Cohen, 2006; Taylor & Brown, 1988; Tesser, 1988;

---

[2] We define culture as "patterns of historically derived and selected ideas and their embodiment in institutions, practices, and artifacts" (Ford & Mauss, 2015, p. 1; see also: Kroeber & Kluckholm, 1952).

Vignoles, 2011; Wills, 1981). In a nutshell, people, no matter the culture they come from, are motivated to self-enhance and self-protect. They desire self-positivity (the "good news," praise, or information about their strengths and virtues) and loath self-negativity (the "bad news," criticism, or information about their weaknesses and vices). People also value having high self-esteem (feeling good about themselves, feeling worthy and liked). For example, they list self-esteem as a key component of their most satisfying life events (Sheldon, Elliot, Kim, & Kasser, 2001) and choose self-esteem boosts over eating favored foods, receiving paychecks, seeing close friends, or engaging in sexual activities (Bushman, Moeller, & Crocker, 2011).

The universality of the self-motives and self-esteem was challenged by the culture movement that flourished in the 1990s. The movement offered a well-reasoned, data-backed thesis. The two motives, along with self-esteem, are culturally bound. They are observed in abundance in the West, but not in the East. For example, Japanese do not possess or wish to possess a positive self (Heine, Kitayama, & Lehman, 2001; Maddux et al., 2010; Markus & Kitayama, 1991) and do not have or wish to have high self-esteem (Heine, 2012; Heine, Lehman, Markus, & Kitayama, 1999), compared to Americans. In fact, Japanese habitually self-criticize rather than self-enhance or self-protect (Heine, Takata, & Lehman, 2000; Kitayama, Markus, Matsumoto, & Norasakkunkit, 1997), and they strive for self-improvement (Heine, Kitayama, Lehman, Takata, et al., 2001). That is:

> The empirical literature provides scant evidence for a need for positive self-regard among Japanese and indicates that a self-critical focus is more characteristic of Japanese...the need for self-regard must be culturally variant...[and] the need for self-regard...is not a universal, but rather is rooted in significant aspects of North American culture.
>
> **Heine et al. (1999, p. 766)**

3. THE CULTURAL RELATIVISM PERSPECTIVE

The cultural relativism perspective posits that Western and Eastern cultural ideas, norms, and practices shape different selves, and this disparity accounts for the ensuing variation in self-motives and levels of self-esteem.

Cultural discrepancy in self-evaluation is purportedly rooted in the way, in which self-construal is forged. Norms, ideals, concepts, beliefs, or values shape the psychological system, and hence the self, via societal institutions and socialization practices (Chiu & Hong, 2006; Morris, 2014; Nisbett, 2003). Of particular interest is the dimension of individualism—collectivism (Hofstede, 1980, 2001; Triandis, 1995; see also Ford & Mauss, 2015).[3] Western culture forges an individualistic self. The culture mandates for independence, distinctiveness, self-sufficiency, emotional expressiveness, personal control, and personal success. East-Asian culture, on the other hand, forges a collectivistic self. The culture mandates for interdependence, cooperation, embeddedness in society, emotional control, relational harmony, and responsibility to the group.

The argument acknowledges nuances in definitions of individualism—collectivism, in the distribution of this dimension across cultures, and in its somewhat varied correlates or consequences (Brewer & Chen, 2007; Oyserman, Coon, & Kemmelmeier, 2002; Shavitt, Zhang, Torelli, & Lalwani, 2006; Van Hoorn, 2015; but see Schimmack, Oishi, & Diener, 2005). Yet, the argument rests on the empirically informed proposition that individualism (observed disproportionately in the West) and collectivism (observed disproportionately in the East) shape self-construal differentially. Individualism forges independent self-construal, whereas collectivism forges interdependent self-construal. Independent and interdependent self-construal may have genetic links. For example, the difference in independence and interdependence between Westerners (European Americans) and Easterners (Asian-born Asians) is accentuated for carriers than noncarriers of the 7- or 2-repeat alleles of the dopamine D4 receptor gene (*DRD4*; Kitayama et al., 2014).

Divergent selves engender markedly different self-motivations and levels of self-esteem. *Individualistic selves* rely on self-expression, validation of internal attributes, and demonstration of innate ability. In a society that values independence and self-sufficiency, the person cannot afford to think lowly of the self—in fact, the astute positioning, if not the acquired motivation, is to think positively of the self and show it to others. It is functional for Westerners to endorse self-enhancement or self-protection strivings and hence to exhibit high self-esteem. *Collectivistic selves*, on the other hand, rely on self-discipline, validation of group membership, and demonstration of

---

[3] We distinguish between Eastern—Western cultures and individualistic—collectivistic cultures. The dimension of individualism—collectivism is broader, as it can incorporate countries that are geographically positioned in the East or in the West. For example, countries high on collectivism (Hofstede, 2011) can be in East-Asia (e.g., Hong Kong, Malaysia) or in the West (e.g., Chile, Serbia). Generally, though, Eastern countries are more individualistic than Western ones.

social utility. In a society that values interdependence and interpersonal harmony, the person cannot afford to stand out and tout superiority to others—in fact, the optimal route is to entertain egalitarian views of the self and convey them to others. It is functional for East-Asians to jettison self-enhancement or self-protection strivings and hence to display low self-esteem.

4. THE EXTENDED SELF-ENHANCEMENT TACTICIAN MODEL (SCENT-R): FOUNDATIONAL TENETS

Our proposal is that culture, a source of normative and informational social influence, can affect self-enhancement or self-protection as observed effects. However, culture cannot affect self-enhancement or self-protection as underlying motives. To use a gastronomic analogy (Sedikides & Gregg, 2008), culture can affect how much one eats (e.g., observed effect: self-criticism), but cannot affect how hungry one will get (e.g., underlying motive: self-enhancement). A person can self-criticize when the person's motive is to self-enhance. That is, even when members of East-Asian culture are observed to display lower levels of self-positivity than their Western counterparts (Heine & Hamamura, 2007; Heine et al., 2000; Kitayama et al., 1997), this observation does not imply that they lack the motive to self-enhance or that the motive to self-enhance is weaker. They may simply manifest the motives differently. A theory is needed, then, that will account for (1) equivalence of motive strength and desire for self-esteem across cultures, but (2) differential manifestations of self-motives and self-esteem across cultures. This theory is the Extended Self-Concept Enhancing Tactician (SCENT-R) model (for its initial formulation, see: Sedikides & Strube, 1997).

The gist of the SCENT-R model is that people in the East and West satisfy the two self-motives and their desire for self-esteem differently. The model consists of four foundational tenets that transcend contextual considerations. The tenets are as follows: Universal valuation of the individual self over the relational or collective self, universal strength of self-enhancement and self-protection motivation, universality of self-enhancement and self-protection strategies, and universality of desire for self-esteem. We elaborate on these tenets below.

4.1 Universal Valuation of the Individual Self over the Relational Self or Collective Self

The SCENT-R endorses the idea that the individual (or personal) self is valued not only to the same degree across cultures, but also to a higher degree than the relational or collective self across cultures. The individual self represents the unique side of the person and comprises aspects (e.g., traits, roles, experiences) that differentiate the person from others. The relational self refers to attachments with close others and comprises aspects shared with these others, and aspects that are associated with role obligations. Lastly, the collective self refers to identification with important social groups and comprises aspects that define the in-group and differentiate it from the relevant, antagonistic out-group (Sedikides, Gaertner, Luke, O'Mara, & Gebauer, 2013). We assumed, in line with past research (Lea & Webley, 2006), that the value of each self can be conveyed monetarily, with the more important group being worthy of a higher amount. We allocated to Chinese and American participants a putative sum of money and asked them to distribute it, in any way they wished, to the three selves (which we defined for participants in advance). Irrespective of culture, participants allocated the highest monetary amount to the individual self, followed by the relational self and then by the collective self (Gaertner, Sedikides, Luke, et al., 2012; Study 3).

In a follow-up study (Gaertner, Sedikides, Luke, et al., 2012; Study 4), we examined whether Westerners and Easterners value characteristics (i.e., goals) of the future individual self more so than characteristics of the future relational or collective self. We assumed that the more primary a self was, the more this self would be associated with future goals (Emmons, 1986). We instructed Chinese and American participants to write a narrative describing their individual, relational, or collective self. For example, the third of participants who were in the individual-self condition read: "Being a unique individual is an important part of life. Indeed, you are a unique individual with your own unique background, personality traits, skills, abilities, interests, and hobbies. Please take a few minutes and describe what makes you unique" (p. 1007). Upon completion of the narratives, participants listed 12 future goals. Subsequently, they indicated whether each goal referred to the individual, relational, or collective self (which we defined for them at that point). Regardless of culture, participants attributed more than twice as many goals to the individual self than either the relational or collective self. Put otherwise, the individual self was associated with over half of the desired goals that Chinese and American participants had.

Collectively, the findings established a cross-cultural motivational hierarchy, with the individual self at the top, followed by the other two selves. Del Prado et al. (2007) reported similar results with the individual self being assigned primacy over the collective self across cultures. Other researchers have also reported results consistent with the primacy of the individual self. Ybarra and Trafimow (1998, Experiment 3) primed either the individual self or the collective self, and found that participants in both conditions wrote down more descriptions pertaining to the individual than the collective self (see also Gaertner, Sedikides, & Graetz, 1999; Experiment 4). Finjeman, Willemsen, and Poortinga (1996) assessed expected inputs to and outputs from various kinds of relationships (e.g., parents, siblings, cousins, friends, acquaintances, strangers) in both individualistic (The Netherlands and United States) and collectivistic (Hong Kong, Greece, Turkey) cultures, and found that, regardless of culture, the willingness to provide for others was related to expectations of what would be received from others. Aarts, Oikawa, and Oikawa (2010) found that the experience of self-agency consists of a nonconscious and universal (i.e., observed both in Japan and The Netherlands) component. Further, Japanese, when asked to describe their ideal self, express a stronger desire to be independent than interdependent (Hashimoto, Li, & Yamagishi, 2011), South Koreans regard themselves as less collectivistic than their peers (Shteynberg, Gelfand, & Kim, 2009), Japanese and Americans have an equally strong need for uniqueness (Kim & Markus, 1999), and Japanese are even more likely than Americans to free ride, that is, exit the group in the absence of mutual monitoring or sanctioning (Yamagishi, 1988; see also Parks & Vu, 1995).

4.2 Universal Strength of the Self-enhancement and Self-protection Motives

The SCENT-R model endorses the notion that the self-enhancement motive is potent among Westerners and Easterners. To be more precise, the model rejects the notion that this motive is stronger in the West than the East. We addressed these issues empirically (Gaertner, Sedikides, & Cai, 2012). We operationalized self-motivation in terms of what people desire or want for themselves (Hepper, Hart, Gregg, & Sedikides, 2011). To return to the gastronomic analogy, just as persons driven by hunger desire food, persons motivated by self-enhancement would desire positive distinctiveness. Chinese and American participants rated the extent to which they wanted to receive self-enhancing feedback, and also self-improving and self-effacing feedback, from multiple sources (friends, parents, teachers, classmates). The inclusion of two additional types of feedback—self-improving and self-effacing—allowed us to test whether Chinese, more than Americans, are motivated by self-improvement or self-criticism. We also incorporated a no-feedback control condition. As an example of the format in which participants received the feedback, the items pertaining to friends (with feedback type, in italics, unseen by participants) were: "I want my friends to tell me..." "(a) I am a great friend (*self-enhancing*), (b) how to be a better friend (*self-improving*), (c) I am an average friend (*self-effacing*), and (d) nothing about the kind of friend I am (*no feedback*)." We adapted the feedback format and feedback items from Neiss, Sedikides, Shahinfar, and Kupersmidt (2006; see Gregg, Hepper, & Sedikides, 2011, for additional validation). Further, we operationalized self-effacement in accordance with Heine and Lehman's (1995) suggestion that, for East-Asians, "self-effacement, in the form of seeing oneself as average...would more likely serve the cultural mandate of maintaining interpersonal harmony" (p. 596). Being average implies higher similarity to others (Ott-Holland, Huang, Ryan, Elizondo, & Wadlington, 2014), compared to any other position in the distribution, thus capturing the essence of East-Asian self-effacement (e.g., being like others or being connected to others).

The results of our investigation (Gaertner, Sedikides, & Cai, 2012) were revealing. Chinese and American participants overwhelmingly desired self-enhancing and self-improving feedback more than any other kind of feedback. Persons, regardless of culture, wanted feedback that extolled their virtues and ensured that they could become even better. Moreover, neither Chinese nor American participants desired self-effacing feedback; they both deemed self-effacing feedback to be as undesirable as no feedback. In short, the findings are consistent with the idea that the self-enhancement motive is vibrant in both cultures (for similar conclusions, see: Becker et al., 2012; Church et al., 2012; Niiya, Crocker, & Mischkowski, 2012). The findings also indicate that the Chinese are as motivated to self-improve, and as unmotivated to self-criticize, as Americans.

The SCENT-R model capitalizes on the notion that not only the self-enhancement motive, but also the self-protection motive is potent across cultures. Again, to be precise, the model rebuffs the notion that this motive is stronger in the West than the East. As we mentioned,[1] self-protection is a specific case of avoidance motivation (Elliot & Mapes, 2005). Avoidance goals are stronger in East-Asian than in Western culture (Elliot, Chirkov, Sheldon, & Kim, 2001; Elliot et al., 2012; Hamamura, Meijer, Heine, Kamaya, & Hori, 2009). East-Asians score higher on prevention focus (an instance of avoidance motivation) than promotion focus (an instance of approach motivation) (Hepper, Sedikides, & Cai, 2013; Kim, Peng, & Chiu, 2008; Lalwani, Shrum, & Chiu, 2009). Likewise, self-protection motivation is stronger in East-Asian than Western culture. To begin, collectivism or interdependence involves rejection avoidance along with harmony seeking (Hashimoto & Yamagishi, 2013). Further, East-Asians manifest excessive concern with face saving or embarrassment avoidance (Ho, 1976; Hwang, 1987; Triandis, 1995) and show conformity in a strategic attempt to avoid a negative reputation (Yamagishi, Hashimoto, & Schug, 2008). The modesty norm is indeed stronger in East-Asian than Western culture (Sedikides, Gregg, & Hart, 2007), with East-Asians favoring modesty in self-presentation to a greater extent than Americans (Bond, Leung, & Wan, 1978) and perceiving Americans as immodest (Terracciano & McCrae, 2007). As supplementary evidence for the relative vigor of the self-protection motive, East-Asians are more likely to render positive self-judgments by repudiating negative self-qualities (e.g., "I am flawless") than by affirming favorable self-qualities (e.g., "I am perfect"), whereas the reverse pattern is observed among Westerners (Kim, Chiu, Peng, Cai, & Tov, 2010).

The domain of memory is well suited for the investigation of self-protection motivation (Sedikides, 2012; Skowronski, 2011). Here, the findings also attest to panculturality. The fading affect bias, whereby negative affect associated with autobiographical events fades faster than positive affect associated with such events, is present both in Western and Eastern cultures (Ritchie et al., 2015). Moreover, mnemic neglect, whereby negative feedback about important self-attributes (but not negative feedback about unimportant self-attributes or about attributes pertaining to another person) is remembered poorly compared to positive feedback about important self-attributes (Sedikides & Green, 2009), is observed both in the West and the East (Tan, Newman, & Zhang, 2014). In short, the evidence is congruent with the notion that the self-protection motive is at least as powerful in the East as it is in the West—and, in fact, may be more powerful in the former than the latter.

4.3 Universal Structure of Self-enhancement and Self-protection Strivings

The SCENT-R model posits that, not only the underlying self-motives, but also the corresponding strivings are found cross-culturally. However, the model distinguishes between structural and content manifestation. In particular, the model posits cultural invariance in the structural manifestation of the self-motives; that is, as we advocate below, the self-motives are characterized by a universal structure of four strivings: defensiveness, positivity embracement, favorable construal, and self-affirming reflections. However, as we will discuss in a later Section 5.1, the model proposes cultural variability in content manifestation of the two self-motives; that is, the content of these strivings may be expressed differently, depending on culture.

We put the proposition of universality in structural manifestation of self-enhancement/self-protection strivings to test (Hepper, Gramzow, & Sedikides, 2010). Following a literature review, we compiled an exhaustive list of cognitive, affective, and behavioral strivings of self-enhancement or self-protection motivation. For each striving, we wrote a representative item. For example, for "better-than-average beliefs" we wrote "Thinking of yourself as generally possessing positive personality traits or abilities to a greater extent than most people," and for "self-serving bias" we wrote "When you achieve success or really good grades, thinking it was due to your ability." We generated 60 items in total. Then, we conducted two studies with Western participants.

In Study 1 (Hepper et al., 2010), we instructed participants that they would be presented with "several patterns of thought, feeling, and behavior in which people engage during the course of everyday life" (p. 791), and asked them to indicate the extent to which each pattern (i.e., striving) was characteristic or typical of them. We subjected participants' responses to an exploratory factor analysis, which resulted in four factors (i.e., manifestations). The first factor was *defensiveness*, that is, self-protection strivings triggered by self-threat. Such strivings involve preparing for (behaviorally) and deflecting (cognitively) undesirable feedback (e.g., self-handicapping prior to evaluative settings in order to make an excuse for failure, attributing undesirable feedback to external sources, expending disproportionate cognitive effort toward the discounting of undesirable feedback). The second factor was *positivity embracement*, that is, self-enhancement strivings triggered by positive feedback opportunities. Such strivings involve obtaining (behaviorally) and making the most of (cognitively) desirable feedback (e.g., selectively interacting with persons likely to provide positive feedback, self-presenting favorably in social interactions, taking credit for group success). The third factor was *favorable construal*, that is, chronic self-enhancement strivings. These strivings involve self-serving cognition about the social world (e.g., believing one is better-than-average on important traits, anticipating a rosier future for the self than for others, interpreting ambiguous feedback as favorable). The fourth and final factor was *self-affirming reflections*, that is, self-enhancement strivings triggered by self-threat. These strivings entail the preservation of self-integrity in the face of imminent or past threat (e.g., bringing to mind one's values when confronted with failure, comparing favorably one's present to one's own past, engaging in counter-factual thinking about worse alternatives).

In Study 2 (Hepper et al., 2010), we validated the four-factor manifes-tation structure via a confirmatory factor analysis, ruling out alternatives (i.e., one-factor and two-factor models). In addition, we obtained theory-consistent associations between the factors and individual differences such as regulatory focus, self-esteem, and narcissism. Defensiveness (a family of strivings relevant to actual or anticipated self-threat) was positively related to prevention focus, whereas the other three factors (families of enhance-ment-oriented strivings) were positively related to promotion focus (Higgins, 1998). Self-esteem was negatively related to defensiveness, congruent with findings that persons with high self-esteem are less prone to self-protection (Tice, 1991), but was positively related to the other three factors, congruent with findings that persons with high self-esteem are more prone to self-enhancement (Tice, 1991). Finally, narcissism was related positively both to defensiveness and the other three factors, congruent with findings that narcissists respond self-protectively to failure and self-enhance at any opportunity (Morf, Horvath, & Torchetti, 2011).

More important, we wondered whether the four-factor configuration of self-enhancement and self-protection manifestations, as well as pertinent links with individual differences, is applicable to Eastern culture. For that purpose, we (Hepper et al., 2013) recruited a Chinese sample and compared it to a Western sample, namely that of Hepper et al.'s (2010) Study 2. We assessed self-enhancement and self-protection expressions not with the full 60-item set used in Hepper et al. (2010), but rather with an abbreviated 20-item scale comprising the five items that loaded the highest on each of the four factors (i.e., defensiveness, positivity embracement, favorable construal, self-affirming reflections). We also assessed regulatory focus, self-esteem, and narcissism with scales validated in China. The factor structure of the manifestations was similar in the two samples: the four-factor model fits well and fits better than alter-natives (one-factor or two-factor) models. The four-factor model exhibited scalar invariance (Cheung & Rensvold, 2002), which is a strong form of mea-surement invariance across cultures (Meredith, 1993). Specifically, it indicates that a researcher can legitimately compare each factor's correlations, and even each factor's latent mean, across cultures (Horn & McArdle, 1992). Further, and in replication of past findings (Kim et al., 2010; Lalwani et al., 2009), Chinese, compared to Westerners, scored higher on defensiveness (a family of self-protective strivings), but lower on positivity embracement (a family of self-enhancement strivings). Yet, Chinese scored higher on favorable self-construal, an enhancement-oriented family of strivings. This finding broadly contradicts prior results suggesting that East-Asians, relative to Westerners, manifest lower levels of the better-than-average effect (BTAE) and unrealistic optimism (Heine & Hamamura, 2007). The finding, though, is reminiscent of "spiritual victories," a prominent concept in Chinese literature, denoting attempts to convince oneself of one's goodness and superiority. Spiritual victories are famously epitomized in Lu Xun's *The Real Story of Ah-Q* (trans. Lovell, 2010), written in the early twentieth century and still considered a reflection of national character. Such a finding is a step toward legitimizing the use of such measures as better-than-average judgments to assess Chinese self-enhancement. Finally, the associations between the three individual difference variables (regulatory focus, self-esteem, and narcissism) and the four families of strivings (defensiveness, positivity embracement, favorable construal, and self-affirming reflections) evinced a similar pattern in the Chinese and Western sample. In all, members of both cultural groups manifest the self-enhancement and self-protection motives, and arguably satisfy these motives, using similar strivings. Also, individual-level variation in the reported use of these expressions is comparable across cultures.

4.4 Universality of Desire for Self-esteem

The fourth and final foundational tenet of the SCENT-R model is that the desire for self-esteem is universal. Although Easterners score lower on explicit self-esteem scales (e.g., Rosenberg's (1965) Self-esteem Scale or RSES) than Westerners, they typically score above the theoretical midpoint of the rating scale (Brown, Cai, Oakes, & Deng, 2009; Cai et al., 2011; Cai, Wu, & Brown, 2009; Kwan, Kuang, & Hui, 2009; Schmitt & Allik, 2005; Yamaguchi et al., 2007; but see Diener & Diener, 1995) indicating universally positive self-attitudes or self-love. Also, East-Asians (i.e., Japanese) regard self-esteem to be as desirable as Westerners (i.e., Americans), emphasizing its role in healthy child development (Brown, 2008a) and good mental health (Brown, 2008b).

But why do Easterners report lower self-esteem than Westerners? A key reason is modesty, a pervasive norm in the East (Chiu & Hong, 2006; Shikanai, 1978; Yamaguchi, Lin, & Aoki, 2006). Japanese children, as young as eight years old, internalize the modesty norm (Yoshida, Kojo, & Kaku, 1982). Chinese children claim it is moral not only to underreport one's good deeds but also to lie about them (Lee, Xu, Fu, Cameron, & Chen, 2001). More generally, in China the modesty norm (reflecting the Confucian proverb "haughtiness invites loss while modesty brings benefits") is considered a powerful deterrent to positive self-attitudes and self-love in China (Bond et al., 1978; Kwan, Bond, & Singelis, 1977; Tseng, 1973). Indeed, modesty among Chinese is negatively correlated with explicit self-esteem (Cai, Brown, Deng, & Oakes, 2007; Cai et al., 2011; Study 1).

Furthermore, self-esteem is universally derived from fulfillment of one's cultural value priorities. Relying on cross-sectional and longitudinal samples of 20 cultures that varied on individualism—collectivism, Becker et al. (2014) examined the influence of four self-evaluative bases (achieving social status, controlling one's life, doing one's duty, benefiting others) on self-esteem. Participants derived self-esteem from all four self-evaluative bases, but particularly from adhering to the bases that were prioritized highly by others in their own cultural milieu. Likewise, Kwan et al. (2009) found that both Chinese and American participants relied on the same three sources of self-esteem, namely benevolence (positive perceptions of self and others), merit (noteworthy accomplishments), and bias (self-positivity).

Evidence from the literature on mortality coping is also indicative. Terror management theory (Greenberg, Solomon, & Pyszczynski, 1997; Pyszczynski et al., 2004) proposes that the universal desire for self-esteem is underpinned by the fundamental need for psychological security that arises from one's vulnerability, existential angst, and mortality awareness. In support of these ideas, the literature has established that mortality reminders strengthen attempts to defend or elevate self-esteem, and that self-esteem acts as a vital resource that buffers anxiety and reduces defensiveness against mortality. Crucially to our argument, these effects are obtained both in Western cultures (Burke, Martens, & Faucher, 2010; Greenberg, 2008) and in East-Asian cultures (Heine, Niiya, & Harihara, 2002; Kashima, Halloran, Yuki, & Kashima, 2004; Nodera, Karasawa, Numazaki, & Takabayashi, 2007; Tam, Chiu, & Lau, 2007; Wakimoto, 2006).

4.5 Summary and Conclusions

The SCENT-R model is built on four tenets that aim to highlight the equivalence across East and West of the strength of self-enhancement/self-protection and of the desire for self-esteem. We reviewed evidence consistent with these four foundational tenets. First, the individual self is universally valued, and is also valued universally over the relational or collective self. Second, the strength of self-enhancement and self-protection motivation is equivalent across Eastern and Western cultures. Third, members of both cultural groups rely on the same expressions of the self-enhancement and self-protection motives. Finally, the desire for self-esteem is universal. Having articulated the foundational tenets and reviewed empirical support for them, we proceed to a consideration of the model's key postulates.

5. THE EXTENDED SELF-ENHANCEMENT TACTICIAN (SCENT-R) MODEL: KEY POSTULATES

The SCENT-R model comprises four key postulates. These postulates refer to context-sensitive or tactical; yet still universal, content manifestations of self-enhancement, self-protection, and self-esteem. The first postulate builds on the principle "self-centrality breeds self-enhancement" and focuses on the role of attribute centrality or importance in the East and the West. The second postulate refers to the role of modesty and its differential relevance in the two cultural groups. The third postulate concerns implicit self-esteem across cultures, and its motivational significance in the East. The fourth and final postulate advocates the functionality of self-esteem and self-motives across the East/West divide. We elaborate on these postulates below.

5.1 Self-centrality Breeds Self-enhancement: The Role of Domain Importance

William James (1907) was the first to articulate the principle "self-centrality breeds self-enhancement," namely that self-enhancement and self-protection occur mainly in domains that matter to the self. James stated (p. 31): "I, who for the time have staked my all on being a psychologist, am mortified if others know much more psychology than I. But I am contended to wallow in the grossest ignorance of Greek." The principle has a venerable tradition in psychology (Crocker & Wolfe, 2001; Greenberg et al., 1997; Harter, 1993; Sedikides & Strube, 1997; Tesser, 2000). A recent empirical example is the work of Gebauer, Wagner, Sedikides, and Neberich (2013). They focused on agency, a construct homologous to individualism, which they operationalized with a set of 10 adjectives (e.g., ambitious, dominant, leader) and on communion, a construct homologous to collectivism, which they operationalized with another set of 10 adjectives (e.g., caring, compassionate, understanding). (For a review of agency and communion, see: Abele & Wojciszke, 2014.) Gebauer et al. hypothesized that agency would predict self-esteem strongly in individuals for whom agency was central, whereas communion would predict self-esteem strongly in individuals for whom communion was central. The results were consistent with the hypotheses. Another example is the work of Lönnqvist et al. (2009). Endorsement of achievement and universalism values predicted self-esteem among persons, who considered these values important, whereas endorsement of self-direction and hedonism values predicted self-esteem among persons, who considered these values important.

5.1.1 Self-esteem

The "self-centrality breeds self-enhancement" principle is relevant to the issue of panculturality of self-esteem. Adhering to standards of high self-centrality is the primary source of self-esteem (Brown, 2010a; Greenberg et al., 1997; Yamaguchi, Lin, Morio, & Okumura, 2008). However, as we have discussed, different sources are primary in the West and the East. Tafarodi and colleagues (Tafarodi & Milne, 2002; Tafarodi & Swann, 1996) distinguished between self-esteem based on self-competence (i.e., feeling that one is capable and efficacious) and self-esteem based on self-liking (i.e., feeling that is relationally skillful and accepted by others). Further, Tafarodi et al. proposed that individualistic cultures would assign foremost importance to competence-based self-esteem and collectivistic cultures to liking-based self-esteem. It follows that members of individualistic (e.g., Western) cultures would report higher levels of competence-based self-esteem, whereas members of collectivistic (e.g., Eastern) cultures would report higher levels of liking-based self-esteem. This pattern has been obtained consistently across Eastern and Western cultures (Baranik et al., 2008; Kwan et al., 2009; Nezlek et al., 2008; Schmitt & Allik, 2005; Tafarodi, Lange, & Smith, 1999; Tafarodi & Swann, 1996; Tafarodi & Walters, 1999).

5.1.2 Self-enhancement and Self-protection

The "self-centrality breeds self-enhancement" principle is also highly relevant to the issue of panculturality of self-motives. The SCENT-R model assumes that self-enhancement (or self-protection) can be either candid or tactical. Candid self-enhancement is expressed directly and immediately. However, tactical self-enhancement is more susceptible to acute concerns and often forgoes immediate aggrandizement for long-term gain. In this section, we are concerned with candid self-enhancement (and self-protection).

The SCENT-R model posits that individuals will self-enhance or self-protect on domains that are important (rather than unimportant) to them (Sedikides, 1993). Self-enhancing or self-protecting on personally important attributes (e.g., traits or behaviors) allows individuals to feel that they adhere to culturally prescribed roles. Indeed, to a substantial degree, the personal importance of an evaluative domain is prescribed by culture (Fischer, 2006). In a cross-cultural context, the implication is that Westerners will self-enhance or self-protect on individualistic attributes (due to the personal importance of these attributes), whereas Easterners will self-enhance or self-protect on collectivistic attributes (due, again, to the personal importance of such attributes).

Sedikides, Gaertner, and Toguchi (2003) documented this pattern. In Study 1, American and Japanese participants imagined being a member of a 16-person task force, whose mission was to solve four types of business problems (advertising, planning, personnel, and budget). All group members were to be of the same ethnicity as well as demographics (age, gender, educational level). Then, participants spent 10 min imagining and writing down ideas and solutions to the business problem for hypothetical sharing with other members. Finally, participants were presented with a set of individualistic traits (e.g., independent, original, self-reliant) and behaviors (e.g., trust your own instincts rather than your group's instincts, disagree with your group when you believe the group is wrong, desert your group when the group does not represent you anymore), and also with a set of collectivistic traits (e.g., cooperative, compromising, loyal) and behaviors (e.g., conform to your group's decisions, avoid conflict with your group at any cost, do anything for your group). Pretesting had determined that individualistic attributes had been rated by participants as more "individualistic" than "collectivistic" (according to definitions provided), and vice versa. On each set, participants compared themselves to the typical group member. They indicated how well each trait described them, and how likely they were to enact each behavior, relative to the typical member of the task force. In support of the SCENT-R model, Americans self-enhanced (or self-protected) more strongly than Japanese on individualistic than collectivistic attributes, whereas Japanese self-enhanced more strongly than Americans on collectivistic than individualistic attributes. In all, self-enhancement took a tactical form. Both cultural groups self-enhanced (thus demonstrating equivalent strength of underlying motive), but on different domains (thus demonstrating distinct motive manifestation).

In Study 1, we (Sedikides et al., 2003) assumed but did not test the idea that self-construal (independent vs interdependent) is responsible for the obtained effects (Matsumoto, 1999). We also did not test directly the idea that personal importance drives the influence of self-enhancement motivation on self-evaluative judgments. We addressed these issues in Study 2

(Sedikides et al., 2003). We engaged, in particular, in a within-culture test, with all participants being from the United States. In the first phase of the study, we administered to a large group of participants the Singelis (1994) self-construal scale. On this basis, we divided participants into two groups: a sample that scored high on independence but low on interdependence (analogous to Study 1's American participants) and a sample that scored low on independence but high on interdependence (analogous to Study 1's Japanese participants). Four to eight weeks later, we randomly drew from each sample 48 participants (henceforth "independents" and "interdependents") and invited them to the laboratory for a second session, where we tested them individually. The procedure was the same as in Study 1, with a key addition: Participants rated the personal importance of the trait or behavior. The results, once again, were consistent with the SCENT-R model. Independents self-enhanced (or self-protected) more than interdependents on individualistic than collectivistic attributes, whereas interdependents self-enhanced more than independents on collectivistic than individualistic attributes. In addition, independents considered individualistic attributes more personally important than collectivistic ones, whereas the reverse was true for interdependents. Finally, attribute personal importance mediated the influence of the self-enhancement motive on self-evaluative judgments. Independents self-enhanced on individualistic attributes due to the personal importance that such attributes had, and likewise interdependents self-enhanced on collectivistic attributes due to the personal importance of such attributes. Both self-construal groups self-enhanced on personally important domains, albeit distinct ones. As predicted by SCENT-R, what matters is not the domain per se but rather whether the domain is tethered to the self.

These findings were not idiosyncratic, confined to our own laboratory. We replicated them by meta-analyzing the extant literature. In line with the specifications of the SCENT-R model, we searched for studies in which participants (1) rated the self (on positive or negative attributes) in comparison to another person (2) on a domain that was empirically validated a priori by researchers to be personally important or unimportant to participants (Sedikides, Gaertner, & Vevea, 2007b, 2007a). In one meta-analysis (Sedikides, Gaertner, & Vevea, 2005; Experiment 1), we demonstrated that Western participants indeed self-enhanced (or self-protected) on individualistic attributes, whereas East-Asian participants self-enhanced on collectivistic attributes. In another meta-analysis (Sedikides et al., 2005; Experiment 2), we demonstrated that members of each cultural group

self-enhanced on the corresponding domain—individualistic for Westerners, collectivistic for Easterners—because that domain was personally
important to them.

5.1.3 The BTAE as an Index of Self-enhancement or Self-protection Motivation

The results of the above-described program of research (Sedikides et al., 2003,
2005, 2007b, 2007a) were based on the BTAE, whereby people overestimate
their merits (or underestimate their liabilities) in comparison to their peers.
The effect is robust and pervasive, found across a wide range of samples,
ages, and evaluative domains (Alicke & Govorun, 2005). People truly believe
in their better-than-average judgments, betting money on them (Williams &
Gilovich, 2008). Crucially, the BTAE reflects motivation and indeed may be
the single best index of (explicitly expressed) self-enhancement motivation
(Guenther & Alicke, 2010; cf. Hamamura, Heine, & Takemoto, 2007). It
may also be suitable for capturing self-enhancement in the East, or at least
in some (e.g., Chinese) Eastern cultures due to the similarity between the
BTAE and the construct of "spiritual victories" (Lovell, 2010). We have
reviewed elsewhere the reasons why the BTAE is motivated (Sedikides &
Alicke, 2012), and recapitulate below.

The BTAE varies in accordance to principles of motivation theory. First,
the BTAE is stronger on personally important than personally unimportant
traits (Brown, 2012; Studies 1—4). For example, people regard themselves
as superior to others on trustworthiness but not necessarily on punctu-
ality—a sign of self-enhancement motivation. Second, the BTAE varies as
a function of attribute valence and controllability (Alicke, 1985). The effect
is stronger on positive traits on which people have high control (e.g.,
resourceful) than low control (e.g., mature), and it is stronger on negative
traits on which people have high control (e.g., unappreciative) than low control (e.g., humorless). Stated otherwise, people regard themselves as more
resourceful, but not necessarily more mature, than others, and they regard
themselves as less unappreciative (or more appreciative), but not necessarily
as less humorless (or more humorous), than others. The former pattern is a
sign of self-enhancement motivation, the latter of self-protection motivation.
Third, the BTAE varies as a function of attribute verifiability (Van Lange &
Sedikides, 1998). It is stronger on attributes that cannot be objectively verified
(where the individual can claim superiority with relative impunity, as in the
moral or social domain), but it is weaker on attributes that can be objectively
verified (where the individual may be threatened with ridicule or exclusion, as

in the athletic performance or intelligence domain). Finally, the BTAE varies as a function of self-threat (Brown, 2012; Study 5). Self-threat, where participants receive negative feedback (vs no feedback) on a domain important to them (i.e., intellectual ability) before engaging in self-other comparisons, intensifies the effect—a sign of self-protection motivation.

We have also refuted purely nonmotivational accounts of the BTAE (Sedikides & Alicke, 2012). The most prominent of them are egocentrism, focalism, individuated-entity versus aggregate comparisons, and assimilation/contrast. *Egocentrism* (Champers, Windschitl, & Suls, 2003) states that, when comparing themselves to peers, people think selectively about their strengths or about their peers' weaknesses. However, selective thinking can itself be a mark of self-enhancement or self-protection motivation (Sanitioso, Kunda, & Fong, 1999). Also, egocentrism cannot explain why the BTAE emerges in cases in which the behavioral evidence for traits relevant to the self and relevant to the typical peer is standardized (Alicke, Vredenburg, Hiatt, & Govorun, 2001). Finally, egocentrism cannot explain (1) why the BTAE emerges (Alicke & Govorun, 2005), and does so cross-culturally (Brown & Kobayashi, 2002, 2003), not only with direct measures (participants rating the self against peers on a single scale), but also with indirect measures (participants rating the self, their best friend, and other people on separate scales), and (2) why the BTAE is stronger on unverifiable than verifiable attributes (Van Lange & Sedikides, 1998). *Focalism* states that individuals, when comparing themselves to the average peer, place the self or the self-relevant attributes in a focal position, thus highlighting their unique attributes and consequently perceiving the self as less similar to the peer (Paul & Eiser, 2006). However, focalism cannot explain why the BTAE is obtained even when the peer is a highly concrete other (rather than the average or typical other) and is known to them through personal contact (Alicke, Klotz, Breitenbecher, Yurak, & Vredenburg, 1995), when the behavioral evidence relevant to the judgment is standardized for self and others (Alicke et al., 2001), and when the measures are indirect rather than direct (Alicke & Govorun, 2005). Also, focalism cannot explain why the BTAE varies as function of attribute importance, valence, controllability, and verifiability (Alicke, 1985; Brown, 2012). *Individuated-entity versus aggregate comparisons* states that any member of a liked group (e.g., soap fragrance) is rated more positively than the aggregate or group average (e.g., average fragrance), whereas the inverse occurs for disliked groups (Klar, 2002). The implication is that the self is seen as an individuated entity, whereas the average is seen as an aggregate. However, individuated-entity versus aggregate comparisons cannot explain why the BTAE emerges when the self is compared to another highly individuated-entity (Alicke et al., 1995), why the effect emerges even when participants are under cognitive load (Alicke et al., 1995; Study 7)—a pattern indicative of self-enhancement (Paulhus, 1993), why the effect is stronger on important than unimportant attributes when the comparison target is a single person (Brown, 2012), and why the effect varies according to the motivational significance of the judgment (i.e., attribute valence, controllability, verifiability; Alicke, 1985). Finally, *assimilation/contrast* states that the BTAE involves anchoring the self and contrasting the average peer from that point (Kruger, 1999). However, judgments of the average peer are assimilated toward, not contrasted from, the self (Guenther & Alicke, 2010).

5.1.4 Self-enhancement and Self-protection Motivation in Socially Desirable Responding

The postulate that individuals will self-enhance or self-protect on domains that are important (rather than unimportant) to them has been replicated in several independent laboratories (Kam et al., 2009; Tam et al., 2012; for an earlier review, see Sedikides et al., 2005). For illustration purposes, we will focus on the work of Shavitt and colleagues (Johnson, Holbrook, & Shavitt, 2011; Shavitt, Torelli, & Riemer, 2011). They proposed that cultures assign different importance to self-presentational styles. East-Asian or collectivistic cultures, compared to Western or individualistic cultures, are avoidance-oriented and emphasize face-saving, while valuing honesty less and tolerating lying more in social interactions (Triandis et al., 2001; Van Hemert, Van de Vijer, Poortinga, & Georgas, 2002). As such, East-Asians will be likely to dissemble and provide false or deceptive responses to questionnaires in adhering to the cultural value of harmonious fit with their social surroundings. For example, they will score relatively high on impression management (IM), denoting attempts to present oneself in such a manner as to create a favorable impression (Paulhus, 1984). IM is related to faking (i.e., dissimulation or deception), as it entails "an attempt to control images that are projected in real or social interactions" (Schlenker, 1980, p. 6). Typical scale items are "I have never dropped litter on the street" and "I sometimes drive faster than the speed limit" (reverse scored; Paulhus, 1988). Westerners, on the other hand, will be likely to present themselves as better or loftier than others in adhering to the cultural value of distinguishing oneself from others. For example, they will score relatively highly on self-deceptive enhancement (SDE), denoting the proclivity to furnish overly positive, if not grandiose, self-descriptions in questionnaire responses (Paulhus, 1984). Typical scale items are "I am very confident of my judgments" and "My first impressions of people usually turn out to be right" (Paulhus, 1988). In all, the two cultural groups will be equally motivated to self-enhance (or self-protect), but they will do so in distinct ways.

Results were consistent with the reasoning of Shavitt et al. East-Asians scored higher on IM, and lower on SDE, than Westerners. Correspondingly, collectivism predicted IM, and individualism predicted SDE (Lalwani, Shavitt, & Johnson, 2006; Studies 1—4). Further, collectivism (but not individualism) was linked with favorable responding to behavioral scenarios of image protection, whereas individualism (but not collectivism) was linked with favorable responding to behavioral scenarios of self-reliance (Lalwani et al., 2006; Study 4). Likewise, interdependent self-construal was related to IM and the proclivity to present oneself as competent and skillful (i.e., in terms of test choice, gift-giving scenarios, and performance), whereas interdependent self-construal was related to SDE and the proclivity to present oneself as appropriate and socially sensitive (Lalwani & Shavitt, 2009).

5.2 Constraints on Candid Self-enhancement: Modesty, Setting Orientation, and Other-Mediation

As stated above, the SCENT-R model distinguishes between candid and tactical self-enhancement (or self-protection). In this section, we focus on constraints upon candid self-enhancement as imposed by normative or contextual influences. In particular, we consider three forms of tactical self-enhancement: modesty, setting orientation, and other-mediation.

5.2.1 Modesty

Modesty is a more prevalent norm in the East than the West (Bond, Leung, & Wan, 1982; Shikanai, 1978; Yoshida et al., 1982; for a review, see Sedikides, Gregg, & Hart, 2007). As such, the SCENT-R model postulates that acute modesty concerns will influence strongly the self-evaluation judgments of Easterners. Cai et al. (2007, Study 2) put that idea to test. East-Asian and Western participants completed the 9-item Inclination Toward Modesty subscale of the Modest Responding Scale (Whetsone, Okun, & Cialdini, 1992). Sample items are: "It's difficult for me to talk about my strengths to others even when I know I possess them" and "I believe it is impolite to talk excessively about one's achievements, even if they are outstanding." Participants also completed two measures of self-esteem, the RSES and a 4-item scale (proud, pleased with myself, ashamed, humiliated) introduced by Brown and Dutton (1995). In replication of past findings, East-Asians reported higher modesty and lower explicit self-esteem than Westerners. Of interest, though, when modesty scores were statistically controlled, the two cultural groups ceased to differ on self-esteem.

These findings are backed by research that Kurman et al. reported. Overall, members of East-Asian cultures reported higher levels of modesty and lower levels of self-enhancement than members of Western culture. However, cross-cultural differences in self-enhancement (academic self-evaluation, ratings on erudition and athleticism) reflected cross-cultural differences in modesty (Kurman, 2002; Study 2), modesty predicted negatively self-enhancement (academic self-evaluation; Kurman & Sriram, 2002), and modesty mediated (i.e., reduced) cultural influences on self-enhancement (academic self-evaluation, the BTAE; Kurman, 2003; Study 2).

Easterners manifest substantially lower self-enhancement or self-protection strivings in public than in private (Crittenden, 1991). Due to self-presentational concerns, modesty will lessen, if not diminish, self-enhancement and self-protection strivings in public forums. The evidence is consistent with this idea. Tafarodi, Shaughnessy, Yamaguchi, and Murakoshi (2011) found that, when self-inflation was legitimized (and thus the modesty norm relaxed), Japanese participants reported higher self-esteem compared to when self-inflation was condemned. Han (2010) demonstrated that Chinese participants self-enhanced, that is, made internal (ability and effort) attributions for their successes in the presence of an acquaintance, but self-effaced, that is made external (luck) attributions for their successes in the presence of an intimate other. In an effort to reduce Japanese participants' self-presentational concerns, Kudo and Numazaki (2003) assured them that their responses would be anonymous and confidential. Subsequently, the researchers provided participants with bogus success or failure feedback on a social sensitivity task and assessed their attributional style, that is, whether they attributed the task outcome to internal factors (effort and ability) or external factors (task difficulty and luck). In contrast to findings from studies that did not control for self-presentational concerns (and thus the potency of the modesty norm; Heine & Hamamura, 2007), participants displayed the self-serving bias. They took more credit for their successes than their failures.

Yet, there is evidence that East-Asians (e.g., Chinese) manage the modesty norm intricately and skillfully. Chen (1993) pointed out that, although societal norms mandate modesty, this does not mean that the Chinese refrain from self-positivity. "All they need to do," he stated, "is to appear humble, not necessarily think humbly of themselves" (p. 67). Indeed, an investigation of evaluative judgments of compliments revealed that Chinese do appreciate and attempt to elicit compliments (Spencer-Oatey & Ng, 2001). Wu (2011) drew similar conclusions in her investigation of self-praising in everyday social interactions. She identified three practices that Chinese use in the service of self-praise. First, the speaker offers self-praise (by directing the listener's attention to a presumably worthy quality of her or him), but immediately retracts it or qualifies it (thus face saving or reducing the need for verifiability or accountability). Second, the speaker praises the self not as best, but as second best; however, the comparison group is an extreme case scenario. Finally, the speaker raises a complaint, but only ostensibly so; in actuality, the complaint is meant to highlight a positive aspect about him or her. In this way, the speaker attempts to reduce the risk of being seen as a braggart.

5.2.2 Setting Orientation

A social behavior setting can range along the competitiveness—cooperativeness continuum. Self-enhancement strivings can be rewarded in competitive, but not in cooperative, settings. Hence, according to the SCENT-R model, East-Asians (who do not lack competitive cognitions; Shwalb, Shwalb, & Nakazawa, 1995; Tang, 1999) will be more likely to self-enhance in competition-oriented situations than in cooperation-oriented situations.

The evidence is consistent with this prediction. Chinese make more self-enhancing predictions of their performance in private than in public (Kim et al., 2010; Study 1). Japanese self-enhance at job interviews, a prototypically competitive setting. Specifically, when requested to generate their self-presentational strategies at prospective job interviews, participants mentioned touting their competence and highlighting their sunny disposition (Matsumoto & Kijima, 2002). Likewise, when a work or professional (school, in this case) setting is salient, Chinese rate themselves highly on the domain of competence (Fahr, Dobbins, & Cheng, 1991) and Taiwanese rate themselves more favorably than their employers do (Falbo, Poston, Triscari, & Zhang, 1997).

The relevance of setting orientation has been documented experimentally. In research by Chou (2002), Chinese participants made internal attributions (ability and effort) for their academic accomplishments in a competitive context, but made external attributions (luck) for the same accomplishments in a cooperative context. Also, in research by Takata

(2003), Japanese participants self-enhanced when they received performance feedback in comparison to a relationally distant partner (competitive situation), but self-effaced when they received performance feedback in comparison to a relationally close partner (cooperative situation). These findings are remarkably similar to those obtained in Western cultures under virtually identical conditions (Sedikides, Campbell, Reeder, & Elliot, 1998). Additionally, Japanese self-enhance more when self-interest (e.g., a monetary reward) is at stake. In an experiment by Suzuki and Yamagishi (2004), participants who had taken a bogus intelligence test were asked whether their performance fell below or above that of their peers. Over two thirds of participants judged their performance to be below average. However, when offered a bonus for making a correct decision, over two-thirds of them judged their performance to be above average. Yamagishi et al. (2012, Study 1) replicated these findings using different experimental tasks, namely an embedded figure test and a trustworthiness judgment task.

5.2.3 Other-Mediation

Theorists have argued that Japanese often prefer other-mediated self-enhancement (Kuwayama, 1992; Lebra, 2004; Mouer & Sugimoto, 1986; Yum, 1985). Stated otherwise, they may self-enhance more through others (given how prominently others are represented in interdependent self-construal) than through own-initiated action. Research by Muramoto (2003) has demonstrated this form of self-enhancement. Japanese participants brought to mind a time when they had succeeded or failed. Subsequently, they attributed this outcome to various factors, and then indicated how they thought their family, friends, peers, and strangers would attribute the same outcome. Participants refrained from making self-serving attributions (i.e., taking personal responsibility for success while displacing the blame for failure). However, they expected that their family and friends would do so. They expected their loved ones to credit them for successes and blame situations for failures in order to protect them, enhance them, or preserve their self-esteem. In a conceptual replication of these findings, Dalsky, Gohm, Noguchi, and Shiomura (2008) showed that Japanese engage in "mutual self-enhancement," a social dance in which they give and receive praise from close others.

Theorists have also argued that Chinese make ample use of other-mediation. As Yang (1985) put it evocatively in regards to Taiwanese: "…if someone invites me for a speech, and I say: Oh, no, I am not really good at speech! However, if that one does not keep on inviting me, maybe

I will throw him a brick next time I see him in Taipei" (p. 30). Han (2008) reported that, although Taiwanese interviewees made external (luck) attributions for their successes, they expected that the interviewer would praise them and even express admiration for them. Han (2011) demonstrated compellingly other-mediation in three studies. In Study 1, participants recorded in writing their conversations between achievers and admirers. When receiving a compliment from an admirer, achievers responded modestly by denying their accomplishments. Achievers, however, rejected admirer's modest responding and intensified their compliments. In Study 2, observers approved both achievers' modest responding to admirers' compliments and admirers' increasing compliments. In Study 3, admirers' compliments following achiever's modest responding gave a boost to achievers' self-esteem. Finally, it is worth noting that Taiwanese and China (including Hong Kong) perceive themselves as making more use of other-mediation than Americans do (Fong, 1998).

5.3 Implicit Self-esteem: Manifestations and Motivational Significance

So far, we have been concerned with explicit self-evaluation. We now turn to implicit self-evaluation, and in particular, to implicit self-esteem. Measures of implicit self-esteem have the potential to capture the influence of self-enhancing or self-protective motivation (i.e., self-positivity) more purely, given that they minimize cultural constraints known to undermine the validity of self-report measures (e.g., modesty, self-presentation, other-mediation).

5.3.1 Implicit Self-esteem in the East and the West

The literature on implicit self-esteem strongly suggests that Easterners are, in an absolute sense, not short on positive self-attitudes or self-love. This conclusion is based on a variety of implicit measures deployed across an array of different countries. In particular, evidence based on the Implicit Association Test (IAT; Greenwald, McGhee, & Schwartz, 1998) has been gathered in both China (Cai, Kwan, & Sedikides, 2012, Studies 1−2; Cai, Wu, Luo, & Yang, 2014; Yamaguchi et al., 2007) and Japan (Szeto et al., 2009; Yamaguchi et al., 2007), and is supplemented by evidence based on semantic priming tasks from the latter country (Hetts, Sakuma, & Pelham, 1999). In addition, evidence based on name-letter preferences or whole-name liking has been gathered in China (Cai et al., 2012; Study 2), Thailand (Hoorens, Nuttin, Erderlyi-Herman, & Pavakanum, 1990), Singapore

(Pelham et al., 2005), and Japan (Kitayama & Karasawa, 1997; Komori & Murata, 2008), and is supplemented by evidence based on birthday-number preferences from the latter country (Kitayama & Karasawa, 1997). Moreover, using an alternative index of implicit self-esteem, the Go/No-Go Association Task (Nosek & Banaji, 2001), Boucher, Peng, Shi, and Wang (2009) found that Chinese evinced higher positive and higher negative implicit self-esteem than Americans.

Crucially, the literature on implicit self-esteem has shown that Easterners and Westerners are equally prone to exhibit positive self-attitudes or self-love. Evidence derived from the IAT indicates that the Chinese and Japanese, like Westerners, have more positive, and/or less negative, associations toward themselves than toward others (Cai et al., 2012; Study 2; Falk, Heine, Takemura, Zang, & Hsu, 2014; Kitayama & Uchida, 2003; Kobayashi & Greenwald, 2003; but see Szeto et al., 2009). Furthermore, the Chinese and Japanese, like Westerners, would appear to regard the self more favorably than they regard their best friend or their in-group (Yamaguchi et al., 2007). In a conceptual IAT replication and extension with a Western sample, participants also preferred themselves over their romantic partner or even their own child (Gebauer, Göritz, Hofmann, & Sedikides, 2012). A meta-analysis (Heine & Hamamura, 2007) has indeed reported no significant differences in self-positivity when comparing East-Asians with Westerners on implicit self-esteem measures.

5.3.2 Validity of the Self-esteem IAT

The above arguments hinge on the validity of the IAT as an index of cross-cultural differences in self-esteem (and, more broadly, of self-evaluation). This validity has been questioned recently (Falk & Heine, 2015). Although a detailed consideration of this critique is beyond the scope of the present article, we wish to point out that, even if some concerns about validity are justified, any confounds would likely apply equally to Easterners and Westerners. At the very least, anyone claiming that the former self-enhanced less than the latter, on the basis of IAT evidence suggesting parity, would be obliged to specify how a confound applied more in one culture than another, a nontrivial challenge.

More importantly, though, ample evidence exists for the validity of the IAT—evidence that Falk and Heine (2015) do not review. Specifically, the validity of implicit self-esteem has been documented in the balanced identity theory literature involving IAT measures. One example is the studies supporting the balance—congruity principle of balance identity theory (Greenwald et al., 2002). The second example involves studies among children documenting the validity of the self-esteem IAT in the context of support for the balance—congruity principle (Cvencek, Greenwald, & Meltzoff, submitted for publication). The third example is a small meta-analysis that reinforces support for the balance—congruity principle (Cvencek, Greenwald, & Meltzoff, 2012). The fourth and final example is a larger scale meta-analysis that cements support for the principle (Cvencek et al., submitted for publication). Interestingly, this meta-analysis, which includes a few Asian-born participant samples, evinced support of the balance—congruity, the principle from IAT measures but not from self-report measures. Indeed, explicit self-esteem measures have also come under similar validity criticism (Baumeister, Campbell, Krueger, & Vohs, 2003). We duly acknowledge that all measures of self-esteem, implicit or explicit, are subject to confounds that compromise their validity, which should be duly borne in mind. However, we would like to reassure investigators that implicit measures such as the IAT exhibit discriminative predictive validity in general (Greenwald, Poehlman, Uhlmann, & Banaji, 2009; Yang, Shi, Luo, Shi, & Cai, 2014), as well as in other specific domains (Gregg & Klymowsky, 2013), and that IAT measures of implicit self-esteem also show such discriminative predictive validity (Conner & Barrett, 2005; DeHart, Tennen, Armeli, Todd, & Mohr, 2009), as do other implicit measures of self-esteem (Hoorens, 2014).

5.3.3 Self-esteem IAT and the Motivational Dynamics of Self-evaluation

Not only do implicit self-esteem measures have sufficient degree of validity, they are also capable of capturing the motivational dynamics of self-evaluation. Chinese and American participants in an investigation by Cai et al. (2012, Study 3) were placed in private cubicles and were informed they would rate themselves on several trait characteristics in an impending task. Before this self-evaluation task, participants were subjected to a modesty manipulation. In particular, they were assigned to one of three experimental conditions. In the modesty condition, participants were instructed: "When rating yourself, please try to be as modest as possible." In the self-enhancement condition, they were instructed: "When rating yourself, please try to enhance yourself as much as possible." In the control condition, they were instructed: "please rate the extent to which the traits describe you." The self-evaluation task—in actuality the modesty manipulation check—followed. Finally, participants completed a self-esteem IAT.

The results indicated that the manipulation of modesty was successful. Participants in the modesty condition assigned themselves lower self-evaluation scores than those in the control condition, who in turn assigned themselves lower scores than those in the self-enhancement condition. Moreover, these findings generalized across cultural groups. However, the implicit self-esteem results differed for Chinese and Americans. The manipulation of modesty raised the implicit self-esteem of Chinese, but not of American, participants. Specifically, in comparison to Americans, Chinese participants manifested higher implicit self-esteem in the modesty condition, equivalent self-esteem in the control condition, and lower self-esteem in the self-enhancement condition.

The last set of findings is worth further consideration. Implicit self-esteem, as assessed by the IAT, can be manipulated, and, when it does so, it fluctuates according to theoretical predictions. Modesty is a prevailing norm in China. Due to strong, if not prohibitive, socialization pressures, modesty would be associated with relatively low explicit self-esteem: modesty would dissuade Chinese people from touting their achievements or flaunt their self-love. Indeed, modesty is negatively associated with explicit self-esteem (Cai et al., 2012; Studies 1–2). However, being modest would privately make Chinese individuals feel that they are fulfilling cultural norms of what it means to be a "good person." As such, acting modestly would elevate implicit self-esteem. This is what Cai et al. (Study 3) observed. Notably, this pattern of results was exclusive to Chinese participants, and is thus a conceptual replication of Han's (2011) Study 3, where admirers' in reaction to achievers' modesty increased achievers' self-esteem. American participants, on the other hand, who are subject to different cultural norms or socialization pressures, reported lower implicit self-esteem under modesty conditions, but reported higher implicit self-esteem under self-enhancement conditions. Such studies are flanked by others implicating implicit self-esteem in motivational dynamics (Weisbuch, Sinclair, Skorinko, & Eccleston, 2009).

5.4 Functionality of Self-esteem and Self-motives: Equivalence across East and West on Psychosocial Health

We will be concerned, in this section, with three instances of functionality of self-esteem, and the two self-motives, across the East and West. The instances refer to the relation between self-esteem and self-enhancement, the relation between self-esteem and psychosocial health, and the relation between self-motives and psychological health.

5.4.1 The Relation between Self-esteem and Self-enhancement

Self-esteem and self-enhancement vary predictably, and similarly, in Eastern and Western samples (Kurman, 2003; Study 1; but see Kitayama et al., 1997). Of interest, high-self-esteem persons are more likely to manifest self-enhancement strivings (e.g., the BTAE, the self-serving bias) than low-self-esteem persons (Campbell & Sedikides, 1999; Kurman, 2003; Study 1; Sedikides & Gregg, 2008). In work by Kobayashi and Brown (2003), Japanese and Americans regarded themselves (and their best friends) as superior to others. Importantly, this pattern was more evident among high self-esteem than low self-esteem participants from both cultures.

Work by Brown et al. (2009) extended these findings. In Study 1, Chinese and American participants engaged in a social sensitivity task and subsequently received false success or failure feedback. Overall, participants made self-serving attributions, that is, they took more personal credit for task success than task failure. However, this pattern was stronger among high self-esteem than low-self-esteem participants, irrespective of culture. In Study 2, Chinese and American participants engaged in an intellectual ability ("integrative orientation") task, and then received bogus success or failure feedback. Again, regardless of culture, participants made self-serving attributions, with high-self-esteem participants making stronger such attribution than their low-self-esteem counterparts. Furthermore, both Chinese and Americans felt momentarily worse about themselves (i.e., reported lower state self-esteem) when they failed than when they succeeded. Brown and Cai (2009) replicated these findings. Following a social sensitivity or intellectual task, Chinese and American participants received false success or failure feedback. All participants displayed the self-serving bias, and this bias predicted corresponding fluctuation in state self-esteem.

5.4.2 The Relation between Self-esteem and Psychosocial Health

Self-esteem and psychological health also vary predictably, and similarly, in Eastern and Western culture. In Western culture, high self-esteem predictably varies with indices of psychologically health, such as lower depression and anxiety, and higher subjective well-being (Brown, 1998; Sedikides & Gregg, 2003; Sedikides, Rudich, Gregg, Kumashiro, & Rusbult, 2004). Cai et al. (2009, Study 2) documented this pattern in China. In a meta-analysis of 50 independent samples involving approximately 22,000 participants, higher self-esteem was associated with lower depression, lower anxiety, and higher subjective well-being. Yamaguchi (2013; see also Yamaguchi, Morio, & Sedikides, Unpublished manuscript) established the same pattern in Japan. In a meta-analysis of 239 independent samples with more than 60,000 participants, self-esteem was positively associated with psychological well-being (subjective well-being and positive mood) and was negatively associated with depression and anxiety.

Further, self-esteem predicts happiness (e.g., "I generally consider myself a happy person") and job satisfaction in Japan (Piccolo, Judge, Takahashi, Watanabe, & Locke, 2005), and predicts life satisfaction in Hong Kong (Kwan et al., 1977). Finally, self-esteem is inversely related to neuroticism (a marker of psychological distress) and is positively related to extraversion (a general marker of psychological well-being) in both Eastern and Western samples (Diener & Diener, 1995; Kim et al., 2008; Schmitt & Allik, 2005).

In a review of the literature, Baumeister et al. (2003) showed that self-esteem is positively related to several indices of social health (i.e., sociocultural adjustment; Ward & Kennedy, 1994) in Western culture. Yamaguchi et al. (2008) relied, when possible, on Baumeister et al.'s classification scheme in examining the association between self-esteem and social health in Japan. Their findings paralleled those of Baumeister et al. First, Japanese self-esteem was related to school performance. In particular, it was positively related to self-perceptions of ability, actual school performance, achievement motivation, persistence in learning, and optimism, whereas it was inversely related to procrastination and the planning fallacy. Second, Japanese self-esteem was related to group behavior. In particular, it positively predicted in-group favoritism. Third, Japanese self-esteem was related to perceptions of physical appearance. In particular, it was positively related to satisfaction with physical appearance, and was inversely related to concern about body appearance. Tanchotsrinon, Maneesri, and Campbell (2007) drew a similar conclusion from their investigation of narcissism (excessive self-love) and romantic attraction in Thailand. That is, narcissism functioned in Thailand as in the Western culture: High (compared to low) narcissists were more attracted to admiring and high status others. Finally, in a meta-analysis based on 76 independent samples that included more than 17,000 participants, Yamaguchi et al. (Unpublished manuscript) found that self-esteem was positively associated with higher quality of interpersonal relationships.

5.4.3 The Relation between Self-motives and Psychological Health

Not only self-esteem, but also self-enhancement varies predictably, and similarly, across cultures. In Western culture, self-enhancement (e.g., self-serving attributions, perceptions of self-efficacy, optimism) has been positively linked with many indices of psychological health (Alicke & Sedikides, 2009;

Sedikides & Gregg, 2008; Taylor, Lerner, Sherman, Sage, & McDowell, 2003). The same is true for Eastern culture. For example, comparative studies indicate that self-serving attributions, perceptions of self-efficacy, and optimism are related to lower depression and life satisfaction among Chinese and Westerners (Anderson, 1999), Japanese and Westerners (Kobayashi & Brown, 2003), Singaporeans and Westerners (Kurman & Sriram, 1997), and Singaporeans, Chinese, and Westerners (Kurman, 2003). Optimism, in particular, is positively and strongly associated not only with subjective well-being but also with perceived physical health across a wide range of 142 cultures (Gallagher, Lopez, & Pressman, 2012). As another example of equivalency of the relation between self-enhancement and psychological health, self-enhancement (academic self-evaluation and the BTAE) is associated with positive affectivity, and is inversely associated with negative affectivity and emotional self-criticism, in both cultural contexts (Kurman, 2003; Study 1). Also, autonomy motivation, a correlate of self-enhancement motivation (Bridget & O'Mara, 2015) is linked to psychological well-being similarly across cultures (Church et al., 2012).

A key postulate of the SCENT-R model is that Easterners self-enhance on collectivistic attributes due to the personal importance ascribed to them, whereas Westerners self-enhance on individualistic attributes due, similarly, to the personal importance ascribed to them (*Self-centrality Breeds Self-enhancement: The Role of Domain Importance*). Gaertner, Sedikides, and Chang (2008) conducted a test of the implications of this postulate for psychological health using a Taiwanese sample. Participants filled out a measure of self-enhancement. That is, they completed better–than–average ratings (i.e., "rate yourself in comparison to your peers") on seven collectivistic attributes (i.e., traits) and seven individualistic attributes. Both sets of attributes were selected for their relevance to Taiwanese culture. Next, participants' rated the personal importance of each attribute. Finally, they responded to four psychological health indices: depression, stress, subjective well-being, and satisfaction with life. Gaertner et al. hypothesized that participants' who self-enhanced to a greater degree on more personally important attributes would evince the highest level of psychological health (i.e., lowest depression and stress, highest subjective well-being and satisfaction with life). The results were consistent with the hypothesis. (For conceptual replications, see: Kitayama, Karasawa, Curhan, Ryff, & Markus, 2010; Kwan et al., 1977; Li, Be, & Rao, 2011; Stewart et al., 2003.)

Although Gaertner et al. (2008) showed links among self-enhancement, attribute personal importance, and psychological health, their results were correlational. The results do not establish that self-enhancement promotes psychological health. In search of causality, O'Mara, Gaertner, Sedikides, Zhou, and Liu (2012) extended these results with a longitudinal-randomized-experimental design. At Time 1 (baseline), Chinese and American participants responded to 5 indices of psychological health: depression, anxiety, stress, subjective well-being, and satisfaction with life. At Time 2, 1 week later, participants listed an attribute they regarded as personally important. A manipulation of self-enhancement followed. Participants were assigned to one of two conditions. In the self-enhancement condition, participants wrote about how their experiences in the preceding week demonstrated that this important attribute is more characteristic of them than their peers. In the self-effacement condition, participants wrote about how their experiences over the last week demonstrated that the important attribute is less characteristic of them than their peers. Finally, participants responded again to the above-mentioned five indices of psychological health. Self-enhancement increased significantly psychological health from baseline among both Chinese and Americans, whereas self-effacement had no effect on psychological health. The results establish that self-enhancement promotes psychological health in both cultural groups.

5.5 Summary and Conclusions

The SCENT-R model offers four key postulates to highlight the tactical, or context-sensitive, manner in which self-enhancement, self-protection, and self-esteem are expressed across cultures. The first postulate relies on the "self-centrality breeds self-enhancement" principle in emphasizing the cross-cultural relevance of domain importance. Collectivistic cultures assign relative importance to, and report higher levels of, liking-based self-esteem, whereas individualistic cultures assign relative importance to, and report higher levels of, competence-based self-esteem. In a similar vein, Easterners regard collectivistic attributes as personally important and self-enhance (or self-protect) on them, whereas Westerners regard individualistic attributes as personally important and self-enhance on them. A good deal of evidence for the latter findings is based on the BTAE, a valid index of self-enhancement/self-protection motivation, although evidence involving alternative measures is also supportive. The second postulate explicates cultural constraints on candid self-enhancement. One constraint is modesty. East-Asians report higher modesty and lower self-esteem than Westerners. When modesty is controlled for, however, East-Asians and Westerners do not differ on explicit self-esteem. An additional constraint is setting orientation. East-Asians display substantially stronger self-enhancement or self-protection striving in competitive than in cooperative settings. Yet another constraint is other-mediation. East-Asians profit from other-mediated self-enhancement, that is, from self-enhancing or self-protecting through others (especially close ones) than through own-initiated strivings. The third postulate refers to implicit self-esteem, which is relatively free of cultural mandates and pressures. Evidence indicates that implicit self-esteem is high in the East, and is equivalently high between cultures. Evidence also vouches for the validity of implicit self-esteem indices, including IAT. The motivational significance of implicit self-esteem is illustrated by findings that implicit (but not explicit) self-esteem is augmented among self-enhancing Chinese (but not self-enhancing Americans). Finally, the fourth postulate advocates parallel functionality (i.e., health benefits) of self-esteem and self-enhancement/self-protection across East–West. Irrespective of cultural background, people with high self-esteem are more likely to self-enhance than people with low self-esteem. Also irrespective of culture, high self-esteem predicts improved psychological health (i.e., lower depression and anxiety, higher subjective well-being) and improved psychosocial health (i.e., school performance, group behavior, perceptions of physical appearance). And irrespective of cultural group, self-enhancement predicts, and indeed leads to, better psychological health.

6. DISCUSSION

The universalism versus cultural relativism debate on self-enhancement/self-protection motivation and desire for self-esteem shows no signs of abatement (Boucher, 2010; Brown, 2010a; Chiu, Wan, Cheng, Kim, & Yang, 2011; Falk et al., 2014; Hepper et al., 2013; Kurman, 2010). The debate is somewhat reminiscent of the interminate controversy between objectivism or realism on the one hand and relativism or constructivism on the other (Rorty, 1979; Searle, 1997). Are self-enhancement/self-protection and self-esteem fundamental human attributes with a permanent presence or are they merely contingent human practices with an ephemeral presence?

For self-enhancement/self-protection and self-esteem to qualify as fundamental human attributes, they ought to reflect the characteristics of basic human needs. They ought to be universal rather than culturally specific, not necessarily pursued or valued at the conscious level, and natural rather than acquired (Baumeister & Leary, 1995; Deci & Ryan, 2000). In an attempt to advance the debate toward a possible resolution, we proposed the SCENT-R model. The model acknowledges the lower overall levels of content manifestations of self-enhancement (but not necessarily self-protection) and of explicit self-esteem in East-Asian than Western samples. However, on the basis of this empirical pattern, it cannot be logically concluded that the self-enhancement motive and the desire for self-esteem do not exist in East-Asia or that they are weaker. Such a conclusion would be as fallacious as deducing that, in the United States, Southerners lack the motive to self-enhance and the desire for self-esteem because they project a more modest demeanor than Northerners (Nisbett & Cohen, 1996). Discrepancies in the manifestation of the self-motives or self-esteem have no implications for their potential existence or nonexistence or for their strength.[4] The SCENT-R model, then, aspires to reconcile two seemingly contradictory empirical phenomena: differential manifestation of the two self-motives and self-esteem across cultures (i.e., cross-cultural variability) and equivalence of motive strength and desire for self-esteem across cultures (i.e., cross-cultural invariance).

6.1 Are the Self-motives and Self-esteem Universal or Culture Bound?

We amassed evidence in favor of the view that the self-motives and self-esteem are universal or pancultural. In particular, the four foundational tenets of the SCENT-R model summarized the evidence for cross-cultural invariance. The referent of these motives is the individual self, and this type of self is primary across cultures over other types of self (i.e., relational, collective). Further, the strength of the two self-motives, their expression, and the desire for self-esteem are comparable across East and West. We also amassed evidence in favor of the view that the manner, in which the self-motives and self-esteem follow, is manifested is universal and tracks motivational principles. In particular, the four key postulates of the SCENT-R model summarized the evidence for cross-cultural variability.

---

[4] Loughnan et al. (2011) made a similar argument. They demonstrated that self-enhancement varies among nations: it is higher in nations with larger than smaller income inequality. Stated otherwise, self-enhancement is differentially adaptive, depending on national income inequality. In nations with a relatively large income inequality, it is adaptive for people to "tout their own horns" (i.e., emphasize positive distinctiveness) as a way to advance themselves. However, in nations with a relatively small income inequality, it is adaptive for people to adopt a modest demeanor (i.e., emphasize communality) as a way to advance themselves.

East-Asians assign personal importance to liking-based self-esteem, where they score higher, and to collectivistic attributes, where they self-enhance, whereas Westerners assign personal importance to competence-based self-esteem, where they score higher, and to individualistic attributes, where they self-enhance. When the pressure of cultural norms diminishes, East-Asians report equivalent self-esteem with Westerners and self-enhance in competitive settings while self-effacing in cooperative settings; also, they strategically engage in more other-mediated than own-initiated self-enhancement. Additionally, East-Asians reap the same psychosocial health benefits from self-esteem and self-enhancement/self-protection that Westerners do. In all, our review suggested that the motives are universal and their manifestations vary in universal (and theory-specific) ways.

6.2 Are the Self-motives or Self-esteem Necessarily Pursued or Valued at the Conscious Level?

We accumulated evidence in favor of the position that the self-motives or self-esteem are not necessarily pursued or valued exclusively at the conscious level. This evidence derives from studies of implicit self-esteem among Easterners and Westerners. Regardless of assessment method (i.e., name-letter preferences, birthday-number preferences, semantic priming, the IAT), the two cultural groups manifest similar levels of implicit self-esteem. East-Asians and Westerns are equally prone to unconscious self-love.

6.3 Are the Self-motives and Self-esteem Natural rather than Acquired?

We have not discussed work relevant to this question in the context of the SCENT-R model. However, drawing on several evidentiary domains, we are led to the conclusion that the two self-motives and self-esteem are natural. These domains concern subjective pleasantness, brain regions underlying self-enhancement/self-protection strivings and self-esteem, as well as evolutionary perspectives.

First, as we have mentioned, the self-enhancement/self-protection bifurcation has its origins in the distinction between approach and avoidance motivation, which relies on a more primitive system of pleasantness/unpleasantness. Humans show an overwhelming preference for pleasantness and derive meaning from it (Osgood, 1979). Self-positivity and self-esteem, reflecting pleasantness for arguably the most cherished entity (Gebauer, Göritz, et al., 2012), are likely to reflect fundamental and natural, rather than acquired, processes. Indeed, such processes are marked by physiological correlates. For example, threat (but not challenge) increases cardiac contractility (Blascovich & Mendes, 2000), and failure (but not success) feedback leads to a heightened cortisol response (Pruessner, Hellhammer, & Kirschbaum, 1999).

Second, a specific site in the brain has been implicated in serving self-enhancement dynamics. In particular, studies in Japan and the United States show that ventral striatum, the part of the brain that responds to all of the primary rewards (e.g., sugar, sex) also responds to self-positivity (e.g., positive feedback or regard from others; Izuma, Saito, & Sadato, 2008; Lieberman & Eisenberger, 2009; for a more general discussion, see: Kühn & Gallinat, 2012). Studies in the US indicate that self-protective responding in the presence (but not absence) of self-threat is associated with increased activation of the orbitofrontal cortex (Hughes & Beer, 2012, 2013). Thus, the self seems to have a locatable physical substratum. Also, a study in Japan (Onoda et al., 2010) suggested that heightened activity of the dorsal anterior cortex (dACC) may underlie the more intense feelings of worthlessness that low (compared to high) self-esteem persons experience as a result of negative feedback (e.g., social exclusion). The dACC is involved in the experience of both physical and social pain (Eisenberger & Lieberman, 2004; Price, 2000). In general, different neural correlates underlie high and low self-esteem (Chavez & Heatherton, 2015). Somewhat relatedly, self-esteem is genetically based (Neiss, Sedikides, & Stevenson, 2002; Neiss et al., 2005) and so is its correlate, narcissism (Luo, Cai, Sedikides, & Song, 2014; Vernon, Villani, Vickers, & Harris, 2008). Of course, genes can be distributed differentially across cultures (Kitayama et al., 2014; see also Dar-Nimrod & Heine, 2011), but arguably the genetic underpinnings of self-esteem are indicative of its fundamental character. Stated otherwise, how could the argument "…the need for self-regard…is not a universal, but rather is rooted in significant aspects of North American culture" (Heine et al., 1999, p. 766) be supported by evidence for the genetic basis of self-esteem?

If the self-motives and self-esteem are natural, what is their role in human evolution? Self-enhancement and self-esteem can be conceptualized as adaptations evolved to promote reproductive fitness (Barkow, 1989; Gilbert, Price, & Allan, 1995; Hill & Buss, 2008; Sedikides & Skowronski, 1997). Indeed, researchers have constructed theoretical models, supported by empirical evidence, that specify the kind of adaptation self-enhancement/ self-protection and self-esteem are. Specifically, they are specified as: an energizing principle that assists in goal-setting and persistence (Alicke &

Sedikides, 2009; Sedikides & Skowronski, 2000), a system that permits failure without lingering and debilitating negative feelings (Brown, 2010b; Campbell & Foster, 2006; Sedikides, Skowronski, & Dunbar, 2006), an index of mate value (Baumeister & Tice, 2000; Holtzman & Strube, 2011; Sedikides & Skowronski, 2000), a symbol of relational value (Leary & Baumeister, 2000), a monitor of prestige or status hierarchies (Cameron, Hildreth, & Howland, 2015; Kirkpatrick & Ellis, 2001; Mahadevan, Gregg, Sedikides, & De Waal-Andrews, submitted for publication), a defense against mortality (Pyszczynski et al., 2004), and a mechanism working to convince others that the self is better than it really is (von Hippel & Trivers, 2011).

7. RESEARCH AGENDA

Research on cultural self-evaluation has an exciting future. We highlight two sets of issues. One set is related to the universalism of the two self-motives and self-esteem, whereas the other set is more general.

7.1 Self-motive and Self-esteem Universalism

There are several paths research can take to clarify further the universalism of the two self-motives and self-esteem while enriching the SCENT-R model. The scope of the empirical agenda would need to be expanded to address differences between East-Asian cultures and also to include other "Eastern" countries, such as Latino or Middle-Eastern cultures. Similarly, more refined theoretical formulations would need to be developed to account for within-culture variation in collectivism (Yamawaki, 2012) or independence (Kitayama, Ishii, Imada, Takemura, & Ramaswamy, 2006). And more attention would need to be paid to rising individualism and narcissism in East-Asian cultures (Cai et al., 2012; Hamamura, 2012).

Some self-enhancement indices, such as the self-serving bias, seem to be more amenable to cultural influences than other indices, such as optimism or overconfidence. For example, although in a meta-analysis (Mezulis, Abramson, Hyde, & Hankin, 2004) the effect size of the self-serving bias in China and Korea was found to be comparable to that in the United States, the corresponding effect size in Japan was substantially lower. However, optimism (Gallagher et al., 2012; Li et al., 2011) and overconfidence (Stankov & Lee, 2014) appear to be equally strong across Eastern and

Western cultures. More generally, additional research is needed into the psychometric properties of explicit measures of self-enhancement.

Self-enhancement has been operationalized in many ways. Two broad approaches involve social comparison and self-insight (Kwan, John, Kenny, Bond, & Robins, 2004). In social comparison, people perceive themselves more favorably than they perceive others. In self-insight, people perceive themselves more favorably than they are perceived by others. The social comparison approach has been by far the more popular in the cultural self-evaluation literature. Future research should consider the implications of self-insight for cultural universalism versus relativism. For example, what is the relation between self-insight and psychological health, and does this relation generalize across cultural context?

7.2 Broader Issues

Although the weight of the evidence is in favor of the panculturality of self-enhancement and self-protection, there are other cultural differences worth examining as potential moderators of the manifestation of the two motives. For example, dialecticism, defined as managing contradicting views about oneself, may be a stronger norm in East-Asian than Western culture (Spencer-Rodgers, Boucher, Mori, Wang, & Peng, 2009). This would explain the findings of Boucher et al. (2009), whereby Chinese participants reported both higher positive and higher negative implicit self-esteem than American participants. Also, viewing oneself from the perspective of others may be a stronger norm in East-Asian than Western culture (Cohen & Gunz, 2002), a norm that, when salient, would tone down East-Asian self-enhancement (Heine, Takemoto, Moskalenko, Lasaleta, & Henrich, 2008). More generally, momentarily activated norms (or mind-sets, to be exact) are likely to moderate self-enhancement. Indeed, bilingual Hong Kong students primed with an individualistic mind-set (e.g., writing in English, thinking of a time when they resisted temptation) versus a collectivistic mind-set (e.g., writing in Chinese, thinking of a time when they succumbed to temptation) self-enhanced to a great extent, that is, they displayed a stronger BTAE and greater distancing from competitors who outperformed them (Lee, Oyserman, & Bond, 2010).

It is also worth speculating about other cultural dimensions, besides individualism—collectivism. Gelfand et al. (2011) drew a distinction between loose and tight cultures. Loose cultures are characterized by weak norms and a tolerance for anti-normative behavior, whereas strong cultures are characterized by strong norms and a punitive attitude toward anti-normative behavior. Self-enhancement strivings might be stronger in loose than tight cultures, whereas self-protection striving might be stronger in tight than loose cultures. Such a finding would be consistent with evidence that lack of mobility strengthens adherence to cultural norms and decreases expressions of one's distinctive qualities (Chen, Chiu, & Chan, 2009). Low-mobility cultures are likely to be tight cultures.

Recent research has started to highlight the relevance of a match between the person and the culture in influencing the person's self-esteem. In particular, the relation between one's personally important attributes (e.g., agency, communion, religiosity, extraversion) and self-esteem is higher in cultures that value that attribute compared to cultures that do not value it (Fulmer et al., 2010; Gebauer, Sedikides, & Neberich, 2012; Gebauer et al., 2013). Research has also started to highlight the complex interplay among self-enhancement/self-protection strivings, cultural goal congruence, and personality differences. Leung, Kim, Zhang, Tam, and Chiu (2012) tested Chinese and American participants in the context of a reward allocation task. Self-enhancement/self-protection strivings were influenced by culture: Chinese participants rewarded the group more than the self, but American participants rewarded the self more than the group. However, these strivings depended on cultural goal congruence: They emerged among Chinese, who considered avoidance (vs approach) goals a success experience and among Americans, who considered approach (vs avoidance) goals a success experience. This pattern, in turn, was moderated by need for closure (Webster & Kruglanski, 1994): It was obtained only among participants (Chinese or Americans) high in need for closure, who exhibited culturally typical behavior. This study is illustrative, because it places self-enhancement/self-protection striving in a broader nexus of cultural, motivational, and personality influences, and, by so doing, calls for more fine-tuned research in that direction.

8. CODA

The self is immersed in motivation and imbued in affect. We focused on two self-motives, self-enhancement and self-protection, and on a self-relevant affect, self-esteem, in charting the evaluative territory of the cultural self. We conclude that the motives to enhance or protect the self, and the desire for self-esteem, are pancultural. We also conclude that the manifestations of self-enhancement and self-protection, and the strivings to increase or protect self-esteem, are influenced by culture, but in predictable ways.

These conclusions have implications for the nature of motivation and the nature of personhood. In regards to motivation, self-enhancement and self-protection are appetitive motives. They require satiation either in a direct (candid) manner or an indirect (tactical) manner. In regards to the person, he or she is an active agent, fully aware of the subtleties surrounding cultural norms and constraints, and at the ready for exploiting these cultural contingencies to their benefit. Persons may be influenced by culture, but they often manage to protect and advance their wishes and desires as to avoid punishment, exclusion, or humiliation and to maximize reward, inclusion, and pride.

REFERENCES

Aarts, H., Oikawa, M., & Oikawa, H. (2010). Cultural and universal routes to authorship ascription: effects of outcome priming on experienced self-agency in The Netherlands and Japan. *Journal of Cross-Cultural Psychology, 41*, 87—98.
Abele, A. E., & Wojciszke, B. (2014). Communal and agentic content. A dual perspective model. *Advances in Experimental Social Psychology, 50*, 195—255.
Alicke, M. D. (1985). Global self-evaluation as determined by the desirability and controllability of trait adjectives. *Journal of Personality and Social Psychology, 49*, 1621—1630.
Alicke, M. D., & Govorun, O. (2005). The better-than-average effect. In M. D. Alicke, D. A. Dunning, & J. I. Krueger (Eds.), *The self in social judgment* (pp. 85—106). Philadelphia, PA: Psychology.
Alicke, M. D., Klotz, M. L., Breitenbecher, D. L., Yurak, T. J., & Vredenburg, D. S. (1995). Personal contact, individuation, and the better-than-average effect. *Journal of Personality and Social Psychology, 68*, 804—825.
Alicke, M. D., & Sedikides, C. (2009). Self-enhancement and self-protection: what they are and what they do. *European Review of Social Psychology, 20*, 1—48.
Alicke, M. D., & Sedikides, C. (Eds.). (2011). *Handbook of self-enhancement and self-protection*. New York, NY: Guilford Press.
Alicke, M. D., Vredenburg, D. S., Hiatt, M., & Govorun, O. (2001). The "better than myself effect." *Motivation and Emotion, 25*, 7—22.
Allport, G. W. (1937). *Personality: A psychological interpretation*. New York, NY: Holt.
Allport, G. W. (1954). The historical background of modern social psychology. In G. Lindzey (Ed.), *The handbook of social psychology* (Vol. 1, pp. 3—56). Cambridge, MA: Addison-Wesley.
Anderson, C. A. (1999). Attributional style, depression, and loneliness: a cross-cultural comparison of American and Chinese students. *Personality and Social Psychology Bulletin, 25*, 482—499.
Banaji, M. R., & Prentice, D. A. (1994). The self in social contexts. *Annual Review of Psychology, 45*, 297—332.
Baranik, L. E., Meade, A. W., Lakey, C. E., Lance, C. E., Hua, W., & Michalos, A. (2008). Examining the differential item functioning of the Rosenberg self-esteem scale across eight countries. *Journal of Applied Social Psychology, 38*, 1867—1904.
Barkow, J. (1989). *Darwin, sex, and status*. Toronto: University of Toronto Press.
Baumeister, R. F. (1998). The self. In D. T. Gilbert, S. T. Fiske, & G. Lindzey (Eds.), *Handbook of social psychology* (4th ed.), (Vol. 1, pp. 680—740). New York, NY: McGraw-Hill.

Baumeister, R. F., Campbell, J. D., Krueger, J. I., & Vohs, K. D. (2003). Does high self-esteem causes better performance, interpersonal success, happiness, or healthier lifestyles? *Psychological Science in the Public Interest, 4*, 11–44.

Baumeister, R. F., & Leary, M. R. (1995). The need to belong: desire for interpersonal attachments as a fundamental human motivation. *Psychological Bulletin, 117*, 497–529.

Baumeister, R. F., & Tice, D. M. (2000). *The social dimension of sex*. New York, NY: Allyn & Bacon.

Becker, E. (1968). *The structure of evil*. New York, NY: George Braziller.

Becker, M., Vignoles, V. L., Owe, E., Brown, R., Smith, P. B., Easterbrook, M., et al. (2012). Culture and the distinctiveness motive: constructing identity in individualistic and collectivistic contexts. *Journal of Personality and Social Psychology, 102*, 833–855.

Becker, M., Vignoles, V. L., Owe, E., Easterbrook, M., Brown, R., Smith, P. B., et al. (2014). Cultural bases for self-evaluation: seeing oneself positively in different cultural contexts. *Personality and Social Psychology Bulletin, 40*, 657–675.

Blascovich, J., & Mendes, W. B. (2000). Challenge and threat appraisals: the role of affective cues. In J. Forgas (Ed.), *Feeling and thinking: The role of affect in social cognition* (pp. 59–82). New York, NY: Cambridge University Press.

Blascovich, J., & Tomaka, J. (1991). Measures of self-esteem. In J. P. Robinson, & P. R. Shaver (Eds.), *Measures of personality and social psychological attitudes* (pp. 115–160). San Diego, CA: Academic Press.

Bond, M. H., Leung, K., & Wan, K.-C. (1978). The social impact of self-effacing attribution: the Chinese case. *Journal of Social Psychology, 118*, 157–166.

Bond, M. H., Leung, K., & Wan, K. C. (1982). The social impact of self-effacing attributions: The Chinese case. *Journal of Social Psychology, 118*, 157–166.

Boucher, H. C. (2010). Understanding Western-East Asian differences and similarities in self-enhancement. *Social and Personality Psychology Compass, 4*, 304–317.

Boucher, H. C., Peng, K., Shi, J., & Wang, L. (2009). Culture and implicit self-esteem: Chinese are "Good" and "Bad" at the same time. *Journal of Cross-Cultural Psychology, 40*, 24–45.

Brewer, M. B., & Chen, Y. R. (2007). Where (who) are collectives in collectivism? toward conceptual clarification of individualism and collectivism. *Psychological Review, 114*, 133–151.

Bridget, P. L., & O'Mara, E. M. (2015). Do autonomous individuals strive for self-positivity? Examining the role of autonomy in the expression of self-enhancement. *Self and Identity, 14*, 403–419.

Brown, J. (1998). *The self*. New York, NY: McGraw-Hill.

Brown, J. (2003). The self-enhancement motive in collectivistic cultures: the rumors of my death have been greatly exaggerated. *Journal of Cross-Cultural Psychology, 34*, 603–605.

Brown, J. D. (2010a). Across the (not so) great divide: cultural similarities in self-evaluative processes. *Social and Personality Psychology Compass, 4*, 318–330.

Brown, J. D. (2010b). Positive illusions and positive collusions: how social life abets self-enhancing beliefs. *Brain and Behavioral Sciences, 32*, 514–515.

Brown, J. D. (2012). Understanding the better than average effect: motives (still) matter. *Personality and Social Psychology Bulletin, 38*, 209–219.

Brown, J. D., & Cai, H. (2009). Thinking and feeling in the People's Republic of China: testing the generality of the "laws of emotion". *International Journal of Psychology, 44*, 1–11.

Brown, J. D., Cai, H., Oakes, M. A., & Deng, C. (2009). Cultural similarities in self-esteem functioning: east is east and west is west, but sometimes the twain do meet. *Journal of Cross-Cultural Psychology, 40*, 140–157.

Brown, J. D., & Dutton, K. A. (1995). The thrill of victory, the complexity of defeat: self-esteem and people's emotional reactions to success and failure. *Journal of Personality and Social Psychology, 68*, 712–722.

Brown, J. D., & Kobayashi, C. (2002). Self-enhancement in Japan and America. *Asian Journal of Social Psychology, 5*, 145–167.

Brown, J. D., & Kobayashi, C. (2003). Motivation and manifestation: the cross-cultural expression of the self-enhancement motive. *Asian Journal of Social Psychology, 6*, 85–88.

Brown, R. A. (2008a). American and Japanese beliefs about self-esteem. *Asian Journal of Social Psychology, 11*, 293–299.

Brown, R. A. (2008b). Equivalence of serufuesutei-mu (self-esteem) and jisonshin in Japan. *Asian Journal of Social Psychology, 1*, 300–304.

Burke, B. L., Martens, A., & Faucher, E. H. (2010). Two decades of terror management theory: a meta-analysis of mortality salience research. *Personality and Social Psychology Review, 14*, 155–195.

Bushman, B. J., Moeller, S. J., & Crocker, J. (2011). Sweets, sex, or self-esteem? Comparing the value of self-esteem boosts with other pleasant rewards. *Journal of Personality, 79*, 993–1012.

Cai, H., Brown, J. D., Deng, C., & Oakes, M. A. (2007). Self-esteem and culture: differences in cognitive self-evaluations or affective self-regard? *Asian Journal of Social Psychology, 10*, 162–170.

Cai, H., Kwan, V., & Sedikides, C. (2012). A sociocultural approach to narcissism: the case of modern China. *European Journal of Personality, 26*, 529–535.

Cai, H., Sedikides, C., Gaertner, L., Wang, C., Carvallo, M., Xu, Y., et al. (2011). Tactical self-enhancement in China: Is modesty at the service of self-enhancement in East-Asian culture? *Social Psychological and Personality Science, 2*, 59–64.

Cai, H., Wu, M., Luo, Y. L. L., & Yang, J. (2014). Implicit self-esteem decreases in adolescence: a cross-sectional study. *PLoS One, 9*, e89988.

Cai, H., Wu, Q., & Brown, J. D. (2009). Is self-esteem a universal need? Evidence from the People's Republic of China. *Asian Journal of Social Psychology, 12*, 104–120.

Cameron, A., Hildreth, J. A. D., & Howland, L. (2015). Is the desire for status a fundamental human motive? A review of the empirical literature. *Psychological Bulletin, 141*, 574–601.

Campbell, K. W., & Sedikides, C. (1999). Self-threat magnifies the self-serving bias: a meta-analytic integration. *Review of General Psychology, 3*, 23–43.

Campbell, W. K., & Foster, J. D. (2006). Self-esteem: evolutionary roots and historical cultivation. In M. Kernis (Ed.), *Self-esteem: Issues and answers* (pp. 340–346). New York, NY: Psychology Press.

Champers, J. R., Windschitl, P. D., & Suls, J. (2003). Egocentrism, event frequency, and comparative optimism: when what happens frequently is "more likely to happen to me." *Personality and Social Psychology Bulletin, 29*, 1343–1356.

Chavez, R. S., & Heatherton, T. F. (2015). Multimodal frontostriatal connectivity underlies individual differences in self-esteem. *Social Cognitive and Affective Neuroscience, 10*, 364–370.

Chen, J., Chiu, C.-Y., & Chan, F. S. F. (2009). The cultural effects of job mobility and the belief in a fixed world: evidence from performance forecast. *Journal of Personality and Social Psychology, 97*, 851–865.

Chen, R. (1993). Responding to compliments: a contrastive study of politeness strategies between American english and Chinese speakers. *Journal of Pragmatics, 20*, 49–75.

Cheung, G. W., & Rensvold, R. B. (2002). Evaluating goodness-of-fit indexes for testing measurement invariance. *Structural Equation Modeling, 9*, 233–255.

Chiu, C.-y., & Hong, Y. (2006). *Social psychology of culture.* New York, NY: Psychology Press.

Chiu, C.-y., Wan, C., Cheng, S. Y. Y., Kim, Y.-H., & Yang, Y.-J. (2011). Cultural perspectives on self-enhancement and self-protection. In M. D. Alicke, & C. Sedikides (Eds.), *Handbook of self-enhancement and self-protection* (pp. 425–451). New York, NY: Guilford Press.

Chou, S. H. (2002). *Attribution patterns in situations of interpersonal competition and harmony.* Unpublished master's thesis, National Taiwan University.

Church, A. T., Katigbak, M. S., Locke, K. D., Zhang, H., Shen, J., Vargas-Flores, J., et al. (2012). Need satisfaction and well-being: testing self-determination theory in eight cultures. *Journal of Cross-Cultural Psychology, 44,* 507–534.

Cohen, D., & Gunz, A. (2002). As seen by the other: perspectives on the self in the memories and emotional perceptions of Easterners and Westerners. *Psychological Science, 13,* 55–59.

Conner, T., & Barrett, L. F. (2005). Implicit self-attitudes predict spontaneous affect in daily life. *Emotion, 5,* 476–488.

Crittenden, K. S. (1991). Self-effacement or feminine modesty? Attributional patterns of women university students in Taiwan. *Gender and Society, 5,* 98–117.

Crocker, J., & Wolfe, C. T. (2001). Contingencies of self-worth. *Psychological Review, 108,* 593–623.

Cvencek, D., Greenwald, A. G., & Meltzoff, A. N. (2012). Balanced identity theory: review of evidence for implicit consistency in social cognition. In B. Gawronski, & F. Strack (Eds.), *Cognitive consistency: A fundamental principle in social cognition* (pp. 157–177). New York, NY: Guilford Press.

Cvencek, D., Greenwald, A. G., & Meltzoff, A. N. *Implicit measures for preschool children confirm self-esteem's role in maintaining a balanced identity.* University of Washington, submitted for publication.

Cvencek, C., Greenwald, A. G., Meltzoff, A. N., Maddox, C. D., Nosek, B. A., Devos, T., et al. *Multi-laboratory meta-analytic evaluation of balanced identity theory,* University of Washington, Unpublished manuscript.

Dalsky, D. J., Gohm, C. L., Noguchi, K., & Shiomura, K. (2008). Mutual self-enhancement in Japan and the United States. *Journal of Cross-Cultural Psychology, 39,* 215–223.

Dar-Nimrod, I., & Heine, S. J. (2011). Genetic essentialism: on the deceptive determinism of DNA. *Psychological Bulletin, 137,* 800–818.

Deci, E. L., & Ryan, R. M. (1995). Human autonomy: the basis for true self-esteem. In M. Kernis (Ed.), *Efficacy, agency, and self-esteem* (pp. 31–49). New York, NY: Plenum Press.

Deci, E. L., & Ryan, R. M. (2000). The "what" and "why" of goal pursuits: human needs and the self-determination of behavior. *Psychological Inquiry, 11,* 227–268.

DeHart, T., Tennen, H., Armeli, S., Todd, M., & Mohr, C. (2009). A diary study of implicit self-esteem, interpersonal interactions, and alcohol consumption in college students. *Journal of Experimental Social Psychology, 45,* 720–730.

Del Prado, A. M., Church, A. T., Katigbak, M. S., Miramontes, L. G., Whitty, M. T., Curtis, G. J., et al. (2007). Culture, method, and the content of self-concepts: testing trait, individual-self primacy, and cultural psychology perspectives. *Journal of Research in Personality, 41,* 1119–1160.

Diener, E., & Diener, M. (1995). Cross-cultural correlates of life satisfaction and self-esteem. *Journal of Personality and Social Psychology, 68,* 653–663.

Dollard, J., & Miller, N. E. (1950). *Personality and psychotherapy.* New York, NY: McGraw-Hill.

Dunning, D. (1993). Words to live by: the self and definitions of social concepts and categories. In J. Suls (Ed.), *Psychological perspectives on the self* (Vol. 4, pp. 99–126). Hillsdale, NJ: Erlbaum.

Eisenberger, N. I., & Lieberman, M. D. (2004). Why rejection hurts: a common neural alarm system for physical and social pain. *Trends in Cognitive Sciences, 8,* 294–300.

Elliot, A. J., Chirkov, V. I., Sheldon, K. M., & Kim, Y. (2001). A cross-cultural analysis of avoidance (relative to approach) personal goals. *Psychological Science, 12,* 505–510.

Elliot, A. J., & Mapes, R. R. (2005). Approach-avoidance motivation and self-concept evaluation. In A. Tesser, J. Wood, & D. Stapel (Eds.), *On building, defending, and regulating the self: A psychological perspective* (pp. 171–196). Washington, DC: Psychological Press.

Elliot, A. J., Sedikides, C., Murayama, K., Tanaka, A., Thrash, T. M., & Mapes, R. R. (2012). Cross-cultural generality and specificity in self-regulation: avoidance personal goals and multiple aspects of wellbeing in the U.S. and Japan. *Emotion, 12,* 1031–1040.

Emmons, R. A. (1986). Personal strivings: an approach to personality and subjective well-being. *Journal of Personality and Social Psychology, 51,* 1058–1068.

Epstein, S., & Morling, B. (1995). Is the self motivated to do more than enhance and/or verify itself? In M. H. Kernis (Ed.), *Efficacy, agency, and self-esteem* (pp. 9–29). New York, NY: Plenum Press.

Fahr, J., Dobbins, G. H., & Cheng, B. (1991). Cultural relativity in action: a comparison of self-ratings made by Chinese and U.S. workers. *Personnel Psychology, 44,* 129–147.

Falbo, T., Poston, D. L., Jr., Triscari, R. S., & Zhang, X. (1997). Self-enhancing illusions among Chinese schoolchildren. *Journal of Cross-Cultural Psychology, 28,* 172–191.

Falk, C. F., & Heine, S. J. (2015). What is implicit self-esteem, and does it vary across cultures? *Personality and Social Psychology Review, 19,* 177–198.

Falk, C. F., Heine, S. J., Takemura, K., Zang, C. X. J., & Hsu, C.-W. (2014). Are implicit self-esteem measures valid for assessing individual and cultural differences? *Journal of Personality, 83,* 56–68.

Finjeman, Y. A., Willemsen, M. E., & Poortinga, Y. H. (1996). Individualism-collectivism: an empirical study of a conceptual issue. *Journal of Cross-Cultural Psychology, 27,* 381–402.

Fischer, R. (2006). Congruence and functions of personal and cultural values: do my values reflect my culture's values? *Personality and Social Psychology Bulletin, 32,* 1419–1431.

Fong, M. (1998). Chinese immigrants' perceptions of semantic dimensions of direct/indirect communication in intercultural compliment interactions with North Americans. *The Howard Journal of Communications, 9,* 245–262.

Ford, B. Q., & Mauss, I. B. (2015). Culture and emotion regulation. *Current Opinion in Psychology, 3,* 1–15.

Fulmer, C. A., Gelfand, M. J., Kruglanski, A. W., Kim-Prieto, C., Diener, E., Pierro, A., et al. (2010). On "feeling right" in cultural contexts: how person-culture match affects self-esteem and subjective well-being. *Psychological Science, 21,* 1563–1569.

Gaertner, G., Sedikides, C., Luke, M., O'Mara, E. M., Iuzzini, J., Jackson, L. E., et al. (2012). A motivational hierarchy within: primacy of the individual self, relational self, or collective self? *Journal of Experimental Social Psychology, 48,* 997–1013.

Gaertner, L., Sedikides, C., & Cai, H. (2012). Wanting to be great and better but not average: on the pancultural desire for self-enhancing and self-improving feedback. *Journal of Cross-Cultural Psychology, 43,* 521–526.

Gaertner, L., Sedikides, C., & Chang, K. (2008). On pancultural self-enhancement: well-adjusted Taiwanese self-enhance on personally-valued traits. *Journal of Cross-Cultural Psychology, 39,* 463–477.

Gaertner, L., Sedikides, C., & Graetz, K. (1999). In search of self-definition: motivational primacy of the individual self, motivational primacy of the collective self, or contextual primacy? *Journal of Personality and Social Psychology, 76,* 5–18.

Gallagher, M. W., Lopez, S. J., & Pressman, S. D. (2012). Optimism is universal: exploring the presence and benefits of optimism in a representative sample of the world. *Journal of Personality, 8,* 429–440.

Gebauer, J. E., Göritz, A. S., Hofmann, W., & Sedikides, C. (2012). Self-love or other-love? Explicit other-preference but implicit self-preference. *PLoS One, 7,* e41789.

Gebauer, J. E., Sedikides, C., & Neberich, W. (2012). Religiosity, self-esteem, and psychological adjustment: on the cross-cultural specificity of the benefits of religiosity. *Psychological Science, 23,* 158–160.

Gebauer, J. E., Wagner, J., Sedikides, C., & Neberich, W. (2013). The relation between agency-communion and self-esteem is moderated by culture, religiosity, age, and sex:

evidence for the self-centrality breeds self-enhancement principle. *Journal of Personality, 81,* 261–275.

Gelfand, M. J., Raver, J. L., Nishii, L., Leslie, L. M., Lun, J., Lim, B. C., et al. (2011). Differences between tight and loose cultures: a 33-nation study. *Science, 332,* 1100–1104.

Gilbert, P., Price, J. S., & Allan, S. (1995). Social comparison, social attractiveness and evolution: how might they be related? *New Ideas Is Psychology, 13,* 149–165.

Greenberg, J. (2008). Understanding the vital human quest for self-esteem. *Perspectives on Psychological Science, 3,* 48–55.

Greenberg, J., Solomon, S., & Pyszczynski, T. (1997). Terror management theory of self-esteem and cultural worldviews: empirical assessments and conceptual refinements. *Advances in Experimental Social Psychology, 29,* 61–139.

Greenwald, A. G. (1980). The totalitarian ego: fabrication and revision of personal history. *American Psychologist, 35,* 603–618.

Greenwald, A. G., Banaji, M. R., Rudman, L. A., Farnham, S. D., Nosek, B. A., & Mellott, D. S. (2002). A unified theory of implicit attitudes, stereotypes, self-esteem, and self-concepts. *Psychological Review, 109,* 3–25.

Greenwald, A. G., McGhee, D. E., & Schwartz, J. L. K. (1998). Measuring individual differences in implicit cognition: the implicit association test. *Journal of Personality and Social Psychology, 74,* 1464–1480.

Greenwald, A. G., Poehlman, T. A., Uhlmann, E., & Banaji, M. R. (2009). Understanding and using the implicit association test: III. Meta-analysis of predictive validity. *Journal of Personality and Social Psychology, 97,* 17–41.

Gregg, A. P., Hepper, E. G. D., & Sedikides, C. (2011). Quantifying self-motives: functional links between dispositional desires. *European Journal of Social Psychology, 41,* 840–852.

Gregg, A. P., & Klymowsky, J. (2013). The implicit association test in market research: potentials and pitfalls. *Psychology & Marketing, 30,* 588–601.

Gregg, A. P., Sedikides, C., & Gebauer, J. E. (2011). Dynamics of identity: between self-enhancement and self-assessment. In S. J. Schwartz, K. Luyckx, & V. L. Vignoles (Eds.), *Handbook of identity theory and research* (Vol. 1, pp. 305–327). New York, NY: Springer.

Guenther, C. L., & Alicke, M. D. (2010). Deconstructing the better-than-average effect. *Journal of Personality and Social Psychology, 99,* 755–770.

Hamamura, T. (2012). Are cultures becoming individualistic? A cross-temporal comparison of individualism-collectivism in the United States and Japan. *Personality and Social Psychology Review, 16,* 3–24.

Hamamura, T., Heine, S. J., & Takemoto, T. (2007). Why the better-than-average effect is a worse-than-average measure of self-enhancement. An investigation of conflicting findings from studies of East Asian self-evaluations. *Motivation and Emotion, 31,* 247–259.

Hamamura, T., Meijer, Z., Heine, S. J., Kamaya, K., & Hori, I. (2009). Approach-avoidance motivations and information processing: a cross-cultural analysis. *Personality and Social Psychology Bulletin, 35,* 454–462.

Han, K.-H. (July 2008). The myth of Chinese modesty: the effect of personal relationships on attribution for achievements. In *Paper presented at the 29th International Congress of Psychology, Berlin, Germany.*

Han, K.-H. (2010). The study of Chinese interpersonal attribution style and motivations for achievement. *Journal of Social Sciences and Philosophy, 22,* 41–76.

Han, K.-H. (2011). The self-enhancing function of Chinese modesty: from a perspective of social script. *Asian Journal of Social Psychology, 14,* 258–268.

Harter, S. (1993). Causes and consequences of low self-esteem in children and adolescents. In R. F. Baumeister (Ed.), *Self-esteem: The puzzle of low self-regard* (pp. 87–116). New York, NY: Plenum Press.

Hashimoto, H., Li, Y., & Yamagishi, T. (2011). Beliefs and preferences in cultural agents and cultural game players. *Asian Journal of Social Psychology, 14,* 140–147.

Hashimoto, H., & Yamagishi, T. (2013). Two faces of interdependence: harmony seeking and rejection avoidance. *Asian Journal of Social Psychology, 16,* 142—151.

Heine, S. J. (2012). *Cultural psychology.* New York, NY: W. W. Norton.

Heine, S. J., & Hamamura, T. (2007). In search of East Asian self-enhancement. *Personality and Social Psychology Review, 11,* 1—24.

Heine, S. J., Kitayama, S., & Lehman, D. R. (2001). Cultural differences in self-evaluation: Japanese readily accept negative self-relevant information. *Journal of Cross-Cultural Psychology, 32,* 434—443.

Heine, S. J., Kitayama, S., Lehman, D. R., Takata, T., Ide, E., Leung, C., et al. (2001). Divergent consequences of success and failure in Japan and North America. An investigation of self-improving motivations and malleable selves. *Journal of Personality and Social Psychology, 81,* 599—615.

Heine, S. J., & Lehman, D. R. (1995). Cultural variation in unrealistic optimism: does the West feel more invulnerable than the East? *Journal of Personality and Social Psychology, 68,* 595—607.

Heine, S. J., Lehman, D. R., Markus, H. R., & Kitayama, S. (1999). Is there a universal need for positive self-regard? *Psychological Review, 106,* 766—794.

Heine, S. J., Niiya, Y., & Harihara, M. (2002). Terror management in Japan. *Asian Journal of Social Psychology, 5,* 187—196.

Heine, S. J., Takata, T., & Lehman, D. R. (2000). Beyond self-presentation: evidence for Japanese self-criticism. *Personality and Social Psychology Bulletin, 26,* 71—78.

Heine, S. J., Takemoto, T., Moskalenko, S., Lasaleta, J., & Henrich, J. (2008). Mirrors in the head: cultural variation in objective self-awareness. *Personality and Social Psychology Bulletin, 34,* 879—887.

Hepper, E. G., Gramzow, R. H., & Sedikides, C. (2010). Individual differences in self-enhancement and self-protection strategies: an integrative analysis. *Journal of Personality, 78,* 781—814.

Hepper, E. G., Hart, C. M., Gregg, A. P., & Sedikides, C. (2011). Motivated expectations of positive feedback in social interactions. *The Journal of Social Psychology, 151,* 455—477.

Hepper, E. G., Sedikides, C., & Cai, H. (2013). Self-enhancement and self-protection strategies in China: cultural expressions of a fundamental human motive. *Journal of Cross-Cultural Psychology, 44,* 5—23.

Hetts, J., Sakuma, M., & Pelham, B. (1999). Two roads to positive regard: implicit and explicit self-evaluation and culture. *Journal of Experimental Social Psychology, 35,* 512—559.

Higgins, E. T. (1998). Promotion and prevention: regulatory focus as a motivational principle. *Advances in Experimental Social Psychology, 30,* 1—46.

Hill, S. E., & Buss, D. M. (2008). The evolution of self-esteem. In M. Kernis (Ed.), *Self-esteem—Issues and answers: A source book of current perspectives.* New York, NY: Guilford.

von Hippel, W., & Trivers, R. (2011). The evolution and psychology of self-deception. *Behavioral and Brain Sciences, 34,* 1—56.

Ho, D. Y. F. (1976). On the concept of face. *American Journal of Sociology, 81,* 867—890.

Hofstede, G. (1980). *Culture's consequences: International differences in work-related values.* Newbury Park, CA: Sage.

Hofstede, G. (2001). *Culture consequences: Comparing values, behaviors, institutions, and organizations across nations* (2nd ed.). Thousand Oaks, CA: Sage.

Hofstede, G. (2011). Dimensionalizing Cultures: The Hofstede Model in Context. *Online Readings in Psychology and Culture, 2*(1). http://dx.doi.org/10.9707/2307-0919.1014.

Holtzman, N. S., & Strube, M. J. (2011). The intertwined evolution of narcissism and short-term mating: an emerging hypothesis. In W. K. Campbell, & J. D. Miller (Eds.), *The handbook of narcissism and narcissistic personality disorder: Theoretical approaches, empirical findings and treatments* (pp. 210—220). Hoboken, NJ: Wiley.

Hoorens, V. (2014). What's really in a name-letter effect? Name-letter preferences as indirect measures of self-esteem. *European Review of Social Psychology, 25*, 228−262.

Hoorens, V., Nuttin, J. M., Erderlyi-Herman, I., & Pavakanum, U. (1990). Mastery pleasure versus mere ownership: a quasi-experimental cross-cultural and cross-alphabetical test for the name letter effect. *European Journal of Social Psychology, 20*, 181−205.

Horn, J. L., & McArdle, J. J. (1992). A practical and theoretical guide to measurement invariance in aging research. *Experimental Aging Research, 18*, 117−144.

Hughes, B. L., & Beer, J. S. (2012). Orbitofrontal cortex and anterior cingulate cortex are modulated by motivated social cognition. *Cerebral Cortex, 22*, 1372−1381.

Hughes, B. L., & Beer, J. S. (2013). Protecting the self: the effect of social-evaluative threat on neural representations of self. *Journal of Cognitive Neuroscience, 25*, 613−622.

Hwang, K. K. (1987). Face and favor: the Chinese power game. *American Journal of Sociology, 92*, 944−974.

Izuma, K., Saito, D. N., & Sadato, N. (2008). Processing of social and monetary rewards in the human striatum. *Neuron, 58*, 284−294.

James, W. (1907). *The principles of psychology* (Vol. 1). New York, NY: Holt.

Johnson, T. P., Holbrook, A., & Shavitt, S. (2011). Culture and response styles in survey research. In D. Matsumoto, & F. van de Vijver (Eds.), *Cross-cultural research methods in psychology* (pp. 130−175). Cambridge, UK: Cambridge University Press.

Kam, C. C.-S., Wilson, A., Perunovic, E., Bond, M. H., Zhang, X., & Zhou, X. (February 2009). *Do Chinese self-enhance? Converging evidence from social comparison and temporal appraisal paradigms.* Tampa, FL, USA: Society for Personality and Social Psychology.

Kashima, E. S., Halloran, M., Yuki, M., & Kashima, Y. (2004). The effects of personal and collective mortality salience on individualism: comparing Australians and Japanese with higher and lower self-esteem. *Journal of Experimental Social Psychology, 40*, 384−392.

Keltner, D., & Beer, J. (1995). Self-conscious emotion and self-regulation. In A. Tesser, J. Wood, & D. Stapel (Eds.), *On building, defending, and regulating the self: A psychological perspective* (pp. 197−216). New York, NY: Psychology Press.

Kerferd, G. B. (1981). *The sophistic movement.* Cambridge, England: Cambridge University Press.

Kim, H., & Markus, H. R. (1999). Deviance or uniqueness, harmony or conformity? A cultural analysis. *Journal of Personality and Social Psychology, 77*, 785−800.

Kim, Y.-H., Chiu, C.-Y., Peng, S., Cai, H., & Tov, W. (2010). Explaining East-West differences in the likelihood of making favorable self-evaluations. *Journal of Cross-Cultural Psychology, 41*, 62−75.

Kim, Y.-H., Peng, S., & Chiu, C.-Y. (2008). Explaining self-esteem differences between Chinese and North Americans: dialectical self (vs. self-consistency) or lack of positive self-regards. *Self and Identity, 7*, 113−128.

Kirkpatrick, L. A., & Ellis, B. J. (2001). An evolutionary-psychological approach to self-esteem: Multiple domains and multiple functions. In G. Fletcher, & M. Clark (Eds.), *The Blackwell handbook of social psychology: Vol. 2: Interpersonal processes* (pp. 411−436). Oxford, UK: Blackwell.

Kitayama, S., Ishii, K., Imada, T., Takemura, K., & Ramaswamy, J. (2006). Voluntary settlement and the spirit of independence: evidence from Japan's "Northern Frontier". *Journal of Personality and Social Psychology, 91*, 369−384.

Kitayama, S., & Karasawa, M. (1997). Implicit self-esteem in Japan: name letters and birthday numbers. *Personality and Social Psychology Bulletin, 23*, 736−742.

Kitayama, S., Karasawa, M., Curhan, K. B., Ryff, C. D., & Markus, H. R. (2010). Independence and interdependence predict health and wellbeing: divergent patterns in the United States and Japan. *Frontiers in Psychology, 1*, 1−10.

Kitayama, S., King, A., Yoon, C., Tompson, S., Huff, S., & Liberzon, I. (2014). The dopamine D4 receptor gene (*DRD4*) moderates cultural differences in independent versus interdependent social orientation. *Psychological Science, 25,* 1169—1177.

Kitayama, S., Markus, H. R., Matsumoto, H., & Norasakkunkit, V. (1997). Individual and collective processes in the construction of the self: self-enhancement in the United States and self-criticism in Japan. *Journal of Personality and Social Psychology, 72,* 1245—1267.

Kitayama, S., & Uchida, Y. (2003). Explicit self-criticism and implicit self-regard: evaluating the self and friend in two cultures. *Journal of Experimental Social Psychology, 39,* 476—482.

Klar, Y. (2002). Way beyond compare: nonselective superiority and inferiority biases in judging assigned group members relative to their peers. *Journal of Experimental Social Psychology, 38,* 331—351.

Kobayashi, C., & Brown, J. D. (2003). Self-esteem and self-enhancement in Japan and America. *Journal of Cross-Cultural Psychology, 34,* 567—580.

Kobayashi, C., & Greenwald, A. G. (2003). Implicit-explicit differences in self-enhancement for Americans and Japanese. *Journal of Cross-Cultural Psychology, 34,* 522—541.

Komori, M., & Murata, K. (2008). Implicit egotism in Japan: preference for first and family name initials. *Hitotsubashi Journal of Social Studies, 40,* 101—109.

Kroeber, A. L., & Kluckholm, C. K. (1952). *Culture: A critical review of concepts and definitions.* New York, NY: Random House.

Kruger, J. (1999). Lake Wobegon be gone! the "below average effect" and the egocentric nature of comparative ability judgments. *Journal of Personality and Social Psychology, 77,* 221—232.

Kudo, E., & Numazaki, M. (2003). Explicit and direct self-serving bias in Japan: reexamination of self-serving bias for success and failure. *Journal of Cross-Cultural Psychology, 34,* 511—521.

Kühn, S., & Gallinat, J. (2012). The neural correlates of subjective pleasantness. *Neuroimage, 61,* 289—294.

Kurman, J. (2002). Measured cross-cultural differences in self-enhancement and the sensitivity of the self-enhancement measure to the modesty response. *Cross-Cultural Research, 36,* 73—95.

Kurman, J. (2003). Why is self-enhancement low in certain collectivistic cultures? an investigation of two competing explanations. *Journal of Cross-Cultural Psychology, 34,* 496—510.

Kurman, J. (2010). Good, better, best: between culture and self-enhancement. *Social and Personality Psychology Compass, 4,* 379—392.

Kurman, J., & Sriram, N. (1997). Self-enhancement, generality of self-evaluation, and affectivity in Israel and Singapore. *Journal of Cross-Cultural Psychology, 28,* 421—441.

Kurman, J., & Sriram, N. (2002). Interrelations among vertical and horizontal collectivism, modesty, and self-enhancement. *Journal of Cross-Cultural Psychology, 33,* 71—86.

Kuwayama, T. (1992). The reference other orientation. In N. R. Rosenberger (Ed.), *Japanese sense of self* (pp. 121—151). Cambridge, UK: Cambridge University Press.

Kwan, V. S. Y., Bond, M. H., & Singelis, T. M. (1977). Pancultural explanations for life satisfaction: adding relationship harmony to self-esteem. *Journal of Personality and Social Psychology, 73,* 1038—1051.

Kwan, V. S. Y., John, O. P., Kenny, D. A., Bond, M. H., & Robins, R. W. (2004). Reconceptualizing individual differences in self-enhancement bias: an interpersonal approach. *Psychological Review, 111,* 94—110.

Kwan, V. S. Y., Kuang, L. L., & Hui, N. H. (2009). Identifying the sources of self-esteem: the mixed medley of benevolence, merit, and bias. *Self and Identity, 8,* 176—195.

Lalwani, A. K., & Shavitt, S. (2009). The "me" I claim to be: cultural self-construal elicits self-presentational goal pursuit. *Journal of Personality and Social Psychology, 97,* 88—102.

Lalwani, A. K., Shavitt, S., & Johnson, T. (2006). What is the relation between cultural orientation and socially desirable responding? *Journal of Personality and Social Psychology, 90*, 165–178.

Lalwani, A. K., Shrum, L. J., & Chiu, C.-Y. (2009). Motivated response styles: the role of cultural values, regulatory focus, and self-consciousness in socially desirable responding. *Journal of Personality and Social Psychology, 96*, 870–882.

Lea, S., & Webley, P. (2006). Money as tool, money as drug: the biological psychology of a strong incentive. *Behavioral and Brain Sciences, 29*, 161–209.

Leary, M. R., & Baumeister, R. F. (2000). The nature and function of self-esteem: sociometer theory. *Advances in Experimental Social Psychology, 32*, 1–62.

Lebra, T. S. (2004). *The Japanese self in cultural logic*. Honolulu, HI: University of Hawaii Press.

Lee, K., Xu, F., Fu, G., Cameron, C. A., & Chen, S. (2001). Taiwan and mainland Chinese and Canadian children's categorization and evaluation of lie- and truth-telling: a modesty effect. *British Journal of Developmental Psychology, 19*, 525–542.

Lee, S. W. S., Oyserman, D., & Bond, M. H. (2010). Am I doing better than you? that depends on whether you ask me in English or Chinese: self-enhancement effects of language as a cultural mindset prime. *Journal of Experimental Social Psychology, 46*, 785–791.

Leung, A. K.-y., Kim, Y.-H., Zhang, Z.-X., Tam, K.-P., & Chiu, C.-y (2012). Cultural construction of success and epistemic motives moderate American-Chinese differences in reward allocation biases. *Journal of Cross-Cultural Psychology, 43*, 46–52.

Li, S., Be, Y.-L., & Rao, L.-L. (2011). Every science/nature potter praises his or her own pot—can we believe what he says based on his mother tongue? *Journal of Cross-Cultural Psychology, 42*, 125–130.

Lieberman, M. D., & Eisenberger, N. I. (2009). Pains and pleasures of social life. *Science, 323*, 890–891.

Lönnqvist, J.-E., Verkasalo, M., Helkama, K., Andreyeva, G., Bezmenova, I., Rattazzi, A. M. M., et al. (2009). Self-esteem and values. *European Journal of Social Psychology, 39*, 40–51.

Loughnan, S., Kuppens, P., Allik, J., Balazs, K., de Lemus, S., Dumont, K., et al. (2011). Economic inequality is linked to biased self-perception. *Psychological Science, 22*, 1254–1258.

Lovell, J. (trans. 2010). *The real story of Ah-Q and other tales of China: The complete fiction of Lu Xun*. London, England: Penguin Books.

Luo, Y. L. L., Cai, H., Sedikides, C., & Song, H. (2014). Distinguishing communal narcissism from agentic narcissism: a behavior genetics analysis on the agency-communion model of narcissism. *Journal of Research in Personality, 49*, 52–58.

Macfarlane, A. (1978). *The origins of English individualism: The family, property, and social transition*. New York, NY: Cambridge University Press.

Maddux, W. W., Yang, H., Falk, C., Adam, H., Adair, W., Endo, Y., et al. (2010). For whom is parting with possessions more painful? Cultural differences in the endowment effect. *Psychological Science, 21*, 1910–1917.

Mahadevan, N., Gregg, A. P., Sedikides, C., & De Waal-Andrews, W. *Winner, losers, insiders, and outsiders: Testing hierometer and sociometer theories of self-regard*. University of Southampton, Submitted for publication.

Markus, H. R., & Kitayama, S. (1991). Culture and the self: implications for cognition, emotion, and motivation. *Psychological Review, 98*, 224–253.

Maslow, A. H. (1943). A theory of human motivation. *Psychological Review, 50*, 370–396.

Matsumoto, D. (1999). Culture and self: an empirical assessment of Markus and Kitayama's theory of independent and interdependent self-construals. *Asian Journal of Social Psychology, 2*, 289–310.

Matsumoto, Y., & Kijima, T. (2002). Job hunters' strategic goals of self-presentation. *Japanese Journal of Experimental Social Psychology, 41*, 111–123.

Meredith, W. (1993). Measurement invariance, factor analysis and factorial invariance. *Psychometrika, 58*, 525–543.

Mezulis, A. H., Abramson, L. Y., Hyde, J. S., & Hankin, B. L. (2004). Is there a universal positivity bias in attributions? A meta-analytic review of individual, developmental, and cultural differences in the self-serving attribution bias. *Psychological Bulletin, 130*, 711–747.

Morf, C. C., Horvath, S., & Torchetti, L. (2011). Narcissism and self-enhancement: tales of (successful?) self-portrayal. In M. D. Alicke, & C. Sedikides (Eds.), *Handbook of self-enhancement and self-protection* (pp. 399–424). New York, NY: Guilford Press.

Morris, M. W. (2014). Values as the essence of culture: foundation or fallacy? *Journal of Cross-Cultural Psychology, 45*, 14–24.

Mouer, R., & Sugimoto, Y. (1986). *Images of Japanese society: A study in the social construction of reality*. London, England: KPI Limited.

Muramoto, Y. (2003). An indirect self-enhancement in relationship among Japanese. *Journal of Cross-Cultural Psychology, 34*, 552–566.

Neiss, M. B., Sedikides, C., Shahinfar, A., & Kupersmidt, J. (2006). Self-evaluation in naturalistic context: the case of juvenile offenders. *British Journal of Social Psychology, 45*, 499–518.

Neiss, M. B., Sedikides, C., & Stevenson, J. (2002). Self-esteem: a behavioural genetic perspective. *European Journal of Personality, 16*, 351–367.

Neiss, M. B., Stevenson, J., Sedikides, C., Kumashiro, M., Finkel, E. J., & Rusbult, C. E. (2005). Executive self, self-esteem, and negative affectivity: relations at the phenotypic and genotypic level. *Journal of Personality and Social Psychology, 89*, 593–606.

Nezlek, J. B., Sorrentino, R. M., Yasunaga, S., Otsubo, Y., Allen, M., Kouhara, S., et al. (2008). Cross-cultural differences in reactions to daily events as indicators of cross-cultural differences in self-construction and affect. *Journal of Cross-Cultural Psychology, 2008*, 685–702.

Niiya, Y., Crocker, J., & Mischkowski, D. (2012). Compassionate and self-image goals in the United States and Japan. *Journal of Cross-Cultural Psychology, 44*, 389–405.

Nisbett, R. E. (2003). *The geography of thought: How Asians and Westerners think differently and why*. New York, NY: Free Press.

Nisbett, R. E., & Cohen, D. (1996). *Culture of honor: The psychology of violence in the South*. Denver, CO: Westview Press.

Nodera, A., Karasawa, K., Numazaki, M., & Takabayashi, K. (2007). An examination of the promoter of gender role stereotype-activation based on terror management theory. *Japanese Journal of Social Psychology, 23*, 195–201.

Nosek, B. A., & Banaji, M. R. (2001). The Go/No-Go association task. *Social Cognition, 19*, 625–666.

Onoda, k., Okamoto, Y., Nakashima, K., Nittono, H., Yoshimura, S., Yamawaki, S., et al. (2010). Does low self-esteem enhance social pain? the relationship between trait self-esteem and anterior cingulate cortex activation induced by ostracism. *Social Cognitve Affective Neuroscience, 5*, 385–391.

Osgood, C. E. (1979). *Focus on meaning: Explorations in semantic space*. The Hague, The Netherlands: Mouton Publishers.

Ott-Holland, C., Huang, J. L., Ryan, A. M., Elizondo, F., & Wadlington, P. L. (2014). The effects of culture and gender on perceived self-other similarity in personality. *Journal of Research in Personality, 53*, 13–21.

Oyserman, D., Coon, H. M., & Kemmelmeier, M. (2002). Rethinking individualism and collectivism: evaluation of theoretical assumptions and meta-analyses. *Psychological Bulletin, 128*, 3–72.

O'Mara, E. M., Gaertner, L., Sedikides, C., Zhou, X., & Liu, Y. (2012). A longitudinal-experimental test of the panculturality of self-enhancement: self-enhancement promotes psychological well-being both in the West and the East. *Journal of Research in Personality, 46*, 157–163.

Parks, C., & Vu, A. D. (1995). Social dilemma behaviour of individuals from highly individualistic and collectivistic cultures. *Journal of Conflict Resolution, 38*, 708–718.

Paul, S., & Eiser, J. R. (2006). The focus effect and self-positivity in ratings of self-other similarity and difference. *British Journal of Social Psychology, 45*, 107–116.

Paulhus, D. L. (1984). Two-component models of socially desirable responding. *Journal of Personality and Social Psychology, 46*, 598–609.

Paulhus, D. L. (1988). Interpersonal and intrapsychic adaptiveness of trait self-enhancement: a mixed blessing? *Journal of Personality and Social Psychology, 74*, 1197–1208.

Paulhus, D. L. (1993). Bypassing the will: the automatization of affirmations. In D. M. Wegner, & J. M. Pennebaker (Eds.), *Handbook of mental control* (pp. 573–587). Englewood Cliffs, NJ: Prentice Hall.

Paulhus, D. L., & Reid, D. B. (1991). Enhancement and denial in socially desirable responding. *Journal of Personality and Social Psychology, 60*, 307–317.

Pelham, B. W., Koole, S. L., Hardin, C. D., Hetts, J. J., Seah, E., & DeHart, T. (2005). Gender moderates the relation between implicit and explicit self-esteem. *Journal of Experimental Social Psychology, 41*, 84–89.

Piccolo, R. F., Judge, T. A., Takahashi, K., Watanabe, N., & Locke, E. A. (2005). Core self-evaluations in Japan: relative effects on job satisfaction, life satisfaction, and happiness. *Journal of Organizational Behavior, 26*, 965–984.

Price, D. D. (2000). Psychological and neural mechanisms of the affective dimension of pain. *Science, 288*, 1769–1772.

Pruessner, J. C., Hellhammer, D. H., & Kirschbaum, C. (1999). Burnout, perceived stress, and cortisol responses to awakening. *Psychosomatic Medicine, 61*, 197–204.

Pyszczynski, T., Greenberg, J., Solomon, S., Arndt, J., & Schimel, J. (2004). Why do people need self-esteem? A theoretical and empirical review. *Psychological Bulletin, 130*, 435–468.

Ritchie, T. D., Batteson, T. J., Bohn, A., Crawford, M. T., Ferguson, G. V., Schrauf, R. D., et al. (2015). A pancultural perspective on the fading affect bias in autobiographical memory. *Memory, 233*, 278–290.

Rogers, C. (1961). *On becoming a person*. Boston, MA: Houghton Mifflin.

Rorty, R. (1979). *Philosophy and the mirror of nature*. Princeton, NJ: Princeton University Press.

Rosenberg, M. (1965). *Society and the adolescent self-image*. Princeton, NJ: Princeton University Press.

Sanitioso, B. R., Kunda, Z., & Fong, G. T. (1999). Motivated recruitment of autobiographical memories. *Journal of Personality and Social Psychology, 59*, 229–241.

Schimmack, U., Oishi, S., & Diener, E. (2005). Individualism: a valid and important dimension of cultural differences between nations. *Personality and Social Psychology Review, 9*, 17–31.

Schlenker, B. R. (1980). *Impression management: The self concept, social identity, and interpersonal relations*. Monterey, CA: Brooks/Cole.

Schmitt, D. P., & Allik, J. (2005). Simultaneous administration of the Rosenberg self-esteem scale in 53 nations: exploring the universal and culture-specific features of global self-esteem. *Journal of Personality and Social Psychology, 89*, 623–642.

Schwartz, S. H. (1992). Universals in the content and structure of values: theoretical advances and empirical tests in 20 countries. *Advances in Experimental Social Psychology, 25*, 1–65.

Searle, J. (1997). *The construction of social reality*. New York, NY: Free Press.

Sedikides, C. (1993). Assessment, enhancement, and verification determinants of the self-evaluation process. *Journal of Personality and Social Psychology, 65*, 317–338.

Sedikides, C. (2012). Self-protection. In M. R. Leary, & J. P. Tangney (Eds.), *Handbook of self and identity* (2nd ed.). (pp. 327–353). New York, NY: Guilford Press.

Sedikides, C., & Alicke, M. D. (2012). Self-enhancement and self-protection motives. In R. M. Ryan (Ed.), *Oxford handbook of motivation* (pp. 303–322). New York, NY: Oxford University Press.

Sedikides, C., Campbell, W. K., Reeder, G., & Elliot, A. J. (1998). The self-serving bias in relational context. *Journal of Personality and Social Psychology, 74*, 378–386.

Sedikides, C., Gaertner, L., Luke, M. A., O'Mara, E. M., & Gebauer, J. (2013). A three-tier hierarchy of motivational self-potency: Individual self, relational self, collective self. *Advances in Experimental Social Psychology, 48*, 235–295.

Sedikides, C., Gaertner, L., & Toguchi, Y. (2003). Pancultural self-enhancement. *Journal of Personality and Social Psychology, 84*, 60–70.

Sedikides, C., Gaertner, L., & Vevea, J. L. (2005). Pancultural self-enhancement reloaded: a meta-analytic reply to Heine (2005). *Journal of Personality and Social Psychology, 89*, 539–551.

Sedikides, C., Gaertner, L., & Vevea, J. L. (2007a). Inclusion of theory-relevant moderators yield the same conclusions as Sedikides, Gaertner, and Vevea (2005): a meta-analytic reply to Heine, Kitayama, and Hamamura (2007). *Asian Journal of Social Psychology, 10*, 59–67.

Sedikides, C., Gaertner, L., & Vevea, J. L. (2007b). Evaluating the evidence for pancultural self-enhancement. *Asian Journal of Social Psychology, 10*, 201–203.

Sedikides, C., & Green, J. D. (2004). What I don't recall can't hurt me: Information negativity versus information inconsistency as determinants of memorial self-defense. *Social Cognition, 22*, 4–29.

Sedikides, C., & Green, J. D. (2009). Memory as a self-protective mechanism. *Social and Personality Psychology Compass, 3*, 1055–1068.

Sedikides, C., & Gregg, A. P. (2003). Portraits of the self. In M. A. Hogg, & J. Cooper (Eds.), *Sage handbook of social psychology* (pp. 110–138). London, England: Sage Publications.

Sedikides, C., & Gregg, A. P. (2008). Self-enhancement: food for thought. *Perspectives on Psychological Science, 3*, 102–116.

Sedikides, C., Gregg, A. P., & Hart, C. M. (2007). The importance of being modest. In C. Sedikides, & S. Spencer (Eds.), *The self: Frontiers in social psychology* (pp. 163–184). New York, NY: Psychology Press.

Sedikides, C., Rudich, E. A., Gregg, A. P., Kumashiro, M., & Rusbult, C. (2004). Are normal narcissists psychologically healthy? Self-esteem matters. *Journal of Personality and Social Psychology, 87*, 400–416.

Sedikides, C., & Skowronski, J. A. (1997). The symbolic self in evolutionary context. *Personality and Social Psychology Review, 1*, 80–102.

Sedikides, C., & Skowronski, J. J. (2000). On the evolutionary functions of the symbolic self: the emergence of self-evaluation motives. In A. Tesser, R. Felson, & J. Suls (Eds.), *Psychological perspectives on self and identity* (pp. 91–117). Washington, DC: American Psychological Association.

Sedikides, C., Skowronski, J. J., & Dunbar, R. I. M. (2006). When and why did the human self evolve? In M. Schaller, J. A. Simpson, & D. T. Kenrick (Eds.), *Evolution and social psychology: Frontiers in social psychology* (pp. 55–80). New York, NY: Psychology Press.

Sedikides, C., & Strube, M. J. (1997). Self-evaluation: to thine own self be good, to thine own self be sure, to thine own self be true, and to thine own self be better. *Advances in Experimental Social Psychology, 29*, 209–269.

Sedikides, C., Wildschut, T., Routledge, C., Arndt, J., Hepper, E. G., & Zhou, X. (2015). To nostalgize: mixing memory with affect and desire. *Advances in Experimental Social Psychology, 51*, 189–273.

Shavitt, S., Torelli, C., & Riemer, H. (2011). Horizontal and vertical individualism and collectivism: Implications for understanding psychological processes. In M. Gelfand, C.-Y. Chiu, & Y.y. Hong (Eds.), *Advances in culture and psychology* (pp. 309–350). Oxford, UK: Oxford University Press.

Shavitt, S., Zhang, J., Torelli, C. J., & Lalwani, A. K. (2006). Reflections on the meaning and structure of the horizontal/vertical distinction. *Journal of Consumer Psychology, 16*, 357–362.

Sheldon, K. M., Elliot, A. J., Kim, Y., & Kasser, T. (2001). What is satisfying about satisfying events? Testing 10 candidate psychological needs. *Journal of Personality and Social Psychology, 80*, 325–339.

Sherman, D. K., & Cohen, G. L. (2006). The psychology of self-defense: self-affirmation theory. *Advances in Experimental Social Psychology, 38*, 183–242.

Shikanai, K. (1978). Effects of self-esteem on attributions of success-failure. *Japanese Journal of Experimental Social Psychology, 18*, 47–55.

Shteynberg, G., Gelfand, M. J., & Kim, K. (2009). Peering into the "magnum mysterium" of culture: the explanatory power of descriptive norms. *Journal of Cross-Cultural Psychology, 40*, 46–69.

Shwalb, D. W., Shwalb, B. J., & Nakazawa, J. (1995). Competitive and cooperative attitudes: a longitudinal survey of Japanese adolescents. *Journal of Early Adolescence, 15*, 145–168.

Singelis, T. M. (1994). The measurement of independent and interdependent self-construals. *Personality and Social Psychology Bulletin, 20*, 580–591.

Skowronski, J. J. (2011). The positivity bias and the fading affect bias in autobiographical memory: a self-motives perspective. In C. Sedikides, & M. D. Alicke (Eds.), *Handbook of self-enhancement and self-protection* (pp. 211–231). New York, NY: Guilford Press.

Spencer-Oatey, H., & Ng, P. (2001). Reconsidering Chinese modesty: Hong Kong and Mainland Chinese evaluative judgments of compliment responses. *Journal of Asian Pacific Communication, 11*, 181–201.

Spencer-Rodgers, J., Boucher, H. C., Mori, S. C., Wang, L., & Peng, K. (2009). The dialectical self-concept: contradiction, change, and holism in East Asian cultures. *Personality and Social Psychology Bulletin, 35*, 29–44.

Stankov, L., & Lee, J. (2014). Overconfidence across world regions. *Journal of Cross-Cultural Psychology, 45*, 821–837.

Stewart, S. M., Byrne, B. M., Lee, P. W. H., Ho, L. M., Kennard, B. D., Hughes, C., et al. (2003). Personal versus interpersonal contributions to depressive symptoms among Hong Kong adolescents. *International Journal of Psychology, 38*, 160–169.

Suzuki, N., & Yamagishi, T. (2004). An experimental study of self-effacement and self-enhancement among the Japanese. *Japanese Journal of Social Psychology, 20*, 17–25.

Szeto, A. C. H., Sorrentino, R. M., Yasunaga, S., Otsubo, Y., Kouhara, S., & Sasayama, I. (2009). Using the implicit association test across cultures: a case of implicit self-esteem in Japan and Canada. *Asian Journal of Social Psychology, 12*, 211–220.

Tafarodi, R. M., & Swann, W. B. (1996). Individualism-collectivism and global self-esteem: evidence for a cultural trade-off. *Journal of Cross-Cultural Psychology, 27*, 651–672.

Tafarodi, R. W., Lange, J. M., & Smith, A. J. (1999). Self-esteem and the cultural trade-off: evidence for the role of individualism-collectivism. *Journal of Cross-Cultural Psychology, 30*, 620–640.

Tafarodi, R. W., & Milne, A. B. (2002). Decomposing global self-esteem. *Journal of Personality, 70*, 443–483.

Tafarodi, R. W., Shaughnessy, S. C., Yamaguchi, S., & Murakoshi, A. (2011). The reporting of self-esteem in Japan and Canada. *Journal of Cross-Cultural Psychology, 42*, 155–164.

Tafarodi, R. W., & Walters, P. (1999). Individualism-collectivism, life events, and self-esteem: a test of two trade-offs. *European Journal of Social Psychology, 29*, 797–814.

Takata, T. (2003). Self-enhancement and self-criticism in Japanese culture: an experimental analysis. *Journal of Cross-Cultural Psychology, 34*, 542–551.

Tam, K.-P., Chiu, C.-Y., & Lau, L. Y. (2007). Terror management among Chinese: worldview defense and intergroup bias in resource allocation. *Asian Journal of Social Psychology, 10*, 93–102.

Tam, K.-P., Leung, A. K.-y., Kim, Y.-H., Chiu, C.-Y., Lau, I. Y.-M., & Au, A. K. C. (2012). The better-than-average effect in Hong Kong and the United States: the role of personal trait importance and cultural trait importance. *Journal of Cross-Cultural Psychology, 43*, 915—930.

Tan, M., Newman, L. S., & Zhang, B. (February 2014). A cross-cultural investigation of the processing of self-threatening information. In *Poster presented at the annual meeting of the Society for Personality and Social Psychology, Austin, TX, USA*.

Tanchotsrinon, P., Maneesri, K., & Campbell, W. K. (2007). Narcissism and romantic attraction: evidence from a collectivistic culture. *Journal of Research in Personality, 41*, 723—730.

Tang, S. (1999). Cooperation or competition: a comparison of US and Chinese college students. *Journal of Psychology, 133*, 413—423.

Tangney, J. P., & Tracy, J. (2012). Self-conscious emotions. In M. Leary, & J. P. Tangney (Eds.), *Handbook of self and identity* (2nd ed.). (pp. 446—478). New York, NY: Guilford Press.

Taylor, S. E., & Brown, J. D. (1988). Illusion and well-being: a social psychological perspective on mental health. *Psychological Bulletin, 103*, 193—210.

Taylor, S. E., Lerner, J. S., Sherman, D. K., Sage, R. M., & McDowell, N. K. (2003). Portrait of the self-enhancer: well-adjusted and well-liked or maladjusted and friendless? *Journal of Personality and Social Psychology, 84*, 165—176.

Terracciano, A., & McCrae, R. R. (2007). Perceptions of Americans and the Iraq invasion: implications for understanding national character stereotypes. *Journal of Cross-Cultural Psychology, 38*, 695—710.

Tesser, A. (1988). Towards a self-evaluation maintenance model of social behavior. *Advances in Experimental Social Psychology, 21*, 181—227.

Tesser, A. (2000). On the confluence of self-esteem maintenance mechanisms. *Personality and Social Psychology Review, 4*, 290—299.

Tice, D. (1991). Esteem protection or enhancement? Self-handicapping motives and attributions differ by trait self-esteem. *Journal of Personality and Social Psychology, 60*, 711—725.

Triandis, H. C. (1995). *Individualism and collectivism*. Boulder, CO: Westview Press.

Triandis, H. C., Carnevale, P., Gelfand, M., Robert, C., Wasti, A., Probst, T., et al. (2001). Culture and deception in business negotiations: a multilevel analysis. *International Journal of Cross-Cultural Management, 1*, 73—90.

Tseng, W. S. (1973). The concept of personality in Confucian thought. *Psychiatry, 36*, 191—202.

Van Hemert, D. A., Van de Vijer, F. J. R., Poortinga, Y. A., & Georgas, J. (2002). Structural and functional equivalence of the Eysenck Personality Questionnaire within and between countries. *Personality and Individual Differences, 33*, 1229—1249.

Van Hoorn, A. (2015). Individualistic-collectivistic culture and trust radius: a multilevel approach. *Journal of Cross-Cultural Psychology, 46*, 269—276.

Van Lange, P. A. M., & Sedikides, C. (1998). Being more honest but not necessarily more intelligent than others: generality and explanations for the Muhammad Ali effect. *European Journal of Social Psychology, 28*, 675—680.

Vernon, P. A., Villani, V. C., Vickers, L. C., & Harris, J. A. (2008). A behavioral genetic investigation of the Dark Triad and the Big 5. *Personality and Individual Differences, 44*, 445—452.

Vignoles, V. L. (2011). Identity motives. In S. J. Schwartz, K. Luyckx, & V. L. Vignoles (Eds.), *Handbook of identity theory and research* (pp. 403—432). New York, NY: Springer.

Vignoles, V. L., Camillo, R., Manzi, C., Golledge, J., & Scabini, E. (2006). Beyond self-esteem: Influence of multiple motives on identity construction. *Journal of Personality and Social Psychology, 90*, 308—333.

Wakimoto, R. (2006). Mortality salience effects on modesty and relative self-effacement. *Asian Journal of Social Psychology, 9*, 176—183.

Ward, C., & Kennedy, A. (1994). Acculturation strategies, psychological adjustment, and socio-cultural competence during cross-cultural transitions. *International Journal of Intercultural Relations, 18*, 329—343.

Webster, D. M., & Kruglanski, A. W. (1994). Individual differences in need for cognitive closure. *Journal of Personality and Social Psychology, 67*(6), 1049—1062.

Weisbuch, M., Sinclair, S., Skorinko, J., & Eccleston, C. (2009). Self-esteem depends on the beholder: effects of a subtle social value cue. *Journal of Experimental Social Psychology, 45*, 143—148.

Whetsone, M. R., Okun, M. A., & Cialdini, R. B. (1992). The modest responding scale. In *Paper presented at the convention of the American Psychological Society, San Diego, CA.*

Williams, E. F., & Gilovich, T. (2008). Do people really believe they are above average? *Journal of Experimental Social Psychology, 44*, 1121—1128.

Wills, T. A. (1981). Downward comparison principles in social psychology. *Psychological Bulletin, 90*, 245—271.

Wood, N. (1991). *Cicero's social and political thought*. Oakland, CA: University of California Press.

Wu, R.-J. R. (2011). A conversational analysis of self-praising in everyday Mandarin interaction. *Journal of Pragmatics, 43*, 3152—3176.

Yamagishi, T. (1988). Exit from the group as an individualistic solution to the free rider problem in the United States and Japan. *Journal of Experimental Social Psychology, 24*, 530—542.

Yamagishi, T., Hashimoto, H., Cook, K. S., Kiyonari, T., Shinada, M., Mifune, N., et al. (2012). Modesty in self-presentation: a comparison between the USA and Japan. *Asian Journal of Psychology, 15*, 60—68.

Yamagishi, T., Hashimoto, H., & Schug, J. (2008). Preferences versus strategies as explanations for culture-specific behavior. *Psychological Science, 19*, 579—584.

Yamaguchi, S. (July 31, 2013). Universality of need for high self-esteem and its functions. In *Paper presented at the 121st annual convention of the American Psychological Association, Honolulu, Hawaii.*

Yamaguchi, S., Greenwald, A. G., Banaji, M. R., Murakami, F., Chen, D., Shiomura, K., et al. (2007). Apparent universality of positive implicit self-esteem. *Psychological Science, 18*, 498—500.

Yamaguchi, S., Lin, C., & Aoki, S. (2006). Self-esteem in cultural context: the case of the Japanese. In Q. Jing, M. R. Rosenzweig, G. d'Ydewalle, H. Zhang, C. H.-C. Chen, & K. Z. Zhang (Eds.), *Progress in psychological science around the world* (Vol. 2, pp. 319—330). New York, NY: Psychology Press.

Yamaguchi, S., Lin, C., Morio, H., & Okumura, T. (2008). Motivated expressions of self-esteem across cultures. In R. M. Sorrentino, & S. Yamaguchi (Eds.), *Handbook of motivation and cognition across cultures* (pp. 369—392). San Diego, CA: Academic Press.

Yamaguchi, S., Morio, H., & Sedikides, C. *Self-esteem and psychological health in Japan: A meta-analysis*, Japan: Nara University, Unpublished manuscript.

Yamawaki, N. (2012). Within-culture variations in collectivism in Japan. *Journal of Cross-Cultural Psychology, 43*, 1191—1204.

Yang, B. (1985). *The ugly Chinese*. Taipei, Taiwan: Lin-Bai Press.

Yang, J., Shi, Y., Luo, Y. L. L., Shi, J., & Cai, H. (2014). The brief implicit association test is valid: experimental evidence. *Social Cognition, 32*, 449—465.

Ybarra, O., & Trafimow, D. (1998). How priming the private self or collective self affects the relative weights of attitudes and subjective norms. *Personality and Social Psychology Bulletin, 24*, 362—370.

Yoshida, T., Kojo, K., & Kaku, H. (1982). A study on the development of self-presentation in children. *Japanese Journal of Educational Psychology, 30*, 120—122.

Yum, J. O. (1985). The impact of confucianism on interpersonal relationships and communication patterns in East Asia. *Communication Monographs, 55*, 374—388.

Zeigler-Hill, V. (2013). *Self-esteem*. London, England: Psychology Press.

INDEX

Note: Page numbers followed by "f" indicate figures.

A

Academically disadvantaged students, 154–155
Academically gifted students, 153–154
Academically selective schools, 149–151, 150f
Academic goal theory, 146–147
Academic self-concept (ASC), 128–129
Achievement goals, 13–14
Alternate Uses Task (AUT), 50–51
American Pulpwood Association, 108–109
Approach–avoidance motivational perspective, 13f
  achievement goals, 13–14
  appetitive and aversive motivation, animals/humans
    BAS and BIS, 8–9
    emotional systems, 9
    Higgins' model, 8–9
    neurocognitive evidence, 9–10
    self-regulation model, 8–9
    theorizing and operationalization, 8
  close relationships, potential costs, 5–6
  dating couples, avoidance goals, 15
  emotion regulation, 6–7
  high-quality relationships, 23
  incentives and threats regulation, 7–8, 11–12
  interpersonal relationship, 4
  laboratory-based conflict, 15
  mediating links, social motivation and outcomes
    appetitive and aversive systems, 17–18
    attention, 18–19
    cognitive biases, 19
    incentive-based goals, 17
    positive events, 17
    social information, 20
  moderators, 21–22
  negative emotion, 7
  positive emotion, 7
  psychopathological symptoms, 6
  rejection-based need, 10–11
  rejection sensitivity, 10–11
  reward-based and threat-based social motives/goals, 10
  sacrifice, romantic relationships, 16
  sexual behavior and desire, 16
  social bonds, 13
  social isolation effects
    loneliness and well-being, 3–4
    meta-analysis, 2–3
    mortality, 2–3
    psychological health, 3
  social motivation and outcomes, 14–15
  social, relational and personal outcomes, 16
  stable interpersonal bonds, 5
  strong avoidance motive, 14
Assessment tendency, 76
Attainment expectancy, 92–93
Attentional blink, 56–57

B

Behavioral activation system (BAS), 8–9
Behavioral inhibition system (BIS), 8–9
Behaviorism, Locke, 120
  Ayn Rand's philosophy, 101
  behavior modification, 102
  consciousness, 100
  determinism mitigation, 101
  Free will, 101
  logical positivism, 100
  "mentalistic", 100–101
  observable behavior, 100–101
  projective tests, 102
  reinforcers, 101
  variable-ratio schedule, 102–103
Better-than-average effect (BTAE)
  assimilation/contrast, 205–206
  egocentrism, 205–206
  focalism, 205–206
  individuated-entity *vs.* aggregate comparisons, 205–206

Better-than-average effect (BTAE)
    (*Continued*)
    self-threat, 204–205
    spiritual victories, 204
Big-Fish–little-pond effect (BFLPE)
        model, 129f
    academic ability measure, 138
    academic goal theory, 146–147
    academic self-concept, 128–129
    age, 148
    average-ability student, high-ability
        group, 137
    competence self-perceptions, 128–129
    cross-cultural generalizability, 142–145
    ephemeral effect, 141
    explicit tracking
        academically disadvantaged students,
            154–155
        academically gifted students, 153–154
        de facto selection process, 152–153
        quasi-experimental approach, 153
    generalizability
        academically selective schools,
            149–151, 150f
        moderation and, 145–146
        nonacademic domains, 151–152
        streamed and mixed-ability classes, 149
    global self-esteem, 138–139
    grading-on-a-curve, 162–163
    individual-student ability, 147–148
    individual-student achievement, 139
    limitations and directions, 173–175
    local dominance effects, 155–156
    low-ability groupings, 139–140
    methodological requirements, 140
    multiple reference frames, 134
    nonacademic components, 136
    personality, 147
    PISA studies, 142–143
    policy practice
        labeling theory, 170
        learning disadvantages, 170–171
        motivational climates, 172–173
        negative effects, 171–172
        psychological benefits, 170
    predictions, 137
    research methodology, 130

school-average ability level, 137–138
SCT. *See* Social comparison theory (SCT)
self-concept
    achievement and accomplishments, 131
    dust bowl empiricism, 132
    history, 132
    multidimensional model, 133–134
    positive psychology movement, 131
    self-perceptions, 133
    social and personal adjustment,
        130–131
    SES, 138–139
    teaching style, 149
    TIMSS studies, 143–145
Bilingualism, 56

C
Candid self-enhancement, 207
    modesty, 207–209
    other-mediation, 210–211
    setting orientation, 209–210
Cognitive control, 34–35
    attentional blink, 56–57
    bilingualism, 56
    Buddhism, 59
    global precedence effect, 58–59
    homosexual individuals, 59–60
    learning, 55–56
    passionate love, 55
    religious faith, 57–58
    short-term biases
        Alternate Uses Task, 50–51
        focused-attention meditation, 53
        loose thinking, 50–51
        meditation, 52–53
        RAT, 52
        Stroop/flanker tasks, 51–52
        systematic mood effects, 52
Collective self, universal valuation,
        191–193
Collectivism, 190
COMT Val158Met polymorphism, 50
Conscious/subconscious goals, 119
Control, balance
    dopamine, 43–44
    overdose people, 44–45
    prefrontal cortex and striatum, 44–45

Control State Model (CSM), 46–49, 48f.
See also Cognitive control
Control states, plasticity, 49–50
Control theory, 112–113
Counterfinality configuration, 71f, 94–95
attainment expectancy, 92–93
counterfinal means, 93–94
defined, 71, 88
disfluency, 88–89
domains of applicability, 95
fluency, 88–89
goal magnitude
fitness program, 91
low and high goal magnitude, 90–91, 91f
mouthwash, 90, 90f
tattooing, 92
mental simulation, 89
rational criteria, 88
Critical incident technique (CIT), 104
CSM. *See* Control State Model (CSM)
Cultural relativism perspective, 189–191
Culture mandates, 189–190

D
Deduced theory, 103, 120
Defensiveness, 196–197
Dilution effects, 70
equifinality configuration
eating fish, 81
eating olives, 81
intrinsic motivation, 81–82
spreading activation, 80
multifinality configuration
fan effect principle, 72–73
means–goal association strength, 73–74
one/multiple goals, 73
two goals, 73
unifinal means, 72–73
in social identification
intimacy goal, 82–83
optimal distinctiveness, 83–84
self-identity, 82
uncertainty–identity theory, 84
Dopamine, 43–44
Dopamine D4 receptor gene (DRD4), 190
Dust bowl empiricism, 132

E
Ego
attention theory, 40–41
decision-making, 42
Freudian approach, 41
loans of intelligence, 41–42
Superego, 39–40
Egocentrism, 205–206
Emotional systems, 9
Ephemeral effect, 141
Equifinality configuration, 71f, 87–88, 94–95
defined, 70–71, 78
dilution effects
eating fish, 81
eating olives, 81
intrinsic motivation, 81–82
in social identification, 82–85
spreading activation, 80
goals and means, commitment, 80
expectancy, 79
value goal, 79
means variety
goal progress, 85–86
goal pursuit, 86–87
motivational constructs, 85
substitutability, 78–79
Executive function, 34–35
Expectancy theory, 106
Extended self-concept enhancing tactician (SCENT-R) model, 199–200
candid self-enhancement, 207
modesty, 207–209
other-mediation, 210–211
setting orientation, 209–210
foundational tenets, 191
gastronomic analogy, 191
implicit self-esteem, 211
East and West, 211–212
motivational dynamics, 213–214
self-esteem IAT, 212–214
self-centrality breeds self-enhancement.
See also Self-centrality breeds self-enhancement
10 adjectives, 200–201
self-enhancement and self-protection, 201–204

Extended self-concept enhancing tactician
    (SCENT-R) model (*Continued*)
    self-esteem, 201
    self-esteem and self-motives, 214
        natural/acquired, 221–223
        necessarily pursued/valued conscious
            level, 221
        vs. psychosocial health, 215–218
        vs. self-enhancement, 215
        universal/culture bound, 220–221,
            223–224
    universality, 198–199
    universal strength, 193–195
    universal structure, 195–198
    universal valuation, 191–193

F
Fan effect principle, 72–73
Favorable construal, 196–197
Field experiments, Latham
    assigned *vs.* participatively set goals,
        109–111
    CIT, 108
    criterion problem, 108
    factor analysis, 108
    goal-performance effects, 107–108
    piece-rate basis, 108–109
    self-management, 111
Focalism, 205–206

G
Gastronomic analogy, 193–194
Goal magnitude, counterfinality
    fitness program, 91
    low and high goal magnitude, 90–91, 91f
    mouthwash, 90, 90f
    tattooing, 92
Goal-setting theory, 105
    affect, 107
    behaviorism, Locke. *See* Behaviorism,
        Locke
    commitment, 107
    conscious and subconscious goals, 119
    expectancy theory, 106
    feedback, 105–106
    field experiments, Latham. *See* Field
        experiments, Latham

marshmallow studies, 120
organizational psychology, 111–112
self-development, 120
self-efficacy, 106
self-set goals, 106
theory, 1990
    academic theories, 112
    aim, definition, 113
    categories, 113
    cybernetically based goal model,
        112–113
    goal mediators, 113
    human resource management, 115
    inductive process, 112
    mediators, beneficial effect, 114–115
    meta-analyses, 113
    performance conditions, 114–115
    self-efficacy, 114–115
    System 4 model, 112
theory building
    conceptual clarity, 118
    contextual scientific discoveries, 119
    contradiction elimination, 119
    critical incident technique, 104
    by deduction, 103
    generality evidence, 118
    goal setting, job performance, 104
    Herzberg's theory, 104
    humans and societal actions, 118
    information integration, 119
    job analysis, 104
    key concepts, 118
    post hoc hypothesis, 104
    rapid generalization, 103
    self-esteem, 103
    tunnel vision, 103
theory expanded, 2013
    closed system, 115
    core tenets, 116
    learning goal, 116–117
    performance goal, 116–117
    personal development, 117
    proximal goals, 117
    self-efficacy, 117
    task/job performance, 116–117
    time-frame, 118
trying stuff, 105

Grading-on-a-curve, 162–163
Gratton effect, 37–38

H
Higgins' model, 8–9
Human action control, 34

I
Implicit self-esteem, 211
  East and West, 211–212
  motivational dynamics, 213–214
  self-esteem IAT, 212–214
Incentive-based goals, 17
Individualism, 190
Individual self, universal valuation,
    191–193
Individual-student ability, 147–148
Intrinsic motivation, 81–82

J
Job enrichment theory, 104

L
Labeling theory, 170
Locomotion tendency, 76

M
Means–goal association, 73–74
Mental map, 70
Methodological-substantive synergy.
    See also Big-Fish–little-pond effect
    (BFLPE) model
  longitudinal studies, 169
  multilevel models
    latent, 167–168, 168f
    manifest, 165–166
  quantitative tools, 164
  quasi-experimental studies, 169
  single-level models
    latent, 165
    manifest, 164–165
Moderators, 21–22
Modesty, 207–209
Motivational climates, 172–173
Multifinality configuration, 71f, 94–95
  defined, 70, 72
  dilution effect, 77–78

  fan effect principle, 72–73
  means–goal association strength, 73–74
  one/multiple goals, 73
  two goals, 73
  unifinal means, 72–73
  goal systems, 72
  multifinality constraint effect, 74–75,
    77–78
  multiple active goals, 71
  regulatory mode effects, 76–77
  in unconscious choice, 75–76
Multifinality constraint effect, 74–75

N
Narcissism, 197
Negative emotion, 7
No-feedback control condition, 193–194
Nonandroids, 187

O
Organisation for Economic Cooperation
    and Development (OECD),
    142–143

P
Pan-human theory, 143
PISA studies, 142–143
Plasticity, 49–50
Polymorphism, 50
Positive emotion, 7
Positivity embracement, 196–197
Prevention-focused goals, 8–9
Promotion-focused goals, 8–9

R
Regulatory mode effects, 76–77
Rejection sensitivity, 10–11
Relational self, universal valuation,
    191–193
Remote Associations Task (RAT), 52
Reward-based social motives/goals, 10

S
SCENT-R. *See* Extended self-concept
    enhancing tactician (SCENT-R)
    model
Self-affirming reflections, 196–197

Self-centrality breeds self-enhancement
    10 adjectives, 200–201
    self-enhancement and self-protection
        BTAE, 204–206
        business problems, 202
        candid self-enhancement, 201
        independents and interdependents,
            202–203
        socially desirable responding, 206–207
    self-esteem, 201
Self-concept
    achievement and accomplishments, 131
    dust bowl empiricism, 132
    history, 132
    multidimensional model, 133–134
    positive psychology movement, 131
    self-perceptions, 133
    social and personal adjustment, 130–131
Self-deceptive enhancement (SDE),
        206–207
Self, definition, 187
Self-effacing, 193–194
Self-enhancement
    defined, 187
    universal strength, 193–195
    universal structure, 195–198
Self-esteem, 188–189
    defensiveness, 197
    defined, 187
    self-centrality breeds self-enhancement,
        201
    universality, 189, 198–199
Self-evaluation, 189–190
Self-improvement, 189, 193–194
Self-motives
    universality, 189
    universal structure, 195–198
Self-protection
    defined, 187
    universal strength, 193–195
    universal structure, 195–198
Self-set goals, 106
Setting orientation, 209–210
Short-term biases, cognitive control
    Alternate Uses Task, 50–51
    focused-attention meditation, 53
    loose thinking, 50–51

meditation, 52–53
RAT, 52
Stroop/flanker tasks, 51–52
systematic mood effects, 52
Social comparison theory (SCT), 132
    class-average achievement, 159
    comparative evaluation, 157–158
    double-edged sword, 157
    extensive debate, 156
    integration of, 161–162
    latent-variable multilevel SEM model,
        160–161
    multilevel latent variable analysis,
        158–159
    rank-order paradigm, 157
    school-average ability, 158
    school-/class-average achievement, 157
    target student self-perceptions, 159–160
    total environments, 156–157
Social isolation effects
    loneliness and well-being, 3–4
    meta-analysis, 2–3
    mortality, 2–3
    psychological health, 3
Spiritual victories, 197–198
Stroop effect, 37–38
Substitutability, 78–79
Superego, 39–40

T
Terror management theory, 199
Threat-based social motives and goals, 10
Trends in Math and Science Survey
        (TIMSS) studies, 143–145

W
Weyerhaeuser Company, 103
Will, 39
    automaticity, 36
    classical Rylean category issue, 36–37
    counteracting force, 35–36
    dichotomy, 38–39
    external stimuli, 38
    motor pattern, 35
    reading process, 37–38
    smoking response, 38–39
    Stroop task, 37–38

Edwards Brothers Malloy
Thorofare, NJ USA
September 22, 2015